# RE-PRESENTING THE CITY

# Re-Presenting the City

**Ethnicity, Capital and Culture in the 21st-Century Metropolis**

Edited by

ANTHONY D. KING

NEW YORK UNIVERSITY PRESS
Washington Square, New York

First published in the U.S.A. in 1996 by
NEW YORK UNIVERSITY PRESS
Washington Square
New York, N.Y. 10003

Library of Congress Cataloging-in-Publication Data
Re-presenting the city : ethnicity, capital, and culture in the 21st-century metropolis / edited by Anthony D. King.
p. cm.
Includes bibliographical references and index.
ISBN 0–8147–4678–0 (cloth : alk. paper). — ISBN 0–8147–4679–9 (pbk. : alk. paper)
1. Sociology, Urban.    2. City planning.    3. Urban renewal.
I. King, Anthony D.
HT151.R349    1996
307.76—dc20                                  95–37010
                                                  CIP

Printed in Malaysia

# Contents

*Preface*                                                                    vii

*Acknowledgements*                                                            ix

Introduction: Cities, Texts and Paradigms                                      1
ANTHONY D. KING

PART I   *Ethnicity, Capital and Culture: Representations of*
         *New York City*

1   Rebuilding the Global City: Economy, Ethnicity and Space                  23
    SASKIA SASSEN

2   Space and Symbols in an Age of Decline                                    43
    SHARON ZUKIN

3   Return to the Future: Puerto Rican Vernacular Architecture in
    New York City                                                             60
    JOSEPH SCIORRA

4   After Tompkins Square Park: Degentrification and the
    Revanchist City                                                           93
    NEIL SMITH

PART II   *Ethnicity, Capital and Culture: Writing the City in*
          *Africa and South Asia*

5   Bypassing New York in Re-Presenting Eko: Production of
    Space in a Nigerian City                                                 111
    NKIRU NZEGWU

6   Exploring Colombo: The Relevance of a Knowledge of New
    York                                                                     137
    NIHAL PERERA

7   Mombasa: Three Stages towards Globalization                              158
    ALI A. MAZRUI

PART III   *Urban Con-Texts: Reading and Writing the City*

8   The City Which is Not One                                                179
    JOHN TAGG

9   Analytic Borderlands: Race, Gender and Representation in the
    New City                                                             183
    SASKIA SASSEN

10  Silent Itineraries: Making Places in Architectural History           203
    GREIG CRYSLER

11  A Guide to Urban Representation and What to Do About It:
    Alternative Traditions of Urban Theory                               227
    ROB SHIELDS

12  Me(trope)olis: Or Hayden White Among the Urbanists                   253
    JAMES S. DUNCAN

    *Notes on Contributors*                                              269
    *Name Index*                                                         271

# Preface

Most of the chapters in this book began as papers, or commentaries, at a one-day symposium with the same title, held at the State University of New York at Binghamton (now, Binghamton University, SUNY) on 4 April, 1992. Sponsored by the History and Theory of Art and Architecture Graduate Program of the Department of Art and Art History (now the Department of Art History), the symposium was the fifth in the series, 'Current Debates in Art History' held at the University. Subsequently, Greig Crysler, James Duncan, Nkiru Nzegwu, and Nihal Perera, originally commentators at the symposium, developed full papers for this published edition and Rob Shields, who was also present at the symposium, was also invited to contribute a chapter. Chapter 9 is a revised version of a lecture with the same title delivered at the University some three weeks after the symposium by Saskia Sassen who was the Distinguished Visiting Scholar in Art History for 1992.

In the original proposal for the symposium – on which I draw for the following paragraphs – attention was focused on certain dominant representations of major 'world cities' which had been published in the early 1990s. According to these accounts, a range of economic, social, demographic and cultural transformations had taken place in major world cities – particularly New York, Paris, London, Los Angeles, Tokyo – of which New York was seen as a paradigmatic example – especially since the 1970s. As organizer of the symposium, I highlighted four of these transformations as having special significance: the substantial growth of the producer service sector (particularly banking, financial services, advertising, legal, business services, realty, etc.) and their increasingly dominant role, both internationally and nationally; the increasing importance of the cultural industries and of the cultural economy in general; the immense change in the ethnic and racial composition of the population resulting from recent immigration and out-migration; and with deindustrialisation, the increase in economic and social polarisation, widening the gap between rich and poor.

Not least resulting from the ever-widening economic and social divisions in both the society and the city, and the transformation in its ethnic and cultural composition, a new cultural politics, a new politics of identity had emerged. Far from being subordinated into simple categories of class, diverse social, ethnic, racial, and gendered cultures were gaining increasing visibility, inscribing their presence on the urban scene, not merely in the old form of 'ethnic neighborhoods' but in public art, street life, and the built spaces of the city.

It was these assumptions that were behind the original title: the city was in the process of being 're-presented' to the city's inhabitants as well as to others; the city was 're-presenting' itself to itself. As I discuss in the Introduction, the notion of representation here was understood primarily (though not exclusively) as a physical, spatial, material and visual phenomenon.

The aim of the symposium, therefore, and subsequently of this book, was to provide an opportunity for a group of leading scholars researching and writing on New York, but also other cities in Africa, Asia and North America, to respond to these issues, but also to address some of the theoretical and methodological questions prompted by the task of urban representation itself.

However as Rob Shields implies in his careful deconstruction of the title, the limitation of the discussion of urban representations within these parameters is not so easy, an issue on which John Tagg also comments, the word 're-presenting' broken by a hyphen, perhaps, because of 'the weight of meaning it has to bear' (p. 179). The published outcome of the symposium, therefore, was left open, both to accommodate the theoretical challenges made to some of the assumptions behind the original proposal as well as the contributions of the commentators who, though unfairly limited to ten or fifteen minutes during the proceedings, were subsequently invited to develop their contributions at length. This also enabled a more substantial discussion of issues and theories of representation to be included in the final section.

The degree to which some of the assumptions behind the original proposal have been challenged, and the different discourses and arguments heard during and after the symposium developed, therefore, has exceeded my own expectations. The contributors not only contest many of the conventional social, political, geographical, ideological and cultural positions of what Sassen terms here the 'privileged viewers' of the different processes that make up the city, but more especially, the very practice of representation itself. Many new insights come from the theoretical chapters in the last section of the book; an equal if not greater number, however, come from a critical reading of the different positions and styles of narration of all of the essays themselves.

Finally I have stayed with the original subtitle of the symposium which refers to the 'twenty-first century metropolis'. By the time this book is published and reviewed, the twentieth century will be at an end. Thinking critically about representation in relation to ethnicity, capital and culture in the world cities of the future is one of the most urgent tasks which we will have to address.

*Binghamton and Bristol* ANTHONY D. KING

# Acknowledgements

The symposium from which this book developed was supported by grants from the Office of Sponsored Programs and Research and the Dean of Harpur College of Arts and Sciences. I would like to thank them and also many others who helped to organize and make the conference possible, especially the speakers for their willingness to speak at the event, the chairs of the different sessions, Bat Ami Bar On and Dale Tomich; other discussants, Axel Jerome and Oscar Vázquez, as also Omari Kokoli, for standing in for Ali Mazrui, whose original contribution was made by video. Special thanks are due to the staff of the Art and Art History Department, especially Joan Scott for much correspondence and many other details, but also to Fran Goldman for help in organizing the symposium and also to Judi Bryant. To Don Bell and Shawn Parker I owe my thanks for design work for the symposium; to my Art History colleagues and to the Art History Graduate Student Union I am very grateful for their support, particularly Shawn Parker and Nihal Perera for their help with the organization. Thanks also to Ursula King and Deryck Holdsworth for hidden help. Finally I am grateful to Lisa Fegley and especially Nick Newman, AHGSU President, 1993–4, for his cooperation and computer expertise in putting everyone's disc on a master and much appreciated help in editing these proceedings. Special thanks to Chris Focht for photography and especially, to Martha Cooper of New York, for her generosity and cooperation in supplying the photographs for Joseph Sciorra's chapter on vernacular architecture in New York.

ANTHONY D. KING

# Introduction: Cities, Texts and Paradigms

Anthony D. King

To put it polemically, there is no such *thing* as a city. Rather *the city* designates the space produced by the interaction of historically and geographically specific institutions, social relations of production and reproduction, practices of government, forms and media of communication, and so forth. By calling this diversity 'the city', we ascribe to it a coherence or integrity. *The city*, then, is above all a representation. But what sort of representation? By analogy with the now familiar idea that the nation provides us with an 'imagined community', I would argue that the city constitutes an *imagined environment*. What is involved in that imagining – the discourses, symbols, metaphors and fantasies through which we ascribe meaning to the modern experience of urban living – is as important a topic for the social sciences as the material determinants of the physical environment.

(James Donald, 'Metropolis: The City as Text')[1]

one person's 'text' is another person's shopping center.

(Sharon Zukin)[2]

## CITIES AS TEXTS: PARADIGMS AS REPRESENTATIONS

In the early 1980s, a prominent urban sociologist spelt out what he saw as the distinguishing features of a new paradigm in the study of the city, that had become established over the previous decade. Variously described as 'the new urban studies' or 'urban political economy', the approach was characterised by a number of assumptions: urbanism (and urbanisation) could not just be taken for granted but required definition and explanation, since they took various forms under various modes of social and economic organisation and political control. The approach was concerned with the

1

interplay between relations of production, consumption, exchange and the structure of power manifest in the state. Urban processes – whether community organisation, class and ethnic politics (or physical and spatial urban form), had to be understood in terms of their structural bases, or how they are conditioned by the larger economic, political and socio-cultural milieu. The approach was connected with social change and this was seen as growing out of conflicts among classes and groups. Changes in the economy were socially and culturally generated and mediated.[3]

This essentially sociological and structuralist approach to the study of the city – though also highly influential in geography, politics, and urban studies more generally – was a paradigm particularly associated with the Marxist-inspired writings of David Harvey,[4,5] Manuel Castells,[6] and their followers, and is one that still commands a strong following. Developed especially from the early 1970s when, as part of a global restructuring of capital, labour and industrial production, North American, British and other European cities were experiencing major phases of restructuring with job and capital flight to the Third World and the decay of older industries in the West, the analyses – for the scholars and others committed to them – have had considerable influence.

A decade or more later, another paradigm shift is occurring, not least because the discourse of the city, at one time simply a privileged territory in the social sciences on which generally white, western, and usually male urban sociologists, geographers, anthropologists, or city planners inscribed their theoretical models, or where urban and architectural historians told their different stories, has increasingly become the happy-hunting-ground of film theorists, poets, art historians, writers, television producers, literary critics, and postmodern cultural connoisseurs of all kinds in the humanities.

Indeed the culture of the contemporary city is not just the subject of representations constituted through different categories of knowledge (the humanities as well as the social sciences) and different disciplines (comparative literature as well as sociology), it is also addressed by different genders, ethnicities, ideologies, races, classes, sexual orientations, national-ities, theoretical *differences* of every shape and form – 'across specific discursive regimes', to quote one of the contributors to this volume.[7] Partly because of the different people and subjectivities inhabiting the contem-porary world or global city – (categories I refer to below) though more especially because of different scholars inhabiting the academy and occupying different positionalities and identities within it – *writing about* the city has both immensely increased as well as been transformed. The cultural orthodoxy of older urban representations has been undermined by new heterodoxies generated by the multicultural city itself. There is no better example than the London of Salman Rushdie's *Satanic Verses*.[8] Critiquing the assumptions behind representations, therefore, might well provide one way out of what Thrift sees as an impasse in the study of the city.[9]

It is, however, the 'material shift' in the cultural composition of both the city and the academy which answers the doubts of Australian geographer Jane Jacobs,[10] who suggests that 'it is arguable whether this sudden interest in what might generally be defined as the cultural dimensions of the city is responding to a material shift in cities, or if it is simply the city being seen anew'.[11] Yet one explanation does not necessarily exclude the other. The increasingly differentiated cultural discourse on the city is itself self-generating and part of the accumulation of cultural capital in the city. It is linked to the massive expansion of the cultural industries in (especially) the western metropolis: to publishing, education, the media, the symbolic and representational realms of advertising, and the 'aestheticisation of social life'.[12,13]

The effect of this incestuous, intertextual implosion of representations where architecture becomes the subject of film, film the subject of history, history the subject of criticism, criticism the subject of deconstruction, deconstruction the subject of architecture, and so on ad infinitum, is the emergence of a situation where according to Jacobs, 'the boundary between social reality and representations of that reality has collapsed':[14] or where, in the words of sociologist of culture Janet Wolff, the effect of various poststructuralist theories (deconstruction, semiotics, Lacanian psycho-analytic theory, Foucaultian discourse theory and postmodern theory) has been to seriously problematise the relationship between 'the real city, the discursive city (and) the disappearing city'.[15] Whatever the explanation, 'the city as an object of analysis has been unbound'.[16]

It would, however, be naive to conclude from these apparently new perspectives, that what may appear to be the anonymous, universalising, seemingly 'voiceless' and often empirical and positivist representation of cities, characteristic of some social scientific writing in the 1980s, or even before, was lacking in self-awareness.

Though recent monographs on 'the city as text',[17,18,19] may have destabilized the more positivist accounts of yesteryear, they are not without their predecessors. For example in *Cities of the Mind: Images and Themes of the City in the Social Sciences*,[20] some twenty prominent urbanists reflected both on the metaphors and leading thematic images in geography, economics, political science, anthropology, sociology, history, city planning, and the ways these have changed over time. How such images relate to particular intellectual traditions and techniques in their respective fields forms the substance of these essays. According to sociologist Peter Langer, such metaphors of the city as bazaar, jungle, organism and machine, can be found 'from the time of the classical nineteenth century social analysts to the present day';[21] see also Donald.[22] And as Walton concludes in the passage cited above: the perspective of the new urban studies is tied to the concerns of a normative theory (of how things ought to be) concerned with both drawing out the ideological and distributional implications of '*alternative positions*' but also '*being critically aware of its own premises*'[23] (my emphasis).

What recent feminist, poststructuralist, postcolonialist, cultural and discourse theorists have done is to sharpen the tools of a self-reflective critique, deflecting attention away from the positivist tracking of, for example, the 'global' or 'world city'[24,25] towards the more subjective issue of their discursive construction. As cited above, Donald suggests that 'the discourses, symbols, metaphors and fantasies through which we ascribe meaning to the modern experience of urban living',[26] provide the essential level of analysis. In their edited collection, *Writing Worlds*, Barnes and Duncan[27] invited contributors to focus on the 'discourses, texts and metaphors' in the representation of landscape (see also Duncan and Ley, 1993[28]).

Yet focusing solely on *discursive* representations, the way the city is spoken, read or written, takes our analytical attention from other representational levels as discussed in the following two passages from King, 1995.[29]

The first is the way the built environment, the material, physical and spatial forms of the city, is itself a representation of specific ideologies, of social, political, economic, and cultural relations and practices, of hierarchies and structures, which not only represent but also, inherently constitute these same relations and structures.

And also:

A further symbolic level is constituted through visual representation, the semiotic domain where visual signifiers refer to some other signified, even though signs, of course, can have infinite meanings. A distinction can be made between these two levels by suggesting that a hospital building, for example, may be understood as a spatial representation of social discourses about health but a hospital designed, say, in Europe in the last century, in Gothic style, may be an attempt to infuse these discourses on health with those of religion. Each of these two levels of spatial and symbolic representation is a necessary prerequisite for a third, the mental constructs which form the discourses – through which the hospital is subsequently represented. In this sense, the distinction between a 'real city' and a 'discursive city' is misleading: the one does not exist without the other.

As Shields discusses at some length in his chapter in this volume, words used as signifiers – whether metaphorically or not – require spatialisation to derive their meaning. And such meanings develop within particular social, cultural and historical speech communities and settings – 'communities of discourse' or 'textual communities' which Duncan and Duncan[30], citing Stock,[31] refer to as a group of people 'who have a common understanding of a text, spoken or read, and who organize aspects of their lives as the playing out of a script'. To speak of a 'suburban' mentality, or a 'semi-detached' existence, presupposes the shared cultural, as well as social, experience of a spatialised material reality. The overly logocentric and scriptocentric emphases of some recent writing on representation marginalises these material and spatial aspects. Spatial, building and architectural practices are representations, as also are the material, physical and spatial forms that result. Human action, behaviour, protests, celebrations and contestations, are likewise representational practices making manifest the attitudes, values and priorities which inform them. It is these many levels of representation which the essays in this book bring to our attention.

*    *    *

The tripartite tidiness in the organisation of the contributions, evident from the contents page, belies the contestatory representations contained within them. Unlike many edited books, this one does not represent a single argument but rather offers an interactive debate. Chapters speak to, bounce off, or ignore one another and there is no single conclusion. A criticism reviewers often make of edited collections is that they are 'uneven' – presumably because the reviewer wishes to present the views of contributors as some single uniform discourse: there is, to quote Duncan, 'an urge to simplify in order to generalise';[32] a drive to comprehend that results in reductive reading.

This book sets out to *be* uneven. Though the essays are arranged in three parts – the first in which four chapters deal with New York from different positions and perspectives; the second where three chapters focus on particular African and Asian cities (again from different positions and perspectives), two of them with passing reference to New York; the third addressing issues and theories of representation – the reader may begin anywhere. Indeed, she or he might well be encouraged to move to and fro through the essays, carrying insights back and forth in order to contradict the implied structure of intelligibility suggested by the serial sequence of the chapters.

By uneven, I also mean that not only are some essays long and others short, or that some emerge from locations in philosophy, political science or art history, but that contributors write from quite different theoretical and ideological positions, drawing their arguments from and into quite different discursive as well as geographical spaces. Many edited collections gather their contributors from the same discipline, area of expertise, or perspective. This book has a different objective, one that has consciously promoted a sense of difference in looking at, speaking about, writing and reading the city. That the chapters are contributed by scholars originally from Argentina, Manhattan, Puerto Rico, Scotland, Nigeria, Sri Lanka, Kenya, England or Canada, and from academic disciplines that include urban planning, sociology, folklore studies, geography, philosophy, art history, architecture, international politics, cultural studies and architectural history, and whose contributions are principally based on a commitment to the title, subtitle, and objectives of the book, is therefore, deliberate not an accidental decision.

## THE PAPERS

### I

Whether in terms of theory or practice, few professions have a longer history or (in some cases at least) a more conscious awareness of their own complicity in urban representational practices than city planners. Urban planning is precisely about the imaginary, about competing representations, differing interests, differing ideologies, differing positionalities. Appropriately, therefore, the book begins with a chapter from a professor of urban planning, Saskia Sassen, drawing on work related to the highly influential paradigm and category she has done much to establish, 'the global city'.[33] Not least in comparison to the other contributions, and especially to her second chapter in Part III of this book, Sassen's first chapter is essentially, and consciously, a gendered, economic and spatial narrative. Within such a frame, with its references to 'postindustrial' and 'advanced' city forms, Sassen positions herself firmly within the 'global city' of New York and, only perhaps in comparison to the essays of Nzegwu, Perera, or Mazrui, for example, in the narrative space of 'the West'.

From this particular grid of intelligibility (which, as Nzegwu points out, though apparently 'economic' also represents an ideological and value position), the built form of the global city exists as a representation of its economy: the high-rise corporate offices providing accommodation for those who exercise 'global control capability' stand in comparison to the smoke stacks of the old industrial town. However, in discussing the way in which 'advanced' economies are materialised in space, Sassen also interrogates conventional assumptions made within such economic representations of the city to show the interconnections between that which is typically represented as 'advanced' and 'neutral', and that which is represented as 'backward' and 'particularistic'. Paying particular attention to questions of gender and ethnicity within processes of economic globalization, among other developments, Sassen posits the recovery of urban space for family life in both gentrified as well as poorer areas. Making the point that cities are also represented by people, just as people represent the city, Sassen suggests that the structural shifts in the gender composition of the global city of New York also bring shifts in representations of the city.

Sassen writes here both within and for the particular textual community of urban planning, and within this argues for new forms of *economic* representation within major world cities, demonstrating in her conclusion the central *political* importance of documenting the economic viability of working-class uses of particular areas (in this case, New York's 14th Street). Concluding that a new narrative is needed to rebuild the city, one that shows the interconnectedness of the 'spaces of difference', Sassen's chapter represents a powerful statement positioned in the space of a theorised practice.

Also writing on (especially downtown) New York, Sharon Zukin directs her sociological focus primarily onto the symbolic economy and the visual representation of social groups in the public and private spaces of the city, each battling over 'representational rights' in the symbolic centre of the city. Particularly significant here are those subjects that have historically been absent from formal representations of the city – women, racial minorities, the homeless, and particular types of workers. In a close reading of the architectural and spatial text, Zukin traces the forms of occupation, segregation and exclusion in the global city, practised not only in particular streets and building types, but also in new forms of architecture, zoning laws, and the detailed intersticial spaces of buildings. Visual artefacts of material culture make comments on the social, making social rules legible.

Zukin suggests that as major western cities have shifted to service economies, they have been 'taken hostage by an aesthetic urge', artists becoming handmaidens to the service economy. As in medieval Venice or Bruges, visual representation through a sculptured or artistic presence becomes a means of representing the city's economy. For 'public art', read finance, insurance, real estate. The city's symbolic economy has two parallel production systems: the production of space and the production of symbols, between them constructing a currency of commercial exchange which is simultaneously a language of social identity.

Zukin identifies the particularly significant representational spaces in the new, financial-services dominated, prototypical global city of New York which, to spell out the city's legibility, she examines in detail: the office-building lobby, the multiblock commercial complex, the neighbourhood shopping street. The full significance of these prototypical elements of New York might better be appreciated if compared, for example, to the symbolic elements in Engels' Manchester and his representation of workers' housing, or the faceless bureaucratic blocks of contemporary Moscow. The signs of the symbolic economy are 'the private security firms, consumption space, false gathering spaces, signature architecture styles'. In the neighbourhood shopping streets, ethnicity is 'both promoted and reviled', the various ethnic districts having the potentiality of becoming centres of both solidarity and resistance. Zukin asks, who has the right to inhabit the dominant images of the city? It is a question which resonates through all four essays in this section.

Zukin's carefully detailed architectural and spatial ethnography, with its representations of the macro and microspaces of 'the new city', draws attention to what is absent in the necessary explanation of what is present, to the times of the past and the silences of the present, and the lives and spaces of the absent others which are assumed in the symbolic monuments which inscribe the skyline of Manhattan. In Sciorra's chapter which follows, these absent places and silences are spelt out in more detail. As with other essays in this collection, Zukin's is a chapter that takes on different meanings when re-read in the context of others in this book.

Of these first four essays, Joseph Sciorra's narrative on *puertorriqueño* vernacular architecture in New York City addresses most directly the issue of the spatial representation of 'ethnicity' – a highly contentious and problematic category as I discuss below – in the global city. To grossly oversimplify the issues in this chapter and to skate over its theoretical elaboration: Sciorra engages with the way in which the cultures of new ethnicities have inscribed themselves on the landscape of the contemporary metropolis, but more importantly, he also addresses the unique historical, geographical, political and economic conditions in which this takes place. As I have argued elsewhere in relation to the built and spatial elements of what must be described as the 'imperial industrial city',[34] Sciorra's essay demonstrates the irrelevance of taking either the space of the nation-state or that of the 'autonomous' city, or the equally bounded time of, for example, the nineteenth century, as the unit of analysis. Sciorra's essay weaves an economic, social and architectural-spatial narrative that constitutes the historical development of the space of the Bronx and Puerto Rico, as a single unitary story of an exploitative spatial division of labour character-istic of the colonial relationship. And though it is not on Sciorra's agenda, his detailed historically and ethnographically documented chapter, with its careful evocation of the Puerto Rican *casita* as a distinctive chronotype – a form which is not only a specific place on the New York landscape but also a specific time – gives further support to the critics of a supposedly uniform or even neutral process of 'globalization', whether in regard to assumptions about 'cultural homogenization' or 'neutrality' in regard to the immense imbalances in economic and cultural power.[35]

Sciorra's essay also provides a socio-spatial knitting together of Sassen's two chapters which themselves offer a credible account of Third-World dependence on the dominant financial order of the global city; but it also demonstrates an alternative narrative of and for that city, a landscape of resistance which contests the representations of the dominant culture. This is not only a different story of New York, but it is one told from different perspectives and different positions. More than this, however, Sciorra draws on various theories and modes of representation – poetry, music, visual imagery, and the oral history and stories of particular speech communities – to show how the *casita*, in literature and the visual arts, has become a central, powerful symbol for the *puertorriqueños*, a metaphor of home which is both a domestic dwelling place and national homeland.

Taking a subtly different focus, the last of these four essays on New York City, by geographer Neil Smith, continues the debate on representation at both a spatial as well as strictly discursive level. Smith deals with the public representations of urbanism and how these affect attitudes towards the contemporary city in the Unites States. Replacing one set of metaphors by another, Smith proposes that, with the decline of the positive middle class image of gentrification, the post-gentrification city has now been displaced by the image of the revanchist city, targeting the media representations of middle and ruling-class whites which are presupposed on the existence of the disenfranchised – minorities, immigrants, unemployed, lesbians and gays.

These are all brought into focus by the embattled space of Tompkins Square Park in the now 'degentrifying space' of the Lower East Side. In this new scenario, Smith writes that 'the scripting of the revanchist city is viscerally local and global', with the forces of might (the police) battling with the homeless over the right to the space of Tompkins Square. The razing of shanty towns and police raids on the homeless, not only re-enacts the scenarios played out over the years in so-called Third World cities but also furnishes the imagery for the discourse of the revanchist city to become a national phenomenon in 1993.

Smith's profound comment that, in the wake of the bombing of the World Trade Centre, media self-representations of US cities – apparently the most cosmopolitan in the world – were 'so systematically able to insulate and indeed isolate the triumphs and crises of American life from international events . . . especially from the results of US military, political and economic policy abroad for so long', is one to which I shall later return.

The visions of 'urban reality' which these four essays represent are of the immense social, spatial, political, economic, as well as cultural contra-dictions generated by what is inadequately represented by the emasculated term 'globalization'. The metaphor of a (smooth and spherical) 'global city', first developed as a fertile image to signify the city, its characteristics and functions, and the (mainly socio-economic and financial) space of the world-economy in which it is embedded,[36,37] is too unitary, neutral and balanced for the fragmented, scarred and lopsided social and economic contradictions which the city contains. Approaching the city from the medical condition of the body politic, William Cobbett called early nineteenth century London 'the Great Wen'; cyst, blister, tumour are all potentially powerful metaphors that might be held in reserve to represent future forms of, and in, the 'global city'.

## II

If representations of 'the global city' have exposed its fractures, its sores and raw edges, the following three essays – clustered by convenience rather than affinity into one group – disturb and de-centre the representations of 'world space'[38] which the notion of the global city assumes. Eschewing both conventional as well as revisionary languages for writing about the city, philosopher and art historian Nkiru Nzegwu argues against the implicit economic determinism that drives many accounts of the contemporary city. Invoking Smith to show how socially generated ideologies determine the production of space, how ideational, subjective desires control economic forces and, with reference to her own discussion of the development of Nigeria's colonial capital of Lagos, how racism shaped the way in which city space was produced – a point also made by Perera in the following chapter – Nzegwu both implicitly and explicitly questions the assumptions behind a direct relationship between symbolic forms and economic process.

As befits her background in philosophy, Nzegwu's Afrocentric, gendered narrative springs from a clearly declared moral position, strengthened by sympathy for the human aspirations implicit in both Sciorra's and Smith's essays and often ignored in political economy narratives. Nzegwu questions the relevance of 'western' conceptual categories for the representation of Yoruba space, addressing the symbolic meaning of *Eko* (the local name for Lagos Island) in terms of its inhabitants' self-representations, including the cultural and symbolic beliefs which inform what she terms the 'freestyle' approach to the production of urban space.

It might be worth noting here that, despite the absence in the editorial prospectus of any reference to colonialism, it has become increasingly impossible to ignore the overwhelming importance of the historical, cultural and political significance of (European) colonialism as a major contributing factor in the making of the culture and space of many contemporary cities. This is not only in the obvious cases discussed here of Puerto Rico, Lagos, Colombo or Mombasa, but also in those cities of the United States, whether New York, Washington or Los Angeles, as yet insufficiently examined within a larger global colonial narrative. As suggested above, Smith has merely hinted at the overwhelmingly parochial media self-representations of New York City. A full-blown analysis which gave due attention to both internal as well as external colonialism in the making of New York is long overdue. Ironically, the story of American cities is too often told from the inside out, rather than the outside in (see also Bhabha, 1994[39]).

Much of Nzegwu's historical account of Lagos retells, in particular and distinctive form, an old colonial story: of imperial representations taking over from those of the locals; of dictatorial modes of space and government replacing consensual modes. Socially, physically and spatially, the colonial transformation was especially represented in the introduction of two-storey houses, organizing space along gender and class lines, with 'vertical homes . . . idolized as symbolizing power, privilege and progress', reinforcing patriarchal relations of power and implicitly opposed to earlier forms of Yoruba architecture which diffused power spatially and encouraged collective representations.

In some ways paralleling Perera's account of Colombo, both in relation to colonial and postcolonial representations of the two cities, Nzegwu addresses the post-1977 'modernization' of Lagos through the vehicles of capital, multinational corporations, and the importation of conspicuous consumption in the symbolic form of the department store. Here the postcolonial narrative takes over as the members of Nigeria's military government, their subjective identities geared to representing Lagos in the clothes of a specifically 'western' imperialist and capitalist modernity, 'seek to project Lagos as a major modern city' (sic), principally through government buildings. It is a project stymied, however, by the contradictory shift to the new capital of Abuja and a 'national' future threatened by ethnic fragmentation, regionalism and communal nationalism.

From the viewpoint of conventional 'urbanistic' writing, Nzegwu's refreshingly unorthodox narrative captures much of the presence of contemporary downtown Lagos. Both here, and in the other essays in this section, ethnicity takes on a new and different dimension. Its immense political and cultural significance apparently operating less at the level of the city than at that of the state, its meaning is at once both marginalised as well as magnified, posing serious questions concerning the future role that ethnicity may play as a political force for social and spatial change in American and European cities.

What is generally referred to as the comparative method is a common methodological device, a crude apparatus for the demonstration of both similarity and difference. It is also yet another way of producing representations. However as architect-planner and historian Nihal Perera points out in his chapter on Colombo, the one time capital of Sri Lanka, the various kinds of difference highlighted by such a method are – as in the Derridian insights discussed in Shields' chapter – defined primarily in relation to the first and most powerful unit in the duality being compared. Like Nzegwu, Perera begins by taking issue with the assumptions behind such a method. Unlike Nzegwu, however, he turns the comparison to his own advantage: the question is not what can be learnt about Colombo by seeing it through the lens of New York, but rather what can be learnt about New York by examining the development of Colombo, a question which yields many valuable insights.

Where Perera's narrative is particularly informed by a discourse on colonialism and is told broadly within the same political economy mode of representation as the essays in the first section, he argues strongly that such representations should reach out far beyond the perspective of the 'core'.

What his essay especially highlights is the need to examine not only the *forms* of representation but also the *spaces* of representation; what it is that is being represented, to which audience, and with reference to what larger spatial universe. This applies equally to the universe of language as we shall see below.

Within the political economy mode, Perera's essay also confirms the importance of paying attention to both culturally and politically different spaces, as well as the positions within these which each author occupies and from which he or she writes. Authors not only write from within different disciplines, states and textual communities, they also recognise and move within different metaphorical worlds. Perera contests many conventional western assumptions and presuppositions, including the most fundamental one for this collection – of particular significance for predominantly rural societies such as that of Sri Lanka – of focussing only on representations of *the city*. He also argues that cities exist in many systems, not only in that of a 'world economy', an issue that highlights the inadequacy of existing intellectual tools and languages to address postcolonial space. As Homi Bhabha has recently stated, this is an increasingly pertinent issue, both in regard to the tyranny of the western episteme, and whether 'the "new" languages of theoretical critique (semiotics, poststructuralist, deconstructionist and the rest) simply reflect those geopolitical divisions (of Anglo-American power) and their sphere of influence'.[40] The discussion of this extremely important issue, implicit rather than explicit in the reading of this collection, will have to wait for another occasion. The language of representation is a theme to which we must return.

These boundaries are pushed even further by Ali Mazrui, political scientist and expert in international cultural politics, who writes of Mombasa here across an impressively broad canvas of international cultural history, producing a geocultural narrative untainted by the specialised language of urbanologists. Addressing various aspects of both ethnicity and culture, Mazrui's interpretation of Mombasa locates the city not merely in the space of the Kenyan nation-state (the existence of which it has long preceded) and African continent, but also of continent in relation to continent, and continents in relation to the world. The intermediate position of Africa in the world, both spatially and geoculturally, is represented through the history of Mombasa, the cultural profile and characteristics of which Mazrui sees as produced through a series of long-term, wide-ranging cultural flows. And though, for the Eurocentric or Americocentric reader, representing a particular Afrocentric and Islamo-centric perspective, Mazrui's fast intellectual footwork subtly shifts his positionality as he moves through three geocultural phases of Mombasa's history: the Afro-Oriental phase, the Afro-Occidental phase, and the Afro-Global phase, each bringing a variety of different linguistic, spatial, dietary, religious and other cultural practices to a city which has been multicultural for a millenium.

The scale of Mazrui's narrative draws attention to the immense geopolitical and geocultural vectors which slice through the port city of Mombasa, at times bringing connections via the Portuguese to the Americas in the West (or indeed, Macao in the East), to Islam in the Arabian peninsula, or to Britain in the North. To paraphrase Mazrui, it is these vectors which explain why, within 24 hours the children of Mombasa cross through civilisations several times, exposed to Kiswahili language at home, Arabic or Islamic lessons in the mosque, Indian films at the cinema and obligatory English at school. Colonial links with Britain brought strong cultural influences in the realms of law, education and notions of the nation state; after decolonisation, American influences penetrate through the World Bank, the International Monetary Fund (IMF), and the media.

Mazrui's radically different historical and geocultural framework poses serious challenges to the more conventional ways of representing the city, both in terms of exclusion and inclusion, or the temporal frame in which perceptions of the city are located. Both Mazrui and Perera ask questions about the present political and cultural orientation of the city not only in terms of its historical links but more especially in relation to the political, economic and cultural regions to which the city is likely to relate in future (see also Taylor and Knox[41]).

We might ask what different insights would be gained by applying such long-term, spatially extensive representations to contemporary Los Angeles, Berlin or Manchester. Mazrui's attention to cultural flows contrasts sharply with Castell's attention to informational and economic flows.[42] Mazrui's Mombasa reminds us that the multicultural city has a long history; a phenomenon in Africa, Asia or Latin America long before it occurred in modern Europe or North America – unless, of course, we return historically to the cultural diaspora of imperial Rome or the ethnic mixes arising from Arab expansion through north Africa into Spain. At a time of extensive restructuring of economic, political and cultural alliances, from the North American Free Trade Agreement (NAFTA) and the European Community (EC), to the countries of the erstwhile Soviet Union, thinking about the restructuring and representation of cities becomes an important theoretical as well as political task.

### III

Though some of the essays in this final section elaborate upon earlier issues, they mainly address theories of representation in their own right. Taking his title from Luce Irigary's *This Sex Which Is Not One*,[43] art historian and

cultural theorist John Tagg's response to the original symposium presentations of Sassen and Zukin provides a useful illustration of a methodologically different mode of deconstruction and critique which contrasts
implicitly with the historical and theoretical mode of the papers in the
previous section. As other contributors, Tagg poses questions concerning
the criteria for defining and measuring 'global cities'. On the basis of
conceptualising world space as a world economy and global cities as
representing functions of 'global control capability' within that world
economy, the criteria for definition have been been set out at length
elsewhere.[44,45] However this is not to deny that many alternative
conceptualisations of world space might be made – cultural, linguistic,
religious, political, ecological, informational, or, as the scientist and
visionary Teilhard de Chardin proposed, as a 'noosphere', or global system
of thought and knowledge. If cities are 'worlded'[46] in these different ways,
Rome, Mecca or Soweto may well be considered as global cities, as Tagg
suggests (see also King,[47] Taylor and Knox[48]).

Writing from a social, spatial and geographical position in what he
metaphorically describes as the 'mean streets' of the (presumably, European
or American) 'nineteenth century metropolis', Tagg draws particular
attention to 'the (professional) languages in which the city is taken to be
known' – the languages of economics, sociology, statistics, etc. – 'languages
not only for describing the city but languages *of* the city'.[49,50] The comment
is especially valuable in throwing light on the gap that forever lies between
the conceptual and signifying task of language, including the many
taxonomies and classificatory systems which different textual communities
use and the everyday social, material, physical and spatial environments to
which they refer.[51]

Tagg's brief essay is equally valuable in bringing to our attention the
varied and specialised languages of representation used in the academy
which each of these chapters (as also this introduction) displays, and to
which Crysler refers in chapter 10. Drawing especially on a Foucaultian
mode, Tagg writes that 'to focus on the city as a disciplinary field . . . is to
focus on the production of the city across specific discursive regimes,
articulating the city as a space of new formations of power and pleasure,
domination and desire' – a representation which, from one perspective,
simultaneously and accurately characterises the essays in this collection
though, from another, in so far as the language excludes concepts which
each essay addresses, also tends to misrepresent them. Some of these issues
are taken up again in Shields' chapter.

Remobilizing the apparatus of deconstruction to address the absences of
race and gender in dominant representations of the economy, Saskia Sassen
takes advantage in her second chapter to address the 'positioned viewer'
behind dominant narratives in economics. In order to revalorise specific
places and presences in the economy, Sassen argues strongly for the

recognition of multiple systems of representation emerging from the new cultural politics and politics of identity, and the need for these 'to get out of theoretical texts and onto the streets' (See also Pile and Keith).[52]

Taking the city as a useful place to explore the limitations of mainstream economic narratives, Sassen questions some of their basic assumptions: the political emphasis on 'leading sectors', its implied hierarchy, and the favouring of some (especially corporate) sectors at the expense of others. What Sassen foregrounds with these questions are issues highlighted by Donald's quotation at the beginning of this chapter, that we cannot represent *the city* as such but only some aspects of it, some processes and flows that help to constitute it. Here Sassen questions the relevance of which flows and which sectors we choose to select.

Particularly important for Sassen's argument is what gets narrated under the language of 'immigration' and 'ethnicity', a whole series of processes which have to do, in one representation, with the globalization of economic activity, but under another – as Sciorra demonstrates – with identity formation and cultural politics. 'Ethnicity' becomes another name for 'Otherness', a lack of familiarity which, however, as highlighted by Smith, is seen only from a dominant white, usually male perspective. The concept of internationalization is rooted and positioned in the experience, to use another metaphor, of the centre not the periphery – each of which represents the process in quite different ways.

Sassen argues here for the recognition of globalization as a process comprising people as well as capital; for a revalorisation of the disadvantaged, women, minorities and migrants in global cities; for the city as a place where the forces of capital as well as labour 'come to rest or fight'. Echoing some of Smith's perspectives, despite others' arguments to abandon the city, Sassen argues in its favour, as 'a strategic terrain for the new cultural politics', a place where the two sectors – the corporate center and 'the other' – 'find in the city a strategic terrain for their operations . . . a new frontier . . . charged with the possibility of fundamental transformation in the West . . . a site where battles of identity, rights, space and life itself are being fought out'.

Where earlier essays have aimed to produce, as well as interrogate, a combination of predominantly economic, social, spatial or cultural narratives, representing the history and nature of particular cities, the subject of sociologist and cultural theorist Rob Shields' chapter is urban representation itself, and the way in which particular contemporary western theorists (generally male, though Shields takes up this dimension of gender) have addressed this.[53]

Starting first with the work of Michel de Certeau and Walter Benjamin, Shields selects for us some telling images; like mists or fog, 'representations blanket' the city, constantly changing the way it appears to us; they are 'arrangements of life', 'treacherous models' which displace the city in its complexity. Yet representations do not exist in limbo; just as the city is a representation of (some) people who construct (and reconstruct) it, so also do people think of their world through their environment. The practices involved in the production of meaning are linked inextricably to the realm of ideas and discourses, but also to the realm of the material, physical and spatial world itself.

Shields walks us through the city with some of the more influential of recent city guides: after de Certeau and Benjamin, Jacques Derrida and Michel Maffesoli, Georg Simmel, Henri Lefebvre and Michel Foucault; through Mikhail Bakhtin's 'dialogical city' and Deleuze and Guattari's 'city as a body without organs', concluding with a comment on the city of the Situationists.

Shields' essay is too rich in the ideas he draws from the scholars discussed, to attempt any useful summary. However I shall close with some of his comments following Derrida because they highlight what is often missing from contemporary poststructuralist cultural theory mobilized in the space of the city. The spatial setting, Shields writes, 'inflects the meaning of even the most basic metaphors . . . space has communicative properties . . . representations depend not only on linguistic and other cultural sign systems but also on material culture . . . In the city, people are inscribed but on it, they leave their own everyday traces'.

One of the more prominent and contested spheres in the realm of urban representations is that of 'architecture' and 'architectural history'. In the following chapter, cultural and architectural critic Greig Crysler examines how a range of forces is involved in the production and dissemination of a particular form of scholarly knowledge, namely, architectural history and its institutionalisation both within and outside professional schools of architecture. Drawing particularly on studies in the sociology of knowledge and literary theory, he addresses the origins of the Society of Architectural Historians in the USA, and especially, the constitution of forms of professional knowledge as represented in the Society's journal over a period of 50 years.

Among many insights, Crysler shows how particular discourses develop in relation to specific representations and practices (such as preservation) regarding selected elements in the city. He draws attention to the way in which both the Society and the journal participate in the construction of a professional identity for the architectural historian; of how, in the interests of wider public dissemination, specialised forms of discourse are eschewed in favour of 'ordinary' language; how oppositional social relations work to exclude specific objects, discourses and forms of knowledge resulting in the formation of a nationally-constituted canon that represents, for the journal's readership, the 'official' practice of architectural history.

Highlighting the way that forms of historical knowledge are produced in relation to specific geographical, cultural and political representations of the world, Crysler focuses our attention on the specifically Eurocentric taxonomies and categorisations which classify and locate the traditional objects of architectural history in the US, citing Hayden White to argue that the differing ways in which mimesis is constituted in historical narratives defines differing forms of historical consciousness. As mentioned earlier, Crysler also directs our attention to the specialised languages of different knowledge communities. Despite the increasing degree of social and cultural differentiation in both the public audience and the academy, including differences of ethnicity, class, nationality, gender, sexual orientation or race, specialised languages or the limitation of objects of enquiry can be deployed as a political tactic to maintain cultural hegemony.

As in the original symposium, geographer and cultural theorist James Duncan, whose recent publications have made significant contributions to the theme of this book, brings this collection to a close. Choosing three influential 'city writers', old and new – E. W. Burgess, Mike Davis, and Roland Barthes – Duncan draws especially on the work of Hayden White to examine the particular metaphorical language with which they have mediated their experience of the city. Particularly interesting here is the early and influential work of E.W.Burgess and his urban world of a 'natural' order, ecology and evolution. The theoretical concerns of Burgess and his other sociological colleagues in Chicago were to do much to ensure that 'modern' life in the West was represented as *urban* life. And as Duncan states here, for many years representations of modern cities – irrespective of location – were made to defer to the form of Chicago.

For Davis, writing Los Angeles, the language is one of warfare, the metaphors of invasion; explanations of urban processes are for ever deferred elsewhere. For Barthes, no longer believing that he (or others) can even represent the world, there are no political solutions; one can only celebrate the fragmentary. Inspired by Japan, Barthes' writings have involved a search for emptiness and absence of meaning.

The importance of Duncan's chapter is to underscore the meaning of representation as an essentially intertextual process: writing the city is inevitably linked to any number of different narratives. As Duncan suggests, the city cannot be described in terms of itself alone. Analysis requires that we focus on the rhetorical form of representations.

Combining these insights with those of Shields suggests that we should argue for and celebrate multi-dimensional representations. Rather than striving for monological coherence and closure, we should encourage parallel and conflicting representations to coexist. To quote the suggestion of Shields, this will be the 'trans-discursive city'.

## NOTES

1.    J. Donald, 'Metropolis: The City as Text', in R. Bocock and K. Thompson (eds), *Social and Cultural Forms of Modernity* (Polity Press, Cambridge, 1992), pp. 417–61, p. 427.
2.    S. Zukin in this volume, chapter 2, p. 43.
3.    J. Walton, 'Culture and Economy in Shaping Urban Life: General Issues and Latin American Examples', in J. A. Agnew, J. Mercer and D. Sopher (eds), *The City in Cultural Context* (Allen & Unwin, London, 1984) p. 78.
4.    D. Harvey, *Social Justice and the City* (Edward Arnold, London, 1973).
5.    D. Harvey, *Consciousness and the Urban Experience* (Blackwell, Oxford, 1985).
6.    M. Castells, *The Urban Question* (Edward Arnold, London, 1977).
7.    J. Tagg in this volume, chapter 8, p. 180.
8.    S. Rushdie, *The Satanic Verses* (Viking, New York, 1988).
9.    N. Thrift, 'An Urban Impasse?', *Theory, Culture and Society*, 10 (1993), pp. 229–38.
10.   J. Jacobs, 'The City Unbound: Qualitative Approaches to the City', *Urban Studies*, 30 (1993) 4/5, pp. 827–48.
11.   Ibid. Jacobs provides a valuable overview of recent 'qualitative' research, including 'discursive and representational analyses, a methodological shift which responds in part to poststructuralist and feminist thinking'.
12.   F. Jameson, 'Postmodernism, or the Cultural Logic of Late Capitalism', *New Left Review*, 146 (1984), pp. 53–92.
13.   C. Philo and J. Kearns (eds), *Selling Places: Culture and Capital in the Contemporary City* (Pergamon, Oxford, 1994).
14.   J. Jacobs, p. 830 (see note 10).
15.   J. Wolff, 'The Real City, the Discursive City, the Disappearing City: Post-modernism and Urban Sociology', *Theory and Society*, 21 (1992), pp. 553–60.
16.   J. Jacobs, p. 827 (see note 10).
17.   J. S. Duncan, *The City as Text. The Politics of Landscape Interpretation in the Kandyan Kingdom* (Cambridge University Press, 1990).
18.   J. Donald (see note 1).
19.   C. Smuda (ed.) *Die Grosstadt Als 'Texte'* (Wilhelm Frink Verlag, Munich, 1992).
20.   L. Rodwin and R. M. Hollister (eds), *Cities of the Mind: Images and Themes of the City in the Social Sciences* (Plenum Press, New York, 1984).
21.   P. Langer 'Sociology – Four Images of Organized Diversity: Bazaar, Jungle, Organism, and Machine', in Rodwin and Hollister, pp. 97–118 (see note 20).
22.   J. Donald (see note 1).
23.   J. Walton, p. 78 (see note 3).
24.   S. Sassen, *The Global City. New York, London, Tokyo* (Princeton University Press, 1991). See also A. D. King (note 36).
25.   J. Friedmann, 'The World City Hypothesis', *Development and Change*, vol. 17, no. 1 (1986), pp. 69–83.
26.   J. Donald, p. 6 (see note 1).
27.   T. J. Barnes and J. S. Duncan (eds), *Writing Worlds. Discourse, Text and Metaphor in the Representation of Landscape* (Routledge, London and New York, 1992).
28.   J. S. Duncan and D. Ley (eds), *Culture/Place/Representation* (Routledge, London and New York, 1993).
29.   A. D. King, 'Re-Presenting World Cities: Cultural Theory/Social Practice', in Taylor and Knox (see note 41).

30. J. S. Duncan and N. Duncan, '(Re)reading the Landscape', *Environment and Planning D: Society and Space*, 6 (1988), pp. 117–26.
31. B. Stock, 'Texts, Readers and Enacted Narratives', *Visible Language*, 20 (1986), pp. 294–301.
32. J. S. Duncan in this volume, chapter 12.
33. S. Sassen (see note 24).
34. A. D. King, *Urbanism, Colonialism, and the World-Economy: Cultural and Spatial Foundations of the World Urban System* (Routledge, London and New York, 1990), p. 132.
35. A. D. King (see note 29).
36. A. D. King, *Global Cities. Post-Imperialism and the Internationalisation of London* (Routledge, London and New York, 1990).
37. S. Sassen, *Cities in a World Economy* (Pine Forge, Thousand Oaks CA, 1994).
38. I am indebted to Nihal Perera for this term.
39. H. Bhabha, *The Location of Culture* (Routledge, London and New York, 1994), ch. 9.
40. Ibid., p. 20.
41. P. Taylor and P. Knox (eds), *World Cities in a World-System* (Cambridge University Press, 1995).
42. M. Castells, *The Informational City* (Blackwell, Oxford, 1991).
43. L. Irigary, *This Sex Which Is Not One*, trans. C. Porter and C. Bourke (Cornell University Press, Ithaca, 1985).
44. A. D. King (see note 36).
45. S. Sassen (see note 24).
46. G. S. Spivak, *In Other Worlds* (Routledge, London and New York, 1988).
47. A. D. King 'Identity and Difference: the Internationalization of Capital and the Globalization of Culture', in P. Knox (ed.), *The Restless Urban Landscape* (Prentice-Hall, New Jersey, 1993).
48. P. Taylor and P. Knox (see note 41).
49. J. Tagg in this volume, ch. 8, p. 180.
50. Jacobs (p. 381, note 10) cites F. Choay, 'Urbanism and Semiology', in M. Gottdiener and A. P. Lagopoulos (eds), *The City and the Sign* (Columbia University Press, New York, 1986), pp. 160–75, to make a similar though subtly different point: that 'it is now necessary to replace the idea of "a language *of* the city" with an understanding of the "language *on* the city"'.
51. A. D. King, 'Taxonomies and Types: Making Sense of Some Buildings and Cities', in K. A. Franck and L. H. Schneekloth (eds), *Ordering Space. Types in Architecture and Design* (Van Rostrand Reinhold, New York, 1994).
52. S. Pile and M. Keith (eds), *Place and the Politics of Identity* (Routledge, London and New York, 1993).
53. The sections in Jacobs' article (note 10) on 'Feminist Cities' and 'Sexuality and Cities' provide a useful introduction to the growing literature in these fields.

See also:

- J. Clifford and G. Marcus (eds), *Writing Culture* (University of California Press, Berkeley, 1986).
- P. Rabinow, 'Representations are Social Facts: Modernity and Postmodernity in Anthropology', in Clifford and Marcus, above.
- A. D. King, 'The Times and Spaces of Modernity', in Mike Featherstone et al., *Global Modernities* (Sage, London, Newbury Park, Delhi, 1995), pp. 108–23.

# I
# ETHNICITY, CAPITAL, AND CULTURE: REPRESENTATIONS OF NEW YORK CITY

# 1

# Rebuilding the Global City: Economy, Ethnicity and Space

Saskia Sassen

---

A walk through almost any of today's large modern cities in Western Europe or the USA leaves one with the impression that each contains many cities: the corporate city of high-rise office buildings, the old dying industrial city, the immigrant city. A space of power; a space of labor and machines; a Third World space. Are they indeed three separate cities, each belonging to a different historico/geographic phase? Or do they presuppose each other — the existence of one, a condition for the other? And if so, what is the nature of the dynamic that connects them?

The particular kind of urban form that dominates our image of today's advanced urban economy is the agglomeration of high-rise corporate offices we see in New York, London, Frankfurt or Tokyo. It has emerged as a kind of representation of advanced city form, the image of the postindustrial city. The industrial town of 50 years ago gained its identity from the built forms of manufacturing. There may have been many other activities in some of these towns. Yet the representational forms of the town were smokestacks. The early Soviet experience imbued this form with an epic quality. Today's corporate towers are imbued with the 'neutrality' of advanced engineering and the power of advanced economic operations.

We see a homogenizing in the urban forms of advanced economic sectors in cities with such disparate histories and cultures as New York, London and Tokyo. This pressure towards homogeneity overrides history and culture. But beyond the central urban core of high-rise luxury offices there are discontinuities within each of these cities: a hierarchy of urban forms, from the transnational urban space of finance to the old working-class districts and new immigrant communities.

The corporate complex and the immigrant community today are probably two extreme modes in the formation and appropriation of urban space. The urban form represented by the global city function – the internationalized corporate services complex and the highly paid professional workforce with its high-priced lifestyle – is the one habitually thought to constitute the essence of an advanced postindustrial economy. The urban form represented by the immigrant community, or more specifically, the informal economy, is habitually seen as not belonging to an advanced economy, one to be found here only because it is imported via immigration. These two socio-physical forms are increasingly evident in more and more major cities in developed countries. Large US cities represent a 'vanguard', containing perhaps the most evolved version that these two forms can assume.

These two forms reveal how power and the lack of power inscribe themselves in the urban landscape. There are different narratives attached to each. One represents technological advance and cosmopolitan culture, the other economic and cultural backwaters. One presents itself as part of the global economy, suffused in internationalism; the other, while international in its origin, is promptly reconstituted as a local vernacular form. One is read to be dis-embedded in the way Giddens[1] has described certain aspects of modernity – transterritorial to the point of being thought of as a-spatial through such concepts as the information economy and telematics. The other is read as deeply embedded – in an economic, social and cultural territory of neighborhoods and particularistic traditions.

I should note promptly that the corporate complex and the informal economy are but two of the distinct features of today's large cities in the United States and in other highly developed countries. There are two other categories that are central to any such account: they are race and gender. Their presence and their representations suffuse all else. Their complexity deserves full treatment, which I address in my second chapter in this book.

Here I will argue that not only the corporate complex but also the informal economy and, more generally, certain 'working-class' uses of space are also forms through which the broader economic dynamic typical of advanced economies is materialized in urban space. One can ask what is the place in an advanced urban economy of firms and sectors which appear to be backward or lack the advanced technologies and human capital base of the leading industries? Are they superfluous? And what about the types of workers employed by such firms? It might be that many of the highly differentiated components of the economy – whether firms, sectors or workers – are articulated under forms of extreme segmentation in the social, economic, racial and organizational traits of each component. This raises yet another question. To what extent is this segmentation produced or strengthened by the existence of ethnic/racial segmentation in combination with racism and discrimination? Ethnic/racial segmentation not only produces economic outcomes that devalue some firms and workers and overvalue others, but also produces a narrative about the nature of our large cities which marginalizes the economics and the culture of non-dominant sectors.

I propose to examine the interconnections between that which is represented as advanced and neutral and that which is represented as backward and particularistic. Such a conceptual reconstituting of the urban economy carries theoretical and political implications. The first section of this paper briefly examines the urban economy of large cities to introduce some key trends and critical questions and discusses the internationalization of the leading corporate services complex and its rise to a dominant position in the urban economy. The focus is particularly on New York City but there are references to other major cities. The purpose here is to show how global processes are actually constituted in the urban economy and in urban space. What is the specific economic content and spatial form of internationalization? How is it different from earlier forms? Also of interest here is the attempt to recover the material conditions, including the production process involved in this corporate complex, in order to uncover the connections with other sectors and types of firms and workers.

The second section examines one of the distinct economic spaces associated with immigrant communities, the informal economy – probably one of the most extreme representations of 'backwardness'. The purpose here is to understand what the informal economy is and what fed its growth in advanced urban economies. This should help us see the extent to which the informal economy is indeed a closed system, internal to the immigrant community, as many think, or whether it is at least in part, deeply intertwined with mainstream sectors. One concern here is also to identify the spaces of the informal economy. Are they always inside the immigrant community, as is commonly thought?

The third section of the paper takes a low-income, low-price commercial district in a large city, a type of place that could be found in any major city. In this case it is 14th Street in Manhattan. To the mainstream eye, much of the commercial area looks rundown, economically marginal, a waste of precious urban space better put to use with high-priced office buildings. I examine this space in order to understand its place in the broader city's economy, and in the light of mainstream cultural narratives about what belongs and what doesn't, what can survive and what cannot in a city like New York, and a place like Manhattan. The aim of these sections is to uncover a different story about the nature of an advanced urban economy in today's world, and the articulation of economic place, cultural identity and dominant or mainstream ideas about both.

## A CONCEPTUAL PERSPECTIVE

Major changes in the technical and spatial organization of the economy at the local, national, and global levels have fed the demand for the kinds of services and centralized control operations likely to be concentrated in major cities. Here the constructs 'world city'[2,3] or 'global cities'[4] or 'global city function'[5] are useful. The need for nodal points to coordinate global economic activities contributes to the emergence of world cities. To this coordinating role I add that of sites for the production of a large array of inputs and 'organizational commodities' necessary for global control and coordination.[6,7]

These inputs need to be produced. We can think of the producer services sector as a sort of new basic industry and cities like New York, Los Angeles or London as preferred sites of production for this industry. A concern with production also makes it possible to shift the focus away from the large multinational corporations which dominate the global economic stage, onto the vast array of small firms involved in the production of such services. Furthermore it leads to an investigation of the organization of this industry: its patterns of subcontracting, suppliers, networks, input and output markets, and other key components. That is to say, while large multinationals are the key economic actors in today's national and world economy, there are many economic activities necessary for the type of economic system such corporations engender, but that take place outside those corporations. I thus want to look at cities as sites for the location of this new basic industry, and not only as sites for the location of corporate headquarters.

A question that emerges out of this concerns the consequences of such a new economic core in major cities for the organization of other economic sectors. Specifically, does the existence of a dynamic growth sector feed the expansion of what appear to be declining or backward economic sectors, such as the downgraded manufacturing sector and the informal economy? What are the linkages? To what extent do the most sophisticated white-collar industries that characterize the new economic core need access to a broad range of industrial services located in places with easy access, notably in Manhattan? And when such service firms lack the bidding power to locate there, does operating informally become an option?

More generally, any city demands goods at least some of which benefit from being produced in a city location. Further changes in the economic base of cities have resulted in a growing demand for goods that can be produced by small firms that prefer a city location because of access to suppliers and customers. But the general understanding about manufacturing, and one that is expressed in much policy, is that a large scale and standardization are the only viable forms of organizing production, and that city locations are therefore unfeasible. Forms of manufacturing production that do not respond to these criteria will tend to be seen as backward or marginal, conjuring up the image of the garment sweatshop. Allocating space to manufacturing activities in large cities is consequently viewed as inefficient. Yet the most dynamic sectors of the city's economy require access to local-based manufacturers for certain kinds of customized products for both firms and households.

A related question is the effect of the reorganization of income-earning activities on consumption patterns and life-style issues. There is considerable evidence that a growing share of high-income jobs are going to city residents, more so in New York than in other major cities. This new middle class produced not only a physical upgrading of expanded portions of major cities, but also a reorganization of the consumption structure, both particularly evident in the high-growth years of the 1980s. The high income of the new workers was not sufficient to explain the transformation. Less tangible factors also matter. An examination of this transformation reveals a dynamic whereby an economic potential – the consumption capacity represented by high disposable income – is realized through the emergence of a new vision of the good life.

The immigrants, in turn, have produced a low-cost equivalent of gentrification. Areas of the city once filled with shut-up storefronts and abandoned buildings, are now thriving commercial and residential neighborhoods. The growing size and complexity of immigrant communities have generated a demand and supply for a wide range of goods, services and workers. The separateness of the immigrant community becomes a vehicle to maximize the potential it contains. Small investments become neighborhood upgrading because of the residential concentration of immigrants. This upgrading does not fit the conventional notions of upgrading, notions rooted in the middle-class experience. Its shape, colors and sounds are novel. They, like the cosmopolitan work culture of the new professionals, are yet another form of the internationalization of global cities.

Not unrelated to these questions is the growing incorporation of women both at the high and at the low end of the occupational structure. A larger share of the new job growth in the region from 1985 to 1992 is accounted for by women. Women make up 50 per cent of all city residents employed in the business and professional services. One question concerns the extent to which the new urban 'gentry' is female. A large presence of women in middle-class gentrification may well lead to a renewed urbanization of families, especially female-headed or two-career families. This would engender an expanded demand for various family services. If we add to this the strong family base in immigrant communities, we might posit a recovery of urban space for family life that is female-led in gentrified *and* poverty areas, and immigrant-led in some other areas of the city. Though somewhat speculative, this notion of a new, female and immigrant-led urbanization of families is intriguing.

Finally a question bringing these different strands together is that of the effect of economic restructuring (in its many guises) on the organization of the capital-labor relation. This type of question requires theorizing alongside empirical research. It organizes much of the presentation in the following sections. Informalization and downgrading are, in the last analysis, modes of reorganizing the relationship between capital and labor. And the changes in the sphere of social reproduction described above also have contributed to such a reorganization insofar as consumption and life-style have contributed to a proliferation of small firms. These contain a distinct form of work organization, quite different from the large-scale, standardized firm where unionization and adherence to various regulations are more typical.

One fundamental form of the interaction of space, production and social reproduction is that the economic base in a city requires a supply of both high-income and low-wage workers. Insofar as it is necessary for a city to contain housing appropriate to both types of workers, conflicts may emerge over the access to city land for housing and to all other components of the sphere of social reproduction – shops, schools, services. At the same time that the economy needs these two types of workers, the bidding power of the high-income worker is so much higher that it can spatially displace the low-income worker. Yet if the trip to work for low-income workers becomes unacceptably long or costly to them, the economy of the city would suffer, notably those highly dynamic sectors that generate the greatest value and a critical mass of both high and low-income jobs.

The socio-economic transformation of the resident population has its own 'autonomous' effect on space in the city. One effect of expanding high and low-income populations is the proliferation of small firms; and two very different types of small firms. Some cater to the upscale market, others to the low-scale market, and include not only services and retail, but also certain types of manufacturing. Indeed the existence of high and low-income residential populations may have the effect of promoting certain forms of manufacturing activity in the city because each of these populations in its own way contributes to a growth in the demand for goods produced on a small scale and locally. At the upscale end, these products and services are adequately or conveniently described as customized; on the low scale as extremely cheap. The proliferation of small firms tells us that a city location is feasible and that neighborhood-level firms become more typical at the same time that global market firms dominate the city's economy.

An intermediate variable that is quite significant in facilitating the proliferation of small firms is the existence of immigrant communities, because these tend to have the requisite structures to implement such production. These structures include labor supply networks that are both flexible, reliable and cheap; a supply of skills and entrepreneurial experience with many immigrants having been craft workers in their home countries; and mutual help arrangements essential for securing the necessary capital. Spatially, these immigrant communities emerge as key locations for a range of firms that are actually producing for the mainstream market, for select boutiques, for larger firms and for individual clients.

The overall sense, particularly accentuated in Manhattan, is that residential space has increasingly been occupied by a growing urban gentry and the infrastructure of shops it requires; by a growing number of immigrant communities containing various sub-economies; and by a growing mass of poor, displaced people who occupy devastated areas of the city, some of which eventually become incorporated into the expanding gentrification process or, alternatively, into the expanding immigrant communities. Commercial space is increasingly occupied by the corporate complex and its auxiliary services, by the informal economy and by the downgraded manufacturing sector.

## CITIES IN THE WORLD ECONOMY

### 1. Global Command Centers

Today, the territorial dispersal of economic activity on a national and world scale creates a need for expanded central control and management, if this dispersal is to occur under conditions of continued economic concentration. The domestic and international dispersal of loci of growth and the internationalization of finance bring to the fore questions concerning the incorporation of such growth into the profit-generating processes that contribute to economic concentration. That is to say, while in principle the territorial decentralization of economic activity could have been accompanied by a corresponding decentralization in ownership and hence in the appropriation of profits, there has been little movement in that direction. Though large firms have increased their subcontracting to smaller firms, and many national firms in the newly industrializing countries have grown rapidly, this form of growth is ultimately part of a chain in which a limited number of corporations continue to control the end product and to reap the profits associated with selling on the world market. Even industrial homeworkers in remote rural areas are now part of that chain.

This is not only evident with firms, it is also evident with places. Thus, the internationalization and expansion of finance has brought growth to a large number of smaller financial markets, a growth which has fed the expansion of the global industry. But top level control and management of the industry has become concentrated in a few leading financial centers, especially New York, London and Tokyo. These account for a disproportionate share of all financial transactions and one that has grown rapidly since the early 1980s.

The fundamental dynamic posited here is that the more globalized the economy becomes the higher the agglomeration of central functions in global cities. The extremely high densities evident in the downtown districts of these cities are the spatial expression of this logic. The widely accepted notion that agglomeration has become obsolete when global telecommunication advances allow for maximum dispersal, is only partly correct. It is, I argue, precisely because of the territorial dispersal facilitated by telecommunication advances that agglomeration of centralizing activities has expanded immensely. This is not a mere continuation of old patterns of agglomeration but, one could posit, a new logic for agglomeration.

The space economy of technological innovation appears to follow the same pattern of dispersal and agglomeration. The most encompassing analysis can be found in Castells' major new book *The Informational City*.[8] He posits that restructuring processes under way in the electronics industry produce a locational logic characterized by the strengthening, notwithstanding urban crisis and economic downturns, of centers for high level innovation which will command and be at the heart of a globally dispersed production system. Secondary 'milieux of innovation' will continue to develop, but increasingly not as a function of innovation but of decentralization of some aspects of the process of innovation. And offshore production will continue but with strong upgrading through the automation of routine operations and the increased offshoring of advanced manufacturing processes. Thus a spatial division of labor will remain as a distinct trait of information-technology industries.[9]

The spatial and technical transformation of economic activity includes the geographic dispersion of plant, offices and service outlets, and the sharp rise in the use of highly specialized services frequently associated with the development of micro-electronics. These two processes, dispersal and service specialization, interact and overlap. The global dispersion requires centralized top-level management and control. Firms operating many plants, offices and service outlets must coordinate planning, internal administration and distribution, marketing and other central headquarters activities. As large corporations move into the production and sale of final consumer services, a wide range of activities, previously performed by free-standing consumer service firms, are shifted to the central headquarters of the new corporate owners. A parallel pattern of expansion of central high-level planning and control operations takes place in governments, brought about partly by the technical developments that make this possible and partly by the growing complexity of regulatory and administrative tasks. Finally, the re-concentration of a considerable component of foreign investment activity and transactions in major cities has further fed this economic core of high-level control and servicing functions. In brief, alongside well-documented decentralization tendencies there are new, less well-documented centralization tendencies.

In short, spatial dispersion of production and the reorganization of the financial industry have created new forms of centralization for the management and regulation of a global network of production sites and financial markets. Spatial dispersion of production, in some cases internationally, has stimulated growth of centralized service nodes for its management and regulation, and telecommunications advances have facilitated both dispersal and centralized servicing.

## 2.  Production Sites and Marketplaces for Global Capital

Centralized control and management over a geographically dispersed array of plants, offices and service outlets does not come about inevitably as part of a 'world system'. It requires the development of a vast range of highly specialized services and top-level management and control functions. These constitute the components for 'global control capability'.[10] Such advances in electronics and telecommunication have transformed geographically distant cities into centers for global communication and long-distance management.

Going beyond the domain of the existing literature on cities, I posit that global cities are a specific type of production site and I examine their central command functions as a production process. They are sites for a) the production of specialized services needed by complex organizations, including prominently top level management, control and servicing operations necessary for running a spatially dispersed network of factories, offices and service outlets under conditions of continued economic concentration; and b) the production of financial innovations and the making of markets, both central to the internationalization and expansion of the financial industry.[11]

By focusing on the production of global control capability, I am seeking to displace the focus of attention from the familiar issue of the power of large corporations over governments and economies; or the issue of supracorporate concentration of power through interlocking directorates or organizations such as the IMF. I want to focus on an aspect that has received less attention, which could be referred to as the *practice* of global control: the work of producing and reproducing the organization and management of a global production system and global marketplace for finance, both under conditions of economic concentration. My focus is on production: the production of those inputs that constitute the capability for global control and the infrastructure of jobs involved in this production. This allows me to focus on cities and on the urban social order associated with these activities.

Formally, the development of the modern corporation and its massive participation in world markets and foreign countries has made planning, internal administration, product development and research increasingly important and complex. Diversification of product lines, mergers and transnationalization of economic activities all require highly specialized skills. The development of multi-site manufacturing, service and banking have created an expanded demand for a wide range of specialized service activities to manage and control global networks of factories, service outlets and branch offices. While to some extent these activities can be carried out in-house, a large share is not. High levels of specialization, the possibility of externalizing the production of some of these services and the growing demand by large and small firms and by governments, are all conditions that have both resulted from and made possible the development of a market for freestanding service firms that produce components for what I refer to as global control capability. This in turn means that small firms can buy components of that capability, such as management consulting or international legal advice. And so can firms and governments from anywhere in the world. In brief, while the large corporation is undoubtedly a key agent inducing the development of this capability and is its prime beneficiary, it is not the sole user.

The growth of advanced services for firms, along with their particular characteristics of production, helps to explain the centralization of management and servicing functions that fueled the economic boom of the early and mid-1980s in New York, London, Tokyo, and other international business centers. The face-to-face explanation needs to be refined in several ways. Advanced services are mostly producer services; unlike other types of services, they are often not dependent on proximity to the consumers served. Rather economies occur in such specialized firms when they locate close to others that produce key inputs or whose own proximity makes possible joint production of certain service offerings. Moreover concentration arises out of the needs and expectations of the people likely to be employed in these new high-skill jobs. They are attracted to the amenities and life-styles that large urban centers can offer. The accounting firm can service its clients at a distance, but the nature of its service depends on proximity to specialists, lawyers, programmers. In this sense then, one can speak of *production sites*.

In the case of the financial industry I argue that this dynamic is also central, but that there are two distinct phases. Up to the end of the 1982 Third-World debt crisis, the large transnational banks dominated the financial markets both in terms of volume and the nature of firm transactions. After 1982, this dominance is increasingly challenged by other financial institutions and the major innovations they produce. These lead to a transformation in the leading components of the financial industry, a proliferation of financial institutions and the rapid internationalization of financial markets. The marketplace and the advantages of agglomeration assumed new significance in the 1980s and led simultaneously to a) the incorporation of a multiplicity of markets all over the world into a global system which fed the growth of the industry after the 1982 debt crisis and b) new forms of concentration, specifically the centralization of the industry in a few leading financial centers. Hence, in the case of the financial industry, a focus on the large transnational banks would exclude precisely those sectors of the industry where much of the new growth and production of innovations has occurred and it would, again, leave out an examination of the wide range of activities, firms and markets that constitute the financial industry in the 1980s.

Thus there are a number of reasons to focus on marketplaces and production sites rather than on the large corporations and banks. First, most scholarship on the internationalization of the economy is already focused on the large corporations and transnational banks. Second, there is a wide array of economic activities, many outside the corporation, which contribute to produce and reproduce corporate power; activities mostly concentrated in major cities. Third, in the case of finance, a focus on the large transnational banks would leave out precisely the most dynamic institutional sector of the industry, one where key new components have been invented and put into circulation. Finally an exclusive focus on corporations and banks leaves out a number of issues concerning the social, economic and spatial impact of these activities on the cities that contain them.

A focus on the spatial and organizational forms assumed by economic globalization today and the actual work of running transnational economic operations,[12] has the effect of recovering the centrality of place and work in processes of economic globalization. A concern with place and work opens up the inquiry to components of the urban economy we do not associate with globalization but which may indeed be an integral part of the global city function, such as the informal economy and certain working-class uses, the subject of the next two sections. (See also Brecher et al.[13] for a view from below of global processes.)


## THE INFORMAL ECONOMY

The possibility of an informal economy in highly developed countries is not foreseen in the main theories on economic development generally, and postindustrial society in particular. Such a possibility is, then, highly controversial and demands not only empirical documentation of its existence but also a theoretically specified plausibility. The concept of an informal economy describes a process of income generating activity characterized by the lack of regulation, in a context where similar activities are regulated. Regulation here refers to the institutionalized intervention of the state in the process of income generating activity. Thus while particular instances of informal work in highly developed countries may resemble those of an earlier period, they are actually a new development in the organization of work given decades of institutionalized regulation that had led to a pronounced reduction, and at times virtual elimination, of unregulated income-generating activity. Because the particular characteristics of informal work are derived from the fact of a context where such work is regulated, the informal economy can only be understood in its relation to the formal economy. But the theories that dominate explanations of advanced economies, whether neo-classical or Marxist, posit that as development proceeds, informal income-generating processes and relations of production will disappear. These theories suggest the gradual incorporation of all aspects of work into formalized market relations.

There is a considerable amount of literature on what is referred to usually as the 'informal sector' but it is focused on Third World countries and has, wittingly or not, assumed that as a social type such sectors are not to be expected in advanced economies. And the literature on industrialization has assumed that as development progresses, so will the standardization of production and generalization of the 'formal' organization of work.

The question, then, is how does this process fit in an advanced economy such as that of New York City. Is it a marginal sphere that provides cheap labor to marginal firms, or are there components of the informal economy that are articulated with the major growth sectors? Since much of the expansion of the informal economy in US cities has been located in immigrant communities, it has led to an explanation of its expansion as being due to the large influx of Third World immigrants and their propensities to replicate survival strategies typical of their home countries – in brief, that it is supply-induced. Related to this view is the notion that backward sectors of the economy are kept backward or even alive because of the availability of a large supply of cheap immigrant workers. Both of these views posit or imply that if there is an informal economy in advanced industrialized countries, the sources are to be found in Third World immigration and in the backward sectors of the economy – a Third World import or a remnant from an earlier phase of industrialization.

Rather than assume that Third World immigration is causing informalization, what we need is a critical examination of the role it might or might not play in this process. Immigrants, in so far as they tend to form communities, may be in a favorable position to seize the opportunities represented by informalization.[14] But the opportunities are not necessarily created by immigrants. They may well be a structured outcome of current trends in the advanced industrialized economies. Similarly what are perceived as backward sectors of the economy may or may not be remnants from an earlier phase of industrialization; they may well represent a downgrading of work involving growing sectors of the economy.

The evidence points to several distinctions in the process of informalization in New York City. A first set of distinctions concerns the origin of the demand for informally produced or distributed goods and services. We can identify informal activities that result from the demand for goods and services in the larger economy, either from final consumers or firms. Most of the informal work in the garment, furniture, construction, packaging and electronics industries is of this type. And we can identify informal activities that result from demand internal to the communities where such activities are performed. Immigrant communities are a leading example, and probably account for much of this second type of demand.

Second, an examination of the conditions that may be contributing directly to the demand for informal production and distribution indicates several sources. One of these is competitive pressures in certain industries, notably apparel, to reduce labor costs given massive competition from low-wage Third World countries. Informal work in this instance represents an acute example of exploitation. The fashion industry needs to have producers in close vicinity for many of its items; given high land prices, informal production operations are one answer for the fashion industry in New York, London, Paris and even Tokyo.[15] Another source is a rapid increase in the volume of renovations, alterations and small-scale new construction associated with the transformation of many areas of the city from low-income, often dilapidated neighborhoods into higher income commercial and residential areas. What in many other cities in the US would have involved a massive program of new construction was mostly a process of rehabilitation of old structures in the case of New York City. The volume of work, its small scale, its labor intensity and high skill content, and the short-term nature of each project are all conducive to a heavy incidence of informal work. A third source is inadequate provision of services and goods by the formal sector. This inadequacy may consist of excessively high prices, inaccessible or difficult to reach locations of formal providers, or actual lack of provision. It would seem that this inadequacy of formal provision involves mostly low-income individuals or areas. Examples are gypsy cabs serving areas not served by regular cabs, informal neighborhood child-care centers, low-cost furniture manufacturing shops, informal auto-repair and a whole range of other activities providing personal services and goods. A further source comes from the existence of a cluster of informal shops that can eventually generate agglomeration economies that induce additional entrepreneurs to move in. This is illustrated by the emergence of auto-repair 'districts', vendors' 'districts', or clusters of both regulated and informal shops in areas not zoned for manufacturing, but that are some of the few viable locations for such activity given the increased demand for space by high bidders. Finally the existence of a rather diverse set of informal firms using a variety of labor supplies may lower entry costs for entrepreneurs and hence function as a factor inducing the further expansion of the informal economy; this can be thought of as a type of supply side factor: it signals to employers the existence of an informal 'hiring hall'.

Third, we can distinguish different types of firms in the informal economy in terms of the locational constraints to which firms are subject. For some firms it is access to cheap labor which determines location, because it allows these firms to compete with Third World factories or to compete in markets with rapid production turnover times. In contrast, many of the shops engaged in customized production or operating on subcontracts, evince a whole host of locational dependencies on New York City. These firms are bound to the city (or to any large city they might be located in undergoing the kinds of socio-economic transformations we identified for New York City) due to some or all of the following reasons: demand is local and involves typically specific clients or customers; vicinity to design and specialized services; brief turnover time between completion of design and production; demand is predicated on the existence of a highly dynamic overall economic situation that generates a critical volume of demand and spending capability on the part of buyers; the existence of immigrant communities which have some of the traits associated with enclave economies and hence contain very specific types of markets. In other words, these are firms whose market is right there in New York City. Leaving the city for a lower cost location is not quite an option. In this case informalization functions as a mode of incorporation into an economic system with great inequality in the bidding power of firms for land, and a sharp increase in the demand for space by high-bidding firms, both factors having contributed to reduce sharply the supply of low-cost space.

Fourth, we can distinguish differences in the types of jobs we found in the informal economy. Many are unskilled, with no training opportunities, involving repetitive tasks. Another type demands high skills or acquisition of a skill. The growth of informalization in the construction and furniture industries can be seen as having brought about a re-skilling of the labor force. Some jobs pay extremely low wages, others pay average wages and still others were found to pay above average wages. But typically there seems to be a saving involved for the employers or contractors compared with what would have to be paid in the formal market.

Fifth, we can identify different types of locations in the spatial organization of the informal economy. Immigrant communities are a key location for informal activities meeting both internal and external demand for goods and services. Gentrifying areas are a second important location; these areas contain a large array of informal activities in renovation, alteration, small-scale new construction, woodwork and installations. A third location can be characterized as informal manufacturing and industrial service areas serving a city-wide market.

It would seem, then, that important sources for the informalization of various activities are to be found in characteristics of the larger city's economy. Among these are the demand for products and services that lend themselves to small scales of production, or are associated with rapid transformations brought about by commercial and residential gentrification, or are not satisfactorily provided by the formal sector. This would suggest that a good share of the informal economy is *not* the result of immigrant survival strategies, but rather an outcome of structural patterns or transformations in the larger economy of a city such as New York. Workers and firms respond to the opportunities contained in these patterns and transformations. However in order to respond, workers and firms need to be positioned in distinct ways. Immigrant communities represent what could be described as a 'favored' structural location to seize the opportunities for entrepreneurship as well as the more and less desirable jobs being generated by informalization.

## WORKING-CLASS USES OF SPACE

Major economic forces in today's large cities push towards the decimating of low-cost and generally working-class uses of space, be they individual buildings, commercial districts or manufacturing operations. These are often forced to become informal. And urban governments tend to see only the advantages of high-profit, high-cost uses of space. The rationale is typically put in terms of taxes that can be collected on such uses, though this can be shown to be a short-term view that disregards the longer-term costs associated with the impoverishment that this form of development brings about. The visually dominant categories reinforce these two sets of forces: mainstream society (both its constituents and its representatives such as politicians) tend to see new buildings, modern constructions, the glitter of high-profit/high-cost uses of space (be they homes or commerce) as the desirable visual forms, as representing progress and an advanced economy; working-class uses of space and the associated built forms are seen as backward and not economically very viable.

The case of 14th Street in New York City is interesting in all these aspects. It is the last major working-class commercial center in Manhattan and functions as a very lively public space. There are working-class jobs and shops, and middle-class homes and offices. Visually much of it looks fairly run down, except for the newly gentrified buildings and new construction. Very importantly, it is a space where what is usually referred to as 'working class' makes itself evident in its full complexity: people of generally working-class conditions, who think of themselves in terms of very diverse categories – classes, races, genders and the multiplicity of forms contained in each of these.

We (Sassen and Satler, in preparation) had several questions: Are the working-class uses on the street economically viable in a city like New York? Do the physical characteristics of buildings allow for the upscale office uses that are being proposed by city government and the real estate industry? Is there a connection between these working-class uses of the street, and what we think of as the leading economic sectors: finance and specialized services?

For the past 100 years, 14th Street has been the working class retail center of Manhattan, with Union Square, once the entertainment and political nexus of working-class life in the city, at its center (see Sennett 1992, chapter 6, for a description of this street and its meaning in the city's history).[16] It has two major subway hubs, connecting most subway lines in the city. This partly explains why working-class people today, from all over the city, still buy electronics, clothes, fabrics and inexpensive furniture on 14th Street, and come on weekends to spend time with friends and strangers in the lively discount commercial district, full of street vendors, all adding up to the atmosphere of an open-air bazaar. But the process of gentrification affecting the rest of the city also came, given its convenient location, close to the downtown and midtown corporate office districts. We now see: a new upper-middle class housing project; renovated warehouse buildings for a new publishers' center; areas of the wholesale meat trade now being converted into high-income residential or office lofts; assemblage of lots by large real estate firms.

The most common view, one held by both government officials and the real estate industry, is that the working-class uses of the street – the meat market, the discount shopping center between Seventh Avenue and the Square, the commercial area on the far East side – are obsolete, economically finished in post-industrial Manhattan. In this view the preferred economic and social uses are corporate or professional offices and middle-class housing. The economic, social and visual homogenization that such a replacement of working-class uses would bring about is seen as highly desirable.

In our study we investigated whether this imagery of obsoleteness and decay of the working-class uses on the street could possibly represent one type of visual signification, one conditioned by common images of what is prosperity and what is urbanistically attractive. Could there be another reading about the economic viability of current working-class uses, the physical viability of proposed office uses, and the socio-political viability of a space of diversity, one of mixed economic and social class uses with the attendant visual mix?

This raises several broad questions. Most generally, can 14th Street, and streets like it, remain a space in which the working-class can participate; and what new forms of space can promote a diversity of class use? What is the productive outcome, if any, of social diversity? Does the creation of a common territory have larger implications for the political discourse between classes of unequal power? And it raises more specific questions. Can the current diversity and mix of activities in terms of socio-economic and ethnic characteristics continue, or will gentrification take over and homogenize this space? Is the discount shopping area viable and is it enough to anchor a public space for the working-class? What other activities on the street could serve as such an anchor? Does the diversity of building types on the street contain specific possibilities or constraints on modes of occupation and types of street activity? To what extent is social diversity reflected in building type? To what extent does building type set limits to mode of occupation and range of use?

The overall result of our inquiry points to the possibility of a different reading of the working-class uses on 14th Street: the prevalent imagery of decay and desolateness is inadequate. These are the main findings: first, the building type on much of 14th Street is such that it limits upscale uses and is in fact well-suited for uses that would further anchor the working-class on this street: warehousing and small specialized manufacturing that is beginning to grow again in New York City. Indeed several factories have recently moved in. Even if it once again becomes profitable to renovate buildings for office space, there are very few buildings left in this area that are feasible for upscaling. There is a distinct difference in building style and type between the corner buildings which have been converted to office space and the mid-block structures which remain underutilized. Some are too small or have upper floors accessible only through the retail space on the ground floor, and others are simply too deteriorated. Further, rebuilding is not an option because most of the buildings here are built to more than two-thirds of allowed bulk. Lastly, 14th Street itself deters prospective office tenants. As long as it retains its reputation as a working-class shopping district, other areas in the city will be able to outbid its mid-block spaces for office tenants. These spaces could, however, be profitably filled with small, specialized manufacturers. In fact these blocks already house several such tenants, for example, dental equipment manufacturers as well as numerous makers of fine jewelry.

Most importantly, encouraging this use for presently underutilized space would help to anchor the working-class more firmly on the street, and resist the city's policy of moving manufacturers out of Manhattan to promote the conversion of space to higher use as offices.

Second, the discount shopping center is highly profitable, draws from a broad area of the city, and is generally far stronger than its appearance suggests. The discount store type is intriguing not only for its incredible success as a vehicle for commerce but also for its position in the urban framework of 14th Street (see Gaber 1992 for a detailed account[17]). Discount stores break down the boundary between private and public space for marketing purposes, store managers put tables piled with goods on the sidewalk and arrange with vendors to sell goods in front of their stores. They bring the sidewalk into the building by using their vestibules as selling space or indenting the whole facade of their store to create a kind of super vestibule for open air sales. These physical arrangements create a complexity and depth in the street wall that makes 14th Street a highly charged and effective urban space.

In contrast, the formal 'public' uses on the street, such as the Armory, the Salvation Army building and even Union Square Park give little to the street urbanistically. They meet the street in a way that reflects a perception of the street's users as clients or intruders. New construction on the street has tended to take the same defensive approach constraining the lively interactive techniques of some store managers. Discount stores provide a model of the way buildings could be designed to reinforce 14th Street's role as a street of markets for people throughout the metropolitan area with moderate and lower incomes.

Third, the new middle-income residential towers built on Union Square and the more upscale commercial activity they promote can be thought of as contributing to the diversity of the area, rather than to its inevitable gentrification. Today 14th Street is a highly mixed area. It is zoned for manufacturing, commercial and residential uses. It has low-income tenants, middle-class housing, high-rise luxury apartments and privately owned renovated brownstones. The high rise buildings on the square and on the corners of avenues contain a range of uses from publishers and professional services to manufacturing, and there is far more demand for space than is available. The discount shopping district generates over $200 million in annual sales with 70 per cent of its shoppers coming from outside the area. The street vendors are an integral part of this shopping district, often working in collaboration with the shops; the overall effect is that of a bazaar. The wholesale meat market is the largest in the city and services almost all of the hotels and restaurants. In brief, these working-class uses are in stronger economic shape than is usually thought.

Since there is much underutilized space in what is one of the prime business areas of the city, there would seem to be a vast potential for new, expanding uses, notably offices and professional studios. But we found that the characteristics of the buildings in the key locations for working-class use on the street are such as to constrain upscale uses. Politically it is of central importance to be able to document the economic viability of the working-class uses of 14th Street and the desirability of social and income diversity. Gentrification and offices are *not* the only viable and desirable options for these types of districts. Working-class uses of the street, from shops, to warehousing, meat packing and manufacturing, are viable whether in New York City, London, Frankfurt or any of today's major cities.

## CONCLUSION

It is essential for us to uncover the interconnections between urban forms that present themselves as unconnected in order to begin to understand what our large cities are about today and in the near future, in order to see what constitutes their complexity – in brief to produce a new narrative, to re-build the city. This will matter for a growing number of large cities in other highly developed countries as well: Frankfurt and Berlin in Germany, Paris and Marseille in France, Vienna in Austria, Tokyo and Osaka in Japan. In all these cities we see the emergence of the dualities in economic power and cultural representation so sharply evident in Los Angeles and

New York. It matters also because the distorted representation we have today of the advanced urban economy does not help political efforts to make these cities more manageable, more livable, less hopeless. A large city is a space of difference, in Sennett's words.[18] The inscription of difference into the urban landscape and into urban space is no easy matter; it cannot simply be an enactment of different cultures, the merchandising of subcultures, a simplistic democratic conception of one vote/one space carried onto the group level. It needs to be rooted in the constitution itself of urban space. That is why, I argue, un-covering, making visible the crucial place or role of economic sectors, firms and workers that may appear as marginal and 'imported', as backward and not belonging, is one step in the direction of such a rebuilding.

## NOTES

The author acknowledges the general support of the Russell Sage Foundation while a Visiting Scholar in 1992–93, and thanks Vivian Kaufman, most particularly, for her invaluable assistance with this manuscript.

1. A. Giddens, *The Consequences of Modernity* (Polity Press, Oxford, 1990).
2. John Friedmann and Goetz Wolff, 'World City Formation: An Agenda for Research and Action', *International Journal of Urban and Regional Research*, 6(3) (1982) pp. 309–44.
3. Peter Hall, *The World Cities* (McGraw-Hill, New York, 1966).
4. A. D. King, *Global Cities: Post-Imperialism and the Internationalization of London*, the International Library of Sociology (Routledge, London and New York, 1990).
5. S. Sassen, *The Global City: New York, London, Tokyo* (Princeton University Press, 1991).
6. Ibid.
7. S. Sassen-Koob, 'The New Labor Demand in Global Cities', in M. P. Smith (ed.), *Cities in Transformation* (Sage, Beverly Hills, 1984), pp. 139–71.
8. M. Castells, *The Informational City* (Blackwell, London, 1989).
9. Ibid., chapter 2.
10. S. Sassen (see note 5).
11. This focus illuminates the positions of different types of cities in the current organization of the world economy. A limited number of major cities are the sites of production for specialized services and financial products sold on national and global markets. And a large number of other major cities have lost their role as leading export centers for manufacturing, precisely due to the decentralization of production.
12. S. Sassen (see note 5).
13. Jeremy Brecher, John Brown Childs, and Jill Cutler (eds), *Global Visions: Beyond the New World Order* (South End Press, Boston, 1993).
14. Edwin Melendez, Clara Rodriguez, and Janis Barry Figueroa (eds), *Hispanics in the Labor Force: Issues and Policies* (Plenum Press, New York, 1991).

15.   S. Sassen (see note 5).
16.   R. Sennett, *The Conscience of the Eye: The Design and Social Life of Cities*, paperback edition (Norton, New York, 1992).
17.   Joe Gaber, 'The Vendors' District on 14th Street in Manhattan', in Saskia Sassen, *Social Class and Visual Scale*, final research report presented to the Chicago Institute for Architecture and Urbanism. New York, 1992.
18.   R. Sennett (see note 16).

See also:

- S. Sassen and G. Satler, *Reading the Late Modern City: A View from the Street* (in preparation).
- T. M. Stanback and T. J. Noyelle, *Cities in Transition: Changing Job Structures in Atlanta, Denver, Buffalo, Phoenix, Columbus (Ohio), Nashville, Charlotte* (Allenheld, Osmun, New Jersey, 1982).
- Rebecca Morales and Frank Bonilla (eds), *Latinos in a Changing U.S. Economy: Comparative Perspectives on Growing Inequality*, series on Race and Ethnic Relations, vol. 7 (Sage Publications, Newbury Park, California, 1993).

Morales and Bonilla includes empirical descriptions of the position of immigrants in the US economy and in major cities, as does Melendez et al. (see note 14).

# 2

# Space and Symbols in an Age of Decline

Sharon Zukin

---

There are two schools of critical thought about the city's built environment. One, identified with political economy, emphasizes investment shifts among different circuits of capital that transfer the ownership and uses of land from one social class to another. Its basic terms are land, labor and capital. The other school of thought, identified with a symbolic economy, focuses on representations of social groups and visual means of excluding or including them in public and private spaces. From this view, the endless negotiation of cultural meanings in built forms – in buildings, streets, parks, interiors – contributes to the construction of social identities. Few urban scholars at this point would defend using only one of these ways of looking at the city. The most productive analyses of cities in recent years are based on interpretations and interpenetrations of culture and power.

But one person's 'text' is another person's shopping center or office building, both a lived reality and a representational space of financial speculation. The ambiguity of urban forms is a source of the city's tension as well as of a struggle for interpretation. To ask 'Whose city?' suggests more than a politics of occupation; it also asks who has a right to inhabit the dominant image of the city. This often relates to real geographical strategies as different social groups battle over access to the center of the city and over symbolic representations in the center. At stake are not only real estate fortunes, but also 'readings' of hostility or flexibility towards those groups that have historically been absent from the city center or whose presence causes problems: women, racial minorities, immigrants, certain types of workers, and homeless people. Occupation, segregation and exclusion on every level are conceptualized in streets and neighborhoods, types of buildings, individual buildings and even parts of buildings. They are

43

institutionalized in zoning laws, architecture and conventions of use. Visual artifacts of material culture and political economy thus reinforce – or comment on – social structure. By making social rules legible, they represent the city.

The material reproduction of urban society depends on the continual reproduction of space in a fairly concentrated geographical area. Certainly the prime factors have to do with land, labor and capital. Yet the production of space depends in turn on decisions about what should be visible and what should not; concepts of order and disorder; and a strategic interplay between aesthetics and function. It is notable that as cities have developed service economies, they have both propagated and been taken hostage by an aesthetic urge. On the one hand, there is a tendency to take a connoisseur's view of the past, 'reading' the legible practices of cultural discrimination through a reshaping of the city's collective memory. Historic preservation connects an ecology of urban buildings and streets with an ecology of images of the city's past.[1,2] Historicist post-modern architecture instantly makes the present part of a classical age. On the other hand there is a desire to humanize the future, by viewing artists and art work as symbols of a postindustrial economy.[3] Office buildings are not just monumentalized by height and facades; they are given another embodiment by video artists' screen installations and public concerts. Every well-designed downtown has a mixed-use shopping center and a nearby artists' quarter.[4] The derelict factory district or waterfront has been converted into a marketplace for seasonal produce, cooking equipment, restaurants, art galleries and an aquarium. Economic redevelopment plans have focused on museums, from Lowell, Massachusetts to downtown Los Angeles. Less successful attempts to use museums to stop economic decline in North Adams, Massachusetts and Flint, Michigan only emphasize the influence of cultural strategies in reshaping urban forms.[5] Thus the symbolic economy of cultural meanings and representations implies real economic power.

For at least 100 years, since Engels visited Manchester and Haussmann rebuilt Paris, modern projects of urban renewal have tended to aestheticize the social problems they displace. Since the 1960s, as artists have developed more self-conscious political organization, and allied themselves with elected political officials, they have been co-opted into these projects as actors and beneficiaries, both developers of an aesthetic mode of producing space and investors in a symbolic economy.[6] There are, moreover, special connections between artists and an urban service economy. A concentration of unemployed and underemployed artists represents a labor pool for service employers who want part-time, non-union, 'flexible' and creative employees for jobs ranging from the restaurant and hotel industry to advertising and television production. Artists also represent the claims of a service economy to cultural hegemony. Their visibility in forms of the built environment, in public art, art galleries, museums and studios, emphasizes the moral distance from old, dirty uses of space in a manufacturing economy. In specific cities, the presence of artists documents a claim to these cities' cultural hegemony. The display of art, for public improvement or private gain, represents an abstraction of economic and social power. Among local business elites, those from finance, insurance and real estate are generally big patrons of art museums and firmly committed to showing public art in their commercial spaces, as if to emphasize the prominence of these sectors in the city's symbolic economy.

It was no accident that the boom in these sectors of business services that lasted for most of the 1980s, influenced sharp price rises in the real estate and art markets in which their leading members were so active. Investment in art, for prestige or speculation, represented a collective means of social mobility. At the same time, a collective belief in the growth of the symbolic economy of art represented belief in the growth of the city's economy. Visual representation became a means of financially re-presenting the city.

The symbolic economy thus features two parallel production systems that are crucial to a city's economic growth: the production of space, with its synergy of capital investment and cultural meanings, and the production of symbols, which construct both a currency of commercial exchange and a language of social identity. By the 1990s, it is understood that making a place for art in the city goes along with establishing a place identity for the city as a whole. No matter how restricted the definition of art that is implied, or how few artists are included, or how little the benefits extend to other social groups outside certain segments of the middle class, the visibility and viability of a city's symbolic economy plays an important role in the creation of place.[7]

This is especially important for global cities, those large metropolitan centers where the major share of world financial trade is concentrated. Global cities share with regional and national urban centers a common cultural strategy that imposes a new way of seeing landscape: internationalizing it, abstracting a legible image from the service economy, connecting it to consumption rather than production.[8] But in global cities, the processes of producing space for cultural hegemony are more intense and have greater effect. A vibrant symbolic economy attracts investment capital from the global portfolios of real estate investors, banks, property developers and large property owners. Partly this continues the patterns of the past, with global cities like London and New York transcending the limited life span of colonial and commercial empires.[9] Partly, too, it results from a desire for comparative advantage over a city's rivals. The symbolic economy of a global city shapes the lingua franca of global elites and aids the circulation of images that influence 'climates' of opinion and investment and 'mentalities'. Artists from all over the world (as well as aspiring bohemians who want to live near well-publicized, cutting-edge artists) are attracted to the symbolic economy of global cities. Their presence helps the symbolic economy to continue growing, although whether this economy thrives on the making or the selling of art is a serious question.[10]

The commercial culture of the built environment has specific ways of incorporating cultural capital from the symbolic economy, converting it into visual images, and circulating them to a wider public. Throughout the twentieth century, configurations of built form, glass and light have offered intimations of sacred realms in secular quarters[11] from Times Square to Docklands. The stores, office buildings, and theaters of commercial culture have defined public space for an increasingly mobile public.[12] In commercial spaces the public are simultaneously customers and viewers, spectators and workers, at leisure and on display. The commercial spaces of the largest metropolises have always been gaudiest and most permeated by contradictions. They bear a double burden of representing both a global city and differentiations of power within that city, both a landscape of power and a vernacular.

The economic recession and worldwide retrenchment of the 1990s halted construction of commercial spaces in global cities. Economic conditions also caused the degradation of existing spaces by making owners decrease maintenance services and increase security controls while vacancy rates rose. These changes call for rethinking the relation between commercial culture and public space in the leading urban centers: How does the symbolic economy change public perceptions of commercial spaces? What happens when such spaces no longer represent growth but economic decline? When leading business sectors suffer, what means of representation differentiate landscape from vernacular? Here I can offer no theory of representation that will for ever alter the way we see cities. However, I can present a few preliminary notes on public space and the symbolic economy from the vantage point of New York City in the recession of the 1990s.

### SIGNS OF DECLINE

Crises like the present economic depression are a good time to take stock of cities. Because the overbuilding of the mid 1980s has abated, we can look at the forms that are left behind, judging their aesthetics and uses with more critical detachment. At the same time uses of space are changing, as firms economize or go bankrupt, vacancies rise, and the real estate industry pursues alternatives to new commercial construction. We can also look at the basic scales of the city's social life – buildings, streets and neighborhoods – and try to determine which forms, in which places, are likely to survive, and for which groups of people. Not only building and reuse, but also decline and disuse can tell us something about the resonance between symbols, space and social power.

Financial crisis is also a good time for secrets to come out. It is no longer a secret that a small percentage of people in New York City are exceedingly rich and a large number are very poor. Because all sides make use of this claim, it is also clear that the working people of New York cannot support the non-working population, the bureaucracy, the public services, and the tax benefits to powerful business interests that have deadened the city's responsiveness to economic change (for a liberal view, see Epstein, 1992[13]). Over a million residents of New York City are on a welfare program of some kind, more than at any time since the Great Depression. Neither is it mysterious that the city's pursuit of the middle class – or really, 'people with money' – has improved the quality of private goods and services while it has done nothing to halt the reduction of public goods. In these senses New York is just a microcosm of the United States, with a bloated budget for 'defense', an inferior education system, and an inability to invest capital in physical infrastructure.

Conditions for changing infrastructure are more complex today than in the past. After the Second World War, when federal urban development strategies acknowledged long-term middle-class flight to the suburbs, money was poured into demolishing and rebuilding downtown commercial centers. These projects aimed to protect department stores, which had been losing business to the suburbs since the 1920s, and office-building developers, who from the 1950s faced increasing corporate flight to new offices in the suburbs. During the 1970s and 1980s, public-private partnerships leveraged a dramatically diminished base of federal funding to finance a new round of downtown commercial construction, often with mixed commercial uses. Mainly through the commercial reuse of historic buildings, this spatial redevelopment harnessed an old urban vernacular – wholesale food markets, ports, railroad terminals – to a new sensual appreciation of aesthetic diversity and a related appropriation of nature. Many of these projects resulted in similar festival marketplaces. Most, though not all, relied on a predominantly corporate-owned mix of businesses to minimize financial risk.[14] In general this paradigmatic change in the program of downtown commercial space indicated that the middle class was more diverse than ever before, the investment climate was more competitive, especially within metropolitan regions, and planning was no longer controlled by public agencies.

Abandoned to market competition for an image-conscious public, urban infrastructure focuses on speciality stores, art and food. By this time image is so grounded in the symbolic economy that it serves as an agent of transition, representing potential uses of otherwise vacant space, saving it for another 'landscape'. Nothing could illustrate transition of this sort more visibly than 'Harry, If I Told You, Would You Know?', a display in a vacant bank branch at 58th Street and Madison Avenue, at the core of a high-rent commercial district in midtown.

*Harry* is the name of a set of contemporary abstract paintings by Al Held that have been exhibited since September 1991 in vacant ground-floor retail space. This empty storefront is across the street from the General Motors Building, a block away from the IBM and Sony (formerly AT&T) buildings, and around the corner from a cluster of art galleries on East and West 57th Street that represent well-known artists. The André Emmerich Gallery, which represents Al Held, is on 57th Street. Emmerich got the idea of renting the storefront to show the paintings, which don't fit into the elevator to his gallery. In the old days – the 1970s and 1980s art market – the gallery might have shown these paintings at their SoHo branch, which was opened in 1971 in a loft building configured for wide loads. But that gallery was closed some years ago, and the storefront on Madison Avenue was vacated by the 1991 consolidation of Chemical and Manufacturers' Hanover banks. The sight of the storefront, denuded of tellers' safety glass windows, with makeshift lighting on bare cement floors and thick columns, either evokes the success of an uptown SoHo, with a potential for upgrading property through cultural uses, or suggests a scenario of doom, with unrented commercial spaces used only for symbolic display.

Since about 10 per cent of the ground floor spaces in this neighborhood of Madison Avenue are now unrented, doom it is. *Harry* signals a cross between the derelict urban spaces of *Blade Runner* and gentrification by cultural consumption. But art work could hardly fill all the vacant space in New York's commercial real estate markets. These markets include not only the vacant flagship department stores that have succumbed to falling sales and leveraged buyouts (Macy's, Bloomingdale's and Saks remain, but Altman's and Alexander's are empty), and the one-storey stores of various sizes that have been subdivided into 'indoor malls', but also unrented shops and offices in large mixed-use complexes – like the World Financial Center and Worldwide Plaza – that express a world city's great pretentions. Could 'Harry, If I Told You, Would You Know?' represent the overexpanded, debt-ridden city of the developers of the symbolic economy?

Look what has happened to Olympia & York. This Canadian firm of real estate developers and managers was responsible for some of the most significant new construction in the symbolic economy in the 1980s, including the World Financial Center in New York and Canary Wharf in London's Docklands. Traditionally cautious in diversifying and hedging investments, developing a blue-chip portfolio, engaging signature architects, owning desirable buildings outright, and negotiating favorable deals with government agencies, Olympia & York nonetheless ran out of cash to pay its lenders. Neither could it pay its agreed share of the costs of extending a rail line between the City of London and Canary Wharf, a necessary condition of getting the workforce to their jobs. It is not irrelevant to the overall circularity of the symbolic economy – '. . . If I Told You, Would You Know?' – that while the company's property leases stopped producing enough income to cover debt repayment, Olympia & York's cash-producing investments in oil, gas and newsprint also lost economic value. Moreover the company couldn't sell off two buildings at Canary Wharf as it had planned to do, when first a Japanese pension fund refused to loan money to Morgan Stanley & Co. to buy an office tower, and second the British government rescinded tax breaks for setting up investment trusts so that individual investors could buy another building. With the still incomplete Canary Wharf passing into the reluctant hands of lending banks, the symbolic value of Olympia & York's architectural projects is no greater than their value in the stock and real estate markets.

The purchase by the German media company Bertelsmann of an office building in Times Square is another story of big bank lenders, developers who couldn't hold on to an empty building, delays, and uncertainty surrounding the re-making of a landscape of power. Even when part of the symbolic economy – in this case publishing and music distribution – continues to flourish under foreign ownership, real estate markets operate at a loss.

But these are current events. Considering space, symbols, and power demands both a short and a long-term view. In the long run vacant and undervalued space is bound to recede into the vernacular landscape of the powerless and be replaced by a new landscape of power. Not so long ago the image and economic value of urban factories were diminished by the rise of the service economy and rose again – in the spatial form of living lofts. The construction starts and cultural critiques that focused attention on cities' polarized growth during the 1980s only reflect four conditions that have shaped New York City's decline from the 1950s. These are the flight of the middle class, the weakening of place identities of major businesses, the standardization of consumption experiences, and, as the countervailing strategy of patrician elites, the reassertion of centrality as a landscape of power. These conditions define the legibility of urban space.

## LEGIBLE SPACES

Legibility and identity are interdependent. Spaces are formed by capital investment and sensual attachment; both who pays for building and rebuilding and the gut feeling of being in and of a specific city. Legibility also speaks to the greed and exclusion that underlie perennial plans to rid a downtown of 'dirty' manufacturing, low-rent tenants, and all infrastructure connected to the poor, workers, and ethnic and racial minorities outside of tourist zones. Nearly all cities use spatial strategies to separate, segregate and isolate the Other, inscribing the legible practices of modernism in urban form.[15,16,17] But the legibility of New York City is an exercise in contradictions. On the one hand tendencies to segregate are thwarted by a

diversity greater than in other cities: the block-to-block variations in uses
and social classes across Manhattan, the uneasy coexistence of Latinos,
Chasidic Jews, Italians and East Europeans in Williamsburg, of Caribbean
immigrants, American blacks and Chasidic Jews in Crown Heights. On the
other hand, while projects to segregate high-value uses are often defeated by
'community' resistance, they result in establishing markets that undermine
the integrity of place: the legalization of artists' lofts in SoHo, the potential
for another high-income neighborhood in the mixed-use development on the
old West Side railroad yards sponsored by real estate developer Donald
Trump and a coalition of community groups. The basic processes of
incorporating the unique identity of place into real estate markets is always
taken farthest in New York because of the visibility and viability of its
symbolic economy.

In Henri Lefebvre's framework,[18] New York is an example of abstract
space: simultaneously homogeneous and fragmented, subordinated to the
flows and networks of world markets, and divided into units of exchange by
real estate developers. Viewed from the city, however, New York resembles
a dismembered imperial space, an imperium whose tributaries owe less and
less to the center, whose facilities are improved upon in the provinces, and
whose utopian joining of freedom and power looks like a dystopia of dirt,
violence and anarchy. Simultaneously utopia and dystopia, New York
claims a place in America's and the world's moral economy. Does it exert
this claim because it is changing, or has it always been this way?

Much of the change in the legibility of New York reflects the greater
choice that people have about where to live, and the influence of corporate
planning on both cities and suburban or exurban alternatives. Squeezed by
the decentralization of mass individual choice and corporate planning,
design in New York, as in other cities, has become a more important mark
of distinction. Design emphasizes legibility. It enables cities to compete for
'people with money': a representation of a tax base, a class of employers,
and consumers for private markets. The new importance of people with
money is intimately related to the disappearance of urban planning in New
York since the 1960s. Public officials were caught without answers to a
series of questions. Having chased industry out of the city, how can the city
government increase employment? Can the city survive with only a symbolic
economy? How do you plan a postindustrial city with a non-European
population? How do you plan for large businesses when telecommunications make it sensible for them to create their own 'footprint' in the suburbs
and exurbs? How do you plan public goods for a low-income or even
homeless and unemployed population when the rich won't pay for them and
no one else can? Under these conditions it is no suprise that the landscape of
cities has been reorganized for visual consumption, abstracting an image of
freedom and power that commands – in its very abstraction – some degree
of consensus.

Since the 1970s only a handful of public spaces in US cities have been conceived and built as truly public – for neither profit nor market-based consumption, for association rather than individualism, for spending time rather than spending money. Certainly notable public buildings have been, and are still being, built: Michael Graves's Portlandia Building and Phoenix Civic Center, the Harold Washington Library in Chicago. But the State of Illinois Center in Chicago, designed by Helmut Jahn in the early 1980s, signaled a decisive change in the definition of public space. In that mixed-use complex, ground floor spaces are occupied by stores while government agencies occupy the higher floors, accessible by a glass-enclosed elevator. The identity of government is subordinated to the shopping center. If a city's legibility is derived from the design of commercial spaces, then the identity of the urban public is negotiated in those commercial public spaces where ownership, work and consumption interact.

To see how space mediates these issues we should look at commercial spaces on three scales typical of New York City, that span landscapes of power and vernacular. These are the office-building lobby, the multi-block commercial complex, and the neighborhood shopping street. To begin with, New Yorkers spend a great deal of time in all three spaces. Moreover these urban forms are still uniquely New York spaces because you don't need a car to get to them, see them and use them.

### a.  The Office-Building Lobby

Office-building lobbies are interiors for a public in transit. Neither so public as a street, nor so private as an office, office-building lobbies are passageways, waiting rooms and theaters of corporate image. In some ways they recall public spaces built for a newly mobile urban public in the late nineteenth century. Like the comfort stations installed in British underground railway stations in the 1890s and railroad terminals like Grand Central after 1900,[19] office-building lobbies between 1910 and 1970 had shoeshine stands, barbershops, telephones and news-stands. Perhaps the apotheosis of this urban form is in great office building lobbies of the 1920s and 1930s like Rockefeller Center. But the lobby of the Equitable Life Assurance Company headquarters, built a few blocks north of Rockefeller Center in the 1980s, is quite different. The comfort station – that in this case includes a shoeshine stand, xerox store, news-stand, hair salon, fitness center, McDonald's and a computer training school – has been relegated to a subterranean passageway or concourse leading to the subways. The concourse connects the Equitable headquarters to other corporate buildings in the area and to Rockefeller Center. In the lobby of the Equitable building, you see an art gallery run by the Whitney Museum, open exhibition areas for art work, sculptures commissioned by the building's owner, very large paintings (like *Harry*) that fit the lobby's scale, all surrounded by glass and marble. Outside, separate street entrances lead to two elegant restaurants, Le Bernardin and Palio, which lease space on the lobby floor but are not visible from inside the lobby. Although the Whitney also runs two gift stores in the lobby, the Scriptorium and the Treasury, Equitable did not renew the museum's lease when it ran out in 1992. The company planned to organize its own art exhibits.

Walking through this lobby, you feel you are in a public space that is at once open but not anarchic, a non-profit space of cultural production that is dependent in some indefinable way on corporate finance. This perception continues as you walk through to the lobby of the adjoining office building, named for the investment firm PaineWebber, its prime tenant. This lobby contains a PaineWebber art gallery, which mounts exhibits in cooperation with local museums, and a separate gallery space occupied by the archives of the Smithsonian Institution. Together the two lobbies contain a variety of small spaces that humanize their high ceilings and glass walls. They seem to break down hierarchies of outside and inside, corporate and cultural, public and private. They create the sense of a street in their design and of a public good in their function. Indeed zoning incentives have been a major influence on the design of office-building lobbies as public spaces.

In the center of the Equitable lobby is a very tall grey marble bench. It is so tall that passing behind it, you can only see the top of the head of anyone sitting on it. The bench curves inward behind tall plants, providing a somewhat secluded sitting area. At 12.45 p.m. one recent day, two homeless men sat on this bench. They were surrounded by secretaries, a computer repairman, and several Indians, Chinese and Mexicans who were not building employees. Several businessmen in suits sat down for a few minutes. Aside from five uniformed security guards who checked people going into the elevators, these were the only stationary users of the lobby. Two non-rotating surveillance cameras are mounted above one of the entrances, one directed at the lobby and one at the door.

The Philip Morris headquarters building on Park Avenue also has a new type of lobby. This lobby also has a branch of the Whitney Museum. It is much smaller than the Equitable lobby and is set up with 12 round tables. At 11.45 a.m. one day, nine of the tables were occupied. Four men of various ages read newspapers, two older middle-aged men ate lunch bought in the lobby cafe, two white-collar workers ate bag lunches together, an Asian mailcarrier ate a Chinese take-out lunch, two women who could have been students had spread books and papers all over the table and were studying. Most of these people were white and alone. On the benches sat two young people who could have been students, and several elderly men read newspapers. A sign posted in the middle of the front of the lobby prohibits sleeping, alcohol consumption, inappropriate attire, excessive packages, touching the art objects, distribution of leaflets and 'conduct which is inconsistent with a sculpture gallery'. A Whitney Museum employee sits outside the door of the gallery. Nearby are an espresso bar, a news-stand, an arts gift-shop and a chocolate shop. A piano for free public performances stands in front of one of the stores. Four pieces of sculpture are installed on the floor and another piece is mounted on a wall. Three uniformed security guards stand in the lobby, and rotating surveillance cameras overlook the lobby from opposite walls.

## b.  The Commercial Complex

During the last two decades the locus of the symbolic economy moved downtown. The crowded core of the financial district in Wall Street was expanded onto landfill in the Hudson River, capping a 25-year plan to revitalize the downtown commercial real estate market. Yet Battery Park City, the new addition managed by Olympia & York that parallels and rivals London's Docklands, is a curious product of historical compromises. Morphologically it extends the grid pattern of Manhattan's streets to the west, but its wide avenues and openness to the sea contrast with the narrow streets that are the only vestige of New York's colonial trading center. Architecturally it adds to the office space materialized by late Governor Nelson Rockefeller in the World Financial Center, but it contradicts the severe verticality of those modernistic towers by a variety of post-modern designs, with mansard roofs, terracotta colored facades and a glass-enclosed atrium with palm trees, a Winter Garden on the river designed by the architect Cesar Pelli, which the *New York Times*'s architecture critic has described as New York's living room. The mixed uses that were envisioned as enlivening community and supporting middle-class residents when Battery Park City was first planned, in the 1960s, were refashioned to suit an upmarket tenancy oriented towards financial firms and business visitors. Similarly the mixture of social classes that was initially planned – as part of the same new urban community – was shifted off the site itself. A linkage agreement between the city and the developers proposed to transfer a percentage of funds derived from bond sales to the construction of new low-income housing in the outer boroughs, where most poor people already live. By the 1990s it was discovered that none of this money had actually been delivered. The city government was also discussing how to divest itself of its interest in the property to generate a one-time infusion of funds.

As the managers of Battery Park City, Olympia & York organize a constant array of cultural events that are open to the public. From the beginning of these programs in 1987 to the end of 1991, attendance was estimated at over 700 000 people, with another 232 000 at marketing or community events and 29 000 at private events, when the building is rented for dinners or other occasions. The overwhelming attendance is at the free cultural events, which are subsidized by the World Financial Center itself. These events are chosen to appeal to a wide audience. In a typical three-month period (January–March 1992), they included separate ballroom and modern-dance performances, an environmental film festival and tropical rainforest sound installation (which appears to be the *sine qua non* of any 1990s cultural complex), and pop vocal concerts. On sunny weekend afternoons the public space along the private marina on the river attracts a large, well-mannered crowd of men and women and families of various ethnicities. A new playground, open to the public, is very well designed for children of different ages and features a Swedish-made merry-go-round powered by children on bicycles. The Battery Park City security force patrols the entrances to the playground and riverside esplanade. There is an indoor shopping center with an art bookstore, clothing stores and restaurants catering to a knowledgeable group of diners.

This is much the same story as for the Equitable and Philip Morris lobbies. Through a mixture of zoning incentives and a desire to build friendly faces of corporate power, commercial developments cloak corporate identity in consumer marketplaces, large gathering spaces and signature architecture. Prices in the retail stores are often high, and there are always conflicts over people – especially homeless people – using the gathering spaces. If the building provides places to sit, they are not too comfortable, and the architects' work is frequently interchangeable with what they have built in other cities. Private security forces, consumption spaces, false gathering places, signature architectural styles: this is what creates the new urban legibility. But what urban identity does it shape? New Yorkers who admire the public spaces in the World Financial Center and Battery Park City say, 'It doesn't look at all like New York'.

New York has few centers that are not commercial attractions. At the beginning of the twentieth century, Times Square marked a shift in symbolic public spaces from civic arenas or forums, and marketplaces or agoras, to commercial projects.[20] As Times Square declined – a slow decline from the Depression, when many legitimate theaters were shuttered and others replaced by vaudeville theaters, burlesque houses and other tawdry amusements, to the massage parlors and porno-theaters of the 1970s – it was displaced by other symbolic centers. Rockefeller Center, a planned and highly regulated small city without residences, anchored the office market in midtown from the 1930s. As the secular counterpart of St. Patrick's Cathedral across the street, it also demarcated the symbolic processional space of Fifth Avenue, much used for annual ethnic, religious, and patriotic parades.

During the 1970s upper Fifth Avenue became another symbolic center, represented by a new street name, 'Museum Mile'. Under the directorship of Thomas Hoving, the Metropolitan Museum presented blockbuster art exhibits that broke attendance records. The museum also expanded into the public space of Central Park by building new wings, including that which sheltered the Temple of Dendur, transported from Egypt. From the

Guggenheim Museum to the Metropolitan, the public space of the Fifth Avenue side of Central Park became an adjunct of the private museums.

Central Park as a whole has a similar history. From the 1860s to the 1880s, as the definition of the public expanded to include working-class and immigrant groups, the public space of Central Park became more inclusive, less culturally hegemonic and more commercial.[21] Probably the park changed more in those first 20 years than in the following century. Nevertheless public uses of Central Park expanded under the populist first administration of Mayor John Lindsay, in the mid to late 1960s, when Thomas Hoving and August Heckscher served as park commissioners. Central Park became a symbolic staging ground for various 'unifying' events, both paying and free, from rock concerts to protest demonstrations. Central Park is also the site of the start of the New York City Marathon. Similarly the large Prospect Park in central Brooklyn, also designed by Frederick Olmstead and Calvert Vaux, has become a symbolic center too. An annual Caribbean Day parade on Labor Day weekend marches to Prospect Park.

The common point of these symbolic spaces is that they blend public and private uses, and commercial and non-commercial functions. While they are structured by public or governmental incentives to include public uses in the sense of free events, they are also shaped by the fact that people are more active as consumers than as citizens. People are also sometimes afraid of gathering in their neighborhoods. While public space in centrally-located, commercial complexes has increased, and is policed by security guards, people feel that usable public space in ordinary neighborhoods – safe streets and parks – has decreased. Neighborhood public space is dirty or unsafe, or outside effective public controls.

The satisfaction of private needs increasingly drives the construction of significant spaces of public life. This displaces the locus of emotional attachment in the city from the home and the local community to the central commercial complex. It reduces support for commercial spaces that cater to local consumption needs, and attracts support to larger, more diversified but ultimately more standardized spaces of consumption. It drives consumption spaces to incorporate symbols of public fantasy, especially fantasies of public life.

### c. Shopping Streets

While an increasing number of central commercial spaces are controlled by private security staffs, neighborhood shopping streets are considered unmanageable. The city government no longer guarantees sufficient streetcleaning or sanitation pickups. Private carters are said to be connected to the Mafia. Especially in ghetto areas, merchants fear daily theft and occasional community opposition. Ethnicity is both promoted and reviled in neighborhood shopping streets, which can equally become symbolic centers of solidarity or resistance. Yet neighborhood shopping streets are the site of vernacular landscape. Sometimes local merchants represent the vernacular of the powerless against the corporate interests of chain stores and national franchises. The local real estate sector typically includes small landlords and developers. The periodic struggle in New York over commercial rent control – which the city lacks – is a struggle over maintaining the vernacular in a populist sense: small-scale, local ownership, amenities at prices local people can afford, variety. The transformation of shopping streets from vernacular diversity to corporate monoculture is also a reflection of the global and national economies. But as a coherent image of public space, the basis of both a cognitive map and social reproduction, neighborhood shopping streets suggest alternatives to the symbolic public spaces of the office-building lobby and commercial complex.

That shopping streets have also been incorporated into a landscape of power is shown by the rapid growth of business improvement districts (BIDs), which enjoy a special legal status in New York State. These are associations of local business owners who have the legal right to tax themselves over and above city taxes in order to provide their own 'improvements', including street lighting, sanitation, holiday decorations, and street festivals.[22] They may hire their own security force. Local merchant associations but with more clout, the BIDs represent the privatized public space of the current period of public-private partnerships. They compensate for the budget restraints on city government. However by taking responsibility for providing public goods, they also take the opportunity to define them. Their control makes shopping streets into a liminal zone neither public nor private. Moreover the biggest and richest BIDs are the ones with the most ambitious plans for re-making their neighborhood.

Because the 34th Street BID and the Grand Central Partnership (on 42nd Street) represent some valuable commercial properties, including the Empire State Building and Grand Central Terminal, their projects to improve the neighborhood dovetail with those of major property owners. The Grand Central Partnership has assumed responsibilities for the redevelopment of such public spaces as Grand Central Terminal (including lighting the exterior) and the reconstruction of Bryant Park behind the Public Library on 42nd Street. Both have been contentious projects, dragging out over years of city government approvals and requests for funding, and the pursuit of private entrepreneurs to operate public amenities. They share a problem of providing access, especially to the homeless, while sustaining an image of the city that attracts the local workforce and tourists. The homeless used to be swept up by periodic police patrols through Grand Central Terminal; now the doors are closed between late night and early morning. In Bryant Park, a neatly printed sign informs us, only homeless people affiliated with a church in the neighborhood have the right to pick among the trash cans. (Collecting the deposits on discarded beer and soft drink cans and bottles is a major source of income for some homeless people.) The Grand Central Partnership established a subsidiary to manage the redevelopment of the park, which oversees landscaping for a privately-owned restaurant, leases to concession stand operators, programs of public concerts and performances, and the general public order. The new park is less likely to harbor the drug sales for which the previous park became notorious.

It is expensive to manage construction projects, field sanitation crews, and to provide trash cans, benches and other 'street furniture' and new signage. Moreover the group has a mission and a vision. They want to make the midtown area look and work like Disney World. For this aim, the Grand Central Partnership's annual budget of $6 million is not large enough. With the mayor's approval the private group received authorization to issue bonds for up to $35 million (*New York Times*, 2 April, 1992). And the Partnership's credit rating is higher than the city's.[23]

Outside of midtown, shopping streets also represent, by ownership and employment patterns, the social and economic integration of neighborhood residents. But here, in contrast to midtown and downtown, a tension between commercial legibility and community identity creates a highly contested representation that sparks periodic violence. The demonstrations and boycotts on 125th Street in Harlem in the 1920s to protest lack of jobs for neighborhood residents in local stores were early confirmations of the power of this representation. In the last three years, demonstrations and boycotts on Church Avenue in Brooklyn, this time against Korean rather than Jewish storeowners, have shown that the representation still has symbolic force. Even without demonstrations, neighborhood resentment against storeowners is usually high when, as on Pitkin Avenue in Brooklyn, the owners and employees are Indian or Caribbean and most residents are native-born African-Americans. Where storeowners do represent the residential community, shopping streets do not become symbols of decline. By comparison, in the Los Angeles insurrection of 1992, people attacked stores rather than housing, and neither the supermarkets financed by community development corporations nor the 31 McDonald's restaurants in the South Central area were harmed.[24]

In the real estate recession of the early 1990s, major shopping streets in New York's immigrant neighborhoods have not suffered from more vacant storefronts than in the high-rent districts of Manhattan. On Flatbush Avenue between Church Avenue and Hawthorne Avenue, in Brooklyn, 11 per cent of 191 stores are now closed, empty or for rent. Storeowners are Haitian, Chinese and Greek; customers are mainly Caribbean blacks, with some Latinos, African-Americans and Chinese. On a recent Saturday there were no white shoppers or walkers. On Main Street in Flushing, Queens, from Highway to Stanford Streets, 12 per cent of 149 stores were closed, empty or for rent. Most owners here are Chinese, but there are also many corporate franchises. On a recent Saturday mainly Asians were on the street, with some Latinos, Indians, African-Americans and whites. Vacancy rates are similar on Madison Avenue in Manhattan, where storeowners and customers are predominantly white and often European. In 174 stores between 80th and 96th Streets, the vacancy rate is almost 10 per cent. Vacancies decline to 6 per cent in the 90s, which have more neighborhood services, but in the 70s, the vacancy rate is 15 per cent. Between 57th and 69th Streets, where there is a high concentration of European designer clothing and luxury-goods stores, as well as 'Harry, If I Told You, Would You Know?', the vacancy rate of just under 10 per cent is about the same as on Flatbush Avenue.

While these vacancy rates do not indicate a good situation, they compare favorably with vacancy rates in office buildings, which were as high as 16 per cent in Class A buildings in midtown in 1992. This suggests a contradiction between the public space constructed by two symbolic economies, the global and the local. The legibility of central commercial complexes and office-building lobbies differs from the identity negotiated in neighborhood shopping streets. Despite their problems, these streets produce the quality of life that New Yorkers prize, the public space that makes neighborhoods livable, and attaches people to place. A period of economic decline provides an opportunity to think creatively about these representations. When recession makes large projects prohibitively expensive, it is time to bring culture into public space in a different way.

## NOTES

1.  Christine M. Boyer, 'Cities for Sale: Merchandising History at South Street Seaport', in Michael Sorkin (ed.), *Variations on a Theme Park* (Hill & Wang, New York, 1992) pp. 181–204.
2.  Susan Sontag, *On Photography* (Farrar Straus & Giroux, New York, 1977), p. 180.
3.  Sharon Zukin, *Loft Living* (Johns Hopkins University Press, Baltimore, Md., 1982).
4.  Bernard J. Frieden, and Lynne B. Sagalyn, *Downtown Inc.: How America Rebuilds Cities* (MIT Press, Cambridge, Mass., 1989.)
5.  Philip Kasinitz and Sharon Zukin, 'Limits of Post-modernism: Culture, Tourism, and Regional Identity in the Berkshires', in Zukin, *The Culture of Cities* (Blackwell, Oxford, forthcoming).
6.  Rosalyn Deutsche, 'Uneven Development: Public Art in New York City', *October*, 47 (Winter, 1988), pp. 3–52.
7.  Sharon Zukin, 'High Culture and "Wild" Commerce: Developing a Center of the Arts in New York City', in *The Culture of Cities* (Blackwell, Oxford, forthcoming).

8. Sharon Zukin, *Landscapes of Power* (University of California Press, Berkeley and Los Angeles, 1991).
9. Anthony D. King, *Global Cities. Post-Imperialism and the Internationalisation of London* (Routledge, London and New York, 1990).
10. Sharon Zukin (see note 7).
11. Jean-Paul Agnew, 'Times Square: Secularization and Sacralization', in William R. Taylor (ed.), *Inventing Times Square* (Russell Sage Foundation, New York, 1991), pp. 2–13.
12. William Taylor, 'The Evolution of Public Space: The Commercial City as Showcase', in Taylor, *In Pursuit of Gotham: Culture and Commerce in New York* (Oxford University Press, New York and Oxford, 1992).
13. Jason Epstein, 'The Tragical History of New York', *New York Review of Books* (9 April 1992), pp. 45–52.
14. B. J. Frieden and L. B. Sagalyn (see note 4).
15. Richard Sennett, *The Conscience of the Eye* (Norton, New York, 1990).
16. Elizabeth Wilson, *The Sphinx in the City* (Virago, London, 1991).
17. Mike Davis, *City of Quartz: Excavating the Future in Los Angeles* (Verso, London, 1990).
18. Henri Lefebvre, *The Production of Space*, (trans.) Donald Nicholson-Smith (Blackwell, Oxford, 1991 [1974]).
19. W. Taylor, p. 44 (see note 12).
20. William Taylor (ed.), *Inventing Times Square* (Russell Sage Foundation, New York, 1991).
21. Roy Rosenzweig and Elizabeth Blackmar, *The Park and the People: A History of Central Park* (Cornell University Press, Ithaca, New York, 1992).
22. Howard Wolfson, 'New York Bets on BIDs', *Metropolis* (April, 1992), pp. 15–21.
23. *Crane's New York Business*, 6 April 1992.
24. Hugo Lindgren, 'Rethinking Los Angeles', *Metropolis*, January–February 1993, pp. 19, 22.

# 3

# Return to the Future: Puerto Rican Vernacular Architecture in New York City

Joseph Sciorra

---

I think that communities of resistance should be places where people can return to themselves more easily, where the conditions are such that they can heal themselves and recover their wholeness.

(Thich Nhat Hahn, *The Raft is Not the Shore*,
quoted in bell hooks' *Yearning*)

*Entonces yo pensé muchas cosas. Pensé en mi hijo que acababa de nacer y en lo que iba a ser su vida aqui, pensé en Puerto Rico y en los viejos y en todo lo que dejamos allá nada más que por necesidad, pensé tantas cosas que algunas ya se me han olvidado, porque tú sabes que la mente es como una pizarra y el tiempo como un borrador que la pasa por encima cada vez que se nos llena. Pero de lo que si me voy a acordar siempre es de lo que le dije yo entonces a doña Lula, que es lo que te voy a decir ahora para acabar de contarte lo que tú querías saber. Y es que, según mi pobre manera de entender las cosas, aquélla fue la noche que volvimos a ser gente.*

(José Luis González, 'La noche que volvimos a ser gente')

And so I thought of many things. I thought of my new born son and what was to become of his life here, I thought of Puerto Rico and the elders and all that we left behind simply out of necessity. I thought of many things that by now I have forgotten, because, you know, the mind is like a blackboard and time an eraser that passes across it each time we fill it up. But the thing I will always remember is what I told doña Lula, which is what I am going to tell you now to finish what it is you wanted to know. And that is, in my poor way of understanding things, that was the night we became people again.

*Si yo vine a Nueva York con el fin de progresar, si allí lo pasaba mal aqui lo
paso peor.
Unas veces el calor y otras el maldito frío.
A veces parezco un lío por la nieve patinando.
Eso no me está gustando. Yo me vuelvo a mi bohío.*

(Miguel Angel Figueroa (El Jibarito de Adjuntas),
'Yo me vuelvo a mi bohío')

If I came to New York with the intention of getting ahead.
[And] if back home it was bad, here it's even worse.
Sometimes it's the heat and other times this damn cold.
Sometimes I look like a mess slipping and sliding in the snow.
I'm not enjoying this. I'm returning to my *bohío*.

It is difficult to imagine the landscape of New York City's South Bronx
without falling victim to the clichéd phrases and images framed by political
candidates, news reporters and film directors for the world's consumption
and titillation. While large tracts of land were reduced to rubble, the South
Bronx was further reduced to the emblematic in a game of tropes whereby
those in power engaged in the ideological construction of the low, the Other.
At its best, the urban landscape of the South Bronx has been compared to
that of post-World War II Europe; Dresden devastated by fire bombs. At its
worst, the image, devoid of life, was lunar. Depicted as the 'Frontier,' the
edge where the 'Wild' began, the South Bronx was inhabited by 'savages'
who stormed the bastion of civilization in the guise of Fort Apache,
defended by the representatives of 'law and order' who were assigned the
miserable task of protecting property torched by its fleeing owners in order
to collect on insurance. The area's Latino and African-American working
poor were denied access to the political process and the economic resources
that shaped their daily life and physical reality. At the same time members of
the power structure, informed by their own attraction and repulsion, further
marginalized the residents of the South Bronx and similar inner-city
neighborhoods through the manipulation of imagery that represented
minority men and women as nothing less than human in 'the shared
imaginary repertoires of the dominant culture.[1,2]

It is within this imposed economic, political and social marginality that
poor people of color struggle to change the existing conditions in which they
live, by creating spaces of their own design that serve as locations of
resistance to a system of inequity and domination.[3] In the South Bronx,
East Harlem and the Lower East Side, Puerto Rican residents of New York
City appropriate municipal-owned property where multi-storied apartment
buildings once stood. There, people clear the detritus of urban decay to
cultivate bountiful gardens and construct wood-frame structures typical of
the Caribbean (Figure 3.1). These transformed sites serve as shelter for the

(*Photograph: Martha Cooper*)

FIGURE 3.1 An urban lot transformed; Puerto Rico in Nueva York, 1988.

homeless, social clubs, block associations, cultural centers, summer retreats and entrepreneurial ventures. The cultural production of vernacular horticulture and architecture create local landscapes of empowerment that serve as centers of community action where people engage in modes of expressivity that are alternatives to those imposed from above by the dominant culture. In turn these concerted actions pose a direct challenge to official notions pertaining to the status of public land and its future use.

These vernacular forms are united temporally and spatially with the historic dispossession of laboring people by the forces of a global capitalist economy. The displacement of populations and destruction of geography result from the dislocations of capital; the shift from an agricultural economy to an industrial one, from a manufacture-centered society to the current service economy of advanced consumerism uniting the South Bronx, New York with San Juan, Puerto Rico. The colonial domination of Puerto Rico's political and economic life for nearly a century by the United States has created the conditions in which working-class *puertorriqueños* have experienced the coerced migration from countryside to city, colony to metropolis, and neighborhood to neighborhood in search of employment and a better standard of living. These historical connections reverberate in the ongoing reconfiguration of traditional architectural forms, the creative response to the devastation of, and dislocation from, the physical and social landscapes of a remembered past. Knowledge and skills developed amidst this destruction are employed in transforming the rubble and ruin in a conscious rebuilding of urban communities. People are not merely reacting to the fluxes of a capitalist world system, but instead are actively offering indigenous solutions to the exigencies of our cities. This chapter will explore 'the degree to which local societies or cultures maintain control over and modify their . . . distinctive [expressive,] building and urban forms, . . . and hence . . . their own economy and polity . . . in the face of global forces' (King, 1991).[4]

## THE COLONIAL EXPERIENCE AND THE CREOLIZATION PROCESS

In his essay on race and class in the context of Puerto Rico's colonial history entitled *El país de cuatro pisos*, author and cultural critic José Luis González likened the Caribbean island to a building consisting of four storeys.[5] González sought in his essay to critique a prevailing view of Puerto Rican culture and national identity held by island elites and intellectuals that divided island society and history into a neat dichotomy consisting of a united '*familia puertorriqueña*' battling the 'invading *gringos*'. In the nineteenth century, Puerto Rico's two-tier society was occupied on the 'ground floor' by the majority population of black and mestizo laborers.

The country's second storey was occupied by a white, predominantly European immigrant, landowning class. According to González, the third and fourth 'storeys' resulted from the 1898 North American invasion, and the industrialization endeavors begun in the 1940s, respectively.[6,7] He points out that while seignorial economic power and cultural way of life were severely undermined by North American imperialism, working-class vernacular culture, which is fundamentally Afro-Antillean in style and content, came to represent the most vibrant expression of Puerto Rican society in the twentieth century.[8,9] While problematic, González's metaphor serves as a foundation for illustrating the confluence of components that contributed to the development of Puerto Rican vernacular architecture.[10]

When the political and economic forces of colonialism bring together diverse peoples, languages, ideas and objects, as has occurred historically in Puerto Rico, a new synthesis, or creole form of cultural expression emerges. This interaction of divergent and often contentious voices at the crossroads of social discourse is what Russian critic Mikhail Bakhtin referred to as 'heteroglossia'. In his writings, Bakhtin explored language use at those sites of pronounced multivocality and polyvalence such as the European novel, carnival festivities, and the medieval marketplace. His interests led him to those syncretic cultural manifestations and social identities '[b]orn on the confines of languages and cultures, which not only were in direct contact but were in a sense interwoven'.[11] It is on the 'carnivalized' landscape of Puerto Rican colonial society, a politically liminal entity situated historically on the periphery of a world economic order, that an amalgamation of Amerindian, African, Iberian, Caribbean, and now North American elements were and continue to be forged in the creation of a new emerging world.

Bakhtin's linguistic philosophy privileged the actual spoken word, or utterance, in everyday life. This method was in sharp contrast to the Saussurian model of communication that suppressed the context-centered component of language by placing emphasis on the study of the synchronic, static system known as *langue* (Volosnov, 1973[12]). Bakhtin's work illuminates language's subversive powers of creativity and variation to form new alternative meanings and identities in the historically situated production of speech.[13] 'A new type of communication always creates new forms of speech or a new meaning given to the old forms'.[14] According to Bakhtin, everyday speech consists of a number of intersecting languages, dialects and argot of various groups that 'are specific points of view on the world, forms for conceptualizing the world in words, specific world views, each characterized by its own objects, meanings and values'.[15] Language carries the weight of past usage and associations, and each utterance is a unique and novel act attempting to lay claim to words not yet one's own.

> [T]here are no 'neutral' words and forms – words and forms that can belong to 'no one'; language has been completely taken over, shot

through with intentions and accents. . . Each word tastes of the context and contexts in which it has lived its socially charged life. As a living, socio-ideological concrete thing, as heteroglot opinion, language, for the individual consciousness, lies on the borderline between oneself and the other. The word in language is half someone else's. It becomes 'one's own' only when the speaker populates it with his own intention, his own accent, when he appropriates the word, adapting it to his own semantic and expressive intention. . . Language is not a neutral medium that passes freely and easily into the private property of the speaker's intentions; it is populated – overpopulated – with the intentions of others. Expropriating it, forcing it to submit to one's own intentions and accents is a difficult and complicated process. (Bakhtin, 1988)[16]

Hybridization results in the struggle to invest words with one's own intentions and subjectivity in the continuous process of fashioning distinctiveness and identity. 'Difference is an effect of inventive syncretism'.[17] Language's mutability and regenerative characteristics stand in sharp contrast to authoritative attempts to fix, to canonize, the fruits of creolization.[18] Bakhtin's work on the spoken and written word provides us with a useful tool for examining various forms of expressive culture other than language, such as geography and architecture.[19]

We can not forget that the historical processes of creolization in the Americas were acts of creative and dynamic resistance by subjugated peoples to centuries of domination and exploitation based on race, class and gender. Expressive forms embodied and reproduced social identities and corresponding ideologies that existed in tension and conflict between oppressor and the oppressed. Contentions at the local level of cultural production and social relations reveal those moments and locations that intersected with the larger forces of a global political economy.[20,21] Popular forms of music, dance and related religious practices, often African-derived, were violently suppressed by civil and religious authorities throughout the new world. Historically, creolization in the Caribbean was not hailed as the creative 'adaptation of means of diverse provenance to new ends'[22] but rather was devalued and dismissed as the unintentional, 'impure', and by extension 'unclean' product of uneducated social inferiors. Members of the Antillean elite distanced themselves from lower class creole configurations by first denying the African roots of folk forms and then promoting elite European and later North American cultural models.[23] Until recently many twentieth century Puerto Rican intellectuals failed to acknowledge the inventiveness of working-class aesthetics in their nostalgic sense of loss for an 'authentic' rural Puerto Rican culture weakened by an undeniably pervasive and powerful North American imperialism.[24,25] For a time, this perspective stunted any serious discussion of popular aesthetics among a people in exile in the United States.[26,27,28]

## CAPITAL, DISPLACEMENT, AND THE EMERGENCE OF A
## PUERTO RICAN VERNACULAR HOUSE FORM

The architectural roots of popular Puerto Rican housing can be found in a narrow lot squeezed between two apartment buildings on East 119th Street in *El Barrio*. There Antonio Tirado has affectionately named his contribution to the caribbeanization of Nueva York, *Mi Bohío* (Figure 3.2). *Bohíos*, post and beam huts constructed out of wood with bamboo and cane walls, and with thatched gable roof, were used as housing in Puerto Rico as late as the 1940s.[29] Their origin and development are interwoven with the sordid history of European capitalist expansion and conquest, Indian genocide, and African enslavement in the frenetic search for profits in the forms of first gold and later tobacco, coffee, and ultimately sugar.

In the first half of the sixteenth century, Spanish chronicler Gonzalo Fernandez de Oviedo wrote a detailed description of the rectangular *bohío* and the polygonal *caney*, two types of Native American dwellings he encountered among the Taíno in neighboring Hispaniola. It has been suggested by twentieth century scholar Sven Lowen that while the *caney* was a truly pre-conquest house type, the *bohío* was in fact a syncretic blend of native building technology and a European house form.[30,31] According to Loven, the Spaniards' rectangular dwelling with gable roof became associated originally with colonial power and was emulated by Taíno *caciques*, or leaders, who were the first to use the *bohío*. Under the *encomiendo* system that granted Spaniards native land and labor, *caciques* were recruited as overseers of lower-class Indian workers known as *naborías*, forced to herd cattle and work the mines.[32] In turn the *bohío* was adapted and modified by Spanish colonists as well as enslaved and free Africans.[33,34] As rebellious Amerindians and Africans fled to the mountain interior, along with Spaniards escaping civil authorities in San Juan, this rich exchange continued in counter-plantation economies and cultures through a settlement pattern of squatter subsistence farming in the mountainous *altura*, or highland.[35,36,37] More durable materials such as ironwood and mahogany cut into boards came to be used in the construction of such housing.[38] In time the *bohío* became *the* housing type of the island's black, white and mestizo laborers for well over four centuries after the annihilation of the island's original inhabitants, the Taínos.

The inventiveness of popular culture not only continued after the North American invasion and occupation of the Caribbean island in 1898 but took on a distinctively proletarian cast with the influx of US-controlled capitalist modes of production. The sudden and rapid capitalist transformation of the Puerto Rican economy by North American businesses occurred in two major stages. During the first quarter of the twentieth century, absentee US corporations purchased huge tracts of land along the coastal plains to form

(Photograph: Martha Cooper)

FIGURE 3.2  In *El Barrio*, Antonio Tirado and friends play dominoes in his broomstick *bohío*, 1988.

technologically-advanced, mechanized sugar plantations, effectively restructuring Puerto Rico into a monocultural sugar economy in the service of a North American market.[39,40] After the second World War, US capital shifted away from agriculturally-based sugar production to an urban-centered industrial economy consisting of export-oriented factories. Foreign investment succeeded in gaining control of the local economy from the nascent Puerto Rican bourgeoisie thus securing the economic integration of the island into that of the United States and establishing the economic basis for continued colonial rule.

These accelerated economic changes had profound effects on Puerto Rican social life, the most dramatic being major movements of the island's population. Both stages in the capitalist development of Puerto Rican society resulted in a surplus of laborers who were trapped in the new order's structural unemployment.[41] Disinvestment in coffee production at the turn of the century and in the general agricultural economy in the post-World War II era pushed displaced workers first from the highlands to the coast, and later from the countryside to the cities. This internal migration strained local services, which were unequipped to handle the mass influx of people, especially acutely in the area of housing. Relying on a vibrant squatter tradition harkening back to Spanish colonialism, landless workers established *arrabales*, or squatter settlements, on marginal public lands located on the urban periphery where they organized to obtain electricity, sanitation, roads, etc., from the insular government. In places christened *La Perla* (The Pearl) and *El Fanguito* (Little Mud), squatters constructed housing in bricolage fashion from imported North American products, often recycling junk and other found objects; discarded kerosene cans and corrugated metal sheets ultimately replaced thatched roofs; balloon framing using packing crates and pre-cut lumber became the primary method of construction; and exterior decoration was augmented by the use of brilliant hues of paint.[42,43] In this way, the jetsam and flotsam of the colonial endeavor served as 'compost for new orders of difference'[44] in the transformation of the *bohío* into the *casita de madera* (little wood house) at the interval of a rural agricultural past and an industrial urban future.

Migration was not solely an internal phenomenon. Working-class *puertorriqueños* also traveled to the United States in search of gainful employment. Immigration to the mainland was facilitated by the imposition of US citizenship on *puertorriqueños* in 1917 less than a month after America entered World War I. While they now reside in all 50 states of the Union, New York City has historically been the primary point of entry and settlement for *puertorriqeuños* who now number close to a million. This massive movement of labor corresponds to the economic conditions in the homeland and took place primarily in three stages; from 1900–45, aggravated, in part, by the Great Depression of the 1930s; 1946–64, when the largest influx of Puerto Ricans arrived in the city; and 1964 to the present, again exacerbated by the 1970s recession.[45,46] Facilitated by US citizenship and relatively inexpensive air travel, the Puerto Rican experience in the United States has been characterized by a circular migration between the colony and metropolis. This migratory pattern has become an increasingly common one for New York Caribbean migrants as a whole and has served to further link the politics, economies, and cultures of the Caribbean and New York City in a 'transnational socio-cultural system'.[47,48,49] This transmigratory exchange thus redraws the boundaries between the islands of Boriquén and Manhattan, effectively transforming each into a *barrio* of the other.


## NEW YORK'S SCARRED LANDSCAPES

The great wave of post-World War II Puerto Rican migration occurred at a historical juncture in the economic life of New York City. Initially, the 'pull' for Puerto Rican (and also southern African-American) migrants to New York was the demand for unskilled labor in the post-war economic 'boom' that fed the escalating consumerism of an increasingly non-urban middle class. But the nation's economy was in the process of decentralizing industrialization in the transformation to a service economy. The accelerated mobility of capital resulted in a frenzy of destruction of the urban built environment that changed the very face of the Northeast metropolis during the 1960s and 1970s. Geographer David Harvey has addressed the cyclical pattern of demolition and development in the service of continued capital accumulation. The actual physicality of urban life stands as an obstacle to further capitalist investment and potential profits.[50] The devaluation and the resulting upheaval have in turn a devastating impact on the local communities that reside, work, and play in urban neighborhoods.

The history of annihilation of the New York landscape and interrelated social life remains obfuscated by class biases and racist mythologies. Industries which provided entry-level employment and were the foundation of vibrant working-class neighborhoods, relocated to the south or overseas during the 1960s and 1970s.[51] With this loss of jobs came the increasing incidence of structural hard-core poverty.[52] The construction of a labyrinth of federally subsidized highways to service the developing suburban townships obliterated large sections of stable working-class neighborhoods in the post-war era.[53] This forced relocation of tens of thousands of residents was augmented by massive 'slum' clearance which leveled block after block of family-owned homes and salvageable apartment buildings, to erect public housing. The African-American and Latino poor, themselves displaced from urban renewal projects in other parts of the city, were 'dumped' into high-rise public housing constructed in predominantly white working-class communities. The banking and real estate establishment helped fan the fires of fear of black encroachment and encouraged white flight through redlining and the systematic disinvestment of neighborhoods in the name of escalating profits and property turnover. When rental apartments no longer became profitable for landlords, they abandoned them by first cutting the services and eventually torching the buildings for insurance money.[54] Frustration rooted in the dire conditions of inner-city life led to riots that contributed to the destruction of housing and local businesses. The proliferation of the drug trade, first heroin, and most recently crack, and the increasing accessibility of handguns and semi-automatic weapons for use by indiscriminately violent, competitive drug entrepreneurs has created a climate of crime and chaos that has further entrenched itself into the everyday life of many New York City communities.

At the onset of the 1990s, the systemic neglect that characterizes current political policy and economic agendas at both local and national levels has preserved acres of barren city land in a perpetual state of official disuse for well over two decades. As New Yorkers have witnessed in the Lower East Side and now in Black and Hispanic Harlem, land speculation prevents the renovation of existing housing stock and the construction of new housing until gentrification makes it profitable for real estate developers. As the current national recession throws city, state and national governments into fiscal crisis, these areas are subjected to yet deeper reductions of already strained social services and the forfeiting of government-sponsored moderate and low-income housing. As a result expanses of land, some a whole city block long, lie vacant except for the weeds growing among the scattered rubble.

## PUERTO RICO EN NUEVA YORK

It is on this topography of destruction that *puertorriqueños* have claimed a space of their own, much like the fabled phoenix rising from the all-consuming flames. Appropriating land laid waste by the excesses of capital and the neglect of bureaucracy, they construct wood-frame buildings reminiscent of the Caribbean. A panoply of structural forms abound in New York City, with each 'type' containing within it diversity and variations on a theme,each a unique architectural utterance.[55] By far the most predominant manifestation of Puerto Rican vernacular architecture in the city and the focus of this chapter is the one to three-room *casita de madera*.

*Casitas* constructed with the entrance at the gable end are the most numerous, but in a few cases one enters at the long end of the building. These 'little houses' are usually raised off the ground like their counterparts in Puerto Rico which were often constructed on posts for protection from seasonal inundations. The *balcón*, or veranda, a dominant feature of Caribbean popular housing, is the most recurring architectural element of New York *casitas*. While a few buildings have a half *balcón*, usually an internal one, most *casitas* are constructed with a full-width veranda running the length of the building's facade. On occasion the veranda may also run along one or both sides of the building. Railings, in a good number of cases, are finished with X's between the balusters. These last two features are such an integral part of the *casita*'s language and aesthetic that they appear even in the simplest structures as a form of architectural shorthand and iconic referent.

Hybridizations that defy conventional typographies abound in New York City. Antonio Tirado's aforementioned structure is an ingenious synthesis that combines elements of the *bohío* as well as the open-air *templete*. Down the block on East 119th Street, a builder broke up the *casita* roof-line by incorporating a garret similar to the mansard roof of a church located across the street from the lot. In the Lower East Side, Virgilio Burgos included a full picture window into his two-story *casita* in an architectural meeting of Ponce and Levittown.

In New York, as in Puerto Rico, a major source of building materials, as well as exterior decoration, is recycled scrap lumber and other found objects culled from the scoria of arson and abandonment. This accrual mode of construction is testimony to the creativity and resourcefulness of urban pioneers who see the value of waste and integrate it into a cycle of reuse.[56,57,58] Antonio Tirado constructed his open-aired *bohío* with broomsticks salvaged from a bankrupt factory and then supplied this novel building material to three other *casita* builders in the neighborhood. One Lower East Side resident fitted a glass roof from a botanical garden greenhouse onto his structure, making it the only *casita* in New York with a skylight. In addition, builders often invest their own money to purchase building materials. Jesus Valásquez spent $250 on corrugated fiberglass to roof his *casita* in El Barrio; while Virgilio Burgos constructed his two-storey structure entirely of store-bought lumber. More durable materials may also be used: concrete for steps, brick for covering an earthen floor, or cinder blocks for walls in one example from the South Bronx.

In a few instances, a single individual is responsible for constructing a *casita* entirely on his own. It most cases, a group of men organize themselves to raise a building collectively. These concerted efforts are usually under the supervision of a skilled carpenter or craftsman versed in the tradition of *casita* building. The work in all these cases is most often donated, undertaken as a gift to the *casita* membership and the community at large, and as such constitutes a source of non-alienating labor[59] (Figure 3.3). Like their *arrabal* counterparts, New York *casitas* are gradually improved over time.[60] The addition of a veranda or a second room is often made after initial construction. Modifications in furnishings and decoration occur not

(*Photograph: Martha Cooper*)

FIGURE 3.3   After a fire destroyed Villa Puerto Rico in 1990, neighborhood men offered their time and skills to rebuild the Bronx *casita* with new materials donated from neighborhood suppliers.

only from year to year but also in the course of summer months. The open-endedness of architectural activity illustrates that the *casita* is viewed as an unfinished entity involved in the ongoing process of becoming.[61]

*Casita* interior space is furnished with many of the comforts of home; a table and chairs, a couch, and even a television. A number are outfitted with a small but fully operational kitchen complete with a refrigerator, running water and a working stove. Gas is supplied from a refillable tank and the water is obtained from either a rain barrel or a nearby spigot. Electricity may be illegally tapped from a nearby lamppost, or in other cases an agreement is worked out with the superintendant of a neighboring apartment building to whom *casita* members pay a monthly fee for the use of electricity. An adaptation to New York's potentially harsh winters is the installation of electric heaters, wall insulation, and in one case, a working fireplace.

Decoration is a contributing component to the overall *casita* aesthetic. The vibrant colors of the Caribbean are one of the most common methods employed in embellishing the exterior. In addition a host of found objects such as posters, advertisements, salvaged oil paintings and completed puzzles are tacked onto the outside walls. These are not haphazard uses of ephemera reflecting a 'culture of poverty' but like the *casita* itself, are instead a deliberate and conscious manifestation of deeply felt values, beliefs and needs in culturally specific and meaningful ways[62,63] (Figure 3.4). In some cases, this playful juxtapositioning of seemingly disparate objects highlights the *casita*'s convivial role as leisure space while visually proclaiming shared interests and links of affiliation of the *casita*'s membership. Expressions of religious sentiment and Afrocentricity are made visually explicit through ornamentation, signage and statuary.[64] The prominence of national heroes and heroines such as baseball player Roberto Clemente, singer Ismael Rivera, and patriot Lolita Lebron, as well as the ubiquitous Puerto Rican flag and accompanying silhouette of the island, articulate an involvement and commitment to sports, the arts, and politics as it pertains to Puerto Rican history and culture despite nearly a century of North American colonialism.

Reclamation not only involves traditional building skills but also the creative reinterpretation of traditional patterns of land use. Urban horticulturalists cultivate vegetables, fruits, flowers, and/or herbs in dooryard gardens similar to those found in Puerto Rico and throughout the Caribbean.[65,66] Plant varieties are dictated to a large degree by climate and seasonal change and as a result *casita* plots include vegetation suitable to New York weather. In these gardens North American staples such as apples, beets, and collard greens grow near peppers, beans, and cilantro raised for traditional creole cuisine. City farming is done under the auspices of Operation GreenThumb, a community garden program run by the city's Department of General Services. The program allocates short-term leases

FIGURE 3.4 *La Parcela de los Amigos* (The Friends' Parcel of Land) in *El Barrio* is decorated with signs of affiliation referencing, among other things, the city of Ponce in Puerto Rico and the New York Mets baseball team, 1990.

ranging from one to five years for a one dollar annual (waived) fee. The city agency provides material assistance in the form of garden equipment, topsoil, seeds, shrubs, and trees. The resurrection of the rural is recognized by Jesus Valásquez who painted on the wooden entrance to his East Harlem compound the Spanish word for a country parcel, *EL JARAGUAL.*

The non-vegetated yard surrounding the *casita* is referred to by the term *batey* and is where much of the socializing occurs. Historically the *batey* was not considered a separate entity from the house but was in fact its spatial extension. As in Puerto Rico, the garden is fenced off and separated from this clean swept and raked yard. In New York the area usually consists of finely packed dirt, while it may be covered with gravel, filled in with decorative brick work, or paved over with cement. Speaking of the pervasive Caribbean settlement pattern of *casita* and *batey*, anthropologist Sidney Mintz noted, 'Together, house and yard form a nucleus within which the culture expresses itself, is perpetuated, changed, and reintegrated'.[67,68]

Land availability and usage vary from neighborhood to neighborhood and from location to location. The South Bronx contains huge expanses of land in comparison to the smaller and scarcer lots found in the more spatially congested and highly concentrated East Harlem and the Lower East Side. Manhattan *casitas* as a result tend to stand on narrow plots squeezed between abandoned and occupied tenement buildings. Regardless of the existing lot size, rarely is more than one constructed on an individual plot of land. A few exceptions to this pattern do exist. On East 139th Street in the South Bronx, three *casitas* were erected as housing on a single lot but the property was subdivided with fences and each section had its own separate entrance at the sidewalk. In *El Barrio*, a walkway connects over half a dozen buildings and accompanying dooryard gardens in a East 119th Street lot. At *Villa El Gato* on Brooklyn's Columbia Street, homeless men displaced from neighborhood apartments have constructed their dwellings in a semi-circle around a central plaza, or *solar*. All but *Villa El Gato* are sealed with a chain link fence at the sidewalk for protection from vandals.

## THE POETICS AND POLITICS OF MEMORY: THE CASITA AS ARCHITECTURAL CHRONOTOPE

The transformed lot is an attempt not only to inscribe a specific place on the New York landscape but also a specific time, that is, a pre-industrial Puerto Rico of the recent past. The configuration of *casita*, *batey* and garden in New York is what Bakhtin referred to as an artistic chronotope where 'spatial and temporal indicators are fused into one carefully thought-out, concrete whole'.[69] These transposed 'landmarks of memory'[70] are material articulations of a sense of displacement from a familiar and cherished landscape inextricably linked to a loss of an era. This salvaged topography has the evocative power to transport New York *puertorriqueños* back to a place and time they remember. Juan Gutierrez, a regular at the South Bronx *casita Rincón Criollo*, noted:

> You see, when you're there the whole scene transforms. All of a sudden you forget that you are in the South Bronx. You forget that you are in New York City. Your mind travels to Puerto Rico, sometime, somewhere. You know you've been there before. That's the kind of feeling you have. (12 July 1989)

The *casita* is similar to scrap books and quilts in that builders piece together disparate objects into a meaningful whole in order to reclaim a lost world and fix it in our consciousness. This ensemble of recycled materials and memories stands as a kind of physical autobiography composed by immigrants of a specific generation who share similar life experiences.[71]

It is a constellation of culturally significant objects that reconstitutes this remembered Caribbean in New York City. In addition to horticulture and architecture, it is a close attention to detail that creates a sense of authenticity; a non-functioning electricity meter attached to an exterior wall, or a hand-operated water pump in an urban *batey*. Livestock such as chickens, ducks, geese, rabbits and even a goat are kept in *casita* yards. Even the latrine, once a staple of poor peoples' homes on the island, has the ability to evoke memories of an earlier time. Emerging from an outdoor toilet during her first visit to *Villa Puerto Rico* in the South Bronx, Maria Castagena said, 'When I went in there, it was like going back in time'.

In Puerto Rico, these wood structures have slowly been replaced in the past 40 years by reinforced concrete houses and highrise apartment buildings for a predominantly urban population. *Arrabales* were systematically destroyed by the insular government in a campaign of slum clearance when once marginal lands acquired new value in the sprawling metropolis that is San Juan.[72] Residents were relocated to public housing projects called *caserios*, or, if they could afford them, to the 'concretized bleakness and army-barracks uniformity'[73] of the suburban-style developments known as *urbanizaciones*. As in New York, the *casita* has made a surprising comeback in recent years giving an interesting twist to González's architectural metaphor. Prefabricated structures resembling *casitas de madera* are sold and assembled as second storeys to suburban homes in an architectural layering of past and present social lives.

Reproduced in literature and the visual arts, the *casita* is a key symbol for contemporary *puertorriqueños*, summing up in an emotionally powerful way a host of often conflicting ideas and sentiments regarding history, culture, and identity.[74] *Casita* iconography is a semiotic battlefield 'entangled' with warring ideological positions attempting to lay claim to the symbol and render its reading as authoritative.[75] The image is part of a pantheon of secular icons visually manifesting a vision of cultural identity and patriotism against the historical backdrop of colonialism. Bourgeois elites and seignorial intellectuals cultivated national emblems by reducing the highland agricultural laborer, or *jíbaro*, to the realm of the nostalgic and 'folkloric' thus denying colonial and class exploitation.[76] In Puerto Rico this patriotic symbol building was often initiated and promoted by accommodationists to colonial rule, ranging from the painter Francesco Oller (who was aligned politically with the *Partido Autonomista Puertorriqueño*), to governor Luis Muñiz Marin,[77] founder of *Partido Popular Democratico*. The 'cult of the *jíbaro*' placed 'authentic' Puerto Rican culture among the predominantly white highland laborers at the exclusion of blacks and mestizos residing on the coast and in the cities within the discourse on 'national identity'.[78] An alternative image of popular housing emerged in the 1950s as socially engaged visual artists Lorenzo Homar, Carlos Raquel Rivera, Rafael Tufiño, and others began producing explicitly political and anti-imperialist imagery that addressed the subaltern conditions of *arrabal* residents.[79,80]

For New York *puertorriqueños*, the *casita* is a metaphor of home that is both the domestic dwelling space and the national homeland. This is apparent in the names given these sites in keeping with the *arrabal* tradition. Collapsing architectural and national elements into one appellation is not uncommon; buildings and lots have been dubbed, *El Balcón Boricua* and *El Batey Boricano*. It is not merely a Puerto Rican veranda or yard, but rather Puerto Rico inscribed on the architecture and patterned landscape. Direct references to the island and its place in the Greater Antilles is witnessed in names like *Villa Puerto Rico*, *Villa Boriquen*, or *La Brisa del Caribe*. Other names point to regional identities associated with specific towns and cities like *Villa San Germán* or *Caquas Gardens*. The *casita* as architectural metaphor expressing mixed sentiments of longing and national pride is explicitly stated on the gable end of a sky blue *casita* that once stood in the South Bronx, '*AÑORANZAS DE MI PATRIA*' – 'Yearnings For My Homeland'.

For those who have lived the *casita*, pieced together its walls and inhabited its space, the moribundly nostalgic *jíbaro* iconography mass produced in the service of tobacco and alcohol companies as well as the island's tourist industry invades their memories. But for many of the former *casita* inhabitants I spoke with in New York City, the building recounts a history of toil, suffering and struggle that stands in marked opposition to such saccharine imagery. When asked what it was like to live in a *casita de madera*, Félix Rivera remembered growing up on his father's farm in Arecibo where a family of eighteen ate 'corn for breakfast, lunch and dinner'. 'We worked and worked', he told me, 'and we'd sell a hundred pounds of tobacco to Philip Morris for a couple of pennies' (18 June 1989). José Manuel 'Chema' Soto, former resident of Río Piedras, explained the *casita*'s message:

People from New Jersey, people from everywhere come here because it reminds them of the houses in Puerto Rico. They say, 'My grandmother used to have a house like this'. Ismael Rivera, the great Puerto Rican singer, came out of a house like this. When I grew up, we lived in a little house just like this one. All of us did. This reminds me of my childhood. There's still some houses, even poorer than this, in Puerto Rico. The *casitas* are a symbol of poverty, of what we went through. (18 August 1990)

In this way, the history of a laboring people is given aesthetic and social form through the production of working-class culture. The *casita* is constructed by those who have mastered the cultural knowledge and necessary technical skills as part of a legacy offered to a new generation of *puertorriqueños*, many New York-born. The concertive action of collective reminiscences makes the *casita* a place

> . . . where one is able to redeem and reclaim the past, legacies of pain, suffering, and triumph in ways that transform present reality. . . [It is] a politicization of memory that distinguishes nostalgia, that longing for something to be as once it was, a kind of useless act, from that remembering that serves to illuminate and transform the present.
> (hooks)[81]

The New York *casita* is not solely the actual remembered dwelling from the Caribbean but it is also an ideal and imagined site; memory given form to serve future possibilities.[82]

## TRADITION, FOLKLORE, AND A CULTURE OF CONTESTATION

Social historians, folklorists, and other scholars have looked at the specific conditions in capitalist society in which the expressive behaviors of subordinate groups contest dominant class control and power. This approach to history and society 'from the bottom up' relies on the analytical concept of cultural hegemony as articulated originally by Italian Marxist Antonio Gramsci and further developed by British literary critic Raymond Williams. The hegemonic process involves the creation, manipulation, and maintenance of cultural symbols by the dominant class that serves to achieve a consensus among subordinate groups to the legitimization of the existing social order as controlled by the former.[83,84,85] 'Civil society' exerts its hegemony through both formally identifiable institutions such as schools, churches or the media, as well as through artistic, intellectual or scientific trends or 'formations'.[86] It is through institutional and formational socialization that individuals internalize those values and meanings promoted by the dominant culture and come to identify those beliefs, feelings and experiences as their own.[87] It is in moments of crisis when the 'natural' hegemonic order breaks down and everyday consensus is no longer sustainable that the state intervenes to impose its 'legal' rule often through violent means.[88]

Both at the societal and individual levels there exists at any given moment cultural forces in operation that undermine the prevailing hegemony. According to Williams, traditional culture or folklore 'represent[s] areas of human experience, aspiration and achievement which the dominant culture neglects, undervalues, opposes, represses, or even cannot recognize'.[89,90] Folklore's power as a culture of contestation resides in the active process of selection and choice by which individuals call into play a repertoire of past symbolisms and infuse it with new meaning and values. Folklore is not some mental baggage mindlessly perpetuated by 'bearers of tradition' but must be seen instead as 'a process of thought – an ongoing interpretation of the past . . . [that is] symbolically reinvented in an ongoing present'.[91,92] In this way, domestic architecture and landscape once used by Puerto Rico's working and unemployed poor is re-created in New York into community-based mutual-help associations.

One way that individuals and social groups contest the existing hegemony is through alternative forms of cultural expression and ways of being that critique the dominant conception of the world. '[O]pposition to hegemonic domination advances values that are, or become, rooted in the ties people have to one another in daily life and in production'.[93] It is in the use of the *casita* environment that people engage in expressive behavior that reproduces cherished values and ideals concerning sociability. Enclosed by the 20 foot chain-link fence, the *casita* is a haven from the harsh realities of inner city life, an oasis where temporary repose is possible. There, people tend their gardens, men gather to play dominoes, children play within the *batey*, and families simply hang out to enjoy each other's company in the veranda's shade (Figure 3.5). The reclaimed lots are places where one goes for psychological healing, what 'Chema' Soto calls '*Boriqua* therapy' for the mental duress endemic to poor working-class neighborhoods. Olga Padilla, whose mother Nina maintains a garden at East 119th Street, explained:

> I just come here once and awhile. I stay with her. I help out with her garden. And sometimes I just come by myself and just sit and relax. You know, I get away from it all. Like when I have problems, or I feel that I have a lot of tension, you know, that I feel like that, I just come here and just sit and shoot the breeze with myself. And it's nice. It's nice. It's peaceful, it's real peaceful. (17 June 1990)

*Casitas* are that place where one can, in the words of author José Luis González, *volver a ser gente* – become people again.[94]

*(Photograph: Martha Cooper)*

FIGURE 3.5 The game of dominoes is the organizing principle of *El Balcón Boricua* (The Puerto Rican Veranda) in *El Barrio*, 1988.

The built environment is a stage for community celebrations such as rites of passage, religious feasts and ethnic festivities. Various types of Antillean vernacular music provide the aural component to these festivities. In addition these fêtes invariably include the preparation and serving of typical foods; in fact the site itself allows the possibility to prepare certain foods in a traditional manner that would be difficult if not impossible elsewhere. These cultural performances bring together landscape, architecture, music, and foodways in powerful and emotionally charged ways.

Time and time again, frequenters to New York *casitas* maintain that they feel comfortable bringing their families to these transformed environments.[95] The *casita* is a place where children are encouraged to play free from the drugs and violence that plague their communities (Figure 3.6). Members of the *casita Rincón Criollo* train neighborhood children in traditional dance and music in a conscious attempt to provide an antidote to the lure of street life. People attribute the success of these urban sanctuaries to the forces of civility and sociability in operation there. Modesto Coto, president of *El Balcón Boricua*, said, 'We respect each other which is the main thing'. For *puertorriqueños* this key concept of *respeto* 'signifies proper attention to the requisites of the ceremonial order of behavior, and to the moral aspects of human activities'.[96] *Casitas* are strictly policed through an appreciation and adherence to community notions of proper behavior. While the drinking of alcoholic beverages, mostly beer and rum, is an acknowledged part of the *casita* and the festivities held there, men are expected to act courteously both to the women present and to each other in accordance with group standards. Anti-social behavior as it is locally defined, is cause for probation or worst, expulsion.[97]

*Casita* members maintain that their little houses serve the larger community as mutual-aid societies or benevolent associations. Unlike the social clubs founded during the great migration of the 1940s and 1950s, whose memberships were based on hometown affiliations, *casitas* are instead rooted in local, neighborhood concerns. Javier Caraballo and other tenants of 411 East 136th Street in the Bronx, organized a block association and collectively constructed a *casita* in a strategic attempt to rid the lot opposite their multi-unit apartment building from a thriving drug trade. According to its president José Rivera, *Rincón Criollo* is a place where the unemployed can find clothing, help in locating work, and assistance in filling out job applications. This community-based orientation is best exemplified by *Villa Puerto Rico* which offers regular assistance with voter registration, medicare, welfare and housing problems. Social worker Millie Manzanet who stops there once a week after work noted, 'This is my office'. The *casita*'s active role in providing sorely needed social services to neighborhood residents is a poignant commentary on the city's failure to meet the basic needs of poor working-class communities. The *casita* as a base for potential political organization is publicly announced by signs

(*Photograph: Martha Cooper*)

FIGURE 3.6   Building sand castles alongside a *casita* in *El Barrio*, 1988.

posted at two different *casitas*: '*BORICUAS UNIDOS*' (Puerto Ricans United) and 'PUERTO RICAN POWER', emblazoned above crossed machetes and a *jibaro*'s *pava*, or straw hat.

As we have seen, the *casita* is a form of community organization whereby control of one's immediate environment is achieved through the use of traditional expressive culture. Folklore is a guide for transforming order out of chaos that is the postindustrial landscape. Neighborhood residents often construct *casitas* in an attempt to reclaim abandoned city property from persistent dumping, automobile thieves, drug use and sale or prostitution. The accessibility and use of public land is an issue builders and others critically articulate in light of a city government that attempts to maintain control over the ways its potentially profitable but undeveloped property is used by its working-class citizenry. Bronx-resident Carlos Padilla discovered that the simple act of cleaning a refuse-filled lot at private expense, that is burying decomposing animals and hauling 200 bags of garbage plus a refrigerator and sofa, left him vulnerable to city fines and arrest.[98] Municipal attempts to collect back taxes on 'continuous use' of city-owned property as in the case of Felicia Hernandez who was fined $18 796 for her seven-year-old Lower East Side garden is another form of official harassment.[99,100]

In 1978, the Koch administration established the GreenThumb program to regulate the unofficial use of city land by Latinos and African Americans for community gardens. The lease specifies that it will be terminated if there is an 'illegal structure' on the property, an ambiguous term defined as 'any enclosed structure'. Under the former director, many leases were annulled. But since 1984, the program's current director, Jane Weissman, has to a large degree turned a blind eye to gardens with *casitas* and as a result helped to stabilize a number of well-established *casitas* under the protection of the city agency. The director has expressed sympathy with the garden/*casita*'s role in community life and realizes that any attempt to do away with it would drastically reduce Puerto Rican involvement in municipal-sponsored gardening. As a result of increased media attention, city hall pressured GreenThumb to develop an officially-sanctioned, standardized open-air structure in 1991.

A number of *casita* builders see their GreenThumb lease as a step towards legitimization, and, in fact, it has been to a limited degree. People express hope in purchasing the land from the city, ideally at favorable rates. *Casita* builders occasionally attempt to legitimize their presence by requesting services such as electricity from Con Edison (unsuccessful) or mail delivery from the Post Office (successful). But the city's Housing Preservation and Development department regularly demolishes non-GreenThumb *casitas*, especially those erected as housing. For the city government, GreenThumb is an interim program established to deal with the period between 'demolition and development'. The municipality views this innovative use of public land not as long-term improvements of inner city neighborhoods but as a form of temporary custodianship of their neglected property. When the land becomes profitable, the city will simply take it away.[101,102]

The conflict between *casita* members and city officials is evident in the documented case of *Villa Puerto Rico* (Figure 3.7). In 1984, it lost its GreenThumb lease just before the new director's arrival. In 1988, its members responded to a city eviction notice with a petition and a reported 300 letters to former Mayor Koch. *Villa Puerto Rico* president Jarán Manzanet, a community liaison worker employed by Bronx Borough President Fernardo Ferrer, is not only politically astute but well connected. Visitors to the *casita* have included Deputy Fire Commissioner Rafael Esparra, Assemblyman Adam Clayton Powell IV, and Judge Luis Gonzalez of the New York State Supreme Court. In 1989, Manzanet took full advantage of the impending mayoral elections to obtain media coverage of the struggle to save the community center. Two years later, *casita* members fended off a second eviction notice and succeeded in removing the Bronx lot from the auction block.

A number of other factors threaten the existence of *casitas* in New York City. Arson, attributed to vindictive drug dealers or 'envious' neighbors, consume a number of 'little houses'. Fire, an endemic problem for inner-city communities where firefighters are laid off and firehouses closed during an economic crisis, presents a temporary set-back for people willing to rebuild as did the members of *Villa Puerto Rico* in 1990. In addition, *casita* builders are aware of similar structures in the city but they have not organized to collectively fight on behalf of their mutual interest. Finally, middle-class politicians and ethnic leaders for whom the *casita* evokes a nostalgic revelry for a romantic rural past or repulsion of the *casita*'s obvious *arrabal* referent, have failed to champion the *casitas*' cause politically.

## CONCLUSION

In his book *All That Is Solid Melts Into Air*, Marshall Berman notes that capitalism's frenetic drive for profits in the building of the urban environment has perpetually created a category of people 'who are in the way – in the way of history, of progress, of development; people who are classified, and disposed of, as obsolete'.[103] *Casita* builders join a chorus of citizens who demand fair access to use and development of public land. Together with the homeless who erect tents and cardboard lean-tos in Tompkins Square Park and in sprouting 'Dinkinsvilles', the urban home-steaders and squatters battling city police in the Lower East Side and the South Bronx for the right to occupy abandoned apartment buildings, as well as the coalition of churches and grass roots organizations planning and building low-income, owner-occupied 'Nehemiah' houses, *casita* pioneers

85

*(Photograph: Martha Cooper)*

FIGURE 3.7    After the Puerto Rican Day Parade makes its way down Fifth Avenue in Manhattan, marchers who hail originally from the town of Salinas in Puerto Rico travel to the Bronx for the annual celebration at *Villa Puerto Rico*, 1988.

reveal the bankrupt housing policy of a visionless government unable or unwilling to provide decent, affordable housing in a city that has been dubbed 'New Calcutta'. These building strategies point to the inadequacies of an economic system that leaves people unskilled and unemployed in the postindustrial economy. The state's response is demolition and forced removals that ideologically reduce the homeless to so much filth in city 'sweeps' that push people from one makeshift shelter to another.

The vibrant, life-affirming culture of New York *casitas* is a counter voice questioning political negligence and economic tyranny that have left so much destruction in their wake. These creative and courageous alternative behaviors – planting, building, singing, dancing, eating and laughing on embers and ruins – with their potential for becoming stable features on New York's scarred landscape, pose a threat to city officials.

## NOTES

Fieldwork for this paper was conducted in 1988–90 as part of research for two exhibitions: City Lore's 'Welcome to Your Second Home: New York's Ethnic Social Clubs', Museum of the City of New York, 1993; and the Bronx Council on the Arts', 'Las Casitas: An Urban Cultural Alternative', Experimental Gallery at the Smithsonian Institution and the Bronx Museum of Art, 1990–92. I benefitted greatly from discussions with co-members of the research team that documented *casitas* as part of the latter project; architect Luis Aponte-Pares, photographer Martha Cooper, sociologist Juan Flores, visual artist and project director Betti-Sue Hertz, and folklorist Susan Sylmovics. Versions of this paper were read at three conferences: Vernacular Architecture Forum (1991), the Middle Atlantic Folklife Association (1990), and American Folklore Society (1989), where participants contributed useful comments and suggestions. Panel moderators Simon J. Bronner, Barbara Kirshenblatt-Gimblett, Jack Kugglemass, and Mario Montaño offered important insights that were incorporated into this final version. Oscar Vázquez's comments on my presentation at the Binghamton symposium greatly helped me flesh out the section on memory and nostalgia. I would like to especially thank Pedro Angel Rivera for his thoughtful critique of this paper. My thanks to Betti-Sue Hertz and Rebecca Miller for use of supplementary interview material. I am indebted to my wife Zulma Ortiz Fuentes who not only assisted with transcriptions and translations but who has lent her support to my research. Special thanks go to the members of the various *casitas* who welcomed me to their urban oases. *Un abrazo a todos.*

1.    Peter Stallybrass and Allon White, *The Politics and Poetics of Transgression* (Cornell University Press, Ithaca, 1986), pp. 5–6.
2.    For a discussion of negative representations of Puerto Ricans in North American literature and film, see Lewis (note 117) and Pérez (note 120).
3.    bell hooks, *Yearning: Race, Gender, and Cultural Politics* (South End Press, Boston, 1990), pp. 145–53.
4.    Anthony D. King, *Urbanism, Colonialism, and the World-Economy: Cultural and Spatial Foundation of the World Urban System* (Routledge, New York, 1991), p. 99.

5.  José Luis González, *Puerto Rico: The Four Storeyed Country*, trans. Gerald Guinness (Waterfront Press, Maplewood, New Jersey, 1990).

6.  James L. Dietz, *Economic History of Puerto Rico: Institutional Change and Capitalist Development* (Princeton History Press, 1986), p. 259.

7.  J. L. González, pp. 15, 27 (see note 5).

8.  Ibid., p. 18.

9.  J. L. Dietz, pp. 94–6 (see note 6).

10. Critical readings in English of González's essay (see note 5) can be found in Flores (note 110) and Ríos (note 121).

11. Mikhail Bakhtin, *Rabelais and His World* (Indiana University Press, Bloomington, 1984), p. 472.

12. V. N. Volosnov, *Marxism and the Philosophy of Language* (Seminar Press, New York, 1973), pp. 59–63.

13. Ibid, pp. 65–8.

14. M. Bakhtin, p. 16 (see note 11).

15. Mikhail Bakhtin, *The Dialogic Imagination* (University of Texas Press, Austin, 1988), pp. 291–2.

16. M. Bakhtin, pp. 293–4 (see note 15).

17. James Clifford, *The Predicament of Culture: Twentieth-Century Ethnography, Literature, and Art* (Harvard University Press, Cambridge, Mass., 1988), p. 23.

18. Susan Steward, 'Shouts on the Street: Bakhtin's Anti-Linguistics', in *Bakhtin: Essays and Dialogues on His Work*, (ed.) Gary Saul Morson (University of Chicago Press, 1986), pp. 41–57.

19. In this respect, my essay takes the lead from Robert St. George's article (see note 122) on architecture in seventeenth century New England. For an overview of the linguistic paradigm in the study of vernacular architecture, see Williams and Young (note 128).

20. George E. Marcus and Michael M. J. Fischer, *Anthropology as Cultural Critique: An Experimental Moment in the Human Sciences* (University of Chicago Press, 1986), pp. 77–9.

21. Ulf Hannerz, 'Culture Between Center and Periphery: Toward a Macroanthropology', *Ethnos*, 54, 3–4 (1989) pp. 212–14.

22. Dell Hymes, (ed.) *Pidginization and Creolization of Languages* (Cambridge University Press, 1971), p. 76.

23. Gordon K. Lewis, *Puerto Rico: Freedom and Power in the Caribbean* (Monthly Review Press, New York, 1963), p. 43.

24. J. L. González, pp. 18–23 (see note 5).

25. Juan Flores, 'Bambun and the Beginnings of la Plena', *Cantro: Centro de Estudios Puertorriqueños Bulletin*, 2.3 (1988), pp. 16–25.

26. Felix Cortes, Angel Falcón and Juan Flores, 'The Cultural Expression of Puerto Ricans in New York, A Theoretical Perspective and Critical Review', *Latin American Perspectives*, 3.3 (1976), pp. 117–52.

27. Juan Flores, 'Rappin', Writin', and Breakin': Black and Puerto Rican Street Culture in New York', *Dissent*, 34.4 (1987), pp. 580–4.

28. Juan Flores, John Attinasi and Pedro Pedraza Jr., 'La Carreta Made a U-Turn: Puerto Rican Language and Culture in the United States', *Daedalus*, 110.2 (1981), pp. 193–217.

29. Carol F. Jopling, *Puerto Rican Houses in Sociohistorical Perspective* (University of Tennessee Press, Knoxville, 1988), p. 65.

30. Ibid., pp. 7–8.

31. Sven Loven, *Origins of the Tainan Culture, West Indies* (Elander Bokfrycheri Akfiebolog, Göteborg, Sweden, 1935), pp. 339–48.

32.  Moscoso, Francisco, 'Chiefdom and Encomienda in Puerto Rico: The Development of a Tribal Society and the Spanish Colonization to 1530', in *The Puerto Ricans*, (ed.) Adalberto López (Schenkman, Cambridge, Mass., 1980), pp. 3–24. Moscoso maintains that the rectangular *bohío* was a pre-Columbian structure used by *naborías* (Moscoso 1980, 15).

33.  C. F. Jopling, pp. 9, 16–23 (see note 29).

34.  John Michael Vlach, 'The Shotgun House: An African Architectural Legacy', in *Common Places: Readings in American Vernacular Architecture*, (ed.) Dell Upton and John Michael Vlach (University of Georgia Press, Athens, 1986), pp. 58–78.

35.  J. L. González, pp. 9–11 (see note 5).

36.  Sidney W. Mintz, *Caribbean Transformations* (Johns Hopkins University Press, Baltimore, 1984), pp. 86–91.

37.  Angel Q. Quintero Rivera, 'The Rural-Urban Dichotomy in the Formation of Puerto Rico's Cultural Identity', *New West Indian Guide*, 61.3–4 (1987) pp. 127–44.

38.  C. F. Jopling, p. 66 (see note 29).

39.  Virginia E. Sánchez Korrol, *From Colonia to Community: The History of Puerto Ricans in New York City, 1917–1948* (Greenwood Press, Westport, Conn., 1983), pp. 17–28.

40.  J. L. Dietz, pp. 98–113 (see note 6).

41.  Ibid., pp. 111–12, 273–81.

42.  Jesse Walter Fewkes, *The Aborigines of Porto Rico and Neighboring Islands* (Government Printing Office, Washington, D.C., 1907), p. 45.

43.  C. F. Jopling, pp. 56–9, 204–5 (see note 29).

44.  J. Clifford, p. 15 (see note 17).

45.  V. E. Sánchez Korrol (see note 39).

46.  Clara E. Rodríguez, *Puerto Ricans Born in the USA* (Unwin Hyman, Boston, 1989), pp. 3–4.

47.  Constance R. Sutton, 'The Caribbeanization of New York City and the Emergence of a Transnational Socio-Cultural System', in *Caribbean Life in New York City: Sociocultural Dimensions*, (ed.) Constance R. Sutton and Elsa M. Chaney (Center for Migration Studies of New York, Staten Island, 1987), pp. 15–30.

48.  J. Flores et al., p. 200 (see note 28).

49.  Luis Rafael Sánchez, 'The Flying Bus', in *Images and Identities: The Puerto Rican in Two World Contexts* (ed.) Asela Rodríguez de Laguna (Transaction Books, New Brunswick, N.J., 1987), pp. 17–25.

50.  Harvey (note 112) notes:

     'Capital represents itself in the form of a physical landscape created in its own image, created as use value to enhance the progressive accumulation of capital. The geographical landscape that results is the crowning glory of past capitalist development. But at the same time it expresses the power of dead labor over living labor, and as such it imprisons and inhibits the accumulation process within a set of specific physical constraints. And these can be removed only slowly unless there is a substantial devaluation of the exchange value locked up in the creation of these physical assets.

51.  Jim Sleeper, 'Days of the Developers: Boom and Bust with Ed Koch', *Dissent* (Fall 1987), pp. 437–52.

52.  Donald G. Sullivan, '1940–1965: Population Mobility in the South Bronx', in *Devastation/Resurrection: The South Bronx*, exhibition catalogue (Bronx Museum of the Arts, 1979), pp. 37–44.

53. Marshall Berman, *All That Is Solid Melts Into Air* (Penguin Books, New York, 1988), pp. 292–393.

54. Donald G. Sullivan, 'The Process of Abandonment', in *Devastation/ Resurrection: The South Bronx*, exhibition catalogue (Bronx Museum of the Arts, 1979), pp. 69–71.

55. In addition to the *casita*, New York Puerto Rican vernacular architecture consists of three other major types. The enclosed *kiosko*, constructed with its flat roof and window that swings out and upwards, is based on the rural roadside stand. In some cases, the structure may maintain its original function as a place to sell refreshments, such as peeled oranges, cold coconuts, and alcoholic beverages, while doubling as a social club. The open-aired rectangular gazebo, or *templete*, usually accessible from only one side, provides shade for those who use the lot on weekends for cook-outs, music making, and general entertainment. *Friquitins* are food stands that range from simple booths with a counter to structures that house tables, chairs, and even full-length bars. A constellation of some 30-odd *friquitins* known collectively as *Villa Hermosa* or *Villa Allegre* are rebuilt each summer in a South Bronx lot. There, stand owners hire musical groups to compete for the attention of hundreds of potential customers who stroll through the central plaza on summer evenings to play games of chance, or buy fritters and cold beer. See Figueroa (see note 109) for a discussion of the 'survival economy' as practiced in social clubs, car repair shops, and by ambulatory women food vendors in Williamsburg, Brooklyn.

56. Kevin Lynch, *What Time is This Place?* (The MIT Press, Cambridge, Mass., 1990), pp. 190–9.

57. Barbara Kirshenblatt-Gimblett, 'The Future of Folklore Studies in America: The Urban Frontier', *Folklore Forum* 16.2 (1983), pp. 214–20.

58. M. Bakhtin, p. 411 (see note 11).

59. José E. Limón, 'Western Marxism and Folklore: A Critical Introduction', *Journal of American Folklore*, 96.379 (1983), pp. 34–52.

60. C. F. Jopling, p. 59 (see note 29).

61. M. Bakhtin, p. 392 (see note 15).

62. Verni Greenfield, *Making Do and Making Art: A Study of American Recycling* (UMI Research Press, Ann Arbor, Michigan, 1986), p. 2.

63. B. Kirshenblatt-Gimblett, p. 183 (see note 57).

64. Catholic religious imagery appears in the forms of *nichos*, or yard shrines, in the area in front of the *casita* or in the visual pun of a posted lifesaver that reads, '*JESU CRISTO SALVA DE LOS PECADOS/CLAMA A JESUS AHORA*' (JESUS CHRIST SAVES SINNERS/CLAIM JESUS TODAY). An exploration of African aesthetics and religious principles in *casita* yard decoration is sorely needed. African ancestor figures and statuary of North American Indians in keeping with Santería iconography are tacked on to exterior gable walls or placed in the yard. The stuffed dolls perched on window sills and hanging from trees may seem at first innocuous until one notices that they are also used in abandoned buildings in Manhattan to attract media attention and thus make the site undesirable for drug use or sales. The protective powers of the little black dolls sewn by women in Puerto Rico and New York is evoked through these Coney Island talismans in strategic attempts to safeguard neighborhoods. For discussion of African aesthetics in American yard displays, see Thompson (note 125) and the catalogue for the exhibition 'The Migrations of Meaning' (note 119).

65. Clarissa T. Kimber, 'Spatial Patterning in the Dooryard Gardens in Puerto Rico', *Geographical Review*, 63.1 (1973), pp. 6–26.

66. S. W. Mintz, pp. 186–7, 236–38 (see note 36).
67. Ibid., p. 232.
68. For a discussion of the urban *solar*, or patio, see Benítez-Rojo (note 105). Richard Westmacott also explores African-American swept yards in the American South, tracing the practice back to West Africa (see note 127).
69. M. Bakhtin, p. 84 (see note 15).
70. K. Lynch, p. 192 (see note 56).
71. Excellent work has been done recently on the creative role that reflection and remembrance play in the life review process of seniors. See Hufford et al (note 114) and Kirshenblatt-Gimblett (notes 115, 116).
72. Helen Icken Safa, *The Urban Poor of Puerto Rico: A Study in Development and Inequality* (Holt, Rinehart and Winston, Inc., New York, 1974), p. 78.
73. G. K. Lewis, p. 307 (see note 23).
74. Sherry B. Ortner, 'On Key Symbols', *American Anthropologist* 75.5 (1973) pp. 1338–46.
75. M. Bakhtin, p. 276 (see note 15).
76. For further discussion of the use of folklore in romantic nationalist ideologies, see Abrahams (note 104); Fernandez (note 108); Handler (note 91); Herzfeld (note 113); and Wilson (note 129).
77. Oscar E. Vázquez, 'The Birth of an Axiomatic Cultural Symbol: Images of the Puerto Rican "Jibaro" and the 1934 Sugar Workers' Strikes', unpublished paper delivered at the Department of Romance Languages Conference, 'New World Regionalism Versus Old World Domination' (SUNY Binghamton, 1992).
78. J. L. González, p. 26 (see note 5).
79. Marimar Benítez, 'The Special Case of Puerto Rico', in *Latin American Spirit: Art and Artists in the United States, 1920–1970*, exhibition catalogue (The Bronx Museum of the Arts in association with Harry N. Abrams, Inc., New York, 1988), pp. 80–90.
80. Mari Carmen Ramírez, 'Puerto Rican Painting: Between Past and Present', in *Puerto Rican Painting: Between Past and Present* (exhibition catalogue) (The Squibb Gallery, Princeton, N.J., 1987), pp. 21–6.
81. bell hooks, p. 147 (see note 3).
82. Antonio Benítez-Rojo observes:

    Generally, every Caribbean person's present is a pendular present, a present that implies a desire to have the future and the present at once. In the Caribbean one either oscillates toward a utopia or toward a lost paradise, and this not only in the politico-ideological sense, but, above all, in the sociocultural sense. . . (1992, p. 251, note 105).

83. Antonio Gramsci, *Selections from the Prison Notebooks* (Lawrence and Wishart, London, 1976), pp. 12–13.
84. T. J. Jackson Lears, 'The Concept of Cultural Hegemony: Problems and Possibilities', *American Historical Review*, 90 (1985), pp. 567–93.
85. Raymond Williams, *Marxism and Literature* (Oxford University Press, New York, 1988), pp. 108–14.
86. Ibid., pp. 117–20.
87. Ibid., pp. 110, 128–35.
88. A. Gramsci, p. 12 (see note 83).
89. R. Williams, pp. 123–4 (see note 85).
90. Much has been written on folklore's place within a culture of contestation. Byrne (note 106) and Cirese (note 107) elaborate on Gramsci's views on the subject, while Limón (see note 59), Lombardi-Satriani (note 118), and

Thompson (notes 124, 126) have applied this critical approach to contemporary folkloristics.

91.     Richard Handler and Jocelyn Linnekin, 'Tradition, Genuine or Spurious', *Journal of American Folklore*, 97.385 (1984) pp. 273–90.

92.     Dell Hymes, 'Folklore's Nature and the Sun's Myth', *Journal of American Folklore*, 88 (1975), pp. 345–69.

93.     Gerald M. Sider, *Culture and Class in Anthropology and History* (Cambridge University Press, New York, 1989), p. 122.

94.     José Luis González, *Mambrú se fue a la guerra (y otros relatos)* (Editorial Joaquín Mortiz, Mexico City, 1972).

95.     Space limitations prevent a discussion of gender as it pertains to New York City *casitas*. The issue is addressed in an examination of one Bronx *casita* in my unpublished essay, " 'We're not here just to plant. We have culture': An Ethnography of the South Bronx *Casita Rincón Criollo*."

96.     Anthony Lauria, Jr., '"Respeto", "Relajo" and Inter-Personal Relations in Puerto Rico', *Anthropological Quarterly*, 37.1 (1964), pp. 53–67.

97.     *At Rincón Criollo*, core *casita* members who engage in improper behavior are ostracized for a specific period of time; one man who got drunk and urinated in the kitchen was banished from the *casita* for three months, while another was expelled for a year after getting into a fistfight at the site in an attempt to break up an argument between an inebriated guest and a female member. My thanks to Betti-Sue Hertz for sharing this information with me.

98.     Sarah Bartlett, '2 Bronx Messes: One Trash, One Bureaucracy', *New York Times* (29 Nov. 1991) A1, B4.

99.     Curtis Rist, 'City Sues Lady of the Lot', *New York Newsday* (6 June 1991): 4.

100.    Lisa Cashdan, Peter R. Stein and David Wright, 'Roses From Rubble: New Uses for Vacant Urban Land', *New York Affairs*, 7.2 (1982), pp. 89–96.

101.    Ibid.

102.    Alisa Solomon, 'A Fecund Refuge: Gardening on the Lower East Side', *Village Voice* (13 Sept, 1988): 13, 16.

103.    M. Berman, p. 69 (see note 53).

104.    Roger D. Abrahams, 'Phantoms of Romantic Nationalism in Folkloristics', *Journal of American Folklore*, 106.419 (1993), pp. 3–37.

105.    Antonio Benítez-Rojo, *The Repeating Island: The Caribbean and the Postmodern Perspective*. trans. James E. Maraniss (Duke University Press, Durham, N. Carolina, 1992).

106.    Moyra Byrne, 'Antonio Gramsci's Contribution to Italian Folklore Studies', *International Folklore Review*, 2 (1982) pp. 70–5.

107.    Alberto Maria Cirese, 'Gramsci's Observations on Folklore', in *Approaches to Gramsci*, (ed.) Anne Showstack Sasson (Writers and Readers Publishing Cooperative Society, Ltd., London, 1982), pp. 212–47.

108.    James W. Fernandez, 'Folklorists as Agents of Nationalism', *New York Folklore*, 11.1–4 (1985), pp. 135–47.

109.    José E. Figueroa, *Survival on the Margin: A Documentary Study of the Underground Economy in a Puerto Rican Ghetto* (Vantage Press, New York, 1989).

110     Juan Flores, 'The Puerto Rico that José Luis González Built: Comments on Cultural History', *Latin American Perspectives*, 11.3 (1984), pp. 173–84.

111.    Richard Handler, *Nationalism and the Politics of Culture in Quebec* (University of Wisconsin Press, Madison, Wisconsin, 1988).

112.    David Harvey, *The Urbanization of Capital: Studies in the History and Theory of Capitalist Urbanization* (Johns Hopkins University Press, Baltimore: 1985).

113.   Michael Herzfeld, *Ours Once More: Folklore, Ideology, and the Making of Modern Greece* (University of Texas Press, Austin, 1982).

114.   Mary Hufford, Marjorie Hunt and Steven Zeitlin, *The Grand Generation: Memory, Mastery, Legacy*, exhibition catalogue (Smithsonian Institution, Washington, DC., 1987).

115.   Barbara Kirshenblatt-Gimblett, 'Authoring Lives', *Journal of Folklore Research*, 26.2 (1989) pp. 125–49

116.   Barbara Kirshenblatt-Gimblett, 'Objects of Memory: Material Culture as Life Review' In *Folk Groups and Folklore Genres: A Reader*, (ed.) Elliot Oring (Utah State University Press, Logan, Utah, 1989), pp. 329–38.

117.   Marvin A. Lewis, 'The Puerto Rican in Popular US Literature: A Culturalist Perspective', in *Images and Identities: The Puerto Rican in Two World Contexts*, (ed.) Asela Rodríguez de Laguna (Transaction Books, New Brunswick, NJ., 1987), pp. 65–75.

118.   Luigi Lombardi-Satriani, 'Folklore as Culture of Contestation', *Journal of the Folklore Institute*, 11 (1975) pp. 99–121.

119.   *The Migration of Meaning*, exhibition catalogue (INTAR Gallery, New York, 1992).

120.   Richie Pérez, 'From Assimilation to Annihilation: Puerto Rican Images in US Films', *Centro: Centro de Estudios Puertorriqueños Bulletin*, 2.8 (1990) pp. 8–27.

121.   Palmira N. Ríos, Review of José Luis González's 'El país de cuatro pisos y otros ensayos', *Cimarrón*, 1.2 (1986) pp. 97–101.

122.   Robert Blair St. George, 'Bawns and Beliefs: Architecture, Commerce, and Conversion in Early New England', *Winterthur Portfolio*, 25.4 (1990) pp. 241–87.

123.   Joseph Sciorra, ' "We're not here just to plant. We have culture": An Ethnography of the South Bronx Casita Rincón Criollo' (unpublished manuscript).

124.   E. P. Thompson, 'Folklore, Anthropology, and Social History', *Indian Historical Review*, 3.2 (1977), pp. 247–66.

125.   Robert Farris Thompson, *Flash of the Spirit: African and Afro-American Art and Philosophy* (Vintage Books, New York, 1984), pp. 146–58.

126.   E. P. Thompson, *Customs in Common: Studies in Traditional Popular Culture* (The New Press, New York, 1991).

127.   Richard Westmacott, *African-American Gardens and Yards in the Rural South* (University of Tennessee, Knoxville, 1992).

128.   Michael Ann Williams and M. Jane Young, 'Grammar, Codes, and Performance: Linguistic and Sociolinguistic Models in the Study of Vernacular Architecture' (unpublished paper delivered at the Vernacular Architecture Forum 1991 conference in Santa Fe).

129.   William A. Wilson, *Folklore and Nationalism* (Indiana University Press, Bloomington, 1976).

# 4

# After Tompkins Square Park: Degentrification and the Revanchist City

Neil Smith

## THE REVANCHIST CITY

After the stretch-limo optimism of the 1980s was rear-ended in the financial crash of 1987, then totalled by the onset of economic depression two years later, real estate agents and urban commentators quickly began deploying the language of 'de-gentrification' to represent the apparent reversal of urban change in the 1990s. 'With the realty boom gone bust in once gentrifying neighborhoods', writes one newspaper reporter, 'co-op converters and speculators who worked the streets and avenues . . . have fallen on hard times. That, in turn, has left some residents complaining of poor security and shoddy maintenance, while others are unable to sell their once-pricey apartments in buildings where a bank foreclosed on a converter'. 'Degentrification', explains one New York realtor, 'is a reversal of the gentrification process': in the 1990s, unlike the 1980s, 'there is no demand for pioneering, transitional, recently discovered locations'. Those few real estate deals that are transacted, he suggests, have retrenched to 'prime areas'.[1] 'In the 1970s, the theory was that a few gentrified areas would have a contagious effect and pull up neighboring districts' but 'that didn't happen', says another commentator. Most bluntly, in the words of census bureau demograper Larry Long, 'gentrification has come and gone'.[2]

Such media proclamations of the end of gentrification have begun to find broader support in the academic literature, where commentators were in any case usually more bromidic in their rhetoric about gentrification. In a clearly argued essay drawing on a Canadian case study, Larry Bourne anticipates 'the demise of gentrification' in those few cities where, he suggests, it had

93

even a minor significance in the 1980s. Gentrification 'will be of less importance as a spatial expression of social change during the 1990s than it has been in the recent past'.[3] The last decade and a half, he suggests, were:

> a unique period in post-war urban development in North America – a period that combined the baby boom, rising educational levels, a rapid growth in service employment and real income, high rates of household formation, housing stock appreciation, public sector largesse, widespread (and speculative) private investment in the built environment, and high levels of foreign immigration. This set of circumstances, except for the latter, no longer prevails.[4]

The 'post-gentrification era' will experience a much reduced 'rate and impact of gentrification' in favor of a more unevenly developed, polarized and segregated city.

The coining of 'degentrification' and the prediction of gentrification's demise are part of a wider 'discourse of urban decline'[5] that has repossessed the public representation of urbanism in the 1990s, especially in the US. Historically, according to Beauregard, this discourse of decline has been 'more than the objective reporting of an uncontestable reality'; rather the discourse 'functions ideologically to shape our attention, provide reasons for how we should react in response, and convey a comprehensible, compelling, and reassuring story of the fate of the twentieth-century city in the United States'.[6] The recrudescence of this discourse in the 1990s has been dramatic. Gone is the white, upper-middle-class optimism of gentrification which was supposed to reclaim the 'new urban frontier' in the name of largely white 'pioneers';[7,8,9] an optimism that significantly modulated the discourse of decline during the 1980s. In its place, an unabated litany of crime and violence, drugs and unemployment, immigration and depravity – all laced through with terror – now script an unabashed recidivism of the city. The revanchism of contemporary urban management is a visceral component of the new anti-urbanism, a reaction against the 'theft' of the city by variously defined 'others', and in large part a defence of a traditionally white, middle-class world view. This revanchist anti-urbanism of the 1990s portends an occasionally vicious reaction against minorities, the working class, homeless people, the unemployed, women, gays and lesbians, immigrants.

The 'revanchist city' is becoming a powerful reality. More than anything it expresses a race/class/gender terror felt by middle and ruling-class whites who are suddenly stuck in place by a ravaged property market, the threat and reality of unemployment, the decimation of even minimal social services, and the emergence of minority and immigrant groups as well as women as powerful urban actors. The revanchist city is justified by the recidivism of prime time – the local news, 'Cops', 'Hard Copy', 'NYPD

Blue'; it represents a reaction to an urbanism defined by recurrent waves of unremitting danger and brutality fuelled by venal and uncontrolled passion. It is a place, in fact, where the reproduction of social relations has gone stupifyingly wrong,[10] but where the response is a virulent reassertion of many of the same oppressions and prescriptions that created the problem in the first place. 'In the US', says Ruth Gilmore, quoting Amiri Baraka, 'where real and imagined social relations are expressed most rigidly in race/gender hierarchies, the "reproduction" is really a *production* and its by-products, fear and fury, are in service of a "changing same": the apartheid local of American nationalism'.[11]

Two separate events on different coasts, equally coded by race and nationalism entwined with class and gender, have crystallized the revanchism of the so-called post-gentrification city. In Los Angeles, widely heralded in the 1980s as the new, raw, Pacific urbanism for a new century, the 1992 uprising following the acquittal of four police officers in the vicious beating of Rodney King, defied habitual media efforts to explain the 'riot' as a simple black assault on whites. The flood of racial stereotypes as a means to explain the uprising was deafening and in the end unsuccessful, for it was, as Mike Davis put it, 'an extremely hybrid uprising, possibly the first multi-ethnic rioting in modern American uprising'.[12,13] Likewise, the bombing less than a year later of New York City's World Trade Center – simultaneously a symbol of 1970s downtown renewal (and the massive displacement this involved) and the 1980s global urbanism – evoked vivid images of a real life *Towering Inferno*, and unleashed a xenophobic media hunt for 'foreign Arab terrorists'.[14] While the complete failure of the building's security systems led to its depiction as a 'sick building' in a 'sick city', the Trade Center bombing cemented the connection between American urban life and apparently arbitrary but brutal violence (terror) on the international scene. The xenophobic hysteria that followed enlisted even the *New York Times* whose language of blithe exaggeration passed for uncontested fact as they documented the search for foreign conspirators – 'a ring accused of plotting to blow up New York City'.[15] No mere Manhattan Project that.

These are not new themes, of course. Anti-urbanism runs deep in US public culture,[16] and the postwar portrayal of the city as jungle and wilderness was never entirely absent through the 1980s, accompanying as much as contradicting the redemptive gentrification narrative. What *is* new is the extent to which this panoply of 'fear and fury'[17] has again come to monopolize public media visions of urban life, and the extent to which the revanchist American city is now recognized as an inherently international artefact. The safety of US borders, real and imagined, has dissolved. Not since the villainization of the city in the teens and early twenties of this century, when European immigrant socialists were identified as attacking the fabric of urban democracy, has US anti-urbanism involved such an explicitly international recognition. Neither the seeming *deus ex machina* of nuclear attack nor the McCarthyism of the cold war produced comparable visions of a US urbanism vulnerable to foreign attack from within; and for their part, the civil rights uprisings of the 1960s which had a sufficient effect on urban structure to provoke the racist term, 'white flight', was represented as a largely domestic question, connections to the anti-Vietnam War movement notwithstanding.

What *is* surprising, perhaps, is not so much that a new anti-urbanism incorporates a reluctant acknowledgement of the internationalization of local social economies in the last two decades. Rather what is surprising is that media self-representations of US cities – ostensibly among the most cosmopolitan of cities, at least in terms of the flow of capital and culture, commodities and information – were so systematically able to insulate and indeed isolate the triumphs and crises of American urban life from international events in general, but especially from the results of US military, political and economic policy abroad. It is hardly an exaggeration to say that the internationalism of the US city was largely restricted on the one hand to recognizing the connections of capital and the market and on the other to the recognition of nostalgic if palpably real Little Italies, Little Taiwans, Little Jamaicas, Little San Juans that dotted the urban landscape, as if to allow a tokenist internationalism at the neighborhood (working-class) scale while insisting on the Americanism of the city as a whole. The scripting of the revanchist city, however, is viscerally local *and* global, no longer so isolated or insulated, if indeed it ever was.

## TOMPKINS SQUARE PARK AND BEYOND

Shortly after 5.00 a.m. on 3 June 1991, 350 police officers dressed in full riot gear moved into Tompkins Square Park in New York City's Lower East Side, woke more than 200 sleeping residents, and evicted them. Remaining clothes, tents, shanties, other structures and private belongings were bulldozed into several waiting sanitation trucks, and seven protestors were arrested. The 10.5 acre park was then cordoned off with an eight-foot high chain link fence, and most of the 350 officers were left to patrol its perimeter. Access was allowed to only two parts of the park: to the playgrounds, children and their guardians were allowed to pass the police guard; and to the dog run, dogs and their owners were permitted to pass.

Tompkins Square Park became a national symbol[18] of the struggle against gentrification and homelessness on 6 August 1988 when a force of 400 police, ostensibly attempting to re-enforce a nineteenth century curfew in the park, initiated a police riot against homeless residents, protestors, punks and other park users. As a result of that riot, 121 complaints against the police were filed with the Civilian Review Board, but none resulted in a civil conviction. For the next three years, until the final eviction in June 1991, the park became a focal point of resistance in the city, drawing in homeless people and squatters, some housing and anti-gentrification activists, as well as local anarchists. As many as 100 structures were erected in the park at any one time, and nearly 300 people slept there on its busiest nights; squatters took over as many as 50 buildings in the neighborhood, housing as many as a thousand people. Meanwhile the city's homeless population swelled to between 70 000 and 100 000.

Only gingerly at first did the police return to the 'liberated zone' of the park, then more brazenly with three attempted 'sweeps' of Tompkins Square and a series of pitched battles between December 1989 and May 1991. Many of these battles occurred around May Day or Memorial Day celebrations, organized around such demands as 'Housing is a Human Right' and slogans like 'Gentrification is Genocide' and 'Eat the Elite', as well as the original 1988 slogan: 'Whose park is it, it's our fucking park'.

'This park *is* a park. . . It is *not* a place to live', explained Mayor David Dinkins, heralding the park's final closure in June 1991.[19] Dinkins, a Liberal Democrat and sometime member of Democratic Socialists of America, was elected with strong support from New York City's housing and anti-homelessness movement, but quickly sanctioned the first evictions of homeless people from the park in December 1989 only weeks after his election, initiating a four-year corrosion of Dinkins' connections with the mass support that had elected him. As the *Village Voice* noted of the evictions, for 'the homeless residents, many of them now scattered in abandoned lots around the park, the closing of the park was just one more betrayal for an administration they thought would stand up for the rights of the poor'.[20] In finally closing the park, Dinkins borrowed a script not from housing or homeless advocates but from the editorial pages of the *New York Times*, which quoted the Webster's dictionary definition of 'park' then judged that Tompkins Square was no park at all: 'A park is not a shantytown. It is not a campground, a homeless shelter, a shooting gallery for drug addicts or a political problem. Unless it is Tompkins Square Park in Manhattan's East Village'. Homeless residents of the park, according to the *Times*, had 'stolen it from the public' and the park would have to be 'reclaimed'. Just three days before the closure, the newspaper inveighed against further partial solutions, preferring instead a 'clean sweep' as 'the wiser course though riskier politically'. There were, it seems, 'some legitimately homeless people' who 'live in the park', and therefore 'misplaced sympathy abounds'.[21] In an interview for National Public Radio, Parks Commissioner Betsy Gotbaum borrowed from the same script, adding her own racial coding of the urban frontier: 'It was filled with tents, even a teepee at one point . . . It was really disgusting'.

Following the police offensive to close the park in 1991, the historic bandshell – symbolic not just as a cultural icon from the 1960s music scene but as the park's only shelter for homeless residents against the rain – was bulldozed, and a hasty, comprehensive, if unpublicized and probably therefore illegal 'park reconstruction plan' was enacted by the City. Meanwhile the locus of political action spread out from the park as the entire neighborhood became the contested zone and the neighboring streets became a shifting DMZ. In the immediate surrounds of the park, a nightly ritual of 'walk the pig' ensued. It is worth quoting at length from an eyewitness report by Sarah Ferguson of just one incident, which offers a visceral portrait of the agency behind the revanchist city:

Since the police takeover 3 June, there have been nightly gatherings on the steps of St. Brigid's Church on Avenue B [on the southeast side of the park], a focal point of community resistance. On Friday, a dozen parents with their children gathered among the punks and anarchists and tried to march against the line of riot police blocking their way, chanting 'Open the park!' When they were forced back onto the sidewalks, some 800 residents took to the streets, banging on drums and garbage can lids, and leading the police cordon [protecting the park] that dutifully followed them from Loisaida through the West Village and back through the projects off Avenue D – what locals call the nightly 'walk the pig' routine.

They were confronted on the steps of St. Brigid's by at least 100 cops, who beamed blinding high-intensity lights into the crowd. The protesters remained peaceful until two undercover cops shoved their way into the church entrance on Avenue B, claiming they wanted to inspect the roof for bottle throwers. One parishioner, Maria Tornin, was struck in the face and knocked against the stairs by one of the cops, and Father Pat Maloney of Lazaru Community was shoved against the wall. Backed by his parishioners, St. Brigid's Father Kuhn pushed the undercover cops out the door.

'When the law ends, tyranny begins, and these guys are tyrants', shouted Father Maloney, leading an angry mob to the paddy wagon where the undercovers had fled. . .

Last Saturday, as bulldozers rumbled past the ripped-up benches and shattered chess tables [in the cordoned-off park], a second demonstration of over 1000 Lower East Side residents linked arms around the park. As the church bells of St. Brigid's rang out, dreadlocked anarchists in combat boots and nose rings held hands with Jewish grandmothers in print dresses and plastic pearls in a peaceful show of unity not seen since the 1988 police riot.[22]

The closure of Tompkins Square Park marked the onset of a stern anti-homeless and anti-squatter policy throughout the city that betokened the coming of the revanchist city. Spearheaded by 'Operation Restore' in the Lower East Side, this new policy for the 1990s was intended to 'take back' the parks, streets and neighborhoods from those who had supposedly 'stolen' them from 'the public'. With 500 to 700 squatters still in nearly 40 buildings in the Lower East Side at the beginning of 1992, the attack on squatters actually proved too difficult for the City although several buildings in the neighborhood as well as in the Bronx were cleared. The major effort came with what the *New York Times* called a 'crackdown on homeless'.[23] Homeless people had responded to the park closure by immediately establishing shanties and tent-cities on several empty lots in the neighborhood, generally in the poorer, still largely Puerto Rican neighborhood to the east of the park. Several sites, mostly between Avenues B and D, were colonized and were quickly dubbed 'Dinkinsville',[24] adapting the mayor's name to the Hoovervilles of the Depression. Not so much a discrete place, Dinkinsville comprised as many as ten separate encampments and shanty settlements linked by the political history of repeated eviction, the determination to colonize the interstices of private and public space, and resistance to enforced homelessness.

As Dinkinsville grew, the new sites were also subjected to surveillance and eventually bulldozing, beginning in October 1991 with a sweep of three vacant lots and the re-eviction of 200 people.[25] These sites too were fenced in to prevent public squatting by homeless people on empty space. Once again the evictees were moved further east, setting up or joining encampments under the Brooklyn, Manhattan and Williamsburg Bridges, under the FDR Drive, or in any available space defensible from public view, police attack, and bad weather. Fire destroyed the Williamsburg Bridge encampment, killing one resident, and a year later in August 1993, the City bulldozed 'the Hill' beneath the Manhattan Bridge, a well-established shantytown of 50 to 70 residents described as 'one of the most visible symbols of homelessness in Manhattan'.[26] Squeezed further east again, many evictees scattered up and down the waterfront of the East River, into Sara Delano Roosevelt Park, and to sites throughout Manhattan.

Elsewhere in the city, shantytowns under the West Side Highway, at Columbus Circle and in Penn Station were simultaneously razed beginning in the autumn of 1991. And to match emerging hardline policies concerning outdoor public space, the Transit Authority instituted new anti-homeless policies for its major hubs, aimed at beginning to deny homeless people access to indoor public space. At Grand Central Station, a more novel approach was tried. Formed in the wake of Mobil Oil's departure from Manhattan and their parting movie, which depicted the tribulations of a white male Executive trying to commute to work through mobs of harassing homeless people, the 'Grand Central Partnership' was formed to privatize public functions. Funded by levies from local businesses, the Partnership instigated private security patrols, and offered food and shelter to homeless people in a nearby church. The overall object was to 'clean up' the station even if the eviction of homeless people was done with a lighter hand.

Eviction, in fact, represented the only true homeless policy of the Dinkins administration; it was, more appropriately, an anti-homeless policy. As the 'crackdown' began in late 1991, a frustrated Director of the Mayor's Office on Homelessness resigned, and by 1993, with hundreds of homeless people sleeping overnight in City offices, the city administration and several bureaucrats were found in contempt of court for their lack of a homeless policy and failure to provide court-ordered shelter.

Back in the early 1980s, just at the beginning of the gentrification boom, a Lower East Side developer speculated somewhat whimsically that as gentrification swept east through the neighborhood, homeless people would 'all be forced out. They'll be pushed east to the river and given life preservers'.[27] In retrospect, one has to wince at the acuity of his urban political geography. A *New York Times* editorial, sounding not a little like Frederick Engels a century and a half ago, perceived the City's anti-homeless policy with equal clarity:

> Last June, police in riot gear tore down a shantytown in New York's Tompkins Square Park and evicted the homeless. Then they swept through vacant lots to tear down a new shantytown and evict the homeless again. Can't the city do better than chase the homeless from one block to another?[28]

In Engels' words:

> The bourgeoisie has only one method of settling the housing question. . . . The breeding places of disease, the infamous holes and cellars in which the capitalist mode of production confines our workers night after night are not abolished; they are merely *shifted elsewhere*.[29]

Meanwhile back at the park, despite a major City budget crisis, retaking Tompkins Square Park from its homeless residents cost an estimated $14 million dollars – $4 million for the actual renovation and nearly $10 million in police costs.[30,31] Rebuilt over 14 months with railings that kept park users on the concrete paths and with benches sporting wrought iron dividers to prevent anyone from sleeping or even lying on them, the park was reopened in August 1992. Demonstrations met the park reopening; there were several bouts of arrests in the following days and weeks, and protestors and occasional homeless people cautiously began to reuse the renovated park, but a heavy police presence prevented impromptu political gatherings and musical events and prevented the park from again becoming a home for homeless people.

## LOCAL PLACES, INTERNATIONAL SPACES

An immediate pressing question after Tompkins Square Park is how a nominally progressive political administration, strongly supported by the City's housing movement, found itself presiding over a more vicious anti-homelessness than even its predecessor. And how such a seemingly progressive government, headed by an African-American, could become the most accomplished practitioner of the revanchist city.

In the wake of the police riot in 1988, there was broad sympathy in the neighborhood for the homeless residents of the park, and this endured for at least two years despite the lack of effective organization in and around the park. For most people the Park was far from ideal as a solution to homelessness, but surely it was better than forcing people to sleep on grates and in doorways scattered throughout the city. St. Brigid's Church was a central focus of support, as was the Church more broadly. This, for example, from the Episcopal Archdeacon of New York, the Reverend Michael S. Kendall:

> When I was in South Africa last year, I saw much the same tactics used against squatters in Soweto and other townships. To close Tompkins Square Park and squatter camps without providing adequate homes for those who have none is immoral.[32]

Another more colorful story suggests the broad civic distrust of official authority. During a May Day celebration in the Park in 1990 which devolved into a melee, six protestors were arrested and when they came to trial, most of the charges, including riot, were either dropped or reduced by an obviously sympathetic jury. The jury did not at all 'believe the prosecutor's contention that the cops were beneficient public servants' and the protestors 'a crazed mob of political extremists'. Confronted with the prosecutors' defense of a supposedly 'restrained' police force, 'one female juror said, 'Gimme a break, where does he think we live?'' The trial lasted 11 days, and the jury deliberations were contentious, but according to one report, the jurors were sufficiently sympathetic that, during their daily bus ride from courthouse to sequestered hotel and back, they echoed the Park defendants' slogan with their own chant: 'Whose bus is it, it's our fucking bus!'[33]

But it was the opposition that won out. The local Community Board 3 had opposed the curfew in 1988, but several of its members colluded with the police to 'authorize' just such a curfew that led to the police riot. Several community organizations, most notably the innocuous sounding Tompkins Square Neighborhood Association, emerged after the riot to argue vociferously against the presence of homeless people in the park, and they began to organize a broad campaign. These organizations formed what

could be described as a 'restoration coalition', and were variously composed
of recent immigrants into the neighborhood, gentrifiers, homeowners and
developers as well as some longer term residents. While often decrying
homeless residents of the park as drug addicts, they successfully opposed
City plans to build a drug rehabilitation facility and an AIDS treatment
center for addicts in the Lower East Side. They contested elections for the
Community Board, eventually achieving a sympathetic majority, worked
with the local police precinct against the homeless residents of the park, and
applied steady pressure on the City administration to 'clean up' the park.

Community support for those living in the park clearly eroded as the
encampment became more entrenched. The park was workplace and
playspace, living room and bathroom, for hundreds of people daily, and the
result was hardly a salubrious solution to emergency housing and other
social needs. Even a sympathetic observer had to conclude when the park
was closed that 'the situation had reached a crisis point that even the
tolerant Lower East Side milieu could no longer sustain. . . Most residents
are too fed up with the homeless and the park to put up another fight. And
the community surrounding the park has already changed'.[34] This erosion
of sympathetic support and action came in the context of a broad media
discovery that in liberal as much as not-so-liberal neighborhoods, 'a
growing national ambivalence about the homeless' had become pervasive.[35]
Beginning in more conservative cities from Miami to Atlanta, but quickly
adopted in bastions of liberal administration such as Seattle and San
Francisco, cities around the US began enacting harsh measures against
sleeping and camping in public, pavement sitting, panhandling and
windscreen washing.[36] The revanchist city was a national phenomenon.
The national press, in the meantime, was running out of new angles on the
visceral reality of homelessness, and they either continued to run
increasingly anaemic, predictable stories of the streets or else eschewed the
issue altogether.

Much less ambivalent was the public embrace of New York as a 'global
city'. The unprecedented globalization of finance in Wall Street and the
Downtown Financial District was accompanied by the equally unprecedented internationalization of the population as nationally defined
immigrant communities emerged in the outer boroughs and suburbs.
Indians, Jamaicans, El Salvadorans, Mexicans, Chinese, Polish, Koreans,
Barbadians, Russians, Thais, Colombians and many other groups
established new communities in the metropolitan area. These immigrant
groups are variously employed in service and retail jobs that can be traced
directly to the globalization of the financial sector, expansion of middle-
class consumption, and indeed gentrification.[37] The gentrification of the
Lower East Side is equally bound up with the globalization of the city
economy. Beginning a mile to the north-east of the downtown Financial
District, the area's gentrification provided housing for, among others,

young professionals employed downtown. The area was also affected by the continued northward encroachment of Chinatown into the Lower East Side, fueled by massive financial flows and immigration from Hongkong, Taiwan and China. Culturally, the art market that flourished in the 1980s was not just the progenitor of internationally celebrated styles and artists but the object of several international exhibitions, while the club and music scenes are still on the international circuit.

That the restoration coalition in the Lower East Side found their symbolic leader in Antonio Pagan is therefore symptomatic. Pagan's political career in the Lower East Side symbolizes both the rise to power of a more established immigrant group and, anticipating the electoral defeat of David Dinkins, the erosion and transformation of a long time liberal tradition in New York City. Antonio Pagan is no stereotype. A Latino community organizer who moved to the area in the early 1980s, Pagan became a housing developer concerned with housing for the poor and elderly as well as market-rate apartments. He is openly gay yet he also helped to form a pressure group called BASTA (Before Another Shelter Tears Us Apart) which successfully blocked a homeless shelter in the neighborhood for people with AIDS. A zealous neo-conservative Democrat who led the crusade to close Tompkins Square, he is virulently opposed to squatters in the neighborhood. At one point, he even attempted to persuade Cardinal O'Connor to dismiss Father Kuhn of St Brigid's Church because of the latter's support for squatters, but was rebuffed. Pagan capitalized on the closure of the Park in 1991 with a political campaign for the local seat on the City Council. Heavily financed by real estate and contracting interests, and endorsed by the *New York Times*, he blamed liberals and liberal guilt for the destruction of the institutions of social reproduction, and cast the eviction of homeless people from Tompkins Square Park as a victory for poor Lower East Siders who now had their park back. Pagan's rise, concluded the *Voice*, 'has all the standard '90s earmarks of the ambitious ethnic pol who pulls the ladder up behind him'.[38]

Opposed by many gays, by 'a coalition of progressive Latinos' who 'protested his support of gentrification', and by AIDS activists as well as housing activists, who began referring to him as the 'Clarence Thomas of the Lower East Side' – say one thing do the other – Pagan succeeded in fashioning a conservative coalition of property owners, gentrifiers, conservative Jews, and enough old time residents and Puerto Ricans to defeat very narrowly the long-term liberal incumbent, Miriam Friedlander.[39]

If Pagan's political victory in the Lower East Side is in part the result of a changed citizenry due to gentrification, he was also significantly assisted by a dubious re-districting of council seats that brought cries of gerrymandering. Approved by the Dinkins administration on the same day that they closed the Park, this plan split the Lower East Side between two districts, the northern one (Pagan's) appended to the well-off Gramercy Park neighborhood, and the southern one attached to Chinatown and the new corporate condo and co-op neighborhood around Wall Street and Battery Park. Pagan consolidated his victory in the 1993 election.

But more than anything, Pagan's ascent to power in the Lower East Side, complemented by Dinkins' citywide defeat in 1993 by Giuliani (the city's first Republican mayor in a quarter century) corroborated the abject failure of liberal housing and anti-homeless policies. Further, it portends the advent of a more ruthless urbanism, an entrenched revanchism. That Dinkins, the failed liberal, and Pagan, the rising conservative moralist, are respectively African-American and Latino is precisely the point of the revanchist city in which the reassertion of power by the white ruling class takes numerous forms. Pagan wins with the help of Gramercy Park, but Dinkins is ousted by Giuliani. Days after taking power as mayor, and in the midst of a record cold spell, Giuliani was questioned by a reporter about his homeless policies given the severe weather. What did the mayor intend to do, he was asked. 'We're working on the weather', responded the mayor.

## CONCLUSION: DEGENTRIFICATION?

The reopening of the park in 1992 was accompanied by a predictable naturalization of Tompkins Square's history, geography and culture in the press. Noting the parallels with Central Park in the 1930s – read: Tompkins Square Park is an old story – the *New York Times* immediately heralded the reconstructed Tompkins Square as a 'shining emerald'.[40] Within a year, the aestheticization of the neighborhood was in full swing with photographs in the press of young, white middle-class families enjoying the park once again. A fashion article in the *Times* celebrated the neighborhood as virtually an inner city, 'serendipitous, ad hoc mall', noting without any mention of the preceding conflicts, that the rehabilitation of the park was followed by a thorough-going 'fashion rehab'. Despite the lingering depression affecting the region, more than 25 new shops opened in the year after the park's reopening, readying themselves 'for the neighborhood's inevitable onset of young professionals'. 'Since the renovation of Tompkins Square Park . . . the area from Seventh Street to Ninth Street between Second Avenue and Avenue B has become extremely desirable from a commercial point of view . . . With rents from $20 to $30 a square foot (and climbing), there is sudden interest "from successful businesses in the West Village and SoHo who want to relocate",' observes one local broker.[41]

In this context, the argument for 'degentrification' seems at best, premature. Predictions of the demise of gentrification are premised on essentially consumption side explanations of the process, and indeed the conditions of consumption have altered with the maturation of the baby boom generation. But if, as I have suggested, the patterns of capital investment and disinvestment are at least as important in creating the opportunity and possibility for gentrification, then a rather different vision emerges. The decline in housing and land prices since 1989 has been accompanied by a disinvestment from older housing stock – repairs and maintenance unperformed, building abandonment – and these are precisely the conditions which led in the first place to the availability of a comparatively cheap housing stock in central locations. Far from ending gentrification, the depression of the late 1980s and early 1990s may well enhance the possibilities for reinvestment. Whether gentrification resurges following the economic depression now appears to be a significant test of production-side versus consumption-side theories.

The language of degentrification, of course, not only justifies the political momentum behind the revanchist city, but feeds the self-interest of real estate developers and contractors. 'Gentrification' has become a 'dirty word' that expresses well the class dimensions of recent inner urban change, and it is hardly surprising that real estate professionals have taken advantage of a very real slow down in gentrification to attempt to expunge the word and the memory of the word's politics from the popular discourse. But neither the memory nor the profits of gentrification are likely to be erased so quickly. Indeed it may not be too much of an exaggeration to surmise that proclaiming the end of gentrification today may be akin to anticipating the end of suburbanization in 1933.

The continuance of gentrification, possibly at a more intense rate than in the past, will not mean the end of the revanchist city and the return of a kinder, gentler urbanism. The more likely scenario is of a sharpened bipolarity of the city in which white middle class assumptions about civil society retrench as a narrow set of social norms against which the recidivism of the city is found dangerously wanting; and, by way of corollary, we can expect a deepening villainization of working-class, minority, homeless and many immigrant residents of the city, through interlocking scripts of violence, drugs and crime. Gentrification and reactions to it will play a central role in this revanchist city. Now, however, the 'apartheid local of the American national', as Ruth Gilmore[42] so lucidly puts it, is increasingly also an apartheid local of American *internationalism*.

## NOTES

I would like to thank Sharon Zukin for alerting me to some of the initial press reports on 'degentrification'.

1. C. V. Bagli, ' "De-gentrification' Can Hit When Boom Goes Bust', *New York Observer*, 5–12 August 1991, p. 1.
2. E. Uzelac, ' "Out of Choices": Urban Pioneers Abandon Inner Cities', *The Sun*, 18 September 1991, pp. 1, 4A.

3.   L. S. Bourne, 'The Demise of Gentrification? A Commentary and Prospective View', *Urban Geography*, 14 (1993), pp. 95–107.
4.   Ibid., pp. 105–6.
5.   R. A. Beauregard, *Voices of Decline* (Basil Blackwell, Oxford, 1993).
6.   Ibid., p. xi.
7.   N. Smith, 'From Renaissance to Restructuring: Gentrification, the Frontier and Urban Change', in N. Smith and P. Williams (eds), *Gentrification of the City* (Allen & Unwin, London, 1986)
8.   N. Smith, 'Tompkins Square: Riots, Rents and Redskins', *Portable Lower East Side*, 6 (1989), pp. 1–36.
9.   N. Smith, 'New City, New Frontier: The Lower East Side as Wild West', in M. Sorkin (ed.), *Variations on a Theme Park. The New American City and the End of Public Space* (Hill and Wang, New York, 1992), pp. 61–93.
10.  C. Katz, 'A Cable to Cross a Curse', unpublished paper, 1991.
11.  R. Gilmore, 'Terror Austerity Race Gender Excess Theater', in Gooding-Williams (ed.), *Reading Rodney King/Reading Urban Uprising* (Routledge, New York, 1993), pp. 23–37.
12.  C. Katz and N. Smith, 'LA Intifada: Interview with Mike Davis', *Social Text*, 33, 1992, p. 19.
13.  R. Gooding-Williams (ed.), *Reading Rodney King/Reading Urban Uprising* (Routledge, New York, 1993).
14.  A. Ross, 'Bombing the Big Apple', in *The Chicago Gangster Theory of Life* (Verso, London, forthcoming).
15.  R. Blumenthal, 'Tangled Ties and tales of FBI Messenger', *New York Times*, 9 January 1994.
16.  M. White and L. White, *Intellectuals Versus the City* (Oxford University Press, New York, 1977.)
17.  R. Gilmore, p. 26 (see note 11).
18.  Insofar as Lou Reed's 'New York' album included a song entitled 'Meet you in Tompkins Square', the park gained international as well as national notoriety.
19.  J. Kifner, 'New York Closes Park to Homeless', *New York Times*, 4 June 1991.
20.  S. Ferguson, 'Should Tompkins Square be like Gramercy', *Village Voice*, 11 June 1991 p. 20.
21.  Anon., 'Make Tompkins Square a Park Again', *New York Times* 31 May 1991.
22.  S. Ferguson, 'The Park is Gone', *Village Voice*, 18 June 1991, p. 25.
23.  S. Roberts, 'Crackdown on homeless and what led to shift', *New York Times*, 28 October 1991.
24.  S. Ferguson, 'Tompkins Squares Everywhere', *Village Voice*, 24 September 1991.
25.  T. Morgan, 'New York City bulldozes squatters' shantytowns', *New York Times*, 16 October 1991.
26.  I. Fisher, 'For Homeless, A Last Haven is Demolished', *New York Times*, 18 August 1993.
27.  C. Unger, 'The Lower East Side: There Goes the Neighborhood', *New York*, 28 May 1984.
28.  Anon., 'Hide the Homeless?' *New York Times*, 11 November 1991.
29.  F. Engels, *The Housing Question* (Progress, Moscow, 1975).
30.  J. Kifner (see note 19).

31. S. Ferguson, 'Bucking for Realtors. Antonio Pagan: the Clarence Thomas of the Lower East Side?' *Village Voice*, 14 September 1993.
32. M. S. Kendall, 'Military Style Evictions', Letter to *New York Times*, 6 November 1991.
33. S. Ferguson, 'Riot Jury Riots', *Village Voice*, 25 February 1992.
34. S. Ferguson (see note 24).
35. S. Roberts, 'Evicting the Homeless', *New York Times*, 22 June 1991.
36. T. Egan, 'In 3 Progressive Cities, Stern Homeless Policies', *New York Times*, 12 December 1993.
37. S. Sassen, *The Global City* (Princeton University Press, 1991).
38. S. Ferguson (see note 31).
39. Ibid.
40. J. Bennet, 'One Emerald Shines, Others Go Unpolished', *New York Times*, 30 August 1992.
41. J. Servin, 'Mall Evolution', *New York Times*, 10 October 1993.
42. R. Gilmore, p. 26 (see note 11).

# II

# ETHNICITY, CAPITAL, AND CULTURE: WRITING THE CITY IN AFRICA AND SOUTH ASIA

# 5

# Bypassing New York in Re-Presenting Eko: Production of Space in a Nigerian City

Nkiru Nzegwu

## INTRODUCTION: THE CENTRALITY OF HUMAN EXPERIENCE

Working in the fields of art history and philosophy, it is not often that one gets the opportunity to participate in forums where the primary methodological and theoretical issues are those of concern to architects, urban designers, or urban planners. The rarity of such interdisciplinary dialogues is unfortunate since it falsely suggests that issues of interest to social scientists are unimportant to art historians and philosophers. One obvious problem with this falsification is that it obscures areas of conceptual overlap, and in the process, erroneously denies that city planning policies raise similar sorts of racial, cultural and gender representation questions that are germane to art history and philosophy. However while it is necessary to mention the limiting nature of disciplinarity and to underscore the existence of commonalities, it does not necessarily follow that disciplinary differences are illegitimate, nor that they must be downplayed.

I will begin this interdisciplinary 'multi-logue'[1] with some ideas provoked by the papers of Neil Smith and Joseph Sciorra. This will open the door into a discussion of Yoruba's notion of space, and the relationship between economic issues and cultural values in the production of the built environment of Lagos. The purpose of tracing the historical roots of architectural and spatial transformations in Lagos is not simply to make the trivial point that cities exist as more than extensions of, or in relation to, other global cities.[2] The main objective is to question a conventional theoretical wisdom that explains the physical and spatial environment of cities principally in terms of economic indicators: macro-economic laws and

111

forces, banking and finance, international trade and capital, the labour force, statistical indices of gross national product, population size and the presence of major international organizations and agencies. Typically, such econo-explanatory emphases proceed from economic and political economy perspectives,[3,4,5] but these have become so pervasive as to shape social-theory analyses.[6,7] The result is that symbolic representational forms deriving from social and cultural beliefs that are non-quantifiable, or irreducibly economic, are either treated as superficial or hardly merit attention. Where exceptions do occur, as is the case with Simon, they inevitably collapse right back into the economic category.

As an analysis of pre-colonial to post-independence urban space in Lagos will show, it is not at all clear that economic forces *per se* are the primary definers of representational forms that shape physical space. For instance between 1940 and 1950 as the 1949 cartoon by Akinola Lasekan inveighs (Figure 5.1), the racist attitudes of the colonial Surveyor, the European members of the Lagos Town Council and the Rent Assessment Board shaped the character of spatial production in colonial Lagos. From the 1920s on, Lagos was racially zoned into the low-density Government Residential Areas (GRA) for Europeans and the high-density Township for Africans. Living in overcrowded conditions and paying the exorbitant rent demanded by their African landlords, the workers watched with annoyance as European officials were solicitously protected from such vicissitudes by being accommodated in comfortable spacious homes *at public expense*.

The physical effect of ideological positions on spatial and architectural representation occurs not only in colonial Africa. Neil Smith's study of urban culture and politics in New York City shows that such non-economic, social and cultural beliefs also occur in contemporary times, and in a First World city. His work on gentrification reveals that it is the non-economic, ideational subjective desires of people that propel privileged individuals to direct, manipulate, and control economic forces. His paper is important not just because he exposes the presence of classist ideals, but because he establishes that the argument for gentrification which is regularly made on economic grounds, even though the underlying vision and end-product are not entirely economic, is a flamboyant lifestyle that lacks moral justification.

The strength of Smith's analysis is that he correctly recognizes the power of capital even as he highlights the role of mythologizing in re-creating and re-structuring the urban environment. Not only does this save the analysis from the reductive mistake of treating symbolic representation as an economic feature, it makes the important point that to say that a lifestyle has important economic consequences is not to say that it is an epiphenomenal economic phenomenon. The relevance of this is that it hints at the need to critically rethink the conventionally accepted relationship between symbolic forms and economic indices. Since it is people's

(*Akinola Lasekan, West African Pilot, 7 February 1949, p. 2*)

FIGURE 5.1  For Immediate Attention

dreams and not inanimate capital that shape spatial forms, our explanatory emphasis must shift to incorporate this feature in evaluating urban renewal projects.

The utilization of a framework in which issues of visual, spatial and architectural representation forcefully intersect with politics and power gives an immediate sense of cities as sites of contestation and interaction. For this reason, Smith's culturally-situated argument about the correlation between urban planning and gentrification is highly relevant. It is further reinforced by such art-historical investigations as Rosalyn Deutsche's analysis of urban redevelopment politics and public art in New York City.[8] Sketching out the boundary and role of gentry ideology, Deutsche, like Smith, expose how mythologizing works in the context of oppressive power. The two analyses reveal how some of the urban-renewal claims in New York City are ideologically driven and, in a certain sense, are like the former Lagos State Governor Lateef Jakande's Low Cost Housing Development Scheme of the early 1980s. In this highly politicized arena of class and power both programs are fundamentally devices for mobilizing capital, finance, and city council support *for* a classist vision. Regentrification, we learn from Smith as we did from Deutsche, conceals a vainglorious vision of self-aggrandizement in which policies and decisions are underpinned by a privileged group's self-interested mythologizations of itself, its space, and its reality.

Sciorra's paper on Puerto Rican vernacular architecture in New York City persuasively advances Smith's argument by presenting, in concrete terms, the grim underside of gentrification. If anything it shows that gentrification prescribes an egocentric, exploitative ideology that is oppressive in many ways. Sciorra's account provides a touching view of *las casitas* and of how an economically deprived group has had to draw on its symbolic imagery and semiotics to cope with economic handicap, urban neglect, and the searing experience of cultural displacement engendered by immigration.

*Las casitas* is a 'life-affirming' healing structure that validates Puerto Ricans' presence in New York and sharply indicts the City Council for 'political negligence and economic tyranny'.[9] The people's recourse to the imagery and semiotics of their former lives in Puerto Rico is not entirely driven by sentimentality. It is a resistance to cultural marginalization and erasure. Given zoning laws and politics, and the City Council's hostility to ethnic difference, the presence of *las casitas* in New York public space reminds us that the institutionally privileged have unrestricted access to financial and city resources, while the access of the less privileged is severely curtailed. It further asserts that urban decay is not always a symptom of poverty; its manifestation is sometimes the result of a deliberate policy of denial. Thus, mocking the City Council's rhetoric on multiculturalism, the flimsy structure of *las casitas* clearly reveals that Puerto Ricans are perceived by the New York City Council as irrelevant and unworthy of social amenities.

In sum, Sciorra's and Smith's views are important because they foreground the centrality of human aspirations in understanding the visual, spatial, and architectural transformations of cities that a perspective of political economy does not allow. They correctly cast urban decay not just as a problem of inequitable distribution of resources, but as a problem of human neglect that proceeds from an abhorrent, yet 'normalized' view that certain groups of people are expendable. By so doing, they raise the more fundamental question of the nature and function of a city: Is a city an impersonal economic space, in which monuments are built to capital? Or, is it basically a place of domicile where even the high-stakes economic players live, pursue their dreams, and raise their children? Because Sciorra's and Smith's views on the processes of spatial representation reveal the presence of hidden value-systems and their transformatory impact on cultural space, they give a 'humanized' sense of cities as places where people actually live; where residents are alternatively subjects and agents, and where they spiritedly resist laws and ordinances that demean their lives.


## NEW YORK AND EKO: WHERE'S THE CONNECTION?

In his essay on rethinking colonialism, Anthony King[10] contends that postcolonial critiques are often trapped by the colonial, center/periphery logic of scholarly discourse. Arguing that such critiques displace indigenous histories and conceptual signifiers, he states that the displacement unwittingly reinscribes and legitimises colonial categories. Following his logic the question that may rightly be asked is: What relevance does Sciorra's and Smith's analyses of New York City's urban politics have for Lagos? How does the identified concept of ethnicity, for instance, inform or become informed by contemporary social and spatial developments in Third World cities?

To seriously rethink colonialism and its pervasive economic conception of cities, we cannot simply assume that a relevance exists between First World and Third World cities, or that the selected categories of understanding are appropriate. Africa's histories, values and philosophies must define the central concepts of analyses. Z. R. Dmochowski[11] realized while working on Nigerian traditional architecture, that a knowledge of that country's diverse regional, social, cultural, economic, geographical and climatic conditions is critical to understanding that country's architectural and spatial forms. Thus to avoid the theoretical pitfall of excluding Yoruba spatial and architectural values in determining the character of Lagos in the 21st century, we must explicate that city's history, forms and metaphors.

## EKO AS ILE: AN AFRICAN CONCEPTION OF HOMECITY

Lagos at the close of the 20th century is the premier city of Nigeria. Eko is its heart and pulse. *Mo nlo sí Eko* (I am going to Eko) marks a trip not just to a geographical destination but to an important vibrant, economic, and socio-cultural urban space where everything happens and nothing is impossible. Stretching from Adeniji Adele road at the north section of the island, to the ring road at the south, and eastward to Onikan, Moloney and Obalende, Eko is *the* place where opportunities abound, where money can be made, and where '419ers' (Nigerian fraud experts) have perfected a unique system for defrauding both the Nigerian government and foreign-based businesses.

Oral history credits the Aworis, who migrated southward from Ile-Ife through Ijebu, as the first settlers of the area known today as Lagos. By the late 17th century, roughly about 1660, the Aworis had spread from Ebute Metta to Iddo and subsequently to the island known as Oko, a Yoruba word for farm. Following the capture of Oko by the Bini army, the island was renamed Eko, an Edo word for 'war camp'. This too was later changed to Lagos after a town in Portugal, in the late 18th century.[12] The Portuguese name eventually acquired official prominence since that was what European cartographers used in identifying the area on world maps.[13] Its retention as the name for the former federal capital city is a significant fact of self-representation that speaks of the collective desire of Nigerians to remember a vital part of its history.

Lagos is much more than a place of residence or domicile to the Aworis. It is *ile* (home). Thus a recovery of Yoruba ideas of land and *ile* (homespace) is critical to understanding the past, present and future character of Lagos.

In the early period, the Aworis who were predominantly hunters, farmers and fishermen lived in a culturally homogeneous urban setting. Like other Yorubas in Oyo, Abeokuta, Ilesha and Ife, they lived in compact densely populated city-states. In this teeming environment, they lived in compounds built with carefully processed lagoon clay, palm thatch, iroko beams and pillars and which, depending on family resources, varied in length from ten to forty yards.[14] Called *agbo ile* (flock of houses), the cool, well-ventilated interiors of these architectural forms were thermally suited to the moist humidity of the coastal swamplands.[15]

Central to the notion of *ile* as homespace is the notion of family as extending from the ancestors to future generations. In accordance with this expanded view, the indigenous Yoruba architectural style spatially organises families into households and compounds. The typical compound consisted of a group of compartments built around a rectangular open courtyard, and having just one entrance. Parallel to the outer wall and at a distance of six to eight feet, ran an inner wall. Rooms that measure about eight feet were created by connecting the two parallel walls with wall partitions. A spacious verandah was created by resting the overhang of the saddleback pitched roof on caryatids or ornamented house posts. The enclosed perimeter provided a shady space where most of the family work, recreation, and sleeping took place.

Larger compounds such as *iga* (residence of Eko chiefs) differed only in their grander scale and numerous inner courtyards. At the basic level, the interlocking character of the horizontal living space reinforced family ties by naturalizing an expansive conception of family. Not only were several families accommodated in one compound, ownership was shared and extended over generations. A house acquired value by being the locus of ancestors and generations to be born. Contacts were regularly initiated with different members of the household – grandparents, fathers, wives, children, relatives, *iwofa* (one in service in lieu of interest) and slaves. As power was channelled on a seniority basis through different family members, it diffused at diverse levels and centres: grandfathers, grandmothers, fathers, mothers, aunts, uncles, and senior and junior siblings. Since the diffusion occurred at diverse sites, it legitimised multiple forms of power relationships, multiple authority figures, and multiple identities. Fundamentally, homespaces knitted large families into tight cohesive units.

In the Yoruba conception of physical space, the world is multivalent. Land, including *igbo* (forests), *oko* (farmlands), *ile* (lived environment) was viewed as belonging to an entire lineage with the *baale* (father of the land) or Idejo chief as the custodian. *Igbo* is seen as an efficacious zone providing habitation for animals and medicinal plants. Given the idea that land is a sacred place, a habitation of numerous forces and entities, it was never treated as a commodity to be entrusted to the highest bidder. Since land was not defined in terms of economics, the role of Idejo chiefs was custodial rather than proprietorial. No indigene was denied access to lineage land, which was used to empower rather than to disempower. As a result, even non-indigenes had usufructuary rights once permission was granted. Land sale did not begin in Lagos until the replacement of this humanistic view with the proprietorial relationship to land of the British law.

The cultural and symbolic beliefs underpinning this conception of land and space have far-reaching consequences on spatial representation. It encouraged a freestyle approach to urban space that was visually different from the regimented square grid-iron order that exists in First World suburbia. In this physical space, *agbo ile* were made up of a warren of interconnected sub-houses and courtyards, ornately decorated walls, and spectacularly carved caryatids or verandah posts. Its urban contours flow with the curves and obstacles of the natural environment, following footpaths and the geographical features which different lineages have used as points of demarcation. Family compounds stretch a long distance, and since they are built near each other,[16,17] natural pathways or streets were created between compounds. Remains of this approach can still be found in

Isale Eko, Lafiaji, and Campos Square environs where narrow roads wind around extensive compounds.

Because of the lineage emphasis on spatial configuration, the characteristic modernist polarization of cities into separate enclaves for the rich and the poor was absent in this context. The Oba, the Idejo chiefs, and counsellors (both male and female) lived among the people, and were socially obligated to the less-fortunate in ways that attended to their welfare. As the pivotal point of the community, the Idejo chiefs and ultimately the Oba defined a special valuational scheme in which social cohesion – being your brother or sister's keeper – was promoted as the valued ideal.

As Isale Eko grew, lineages expanded into quarters and were administratively governed as such by the resident white-capped Idejo chiefs. Within each quarter or ward the *iga* (residences of the Idejo chiefs) became the central arenas of influence. These in turn revolved around the larger political and spiritual power spot on the island, *Iga Idunganran*, the sprawling residence of the Oba of Lagos. The intersection of the sacred and the social in the personhood of the Oba compelled an architectural design and space that mirrors the Oba's power and role as guardian of the community. In this guardianship role, *Iga Idunganran* served as an administrative centre; it harboured major shrines; and it hosted the Adamu Orisha festival as well as the city's principal *oja* (market).


## COLONIALISM: FROM 'ILE' TO THE MARKET

Up until the beginning of colonial rule, Isale-Eko was an *ile*, a residential environ with clearly defined markets at Ebute Ero, Idumota and Faji. The idea that 'everyone is everybody's keeper' was an important social philosophy that had far-reaching impact on the visual and spatial representation in Old Eko. However, radical changes occurred with colonisation. What needs to be determined is the nature and direction of the change as well as the processes by which they were accomplished.

In 1851, Lagos unofficially became a British colony following the restoration of Oba Akitoye to the throne. The island was formally ceded to the Crown in 1861. The annexation meant the introduction of a land-law system, which treated land as a marketable commodity,[18,19] a phenomenon that triggered the decline of Yoruba visual and spatial values.

Between 1861 and 1865, the colonial government imperiously announced its presence by appropriating Lagos island, including Ikoyi,[20] Victoria Island, and the land around the port at Apapa, the mainland opposite Eko. This act of imperial representation was visually framed in grand spatial terms. Under governor-generals from John Glover, William MacGregor, to Alfred Moloney, major urban restructuring programs were instituted that changed what has been described as the 'disordered' geographical character of Eko. Three main latitudinal thoroughfares were built across the island: the Marina and Broad Street in 1861, and Victoria Street in 1866. Begun in 1895, the completion of the first phase of the railway facilitated the agricultural and mineral exploitation of the territory. By 1901, Idumota, Kokomaiko and Oke Suna swamps were reclaimed. The construction of three bridges – Five Cowrie Creek, Carter and Denton – linked Eko to Victoria Island, and to the mainland.

The commissioning of the Lagos Steam Tram shortly afterwards eased the movement of workers between the mainland and the island. This service facilitated the dramatic change of the culturally homogeneous character of Isale Eko. Once Lagos became the capital of Nigeria in 1914, its new status created a huge demand for workers, and its status as a 'first-class township' set up a demand for a range of service-related activities. From the Yorubaland hinterland came the Egba, Ijebu, Ijesha, Oyo, Ondo and Ekiti; and from the North came the Hausa, Fulani, Nupe, Borguwa and Kanuri. By 1900, such eastward ethnic groups as the Edo, Urhobo, Itsekiri, Igbo, Ibibio and Kalabari had settled in Lagos. Africans arrived from parts of British West Africa, primarily from Sierra Leone, Gambia, the Gold Coast (now Ghana), and Western Cameroon as well as from Niger, Chad, Benin and Togo in French West Africa. Next came the 'Coras' (Lebanese and Syrian merchants) on the heels of the expatriate staff of such European trading firms as G. Gottschalck & Co., Elder Dempster, Miller Bros. Ltd., G. B. Ollivant, John Holt Ltd., W. B. Maciver and Co. Ltd., Société Commerciale et Industrielle de l'Afrique Occidentale (SCOA) and others.[21]

The massive infusion of all these ethnic and racial groups created a huge demand for housing. The colonial response to this housing problem is particularly revealing since it highlights the endemic racism of British colonialism and shows how racist and classist values were injected into the Lagos landscape. To maintain its imperial mystique and power, the colonial government deployed racial superiority arguments to officially separate Europeans from Africans. This segregationist policy resulted in the massive development of Ikoyi and western Marina for Europeans. As Lasekan satirised, salaries and allowances were increased for non-African employees, while Africans were denied (Figure 5.2). Stinting on housing expenditure for the African staff, the Public Works Department (PWD) constructed narrow dwellings for African workers in the Constabulary in Obalende. Not only were these economy homes spatially different from the PWD homes of European staff; these prototypes of today's shanty houses or 'bachas' were inconvenient, having been designed for bachelors rather than for families.

This racialisation of Lagos enabled the colonial government and the Lagos Town Council to bring the city in line with western aesthetics and its conception of space. After the bubonic plague of 1929, the Lagos Executive Development Board (LEDB) was set up a year later to rid Eko of the

120

(*Akinola Lasekan, West African Pilot, 23 May 1949, p. 2*)

FIGURE 5.2   The Beast of Burden!

stagnant swamps that bred mosquitoes and malaria. The new Board also set up building codes and guidelines. It laid down land-use densities, size of rooms and heights of buildings. Since indigenous architecture was perceived as 'shacks and hovels,' and the traditional free-style utilization of space as 'disordered and chaotic,'[22] Idumagbo section of Isale Eko was declared a slum area.

Embarking upon slum clearance and reclamation, the LEDB erased the freestyle Yoruba approach to land utilization that lacked a notion of socially exclusive space. It deployed a negative stereotypical image of 'dirty Africans' to legitimize the mass demolition of houses around Idumagbo lagoon. Although the LEDB and the PWD claimed that the demolitions were health related, the indigenes did not miss the underlying rationale of this urban development policy, which was to make the city more administratively manageable *for the colonial officials*. While appreciative of some of the colonial programmes, the indigenes resented the growing commercialisation of basic amenities like water. They especially resented the fact that colonial rule was achieved by uprooting them, devaluing their lifestyle (Figure 5.3), their customary relationship to land, and their conception of spatial production. In response, the people publicly expressed their frustration in the names they gave some of their resettlement locations. One such name which captured their outrage as well as their feelings on their Oba's collusion with the British was 'Obalende', which means 'the king has driven us to this place'.[23]

Officially, the slum demolition and relocation exercises were successful since they freed up prime real estate for commercial use. However the high population density which was viewed as the root cause of the sanitation problems persisted because inadequate attention was paid to the indigenes' lifestyle. The policy of small resettlement homes for 'the natives' ignored indigenous patterns of inheritance, and preference for large extended family life.

As a condition for their peaceful relocation, families had insisted that traditional land law be upheld which meant that all those who had access to former family homes must have their right observed. Given that the average plot for a family in the resettlement areas of Yaba and Obalende was 30 feet by 100 feet, and since the houses destroyed in the 'slum clearance area' contained large numbers of family homes, once the plots were allocated, high population densities were automatically re-created in the small plot holdings of the new housing areas. Moreover since annexation meant that all rights to land and territories now resided with the colonial government, families in Lafiaji, Idumagbo and Moloney could not freely expand their homes as they would have traditionally done. Trapped in narrow living spaces, the condition deteriorated until they entered the colonial economic system, and earned the necessary money to lease or purchase land from the colonial government.

122

(*Akinola Lasekan, West African Pilot, 11 April 1949, p. 2*)

FIGURE 5.3    African 'Barbarism'?

The effect of this was the sort of low-income housing conditions described by Aina (1990).[24] The failure by the town council to anticipate the heavy emotional investment of people in their family homes exposed their sanitation claims for the mythologizing ploys they were. Had the town council's claims been genuine, they would have realized that moving the people to small plots would cramp extended family life, and re-create the very problem they sought to solve. In fact the oversight showed that council members lacked any real understanding of the people and of their social habits, and revealed that the decisions were essentially driven both by a stereotypical view of Africans and the indigenous way of life. The imperial benefits of the resettlement schemes were to disenfranchise indigenes of their land and make them tenants of the Crown; and in the allocation of the reclaimed plots provide revenue for colonial coffers.

## ELITISM AND GENDER DISPARITY: THE NEW SOCIAL VALUES

There is no question that the cumulative effect of imperial self-representation in physical space was the awareness of the 'natives' of their loss of autonomy. Of prime concern in this analysis, however, is not whether or not colonialism was an unmitigated disaster to Yoruba traditional life as Lasekan has quipped in his 'Modern Partnership' cartoon (Figure 5.4). Rather, the investigation is directed towards understanding how a human-centered conception of urban space was replaced by one that privileged proprietorial relations, and social and economic inequality.[25] As a means of understanding the present situation of Lagos, there is need to appreciate the processes of change and the social values that transformed the indigenous conception of physical space.

As political power shifted away from the traditional administrative centre in Iga Idunganran to the Governor General's office, court house, treasury, police station, and prison, power was transformed from its consensual communitarian mode to an imperial dictatorial mode. This move not only introduced a new style of leadership; it glamourised dictatorial power and legitimised modernity and progress as feasible only in hierarchical contexts of power.

The architectural and spatial design which coded this power relationship, and which greatly disrupted indigenous social norms, was the vertical storey house. Scattered all over Eko by 1920, it was specifically concentrated around Campos Square where the Agudas (Brazilian Yoruba returnees) had settled; Olowogbowo, where the Saros (Sierra Leonean freed slaves of Yoruba descent) lived;[26,27] and along the Marina where the christian missions and such European trading firms as G. B. Ollivant, Paterson & Zochonis (PZ), and Gottschalck & Co. were located. Quite distinctive of this new storey-style design were the corrugated iron roofs, bricks, planks (*ile*

124

(*Akinola Lasekan, West African Pilot, 20 April 1949, p. 2*)

FIGURE 5.4   Modern 'Partnership'

*alapako* – house of planks as in the first storey house, the Mission House),[28] and the gables and ornate Brazilian plasterwork. Through such buildings as the Elephant House[29] of Hon. Samuel Pearse, Branco house on Kakawa street, and Yoyo Araromi house formerly at the junction of Tokunbo and Oshodi streets, Brazilian-Yoruba master builders like Joao (Juan) Baptist da Costa brought about major visual and physical changes in public and domestic space.

Through this architectural innovation western social values began to impact on customary values and life. In contrast to the sprawling *agbo ile* (compound-style) in Isale Eko, the vertical style of the PWD colonial storey houses, and the superlative homes of men like A. W. U. Thomas organised domestic space along gender lines: master bedroom, bedrooms, drawing room, parlour, dining room, kitchen, pantry and shop. As family interaction was hierarchically formalized, prime living space was accorded to men. Male power and mystique increased as men of the elite class represented themselves as 'storeowners', 'agents', 'lawyers', 'doctors', and 'engineers' and removed themselves from the mundane day-to-day running of the home. Disempowered within this spatial scheme, female activities were relegated to the secondary spaces of the backyards, while children's recreational space was displaced into the neighbourhood streets.

Dotting the island landscape by the 1920s, these vertical homes were idolized as symbolizing power, privilege and progress. Their inhabitants emulated Victorian dress, manners and lifestyle and represented themselves by the spatial codes of the architectural style. Aspiring to be Englishmen and women, the pretentious Saros uncritically upheld the patriarchical values and gender relationships that had been sanctioned by the missionaries. As they transformed themselves into patriarchs, the men of this elite class treated women as inferior and condescendingly promoted domesticity as *the* female profession. As this gender identity became fashionable and pervaded the society, it hindered the professional and economic advancement of women.

It is noteworthy that the western constitution of space markedly differed from the Yoruba organization where there are multiple players and multiple sites of power and interaction for both men and women. While in the classical colonial form officers were expected to be single and adequate allowance was hardly made for wives and children, in the indigenous setting the Yoruba extended family consisted of a number of sub-families and kin groups, with members living in the presence of other kin groups. So while the indigenous architectural style diffused power and encouraged collective representation between men and women, in the vertical hierarchical, gender-loaded modern variation, architecture became a valuational tool that both reinforced patriarchal relations of power and fostered female dependency.[30]

For the elites, comprised mainly of intellectuals of Saro descent and wealthy Yoruba professionals and merchants, the vertical storey-style form of their homes asserted their newly acquired values, and normalized gender hierarchy and the subsidiary position of women. Where in indigenous space, women were valued and female activities like meetings, cooking, washing, and the nursing of babies were publicly carried on around the perimeter of the courtyard, in the modern adaptation they were devalued and hidden from view. By contrast, male activities occurred in parlours where they increased in prestige and were publicly endorsed.

With this gender shift, family interaction in the homes of educated christian elites was affected in ways that brought them in accord with the underlying vision of European life. The impact of the new spatial values on social and gender identity can best be seen when we consider what obtained in the homes of the Oba, the chiefs (male and female), the traditional elites, and ordinary citizens who continued to live their customary life. While women in the Saro or '*aje butt*' (butter eaters', privileged) class were encouraged to model their identity after the meek demeanor of a 'civilized' (white) woman, 'local' (non-educated, unwesternised) women who were mainly traders and wealthy merchants preferred the power of an Iyalode/ Iyaloja (Mother of Markets), and the assertive identity of a commercially affluent Madam Tinubu.

## NATURALIZING POVERTY: INDEPENDENCE AND POST

It is often the case in development circles, that the term 'Third World' has come to signify the socio-economic conditions of hopelessness, deprivation, squalor, poverty, high unemployment, and underdevelopment. By focusing on the development marvels of the First World, the term equates material successes with the good life and plays up economic indices over humanistic values. As material poverty is naturalized as a Third World phenomenon, it is insidiously transformed and equated with cultural poverty. The ominous result of this conceptual sleight-of-hand is that human misery *naturally* depicts Third World reality by masking and subsequently erasing that which is socially significant and valuable in Third World realities.

Noting this conceptual masquerading, Lowder[31] rebuffs the attempt to naturalize poverty as a Third World condition. She contends that the socio-economic condition is basically a spin-off of modernization in a context of domination rather than simply of population growth and ignorance. Polemical as the contention may seem, Lowder's statement invites a critical appreciation of the negative effects of modernisation in a dysfunctional context. It is not the cavalier absolution of the shortcomings of Third World societies as it may seem. As will readily be seen in the case of Lagos, the outrageous commercialization of land and housing that occurred in the 1970s arose not from population explosion *per se*, as Lowder has argued, but from the egocentric commodification ideology that abruptly displaced the consensual communalist one.

At independence in 1960, Lagos was a racially divided island plotted out in grid-iron layouts. At the eastern section of the island in Ikoyi were the sprawling low-density, large-sized lots of the European quarters. At Obalende and Moloney are the high-density, mini-sized lots where Africans live in low-quality houses. To the south is the commercial district between Marina and Nnamdi Azikiwe street with Odunlami street at the eastern border. North of Nnamdi Azikiwe and Bamgbose streets all the way to Adeniji Adele road are the small, high-density areas of Isale Eko, Lafiaji, Oke Suna, and Brazilian quarters.

With the demise of colonialism in 1960, class divisions replaced racial divisions as a social ideal, and snobbery became the normal social style of Nigeria's ruling elite. The acceptance of this segregationist ideology meant that egoism and exploitative behaviour became the order of the day. For the Nigerian male heirs of the old political system, the primary goal of public life was not necessarily service, but personal aggrandizement. Anxious to reap the benefits of power and privilege, the new elite represented themselves in oppressive, arrogant ways that continued the discriminatory policies of the departing imperialists. This behaviour translated into a manipulation of public space for personal use. As the former European quarters became vacant, they were hastily occupied by these upper and upper middle-class Nigerian men and their families who meticulously maintained the trappings of colonial life. Drawing on class distinction, they justified the continuation of the separatist housing policy which had begun under colonial rule. Their disdain for the needs of low-income Nigerians meant that low-income areas of Isale-Eko and Lafiaji were neglected.

Following the 1972 indigenisation decree and its 1977 modification, Nigerians had sixty percent control of any foreign business,[32] and commercialization pushed up the retail and rental value of land in central Lagos. Many of the old Brazilian homes and colonial buildings were pulled down in the sixties and seventies as families cashed in on the land boom and either sold or leased their homes. The large multinational corporations that bought up these properties reshaped the spatial environment of central Lagos in the Modernist Movement architectural style. Towering skyscrapers (*onile gògòrò*, that inspired and popularised a head-tie style of that name) and huge department stores were built along Broad street and Marina: Bristol Hotel just off Broad street, Co-operative Bank and Elder Dempster on the Marina, and Western House on Upper Broad street. Major commercial firms and banks followed suit in locating their headquarters on the commercial strip, notably UTC (United Trading Company), Kingsway, Eleganza, PZ, Union Bank (formerly Barclay's Bank), United Bank for Africa (UBA), First Bank, Bank of the North, and Central Bank.

As the economic value of the real estate in the central business district skyrocketed, commercial interest became the paramount consideration in spatial representation. The Lagos Executive Development Board set the pace either by building or approving the building of shops all along the streets from Tinubu Square to Aponpon. With this approach to physical space and spatial representation, the emphasis shifted from Eko as *ile* to Eko as a place of investment. Affluent families moved out to exclusive suburbs, as the migrant workers, low-income employees, and itinerant traders moved in to take their place. Thankful in finding a place to sleep, these new residents crowded seven or more to a room in overcrowded, badly maintained houses. They tolerated these poor living conditions by viewing Eko as a merely temporary place of work; their villages represented home and comfort.

As population pressure increased in and around Isale Eko in the late 1960s, a settlement area was built in Surulere on the mainland to which families were relocated. For those who remained, regulatory bye-laws were passed to monitor housing construction and living conditions in Isale Eko and Lafiaji. These were routinely flouted as landlords colluded with highly placed government officials to exploit people's rental needs. Because these rental ('cut and nail') houses were strictly for profit, they lacked adequate facilities: kitchens, toilets, and bathrooms. For the most part landlords opted for the colonial Constabulary-type design and its 'face me, I face you' storey-style. This disregard for renters' living conditions was a consequence of seeing them solely as commodities.

By the late 1970s, the spatial transformations of the domestic arena by the modernist style were complete. Few notable Nigerians like Chief Tunji Otegbeye built their homes on the indigenous rectangular-courtyard design. The general preference was for new architectural designs that identified people as progressive and different. Though the exterior design of these homes in SE and SW Ikoyi may have a 'Western' resonance, the interior spaces have been culturally adapted to capture the living pattern, cooking habits, and the spatial needs of the diverse social groups. Even the colonial houses in Ikoyi Government Residential Area (GRA), have been remodeled to accommodate customary family values. Many government officials who moved into Ikoyi after independence were either polygamists with large families, or if they were not, they had a large retinue of children, relatives, friends and neighbours.

As revenue from petroleum poured into the national coffers in the 1970s to 1980s, the Nigerian military government sought to project Lagos as a major modern city. This facelift took the form of extensive physical transfiguration in public space. The Tafawa Balewa Square and shopping complex in Onikan was transformed from a little used open cricket field to a heavily utilized centre (Figure 5.5). Massive horses in full gallop guard the gate that leads to the Legislative Assembly. Close by at Awolowo Road, are

(*Photograph: Nkiru Nzegwu*)

FIGURE 5.5    The Tafawa Balewa Complex Seen from the 14th floor of Western House

three blocks of high-rises for Federal Government employees. On the Marina are the towering Nigerian Telecommunications Office (Nitel), the External Affairs ministry, The Federal Mortgage Bank of Nigeria (FMBN), National Electric Power Authority, and the Nigerian Ports Authority (NPA). The Ring Road (locally likened to the wraps of a head-tie, and initiating the popular slogan *Eko won gele*) circled the island in a series of loops and 'flyovers'. Constructed by extensively filling in parts of the lagoon, the Ring Road promised to untie the infernal Lagos go-slows (traffic jams).

During this construction spree, the military government hardly thought about the living conditions of low-income Nigerians as it built accommodation for high-income government officials. As these disadvantaged Nigerians struggled to pay their exorbitant rents, the reclaimed land between the Marina and this ring road was turned into parking lots for the office blocks lining the Marina and Broad Street (Figure 5.6). Openly contesting this allocation, the 'area boys' – who are generally perceived as hoodlums – have turned these car parks into their headquarters. Users have to pay a protection fee if their cars are not to be vandalized. Losing the battle over the control of public space, both the Federal and Lagos State governments find that visual and spatial representation is controlled by the ubiquitous tables and kiosks of the street traders, fleet-footed car-chasing hawkers, 'area boys', and mallams. Broad Street, the major thoroughfare of the financial district, is controlled by the enterprising mallams and alhajis who cannot afford the exorbitant office rents of central Lagos. Defying the Central Bank and audaciously challenging the numerous banks in the district, these financial hustlers have set up a powerful parallel foreign exchange market that sets the real exchange rate of the naira to the dollar, sterling, yen and deutschmark.

The egotistic idea of wealth and property and intense commercialisation of downtown Lagos has turned the entire island into one pulsating sprawling market. With the commodification ideology now at its logical end, Eko is no longer an *ile* (home) but a bustling market. The major textile and fashion accessories market around Balogun, Martin and Nnamdi Azikiwe streets have merged with the wine, liquor and provisions market at Aponpon and Ebute Ero, and with the major motor spare-parts market at Idumota.

These mercantile values have also invaded even the exclusive residential areas of Ikoyi, pushing out former residents who have had to move into the badly built, pre-fabricated homes in the exclusive Dolphin Estate in Ikoyi. The invasion which began with the attempt of poorly paid servants in the 'boys' quarters' (the detached servants' accommodation) to supplement their income, ended up transforming Awolowo Road in SW Ikoyi and large parts of Victoria Island into high-class shopping and banking districts. Driving around this once secluded area, one finds a thriving plantain market

*(Photograph: Nkiru Nzegwu)*

FIGURE 5.6    Government Parking Lots in Lagos Island

under Falomo bridge, and all along Awolowo Road, merchant banks, expensive furniture and audio equipment stores, as well as boutiques proliferate.

The severe economic downturn of the eighties and nineties, caused by the IMF imposed Structural Adjustment Programme (SAP), has socially polarized Nigeria: on the one hand are the wealthy Nigerians in Ikoyi and Victoria Island, on the other the poor in Idumagbo, Lafiaji, Moloney and Obalende. As class polarization widened, armed robbers periodically invaded some of the exclusive neighbourhoods to terrorise inhabitants. The result was the rapid construction of high concrete walls round the premises of most houses in Ikoyi and Victoria Island. Where in the 1960s and early seventies Ikoyi had the look of a lush tropical garden, by the late seventies this former paradise had become a walled city, reminiscent of the old *agbo ile*, but with colonial houses inside.

## FORECAST: TRENDS IN THE 21ST CENTURY

Despite its importance as an economic centre the challenge of Eko is that its future growth would not depend on its national or global economic role but on non-economic considerations. With the institution of the Structural Adjustment Program (SAP), the devaluation of the naira in 1988 and the attendant liberalisation of foreign exchange regulations, banking institutions were given freer access to foreign exchange allocations. A year later, this resulted in the setting up of an unprecedented number of merchant banks, bureaux de change, and credit and finance companies by Nigerians. Primarily engaged in the buying and selling of foreign exchange, the limited service provided by these institutions quickly led to foreign currency speculation and sharp banking practices. Their high-risk investments fuelled the inflationary cycle, and outrageously widened the gap between the rich and the poor.

Before the banking crash in late 1993, the value of real estate on Lagos island had rocketed to unimaginable heights so that only banks, bank CEOs, and retired military generals could afford accommodation in and around Eko. As the inflationary cycle spiralled, crime and homelessness increased. Begging became an accepted way of life and the maimed and the handicapped publicly flaunted their deformities to attract attention and charity. High unemployment and low wages characterised the lot of workers. Workers' morale dropped as many could not afford the high cost of rent, adequate meals for their families, and education for their children. Driven by the commodification ideology, street hawking boomed as people took to it as the fastest way to make some money.

The challenge of Eko as an important social and economic centre lies in its potential decline as Nigeria's premier economic centre. This decline has nothing to do with these economic problems but with deep-seated political and ethnic tensions that trace their roots to colonialism. The political entity known as Nigeria was constructed by the British without any input from the region's 250 ethnic groups. Lumped together since 1910, searing tensions have existed between the groups. These have openly erupted at various times, the most tragic so far being the Biafran war. However, the most significant for Lagos has been the decision by the Federal Military Government to move the federal capital from Lagos to Abuja, and the annulment of the Presidential elections.

The reason for the relocation is basically political. Unhappy with the high investments and revenue being ploughed into Lagos by the Federal Government, the northern faction conspired to get its share of the 'national cake' by insisting on the relocation of the federal capital to a more 'central location'. Abuja in the Suleja emirate was chosen as the most central location. Construction began from ground zero in the early eighties and by late 1991, the move to Abuja commenced. The relocation pace intensified as President Babangida took up residence in Abuja, forcing many federal government ministries, corporations, and para-statals to move. The diplomatic missions, and international agencies followed suit. Lagos will probably feel the social and economic impact of this relocation by the year 2000 when Abuja is expected to become fully operational. Relegated to the level of a state capital, Lagos will have no special privileges and will then feel the loss of revenue that had previously been poured in to enhance its image as the nation's capital.

Some believe that the socio-economic fallout of the relocation will be minimal, and that Lagos will survive as an important financial centre. But the falling price of real estate in Ikoyi and Victoria Island triggered off by the vacancy created by the departing government institutions and the 1993 banking crisis is an ominous sign. Further complicating matters for a rosy forecast is the recent political crisis that has engulfed Nigeria. This has re-opened the age-old question of Nigeria's unity. Where in the past many favoured a strong Federal government, today people are openly advocating the break-up of the country, or a weak confederation at best. The annulment of the 1993 Presidential elections has finally brought it home to the Yorubas that the northern political leadership had no intention whatsoever of handing over political power to any democratically elected leader who is not a northerner. Speaking for and on behalf of the North, Alhaji Maitama Sule, the former Nigerian Ambassador to the United Nations, unequivocally proclaimed that Allah had given the North the talent to rule: to the Yorubas he gave economics, and to the Igbos technology.

Miffed by these developments, the Yorubas are advocating a confederacy system for Nigeria as a means of halting the near monopoly of northern rule. The ethnic rhetoric and polarization is not only whipping up parochial interests, it is intensifying the Federal Government's pace of withdrawal from Lagos. For many the political orchestrations are reawakening memories of the events that led to the civil war. Igbos especially, who dominate the spare-parts markets, the shoes, electronics, clothing and fashion accessories retail, and who bore the brunt of the last war, have seriously begun to reassess their stay in Lagos and other parts of the country. Haunted by memories of their loss in the northern states and the confiscation of their properties and investments by the Rivers and South Eastern state governments, and recalling the periodic destruction of their businesses and properties in the northern states since the war ended, regionalism and communal nationalism are becoming acceptable political options.

The jittery political situation underwriting the Igbo decision to pull back from Lagos has caused many non-Yoruba Nigerians also to reassess their decision of taking Lagos as a permanent home, knowing that in emergency situations it will not be a home to them as it is to the Aworis. Nigerians are aware that ethnic politics will make a positive answer difficult. In the wake of the 1993 Presidential elections, many non-Yoruba traders are quietly relocating their businesses to their states of origin. This relocation will undoubtedly have a more devastating impact on the economic life of Eko than the relocation of the Federal Capital to Abuja. Past history shows the effect of such a boycott on Port Harcourt and Calabar ports. Though nearer to the Igbo commercial centres of Aba and Onitsha, Port Harcourt and Calabar wharves were located in the two states that are hostile to, and had forcibly seized Igbo properties after the civil war. The under-utilization of these ports resulted in the diminished growth of Port Harcourt and its failure to rival Lagos as a major commercial and business centre.

There is no question that regionalism and communal nationalism will have a negative impact on the future growth of Lagos. Already the shift of the Federal Capital to Abuja is seeing the rise of Yoruba parochial interests in Lagos and the re-assessment, by non-Yorubas, of their options. Thus since the continued importance of Lagos as a major economic centre in the twenty-first century will have to depend on these ideological and political issues, it is difficult to determine its visual, architectural and spatial transformations.

## NOTES

1.    The term 'multi-logue' is used to indicate that this interdisciplinary analysis is being carried on from multiple sites; primarily city planning, art-historical, feminist, and critical studies perspectives.

2.    S. Sassen, *The Global City: New York, London, Tokyo* (Princeton University Press, 1991).

3. M. Filani and J. Onyemelukwe, 'Nigeria', in H. de Blij and E. Martin (eds), *African Perspectives* (Methuen, New York, 1981), pp. 3–30.

4. D. Simon, *Cities, Capital and Development: African Cities in the World Economy* (Belhaven Press, London, 1992).

5. Simon (ibid.) describes his perspective as 'an essentially political economy perspective' (p. 6). Because he recognizes the need to include 'the human dimension in critical analysis' (p. 33), he strives to assign '[c]ulture' (read: human nature) a significant role.

6. J. Abu-Lughod, 'New York and Cairo: a view from street level', *International Social Science Journal*, 125 (1990), pp. 307–18.

7. Ibid. I am not sure Abu-Lughod would characterize her position as 'social theory', by which I loosely mean a perspective that substantially factors everyday experiences into theoretical analysis. However her essay takes an econo-oriented stance even though she makes no overt or special claim for the primacy of economic structures and categories in urban analysis. The econo-oriented claim is, however, made in an indirect way when she argues for the 'real' differences between Cairo and New York on the basis of deep economic structures. It is not just that her theoretical divide is drawn on economic lines, but that it is done in a way that privileges economic differences as 'real' difference. The implication of Abu-Lughod's emphasis is, of course, that other differences are basically superficial.

8. R. Deutsche, 'Uneven Development: Public Art in New York City', in R. Ferguson, M. Gever, T. T. Minh-ha and C. West (eds), *Out There: Marginalization and Contemporary Cultures* (The New Museum of Contemporary Art and The MIT Press, New York, 1990), pp. 107–30.

9. J. Sciorra, 'Return to the Future: Puerto Rican Vernacular Architecture in New York' (in this volume, chapter 3).

10. A. King, 'Rethinking Colonialism: An Epilogue', in N. Alsayyad (ed.), *Forms of Dominance: On the Architecture and Urbanism of the Colonial Interlude* (Gower, Aldershot, 1992), pp. 347–63.

11. Z. R. Dmochowski, *An Introduction to Nigerian Traditional Architecture*, vol. 2 (Ethnographica and The National Commission for Museum and Monuments, London, 1990).

12. K. Akinsemoyin and A. Vaughan-Richards, *Building Lagos* (F. & A. Services, Lagos, 1976).

13. The use of the Portuguese name as the official name of Eko references the eurocentrisation of cartography and Nigeria's colonial history. Indigenes and other residents of the city have continued to refer to Lagos Island as Eko, while the sprawling metropolis of close to ten million people retains the European name of Lagos.

14. K. Akinsemoyin and Vaughan-Richards (see note 12).

15. R. Dmochowski (see note 11).

16. F. Coker, *Sir Adetokunbo Ademda: A Biography* (Times Press, Lagos, Nigeria, 1972).

17. S. Johnson, *The History of the Yorubas* (C.S.S. Bookshops, Lagos, rpt. 1976).

18. T. A. Aina, 'Petty Landlord and Poor Tenants in a Low-Income Settlement in Metropolitan Lagos, Nigeria', in P. Amis and P. Lloyd, *Housing Africa's Urban Poor* (Manchester University Press, 1990), pp. 87–101.

19. Aina's study (ibid.) of Olaleye-Iponri, a district within metropolitan Lagos, also confirms this mid-nineteenth century timeframe for the inception of commercial transactions in land.

20. The Onikoyi family land in Ikoyi was appropriated by Governor Glover in 1865.

21. A. Macmillan, *The Red Book of West Africa* (Spectrum Books Ltd., Ibadan, Nigeria, 1993), pp. 63–117.

22. N. S. Miller, 'The Beginnings of Modern Lagos. Progress Over 100 Years', *Nigeria Magazine*, 69 (August 1961), pp. 106-121.

23. This name captures their frustration with the Oba who they felt had caved in to the demands of the British, and thereby participated in driving them to the resettlement area. 'Surulere' was another relocation project with a name that captured the politics of the time. Although carried out under the Federal Government of Nigeria, the logic and process of execution closely followed the guidelines set out by the defunct colonial administration. 'Surulere' means the 'land of patience'.

24. T. A. Aina (see note 18).

25. M. Peil and P. Sada, *African Urban Society* (John Wiley & Sons, Chichester, 1991).

26. A. Mabogunje, 'Lagos-Nigeria's Melting Pot', *Nigeria Magazine*, 69 (August 1961), pp. 128–55.

27. A. B. Laotan, 'Brazilian Influence in Lagos', *Nigeria Magazine*, 69 (August 1961), pp. 156–65.

28. The Mission House was built by the Christian Missionary Society.

29. Elephant House was the home of Samuel Herbert Pearse, a Lagosian of Saro extraction. Other such homes were those of J. H. Doherty, W. A. Dawodu, C. O. Blaize, Ekundayo Phillips, and A. W. U. Thomas.

30. F. Aig-Imoukhouede (ed.), *A Handbook of Nigerian Culture* (Department of Culture, Federal Ministry of Culture and Social Welfare, Lagos, 1991), pp. 92–6.

31. S. Lowder, *Inside Third World Cities* (Croom Helm, London, 1986).

32. The impact of this is that the country's economy has largely been controlled by Nigerians. In 1977, the Nigerian Head of State, General Olusegun Obasanjo nationalised some British investments in Nigeria to bring pressure on the British government to withdraw its support of Ian Smith's regime in Rhodesia, now Zimbabwe. The pressure which resulted in the constitutional conference that led to the independence of Zimbabwe, transferred some multinational holdings into Nigerian hands.

See also:

- N. Miller, 'The Beginnings of Modern Lagos Progress Over 100 Years', *Nigeria Magazine*, 69 (August 1961) 106–21.
- M. Peil, *Lagos: The City is the People* (Belhaven Press, London, 1991).
- N. Smith, 'After Tompkins Square Park: Degentrification and the Revanchist City' (in this volume, chapter 4).

N.B. *A note on the cartoons in this chapter.* Born in 1914 in Owo, Nigeria, Akinola Lasekan was the most prominent Nigerian cartoonist from 1944 to 1966 when he retired from the *West African Pilot*. He died in 1974. Laskan is presently the subject of a major study, by the author, on contemporary Nigerian art, including the impact of colonisation on Nigerian politics, consciousness, social life and art.

# 6

# Exploring Colombo: The Relevance of a Knowledge of New York

Nihal Perera

The first chapters in this volume provide exhaustive evidence, as well as arguments, illustrating the profound restructuring that New York City has been undergoing – at various scales – over the past two decades. They also point to the agencies involved and the conflicts arising from this process. Yet at the same time, their exclusive focus on New York gives the impression that 'the city' in general is in fact New York City. In assessing the relevance of such analyses of New York for the understanding of other cities in the world, I am interested in addressing two questions. How representative is New York of cities in the so-called postcolonial periphery? And, in regard to the first four chapters on New York, what is the relationship between the urban processes discussed, the agencies involved, and transformations in the city as a whole?

In the pages that follow, I shall problematize these issues by exploring the reverse, namely, the relevance of a knowledge of contemporary urban developments in Colombo, the former capital of Sri Lanka, for the understanding of New York. In doing so, I shall first elaborate the two questions raised above in regard to cities in general. I shall argue that New York is too unique to be representative of the large majority of major cities of the world, even so-called 'world cities'.[1] Despite having a broader knowledge of New York, and other major cities of the world-economy, a lack of mediating concepts prevents us making use of such a knowledge to understand other cities. As Sassen's paper – with its conceptualization of the 'global city' and a particular world structure of cities – provides more opportunities for transnational and trans-city explorations, I shall largely draw on this.[2]

Though a knowledge of New York may not be directly relevant for an understanding of developments in Colombo, I shall nevertheless begin by pointing out some similarities. New York and Colombo have at least four or five historic characteristics in common. Both were founded as colonial outposts by Europeans in non-European continents, north America and south Asia. In both cases, the early (if not the first) colonists included the Dutch, followed by the British. As important colonial port cities, both developed, along with Cape Town and Batavia (now Djakarta), as crucial nodes of the seventeenth century Dutch imperial system: New York (as New Amsterdam, between 1626 and 1664, when it was taken over by the British), and Colombo from 1658 (when it was acquired by the Dutch from the Portuguese who had first established it in 1517) to 1796, when it was taken over by the British. Both were later developed as part of the British imperial system, New York for just over a century (1667–1776), Colombo for one and a half centuries (1796–1948). Finally, both are contemporary financial centres – one, long-established and in reference to the global economy; the other, aspiring and recent, with reference to the regional economy.

Here the correspondence between the histories of these two cities tends to fade. Unlike the Dutch in New York, what the Portuguese appropriated in Colombo was an established trading port of the Indian Ocean trade network, displacing the *Marakkala* people who had operated and inhabited it.[3] The most significant difference is, however, in the population that subsequently gained control of and inhabited these cities, as well as the states to which they belonged. Colombo, like New York an essentially foreign implantation, was appropriated by the indigenous population, the Ceylonese in 1948, after 150 years of British political, cultural, and spatial control and 430 years of European colonial presence.[4,5] Yet in New York, as also in the rest of the United States, Canada, Australia, New Zealand and elsewhere, the colonial situation continues, albeit not under the original British, Anglo-Saxon regime, but through a cultural, spatial, if not political conflation of the metropole and the colony.[6,7] The city of New York, therefore, unlike Santa Fe in New Mexico, for example, not only lacks any visible indigenous political, cultural, or spatial presence in the city with an attachment to land or in the vicinity, but there is virtually no material or spatial evidence on the landscape of the once indigenous population. To that extent, New York City approximates a situation of *total* colonial control, with the elimination of the indigenes, a phenomenon that is reflected in the brute gridiron division of space dedicated to the buying and selling of land. As Sennett[8] points out, this represented a straight relationship between capitalist economics and the grid of the city.

The elimination of the indigenous populations, cultures and languages, also provided the linguistic space for the development of one important language – English. It is this which provides a common lingua franca for addressing, in this volume for example, issues concerning New York, Lagos,

Mombasa, Colombo and other cities, by scholars of British, Canadian, Puerto Rican, Nigerian, Kenyan, Argentinean and Sri Lankan origins, in a spatially, politically, and culturally 'native free' environment. This common European, especially Anglo-Saxon colonial past is equally important for the understanding and explanation of certain dominant social, cultural, and political phenomena in these cities, for example, the relevance of a 'foreign', Western and European-oriented Colombo for the construction of an indigenous Other that is represented as 'Sri Lankan' culture. In New York, failing the presence of a 'genuine' indigenous Other, their position is occupied by what Horvath[9] calls 'intervening groups',[10] for example, the Puerto Rican (colonial) immigrants. This no doubt helps to explain the inclusion of a chapter on their particular architectural practices in this volume. As Columbus supposedly 'discovered' the Americas for Europe, so the Portuguese in colonial Ceylon romanized the old name of Kolamba to Colombo in recognition of Columbus.[11] The common European cultural space linking north America and south Asia is therefore reflected in nomenclature and language, among numerous other phenomena.

## THE RELEVANCE OF A KNOWLEDGE OF NEW YORK

To what extent can the analytical frameworks and categories developed to examine New York be useful for understanding other cities? The exclusive focus of the first chapters on New York implies that it can, in some ways, stand as a model or trope for the twenty-first century metropolis. In locating New York within a larger system of cities and addressing it as one of a particular class of 'global cities', Sassen represents New York, along with London and Tokyo, as occupying the top of an economically defined hierarchy of cities of the world. Yet the direct employment of such a framework, which I would call a New York-centric approach, is likely to lead us to recognize in those cities problems, issues and characteristics similar to those of New York.

Here I would suggest an analogy from my own research on Sri Lanka. In early twentieth century Colombo, British municipal officials, drawing on their social and cultural constructions of 'poverty' in what at that time was defined as 'unfit' housing and absence of 'sanitation' in Manchester and London, applied these same culture-specific and particular town-planning perceptions to identify urban and housing problems in colonial Ceylon. What the municipal officials found in Colombo was, naturally, 'poverty', 'overcrowding', and the 'absence of sanitation,'[12] as in Manchester and London. If this approach to the understanding of urban issues was perfectly logical for the colonial British who ran the municipality for their own benefit,[13] it is hardly a model for today.

How useful are the spatial units of 'city' and 'metropolis', the focus of this volume, as concepts for the task of 'representing the city'? We might briefly examine here the main social categories and spatial units employed in the first chapters. These have explored the remodelling of New York City by immigrants of Puerto Rican origin (Sciorra), the marginalized (Zukin), the homeless (Smith), and the corporate sector (Sassen). However, do the activities in these micro sectors of the city actually restructure the 'city' and the 'metropolis' *as a whole*? Or do they only affect a part of it?

What these accounts suggest is that each of the agencies mentioned has conceived particular locales within the city as the domain of their own activities. We might even say that these agencies operate within different cities. Hence the perception and representation of the city and the metropolis prevalent in these accounts is one that somehow provides a neutral and abstract *background* for these practices, not the object in itself. This ambiguity in representation illustrates the fact that cities are not systems; only some systems are usefully identified and designated as the city.[14] What we are looking at therefore is a conflict between the old city and new phenomena. Nonetheless the political meanings invested in the 'city' may have more far-reaching importance for the examination of new urban processes.

Can the phenomenon of locating global economic command functions in New York City, argued by Sassen,[15] be viewed as the production of a 'new city' as such? Or only just a small but central element of it? What we have seen in the 1980s is not the invention of economic command functions, but rather a particular reorganization of those functions in and through new technical and social divisions of labour,[16] separating them from production, distribution and exchange of goods and services, and concentrating them in particular cities. Since most crucial nodes of the contemporary capitalist world-economy, especially the centres of capital accumulation in early modern Europe, were established through the location of economic command functions in already existing cities such as London and Paris, the production of larger imperial (economic, military, political and cultural) command centres based on these cities and their subsequent development are phenomena which require a much better historical explanation than currently exists (see, for example, King's work on London[17]).

The location of particular command functions giving rise to cities can be seen more clearly both in smaller and colonial cities.[18] Colombo for example, did not command or control the economic functions of the entire island territory of Lanka prior to the British conquest of its last kingdom, Kandy. In the nineteenth century, the city – which was neither a mining nor plantation town – was organized by the British to form the command centre of the nascent polity and economy of the colony as well as to function as a node in the imperial system. It is this nucleus that grew into modern Colombo, simultaneously constructing Ceylon around it, as its 'hinterland', by means of a military-administrative system and a plantation complex. Colombo has, however, grown beyond being a simple colonial economic and political command centre through the intervention of Ceylonese entrepreneurs and migrants and successive restructuring by city authorities.[19] Writing of another colonial situation, Mary Karasch[20] suggests that it was Rio de Janeiro that made Brazil, rather than Brazil making Rio. We can similarly ask how far New York City made the (northern) United States rather than the United States making New York City.

Sassen's argument demonstrates the production of a special form of 'city' in New York and a hinterland for particular functions. This is also the case of Colombo. What we see in her argument is the corporate 'adaptive re-use', or recycling of a locale within New York City – and also London and Tokyo – for the superimposition of corporate service complexes over the pre-existing urban infrastructure. One immediate urban outcome has been a particular kind of gentrification within the city, generating very high and very low-income neighbourhoods, new consumption structures, and new kinds of class and ethnic subjects. We are not therefore speaking about the entire city or the metropolis, as it exists, but only about the construction of a new 'urban' nucleus within the old city.

The hinterland of this global city is assumed as 'global', which implicitly includes other cities and territories around the world. Yet how truly 'global' is this 'global hinterland' and New York's 'global command capability' within it? If the economic domain of Tokyo has expanded in certain places during the last decade, New York's has certainly receded in others. The main states that have industrialized, or are in the process of industrializing from the 1970s are located in the south-east Asian region.[21] For enterprises in these states, the USA has increasingly become a consumer of their products rather than an exporter of capital or 'commander' of their economic activity.[22] If transport is an indicator of the economic domain, Keeling's data on the number and frequency of direct flights between major world cities suggests the *absence*, rather than the presence, of direct communication between New York and south-east Asia.[23]

Beginning with Taiwan and South Korea, the industrializing zone has spread as far as Sri Lanka and Mauritius. Capital for this industrialization has largely come from east Asia: first from Japan, and then Taiwan and South Korea. Moreover investments have recently diversified to include, for example, Australia and some Middle Eastern states.[24] With the dramatic appreciation of the Yen, which makes Japanese products decreasingly competitive in the market, this trend of diversification is likely to continue.

What is important here is that it is not only Japan that strives for, and finds, outlets for accumulating capital, but also the Taiwanese who have turned recently to Vietnam, and the Koreans to Myanmar. Since 1987 more than 4000 Taiwanese companies have set up operations in south-east Asia. Moreover within the boom of foreign investment in China, with over $30 billion invested in 1992, the share of south-east Asian capital has increased to 10–15 per cent.[25]

Quite seminal here is the changing control of Subic Bay in the Philippines, vacated by the US navy in 1993. It is not Japanese capital, as one might expect, that is replacing the American presence, but the Taiwanese who have agreed to develop an industrial site there.[26] While it is true that each of these investments is small in quantity compared to global transactions, it is precisely their smallness and the high number of transactions that make this phenomenon qualitatively significant for any understanding of 'world city' developments.[27]

What we see here therefore is the dispersal and reorganization not just of economic activity but of centres that export capital and control economic processes. In addition to the centralizing command over a decentralizing world economy being located in particular cities, such as New York and London, transformations of the world economy in the 1980s and 1990s have also led to a process of decentralization, dispersal and disintegration. Urban economic functions have also multiplied as well as diversified. This is precisely what has not been addressed.

Friedmann's 'world city hypothesis'[28] provides a broader framework for addressing the role of some regional centres in today's world-economy. He takes into account the decentralization and dispersal of economic activity, yet also focuses on the processes of centralization in the world-economy within a larger centralized structure of 'world cities'. We need to carry out our inquiries beyond the global centralization of economic command functions, such as is taking place in Seoul, Taipei, Singapore and Johannesburg, in order to understand the changing roles and forms of these in other cities such as Colombo and Kuala Lumpur. The limitations of concepts such as the 'global city' or 'world city' is in the preoccupation of their protagonists with the centralizing process in a few major nodes of the world economy, while neglecting other components. Yet the understanding of these is essential if we are to address transformations taking place in many other cities, particularly in Asia and Africa.

## CAPITAL AND THE RESTRUCTURING OF COLOMBO

I shall turn now to Colombo and briefly explore the factors governing its economic restructuring in the 1980s and 1990s and their relevance for understanding developments in New York. What we see in Colombo is a profound reorganization of the city through the particular decentralization and recentralization of its activities which have simultaneously redefined 'the city' and also its position within Sri Lanka.[29] The differences between the contemporary processes affecting these two cities are not only the result of their contrasting locations within the world economy – one in the core and the other in the periphery, from a world-systems perspective – but also their geographic location; Colombo is in an expanding economic zone of Asia, and at a juncture of two spatial systems, of cities and of states.

As with New York, the role of both foreign as well as local capital in Colombo has been significant. In the 1980s a prominent space was created in Colombo through the construction of a Central Business District, in the former colonial Fort area, in which were located the reorganized command functions over the Sri Lankan economy. Spatially, this was carried out by separating the institutions of the polity and economy, as well as the economic functions of production, collection and distribution of goods and services, and relocating them outside Colombo municipal limits. The relocated institutions included government department headquarters, warehouses, and the military. New Export Processing Zones were also located outside city limits, beginning with a site near the Colombo International Airport, about 25 kilometers from the Fort area. Most conspicuous was the shifting of governmental functions from the former Parliament, located in the Fort area, to a new complex built at Sri Jayawardanapura-Kotte. In addition to the construction of a central business district in the heart of Colombo, the privatization of state corporations transferred their headquarters in Colombo into private hands, thereby making the new central business district largely the domain of private capital.

Parallel to the separation of these political and economic institutions was their replenishment and reorganization within an expanded city, as compared to a smaller one in New York. Although the municipal boundaries of Colombo were not physically changed, the perception of Colombo was transformed as part of this process. For example, Greater Colombo and Colombo Metropolitan Region were created, expanding their limits to incorporate the decentralized key economic and political activities. Here, the notion of Colombo Metropolitan Region was adopted by the Urban Development Authority; also Greater Colombo, as the jurisdiction of the agency created to establish new Export Processing Zones, the Greater Colombo Economic Commission. In this context, the Export Processing Zones at Katunayake near Colombo airport, warehouses at Peliyagoda outside the northern boundary of the municipality, and the governmental complex at Kotte, were reincorporated into Colombo. Hence shifting the seat of government outside an increasingly commercial Colombo to Kotte – resembling in some ways the distinction between New York and Washington – in fact amounted to a reorganisation of an expanded Colombo, with a distinct area allocated for legislative and executive functions.

The initiative to reorganize the city was taken by the (national) state which invited foreign capital to occupy the central business district as well as invest in Sri Lanka. Although foreign capital has been a crucial agent of change, it was the state which not only reorganized the economic command centre and the national economy but which also had a stake in their development. In this context, the 1977 government which initiated this process, and the two governments which followed it, also established legal havens for investors, creating Export Processing Zones devoid of labour laws, and privatizing state departments and corporations. In contrast in the USA, the principal emphasis of city government policies by the mid 1970s, changed from the direct sponsorship of large-scale planned redevelopment and the production of central business districts, to one of facilitating privatized physical redevelopment and subsidizing private capital accumulation.[30]

Although various spatial systems display a degree of autonomy from each other, in this case an economically defined world system of cities and a system of modern states converge at certain points to produce particular nodes. A particular convergence of the political, economic and cultural realms of a society can be seen in national capitals which are also the economic command centres of those states. In New York however, capital no longer has to seek state-directed redevelopment, in part because the process of making central business districts profitable for investment has already been achieved in the United States.[31] In Sri Lanka however, state intervention was needed to create profitable arenas for capital investment in the 1980s, since the previous governments had substantially destroyed its capitalist infrastructure. For this restructuring of the economy, the state selected Colombo as the central site.

This is very well expressed in terms of space. Although New York's landscape is symbolized by monuments dedicated to capital, until quite recently Colombo's landscape has been dominated by monuments dedicated to the state. It is about fifteen years since the Urban Development Authority of Sri Lanka adopted an explicit policy to create a central business district. Despite substantial foreign investment and the sprouting of a modernist built environment in and around this district, visually, the most dominant building in the area is still the thirty-two storied head office of the state-run Bank of Ceylon.[32]

Although the city governments as well as other public and private agencies in both Colombo and New York might have responded to the same broad world economic conditions, their perception of problems differ due to their contrasting positions in the world economy as well as their geographical location. This results in two fundamentally different spatial solutions carried out by two different agencies. Moreover, in Sri Lanka, the initiative of the 1977 government was largely directed towards rebuilding a capitalist infrastructure in place of what had been destroyed over the three previous decades by nationalist-socialist governments. This had included the nationalization of the British and Ceylonese owned plantations,[33] the main means of production for the 'world market'; the imposition of ceilings on land and house ownership, and the reinforcement of workers', consumers', and tenants' rights.[34] In this context, the 1977 government's open invitation to foreign capital to invest in Sri Lanka was arguably due to the incapacity of the disabled national capitalist class, weakened by the policies of the previous nationalist-socialist governments, to begin the restoration of a privatized 'market' economy.

State policies in the 1980s have been successful in attracting substantial amounts of foreign capital to Sri Lanka as a whole, through Colombo, and this has in effect industrialized Sri Lanka.[35] In the process Colombo has been re-incorporated into the circuits of transnational capital, making the city an important node in the world economy. The particular conjuncture in the world economy that provided for the industrialization of Sri Lanka has been much greater than just a decentralizing of production activity and recentralizing its command functions in the so-called global cities. The loosening grip of the core capitalist states, and cities, over the world-economy and the emergence of centres of capital accumulation in Asia provided an opportunity for more 'independent' economic development in Sri Lanka as well as in the various states of the region.

This economic 'success' has itself transformed Sri Lanka's orientation away from the West, particularly the UK and USA, towards east Asia and the immediate region of south Asia. Intranationally, most crucial was the disorientation of the capitalist planter class which had grown up under colonialism, investing in plantation crops complementary to their larger and dominant British counterpart.[36,37] The nationalization of plantations in 1976, and the severing of vestiges of colonial controls by making Sri Lanka a republic in 1972, weakened this partnership.[38] Free from its old British orientation, the United National Party which formed the government in 1977, principally looked towards the United States for help in reconstructing favourable conditions for capital in Sri Lanka and continued to depend on the World Bank and the International Monetary Fund for loans.[39] Yet capital for the expanding manufacturing sector has largely come from east Asia; Japan, Taiwan and South Korea.[40] The new British focus on Europe, the weakening of the US economy and power worldwide, the inflow of capital from South Korea and Taiwan, the importation of commodities from Japan, and the entry of banks from the Middle East, Malaysia and elsewhere have done much to reorient Sri Lanka towards east Asia.

Since then, industrial enclaves around Colombo have replaced British owned plantations as the main export earner in the country.[41] The flow of consumption goods has been reversed: from importing products from Western core states to the export of Sri Lankan products to them.[42] Instead of rice, Sri Lanka currently imports television sets, stereo sets and cars from Japan, Taiwan and South Korea. In place of her previous policy of strengthening the non-aligned movement by participating in international political efforts to repudiate cold-war politics, Sri Lanka currently spends her energy in building south Asian regional cooperation.[43] In this sense, state programmes have been successful in rebuilding a capitalist infrastructure in place of what was destroyed over decades by nationalist-socialist governments. Simultaneously, Colombo's orientation has changed and also diversified, although not towards the USA and New York as the government had initially desired.

What I am foregrounding here is not the irrelevance of broad frameworks, such as that associated with the 'global city' thesis, to explore the economic dimension of the transformations of cities during the 1980s. On the contrary, Sassen's study provides a particular conceptualization of the world system of cities in the world-economy, making a crucial difference between what she calls 'global cities', where global command functions are already in place or being located, and the rest. Yet the focus is on a particular set of cities located in capitalist centres, and processes that advance their command capability during a time of declining fortunes. In contrast, for Colombo, it is a test of how it will manage a situation of increasing fortunes, and its implications for the future. Hence this focus falls short of providing a framework in which to explore conditions governing the development of other cities. This requires a broader understanding, far beyond a binary opposition of 'global cities' and 'non-global cities'. Moreover although we have been focussing on cities in the world economy, this is only one system of cities among many, and most cities operate within a number of systems simultaneously.

## CULTURE, ETHNICITY, AND CLASS

Let me turn now to ethnicity, culture and the city. The main point I want to make here is that the discursive emphasis on cities, and increasingly on the larger ones, is especially a 'Western' pre-occupation. The notion that the city is a 'crucible of change' is a cultural product of western industrial societies.[44,45] The situation of societies in the world outside Europe and North America, where the majority of people are more intimately tied with the so-called rural, is quite different, even though we recognize that the largest cities in the world are, indeed, increasingly in the 'Third World'.

As in almost every major city,[46,47] Colombo represents a different ethnic and religious composition than the island as a whole. For example, the Singhalese, who are about 77 per cent of the total population of the island, and more than 90 per cent in the surrounding areas, are only about 50 per cent in the city (see Table 6.1). It also accommodates some smaller ethnic groups that are not widespread in the island. Nominal and real religious affiliations of inhabitants enhances this contrast between the city and the state (see Table 6.2). As in other postcolonial or postimperial cities,[48] Colombo too has ethnically defined 'quarters', for example the Tamil quarter of Wellawatta.

TABLE 6.1 *Ethnic Composition of Colombo, Colombo District, and Sri Lanka*
Population (per cent)

|  | Colombo city | Colombo District | Sri Lanka |
|---|---|---|---|
| Singhalese | 51.1 | 77.9 | 74.0 |
| Muslim | 18.8 | 8.3 | 7.1 |
| Sri Lankan Tamil | 17.2 | 9.8 | 12.6 |
| Indian Tamil | 6.6 | 1.3 | 5.5 |
| Burghers | 2.6 | 1.1 | 0.3 |
| Malays | 2.2 | 1.1 | 0.3 |
| Others | 1.5 | 0.5 | 0.2 |
|  | 100 | 100 | 100 |

*Source*: *Census of Population and Housing 1981* (Dept of Census and Statistics, Colombo, 1982).

TABLE 6.2 *Religious Composition of Colombo, Colombo District, and Sri Lanka*
Population (per cent)

|  | Colombo city | Colombo District | Sri Lanka |
|---|---|---|---|
| Buddhist | 43.2 | 70.8 | 69.3 |
| Muslim | 21.5 | 9.9 | 7.6 |
| Christian | 19.7 | 11.4 | 7.5 |
| Hindu | 15.4 | 7.6 | 15.5 |
| Others | 0.2 | 0.3 | 0.1 |
|  | 100 | 100 | 100 |

*Source*: *Census of Population and Housing 1981* (Dept of Census and Statistics, Colombo, 1982).

Although Colombo shares a number of characteristics in common with New York, largely due to its colonial past, the relationship of ethnicity to territory is quite different. In Sri Lanka the attachment of ethnic and cultural groups to their territory of origin is still strong and there is considerable movement of people between the city and ethnically specific rural areas, not least because distances are relatively small. In New York however, while there may be strong ties between ethnic groups and particular territories elsewhere in the world, the connection is more likely to be through memory. This makes the construction of ethnic identity in Colombo somewhat *extrovert*, as compared to New York which is largely *introvert*. By *extrovert* I refer to the outward orientation of particular cultural groups who maintain a continued physical relationship with their 'homeland' outside the city and its culture, as a primary source for the construction and replenishment of their identities. *Introvert*, on the other hand, implies that the primary focus is in the reproduction of a culture and identity within the city but with no direct relation to the place from which the cultural group originally stems.

As in the cultural and spatial practices of Puerto Rican immigrants in New York (Sciorra, this volume, chapter 3), most cultural groups in New York City construct their identities through the reproduction of a distant, sometimes completely unknown homeland and culture, often far from the place of origin. Not least because of distance and high costs of travel compared to the low income of immigrants, but even among the so-called middle classes, there is often little intention to return to their lands of origin. Hence people deploy a cultural past to inscribe a present, a difference in the city.[49] Most inhabitants of Colombo, however, continue to retain strong ties with their *gamas*, or 'home villages', to which they might return after retirement, loss of employment or illness. Their perception of Colombo is therefore largely as a place of temporary residence which, in some cases, is merely a desire, an image of 'the good life'. In these circumstances, there is little need or incentive to inscribe signs of their own ethnic identity.

The poorest strata of migrants to the city, who were largely 'coolies' for the colonial community, and later 'squatters' for urban planners, reproduce in Colombo the built forms and cultures with which they are familiar. They also, however, continue to have one foot in their home village. In Colombo, what are called 'shanties' by urban experts are in fact the urban production of rural house forms, employing similar methods of construction but with urban materials.[50,51] Despite aspirations to build a modern house in the city, they are prevented from doing so by prevailing market conditions.

The aspirations of the middle income strata, largely composed of state and private sector employees, are more ambivalent; mostly, they do not consider Colombo as their home. Middle-level government and private sector employees who occupy ethnically defined 'quarters' also maintain a strong relationship with their home village, one expression of which is building a house there. While in the city, the identity of Colombo's residents is more a result of their employment and economic status, frequently in some form of government service; their cultural identities are produced in Colombo both as part of their class and status identities through the continuing relationship with their home villages. This points to one of the most basic differences between Colombo and New York, namely that the former is the nation's capital city – with all that this implies for the presence of administrators, politicians and bureaucrats, and their effect on the social characteristics of the city – and New York is not.

The complex relationship between culture, territory and the city is expressed in the challenges to Colombo's postcolonial centrality within Sri Lankan society and space. Colombo's role as the principal site of political negotiation has sofar been a short-lived, postcolonial phenomenon. Despite the efforts of the 1977 government to reorganize Colombo's economic centrality within Sri Lanka, its political centrality has waned. This is understandable if we remember its colonial history as a capital imposed from outside to serve the colonizers' interests and not those of Lanka itself. Although the government has built a new government complex at Kotte, the locus of political negotiation, the principal place where political organizations resolve regional and cultural differences within broader national policies, has shifted not to Kotte but to rural areas.

It was only during the first three decades after independence in 1948 that Colombo enjoyed a position as the national centre in which political conflicts were resolved, constitutionally through voting and parliamentary debates, and by representatives sent to Colombo from electorates elsewhere. This was a particular form of decision-making developed in the 'West', known as 'democracy', institutionalized in Ceylon by the colonial government. The major political conflicts during colonial rule, including earlier revolts led by the Kandyan aristocracy and Buddhist clergy and later in the twentieth century socialist led strikes and plantation uprisings, have largely taken place in rural areas. The major political conflicts of the last two decades, one of which calls for a separate Tamil state, Tamil Eelam, led by the Liberation Tigers of Tamil Eelam, and the rebellions led by Janata Vimukti Peramuna between 1971 and 1989, have also taken place in rural areas outside Colombo. Instead of using 'democratic' means of debate and voting, both the Liberation Tigers and the Janata Vimukti Peramuna have resorted to armed struggle, inviting representatives of the state to their own territory to negotiate the outcome. They have thus devalued Colombo's role as the centre of national politics and government. It is the exacerbation of this culture-land-people conflict that is apparent in these two struggles.

It is therefore quite pertinent to ask to whose domain does Colombo belong? Like New York, Colombo was a European implant, a secular and essentially commercial city. It was race and ethnicity which provided the principal criteria for social stratification and segregation in the city, colonial masters from the indigenous population as well as white officials from white business and working classes.[52] Here, the British did not tolerate the close presence of other Europeans, the descendants of the former Dutch and Portuguese colonial communities, later identified as Burghers. In squeezing them out of the fort area – first constructed by the Portuguese and later modified by the Dutch in the mid seventeenth century – the British effectively divided the city into three ethno-racially defined components. In the words of Hulugalle, 'the Fort was chiefly occupied by British residents; the Pettah [area outside the fort] by the Dutch and the Portuguese; and [the 'outer Pettah'] by Singhalese, Tamils, and [Muslims]'.[53]

In the postcolonial city racial segregation has given way to increasing class stratification to which new ethno-linguistic and also caste divisions are being appended. By 'class', I refer to social groups defined primarily along economic and occupational lines vis-a-vis cultural groups defined along ethnic, religious and caste ones, with their accompanying values. This emphasis on class is certainly an outcome of the British colonial system with its large bureaucratic and socio-spatial segregation as well as the hierarchic industry-based culture. Since the colonial division of labour was organized around ethnicity and race, social stratification was based on a combination of race, ethnicity, and class. The economic and political elite who moved into powerful positions as postcolonial administrators in this capital city, and occupied prestigious places such as the suburb of Cinnamon Gardens left by the colonials, had more of an elite outlook than an ethnic or religious one. They were the 'old boys' of elite schools who shared the same culture, cultivating a value system which supported the view of the city as home, promoting secularization and undermining ethnic, religious and linguistic differences.[54,55] By the time of independence, according to Murphy,[56] most of the Ceylonese political, economic and cultural elite were more at home in England and the colonial world of Colombo than in the Singhalese or village-based world, that had once been their own. Hence Colombo is now largely the home of the power elites[57] and capitalists, also executives, bureaucrats and traders – though this is hardly the producer service class of New York. Those who occupy the top rungs of an economically and administratively defined hierarchy of inhabitants of Colombo are the ones who can afford to buy or invest in expensive real estate and share the similar 'introvert' values to those found in New York. That Colombo is still the 'capital' and there is no wholly commercially-oriented city (as represented by the relation of Washington to New York), probably dampens the development of market values in the city.

Elite attitudes towards culture, ethnicity and religion have produced confusion, especially since independence made Colombo more directly a part of larger Sri Lanka, as well as one of its cultural centres, primarily of 'Western' capitalist culture. Hence there is a desire among groups that are culturally and linguistically more close to the 'West', to reproduce ethnic and religious identities acceptable to the Sri Lankan public. This is particularly the case with politicians who, for example, now wear national dress for important political events.

Colombo's political and economic centrality, and cultural supremacy over the crown colony of Ceylon, was a result of British colonialism. It resulted from the incorporation of the island into Colombo's sphere of domination.[58] The independence of Ceylon has not only enabled indigenous religions to play a greater role in the society, but also revived historic ethno-religious centres – the Buddhists in Kandy and Anuradhapura and Hindus in Jaffna – producing a multicentered cultural arena. In this context new cabinet members made pilgrimages to the Temple of the Tooth Relic of Buddha at Kandy, and the first executive president, J.R. Jayawardana, following a former royal tradition chose to address the nation in 1978 from the *pattirippuwa*, the octagonal podium of the temple. Thus governments reinforced this multicentric cultural and spatial formation until the 1980s, even though Colombo still remained the principal centre of accumulation and 'Western' capitalist culture.[59]

The former president, Ranasinghe Premadasa (1988–1993), who was also prime minister under Jayawardena, attempted to promote the Buddhist temple at Gangaramaya to a 'national' level by, among other things, holding an annual procession with elephants, comparable to that held in Kandy. This is perhaps the latest and most profound example of mobilizing historic temples for political means in the vicinity of the municipal area. Attempts to advance Colombo to a significant ethno-religious centre have not been limited to Singhalese-Buddhists, but can also be seen among Hindu-Tamil elites and the upper middle classes of Colombo.[60] It is, therefore, the upper classes and politicians of all ethno-religious groups that have attempted to construct a more consciously 'postcolonial' cultural role for Colombo.[61] It is hardly necessary to point out that, for obvious reasons, there is no comparable resurgence of indigenous cultural expression, either in New York or its vicinity.

Moreover Colombo, where different ethnic groups meet and conflicts arise, is seen by them as common territory. Although the wave of anti-Tamil violence of 1983 caused a large migration of Tamils out from Colombo and its vicinity to the north, as well as emigration out of Sri Lanka, the continuing battle between Tamil separatists and the military, and among militant groups in the north and east, has caused many Tamils to return to the city. Here, the former separatist groups, for example, the Peoples Liberation Organization of Tamil Eelam, also use what they view as the 'neutral territory' of Colombo for political activity and organization.

For the most, the identities constructed in Colombo are not complete; they are only one of a number of other identities that exist in tension. As the majority of Tamils settled in Colombo seem not to favour a separate state, this would suggest that their economic and social identities are also important. Colombo is therefore much more a part of a larger single territory of Sri Lanka, a city that cannot be separated from the state in which it exists. Should there be a separate state of Tamil Eelam, this would oblige the Tamils of Colombo, like the transnational immigrants of New York, to provide a meaning for their lives and culture by referring to an unrelated land.

## THE CULTURE INDUSTRY AND TOURISM

The cultural industries of the 'global cities', particularly in New York, have developed, according to various scholars, mainly to serve the new professionals of the producer service sector as well as domestic and foreign tourists. In the newly independent states, a more general tourist industry can be seen as related. Although art markets and tourism are not new, they have expanded, especially from the 1970s. After the failure of policies directed at economic development, many Third World states developed tourism as a means of earning foreign exchange and balancing trade deficits.

Cultural industries, derived from a particular commodification of culture, have also emerged in Sri Lanka. The cultural artifacts exhibited for the consumption of mainly European and American tourists are located in the ancient metropolitical centres of, for example, Anuradhapura and Polonnaruwa, far away from Colombo which, in this respect remains a somewhat alien port-city of less interest. This exemplifies the stereotypical colonial and postcolonial split site, of the so-called 'traditional' and 'modern' city. This is certainly a departure from an earlier British representation of Sri Lankan cultures through dead artifacts in museums, whether in Colombo or London.[62] Here the Sri Lankan government has restored ancient capitals, historic and architecturally important buildings, as well as culturally significant landscapes in their original sites. Promoted as a foreign exchange earner in the 1970s, tourism has renewed an interest in the past, expressed in the establishment of an institution separate from the Archaeology Department, the Cultural Triangle, which refers to three former Lankan capitals, Anuradhapura, Polonnaruwa and Kandy. Significantly however, the production of this history and the organization of this particular culture industry takes place in Colombo, still reflecting its external origins.

**CONCLUSION**

I have drawn attention in this paper to the inadequacy of the available intellectual tools to address issues of postcolonial space, in this case, cities such as Colombo. It is clear that, apart from some commonalities, frameworks produced for the examination of New York are insufficient to make much sense of contemporary developments in Colombo, even though they do provide some significant insights. New York, as the leading economic centre of the leading economic power of this century and with its continuing colonial situation, is too unique to be directly relevant for the study of many other cities of the world. Despite significant developments in the capacity to explore cities as part of a larger spatial system, particularly through the concepts of the global or world city, much of this theory is inadequate to address the economic restructuring of cities outside the capitalist core, and concerning aspects other than the economic.

Moreover, 'cities of the world economy' is only one among many ways of representing systems of cities. Regional and national as well as cultural and political formations have come to play an increasingly significant role following the independence of a large number of states after the mid twentieth century. This is even more so after the end of the Cold War and the demise of US hegemony. As the case of Colombo demonstrates, it is these different spatial, cultural, and political contexts that produce differences among cities. This is not to reject the importance of studying larger structures of cities and commonalities among those, which, in an increasingly integrated world, are increasingly visible. Nonetheless, this global integration has itself produced more and new differences in seemingly similar spaces. Addressing more carefully the changes taking place in cities outside the capitalist core – which is hardly a unified entity – and relating those to phenomena in that core, however, requires the mediation of more conceptually sophisticated frameworks.

## NOTES

This chapter is based on research from my doctoral dissertation, 'Decolonizing "Ceylon": Society and Space in Sri Lanka', Binghamton University, State University of New York, 1995.

1.  J. Friedmann, 'The World City Hypothesis', *Development and Change*, 17:1 (1986), pp. 69–83.
2.  Saskia Sassen's paper in this volume largely draws on her book, *The Global City: New York, London, Tokyo* (Princeton University Press, 1991).
3.  Anthony D. King *Urbanism, Colonialism and the World Economy: Cultural and Spatial Foundations of the World Urban System* (Routledge, London, 1990), pp. 21–2, discusses typologies of colonial settlement.
4.  Although not central to the argument here, it is important to note the difference between those who were indigenous to Colombo, the *Marakkala* (Muslim) traders, and those indigenous to the rest of Lanka, the Singhalese and Tamil, prior to the Portuguese takeover of Colombo in the early sixteenth century (for example, Azeez, note 5). I employ Lanka to identify the island of Sri Lanka before its European colonization.
5.  Mareena Azeez, 'Early Muslim Settlements', in M. M. M. Mahroof et al. (eds), *An Ethnological Survey of Muslims of Sri Lanka: From Earliest Times to Independence* (Sir Razik Fareed Foundation, Colombo, 1986), pp. 17–42.
6.  I refer to the secession of the thirteen British North American colonies from direct British rule to form what became the United States of America. Wallerstein (see note 7) calls this process, 'settler decolonization'.
7.  Immanuel Wallerstein, 'Cities in Socialist Theory and Capitalist Praxis', *International Journal of Urban and Regional Research*, 8 (March 1984), pp. 64–72.
8.  Richard Sennett, *The Conscience of the Eye* (Knopf, New York, 1992), p. 53.
9.  Ronald J. Horvath, 'In Search of a Theory of Urbanization: Notes on the Colonial City', *East Lakes Geographer*, 5 (December 1969), pp. 69–82.
10.  Horvarth's (ibid.) 'intervening group' refers to a population imported from a third territory in the colonial system, such as the Indians in Uganda.
11.  W. Urwick, *Indian Pictures* (The Religious Tract Society, London, c.1888), p. 19.

12. H. A. J. Hulugalle, *Centenary Volume of the Colombo Municipal Council 1865–1965* (Colombo Municipal Council, Colombo, 1965), p. 167.

13. R. K. Home, 'Town Planning and Garden Cities in the British Colonial Empire 1910–1940', *Planning Perspectives*, 5 (1990), p. 4.

14. Seymour Mandelbaum, 'Thinking about Cities as Systems: Reflections on the History of an Idea', *Journal of Urban History*, 11:2 (February 1985), pp. 139–50.

15. Saskia Sassen (see note 2).

16. R. B. Cohen, 'The New International Division of Labor, Multinational Corporations and Urban Hierarchy', in Michael Dear and Allan J. Scott (eds), *Urbanization and Urban Planning in Capitalist Society* (Methuen, London, 1981), pp. 287–315.

17. Anthony D. King *Global Cities: Post-Imperialism and the Internationalization of London* (Routledge, London and New York, 1990).

18. Joe R. Feagin, *The Free Enterprise City: Houston in Political Economic Perspective* (Rutgers University Press, New Brunswick, N.J., 1989) illustrates how the city of Houston, begun by two New York realtors in 1836, grew into one of the largest cities in the USA.

19. T. G. McGee, *The Urbanization Process in the Third World: Explorations in Search of Theory* (Bell, London, 1971), has addressed the issue of the 'ruralizing' of 'Third World' cities by migrants (pp. 55–8).

20. Mary Karasch, 'Rio de Janeiro: From Colonial Port Town to Imperial Capital', in Robert J. Ross and Gerard J. Telkamp (eds), *Colonial Cities*, (Martinus Nijhoff, Dordrecht, 1985), pp. 123–54.

21. Nigel Harris, *The End of the Third World: The Newly Industrializing Countries and the Decline of an Ideology* (Pelican, London, 1986).

22. United Nations, *Economic and Social Survey of Asia and the Pacific 1992* Part I: *Recent Economic and Social Developments* (United Nations, New York, 1993). See in particular I:61. Also 'USA Becomes Sri Lanka's Major Market', *Economic Review*, 6 (April 1980), p. 22.

23. David J. Keeling, 'Transport and the World City Paradigm: An Agenda for Research', in Peter Taylor and Paul Knox (eds), *World Cities in a World System* (Cambridge University Press, 1995).

24. Japan's share of new investments in the bloc of Association of South East Asian Nations (ASEAN), peaked at 35.6% in 1987. The inflow of capital to these countries between 1985 and 1991 was: Japan 21.2%, Taiwan 17.6% Hong Kong 6%, South Korea 4.8%, Singapore 4.6%, Australia 1.2%, Europe 14.2%, USA 6.7%, Other 23.7% (see 'Investment in Asia: The Yen Block Breaks Open; *The Economist*, 8 May 1993: 70). By the end of the 1980s, however, Japan's rank in investments in this region had dropped significantly and by 1991 it accounted for only 15.2%, whereas Taiwan's share had increased to 15.4%, and that of all four 'dragons' to 29.5% (ibid.).

25. *The Economist*, 18 March 1993; and 8 May 1993, p. 72.

26. 'Taipei's Offshore Empire', *Far Eastern Economic Review*, 18 March 1993, pp. 44–5.

27. See United Nations (1993), particularly the increase in the category of 'others' in its tables (note 22 above).

28. J. Friedmann, 'Ten Years of the World City Hypothesis', in Peter Taylor and Paul Knox (eds), *World Cities in a World System* (Cambridge University Press, 1995). See also note 1.

29. Edward Soja, 'Economic Restructuring and the Internationalization of Los Angeles Region', in Michael Peter Smith and Joe R. Feagin (eds), *The Capitalist City: Global Restructuring and Community Politics* (Basil Blackwell,

Oxford, 1989), pp. 178–198. Soja has argued that in relation to Los Angeles, the restructuring of urban space during economic crises has involved both decentralization and recentralization (p. 185).

30. Norman I. Fainstein and Susan Fainstein, 'Regime Strategies, Communal Resistance, and Ethnic Forces', in Norman Fainstein et al. (eds), *Restructuring the City* (Longman, New York, 1983), pp. 245–67.

31. Ibid., p. 259.

32. After more than a decade, a Singaporean developer has recently proposed to build a speculative building taller than the Bank of Ceylon (Leonard Dissanayake, Urban Development Authority, personal communication).

33. The size of estates privately owned by Sri Lankans was restricted by a ceiling on landownership imposed in 1972. Company-held estates, foreign and local, were nationalized in 1976.

34. As in many other newly independent countries, nationalist and nationalist-socialist governments that were in power for two decades between the mid 1950s and mid 1970s used the state to combat national and foreign capital; they nationalized a large number of private enterprises and new industries were sponsored by the state. These governments not only imposed ceilings on the ownership of housing property (two units per family) and land (50 acres per person), but also on individual expenditure (Rs. 2500 a month) and the price of goods. Strong working class movements also won many rights during this period, including minimum wages.

35. According to economic indicators, the Sri Lankan economy has been growing at a rate of 4–8% during a period of economic recession in the 'advanced' West. The Gross Domestic Product grew at an annual average rate of 6% between 1978 and 1983, more than twice the average rate of 2.9% in the 1970s. After a dip in 1987, in 1990 and 1991 the growth rate has been 6.4% and 4.7%: see 'Sri Lanka: Country Profile 1992–93. Annual Survey of Political and Economic Background' (The Economist Intelligence Unit, London, 1992: World Microfilms), pp. 11, 14.

36. During colonial rule, instead of competing with British capital, as in India, nascent Ceylonese capitalists surreptitiously sneaked into the British dominated plantation economy and invested in crops such as coconut and rubber complementary to British coffee, tea and rubber plantations. This process produced a British oriented Sri Lankan capitalist class which peacefully coexisted with the British planters, and shared their values (see for example Roberts, note 37 following). Despite the postcolonial Sri Lankan refusal to participate in Cold War politics, and the attempt to construct an identity of non-alignment even under nationalist-socialist governments, Sri Lanka has always maintained a close relationship with Britain, particularly through the British Commonwealth.

37. Michael Roberts, 'The Two Facets of the Port City: Colombo in Modern Times', in Frank Broeze (ed.) *Brides of the Sea: Port Cities of Asia from the 16th Century to the 20th Century* (Hawaii University Press, 1989), pp. 173–87.

38. The relationship between Sri Lanka and Britain further deteriorated when the British Ambassador was expelled by the Sri Lankan government in June 1991 after accusing him of interfering in local government elections. The British government reacted by freezing new aid and restricting arms sales. In October 1992, however, a British Minister, Mark Lennox-Boyd, arrived in Sri Lanka on a fence-mending mission to meet the President.

39. For example the leading construction projects such as the Mahaweli river diversion project and the Million Houses Program were largely funded by US and European sources.

40.   Michael Davenport and Sheila Page, *Europe: 1992 and the Developing World* (Overseas Development Institute, London, 1991), p. 95.

41.   Ibid., p. 65.

42.   Sri Lanka's exports to industrialized states have increased three-fold during the last four years. In 1988, Sri Lanka exported goods worth Rs.27 billions to industrialized states, and in 1992 this increased to Rs.82 billions. The largest market for its products is the former largest exporter to Sri Lanka, the USA, which receives 45% of the goods going to 'industrialized' states (*Daily News*, 11 May, 1993). The five major importing countries for Sri Lankan products between 1987 and 1991 were the USA, Germany, the UK, Japan and Belgium; those exporting most to Sri Lanka were Japan, South Korea, India, Hong Kong and Taiwan (*Economist Intelligence Unit*, see note 35). See also, 'USA Becomes Sri Lanka's Major Market', *Economic Review*, 6 (April 1980), p. 22.

43.   Currently most attention from Sri Lanka and the south Asian states is received by the South Asian Association for Regional Corporation (SAARC), the members of which are India, Pakistan, Bangladesh, Nepal, Bhutan, Maldives and Sri Lanka. Ariya Abeysinghe in 'SAARC: From Dhakka to Colombo', *Economic Review*, 18 (1992), p. 25, argues that the success of the Association of South East Asian Nations (ASEAN) as an economically dynamic sub-region advanced an interest among some south Asian leaders to form the SAARC.

44.   T. G. McGee (1971) pp. 25, 58 (see note 19).

45.   Immanuel Wallerstein, 'Cities in Socialist Theory and Capitalist Praxis', *International Journal of Urban and Regional Research*, 8 (March 1984) pp. 64–72.

46.   Hugh Tinker, *Race in the Third World City* (Ford Foundation, New York, 1971).

47.   T. G. McGee, *The South-East Asian City: A Social Geography of the Primate Cities of South-East Asia*, (Praeger, New York, 1967).

48.   Anthony D. King, *Colonial Urban Development: Culture, Social Power and Environment* (Routledge and Kegan Paul, London and Boston, 1976).

49.   As inhabitants of a US colony, Puerto Rican immigrants in New York do have differences when compared to other immigrant communities.

50.   Senake Bandaranayake, 'Form and Technique in Traditional Rural Housing in Sri Lanka', *ASA* 1:1 (1978) pp. 9–13.

51.   T. G. McGee (1971) pp. 51–8 (see note 19).

52.   R. K. Home, p. 10 (see note 13). See also Nzegwu, ch. 5 this volume.

53.   H. A. J. Hulugalle, p. 25 (see note 12).

54.   Mary Anne Weaver, 'The Gods and the Stars – A Reporter at Large', *New Yorker*, 21 March 1988, pp. 40–58.

55.   M. Roberts (see note 37).

56.   Rhodes Murphy, 'Colonial Port Cities and the Reshaping of Asia: Colombo as Prototype', in Dilip K. Basu (ed.), *The Rise and Growth of the Colonial Port Cities in Asia* (University Press of America, Lanham, MD, 1985), pp. 19–21.

57.   Charles Wright Mills, *Power, Politics, and People: The Collected Essays of C. Wright Mills* (Oxford University Press, 1963).

58.   See Paul Bairoch, *Cities and Economic Development: From the Dawn of History to the Present*, trans. C. Braider (Chicago University Press, 1988): '[Colonial cities] became starting points for the network of railroads set up to facilitate the integration of the colonized territory into the world-economy' (p. 508). Colombo was therefore the node from which imperial power and European capitalist culture diffused over the territory, and channelled economic gains from, and domination over, the colony back to the metropole.

For McGee (note 47, p. 57), 'the colonial city was the *nerve centre* of colonial exploitation'.

59. Warwick Armstrong and Terence McGee, *Theatres of Accumulation. Studies in Asian and Latin American Urbanization* (Methuen, London, 1985).

60. Although certain Tamil militant groups have been fighting for over a decade to separate the north and the east of Sri Lanka, areas furthest from Colombo, into a new Tamil state, the Hindu temple of Wellawatta, Colombo has also acquired increased importance among Hindu temples of the island.

61. Such a drive has certainly produced tensions between the desire of the capitalist classes to incorporate cultural activity into the political economy centered upon Colombo, and the ethno-religious leadership which strives to preserve ethno-religious identities based upon historic centres located in what is presently the hinterland.

62. Henry W. Cave, *The Book of Ceylon: Being a Guide to its Railway System and an Account of its Varied Attractions for the Visitor and Tourist* (Cassell, London, 1908).

# 7

# Mombasa: Three Stages towards Globalization

Ali A. Mazrui

Mombasa is Kenya's second city. To that extent it may be worth considering whether second cities generally deserve a different theoretical framework. Do we need to study second cities as special entities? Is Montreal a second city to Toronto? Is Melbourne a second city to Sydney? Should we approach that subject in a different manner?

However Mombasa is also a kind of global city, though it is small as global cities go. It is the second largest city not only in Kenya but in East Africa. But we are still talking about a city of less than a million people. It is the largest seaport of the region, and one of the oldest urban centres in East Africa. It has been around for quite a while. The nature of its globalization had three, fairly distinct and different, phases. But within each of those phases, there were sub-phases or stages.

But first we must bear in mind that Africa as a whole is culturally intermediate between Europe and Asia. There are parts of Africa which are more 'occidental' than is any part of Asia. Then there are parts of North Africa and parts of South Africa which are more Europeanized than you will find anywhere on the Asian continent. Within the African continent you may find bits of Europe which are not reproduced anywhere in Asia. On the other hand there are parts of Africa which have more in common with Asia than have any parts of Europe. Islam for example, is older in parts of Africa than it is in most of Asia. And Christianity is older in Ethiopia than it is in most of western Europe. This essential intermediate position which Africa enjoys between the occident and the orient is captured in the story of Mombasa. This is part of the story of this African city on the Indian Ocean.

As we indicated, there are three distinct phases in the history of Mombasa as a city. The *Afro-Oriental* phase was the period when Mombasa was a small cultural arena where traditions from West Asia and South Asia

158

interacted with African traditions in search of new cultural configurations. This period covered several hundred years, during most of which Mombasa was known as *Mvita*.

The second historical period was the *Afro-Occidental* phase when Mombasa was at last 'discovered' by Europeans. First the Portuguese and later the British initiated the process of reorienting Mombasa away from its traditional links with Asia and more towards a new relationship with Europeans and with Western culture.

The third phase of Mombasa's history is currently in progress – the *Afro-global phase*, when the city feels the pull of both east and west. The old transition from being a city state to being the main port of a nation-state has now greater global repercussions for Mombasa and its people. Let us take each of these phases in turn.

## THE AFRO-ORIENTAL PHASE

Three interrelated factors conditioned the origins of the Afro-Oriental phase. One factor was that Mombasa lay in the path of the monsoon winds, and was therefore reachable by trading sailing ships from parts of Asia using those winds.[1] Secondly, Mombasa itself had a natural harbour which could accommodate those ships, as well as activate a nautical and ship-building tradition of its own. And thirdly, Mombasa was relatively near the Arabian peninsula and was soon to interact *culturally*, as well as *commercially*, with the land which gave birth to the Muslim religion. Mombasa became one of Islam's entry points into eastern Africa.

As a result of this configuration of factors, the *multiculturalization* of Mombasa began quite early. Consumption patterns felt the cultural influences which came with the trading traffic of the monsoons. From Arabia and other ports of Asia came expensive porcelain and plates, brass decorated wooden chests, silks and finery.[2] In East Africa these were sometimes paid for in ivory, copra and animal skins. There was also a limited trade in slaves.

At the more popular level of consumption culture, the Afro-Oriental phase of Mombasa's history produced the increasing use of seasoning and spices in the local cuisine. New spices were imported into Mombasa from Asia and innovative, syncretic and eclectic cuisine developed among the Coastal people generally, combining elements of African, Indian and Arab food cultures.

It was during the Afro-Oriental phase that rice became the staple diet of the people of Mombasa and the surrounding coastline. While the vocabulary of ordinary rice dishes remained completely African (*mpunga* for unhusked rice, *mchele* for uncooked rice and *wali* for cooked rice), dishes for special occasions had such borrowed words as *biriyani* and *pilau* from South Asia. On the other hand, the names of the individual spices used in preparing these quasi-Indian dishes were more likely to be words borrowed from Arabic rather than from any Indian language (*bizari* for curry powder and *thumu* for garlic, for example).

The Afro-Oriental phase also witnessed changes in the musical culture of Mombasa and into the coastal areas. In addition to the traditional African drums, the small Indian drum (*tabla*) found its way into the coastal range of musical instruments. In time the Arabian string instrument, the *Ud*, also entered Swahili culture. So did the dancing drums with small bells attached known as *matari*. Indeed, in some Islamic denominations at the Coast the *matari* were even used in the mosque in accompaniment to certain lively praise songs in honour of the Prophet Muhammad. (More traditionalist Muslim theologians strongly disapproved of the use of drums in the mosque or for any religious purpose).[3]

The flute in Coastal music was a child of all three traditions – African, Arab and Indian – reinforcing each other. But the 'Orientalization' of Mombasa music was still increasing.[4] Over time even the tunes of Swahili songs became strongly influenced by Arab music (especially Egyptian), on one side, and Indian music on the other. At its worst, some so-called Swahili composers simply plagiarized the music of some Indian songs and just substituted Swahili lyrics. Fortunately there always remained a hard-core Swahili tradition which tried to remain authentic against all comers from the Orient![5]

But the most profound changes which came from Asia into Mombasa concerned first *religion*, and secondly *language*. Islam arrived in Eastern Africa while the Prophet Muhammad was still alive. But Islam's first African landing-space was not Mombasa but a part of Ethiopia. Persecuted Muslims from Arabia arrived in Abyssinia in quest of asylum during the Prophet of Islam's own lifetime. It is because of that factor that some have argued that the *Hijjra* (migration for asylum) from Arabia to Africa was almost as early, and in a few respects almost as symbolic, as the Prophet's own *Hijjra* from Mecca to Medina. With the African *Hijjra* a seed was being planted which, by the end of the twentieth century, had turned Africa into the first continent to have an absolute Muslim majority.

Not long after the death of the Prophet Muhammad, Islam got to the part of eastern Africa which is now Mombasa. Mosques were being built in this part of East Africa before they were constructed in parts of what is now the Middle East. Islam in Mombasa is older than Islam in Istanbul and the rest of Turkey. It may be older than Islam in Islamabad and the rest of Pakistan. Is it older than Islam in parts of what is now the Arab world itself? Certainly parts of the Maghreb in North Africa (such as Morocco) were probably penetrated by Islam later than Mombasa, though much of this is in the arena of historical calculation rather than confirmation.

Before long the arrival of Islam in Mombasa and surrounding areas affected diverse areas of the cultural experience of the people.[6] Marriage and kinship relations were changed profoundly, as were the rules of inheritance and succession. African indigenous norms were often in competition with the Islamic rules. In some cases syncretism was the result; in others the indigenous norms still had an edge; but increasingly the Afro-Oriental phase of Mombasa's history witnessed the gradual triumph in precolonial Mombasa of the Islamic rules of marriage, kinship, inheritance and succession.

The arrival of Islam in Mombasa also had a profound impact on dress culture. The concept of *nakedness* was completely redefined for both men and women, with practical consequences for forms of attire for each gender. The *kanzu* entered the scene for men (the long outer garment) which subsequently became religion-neutral in Uganda where both Christians and Muslims accepted it as a kind of national dress. (In Kenya the *kanzu* was still associated with Muslims.)

In Mombasa the womenfolk developed the black *buibui* for outdoor use, intended not only to veil their faces but also to deny shape to their bodies. The *buibui* was worn by Muslim women of Mombasa only out of doors when they visited relatives or went grocery shopping. The shapelessness of the garment was part of Islam's quest for female modesty in public places. 'In public do not emphasize the curves! Conscience begins with avoidance of temptation!' This is a strong Islamic premise. It profoundly affected dress culture in Mombasa during the Afro-Oriental phase.

The arrival of Islam in Mombasa also affected architecture, initially with the minaret and the architectural culture of the mosque. The homes of the people of Mombasa increasingly felt the influence of Islamic conceptions of gender segregation, the courtyard, the use of tiles and clay in construction, and the place of prayer for women with the ablution washroom attached to it.

And then the winds of the western world were at last felt in Mombasa. East was East and West was West – but the twain were indeed about to meet in the African city of Mombasa.

## THE AFRO-OCCIDENTAL PHASE

In the process of the westernization or Occidentalization of Mombasa, there was always one Western power which was the epicentre. Again three phases are identifiable. There is the phase when Portugal was the western epicentre, virtually unchallenged. There was also the more comprehensive phase of European colonialism when Britain was the epicentre of the western presence in Kenya as a whole and in Mombasa. And thirdly, there is now the postcolonial phase when the epicentre of the western world as a whole is the United States of America – and Mombasa has inevitably felt that shift in power and influence.

Vasco da Gama was virtually the first European to disembark in Mombasa. That was in April 1498. The sailors of Mombasa and the rest of this African coast helped him in his efforts to find his way to Calicut in India. Although the people of Mombasa did not realize it at the time, Vasco da Gama was also preparing the ground for the Portuguese imperial incursion into eastern Africa. The Portuguese later came with warships and sought to build coastal African colonies to service their trading fleets in the Orient. In Mombasa they subsequently built Fort Jesus, a fortress to defend and monopolize the old harbour, and from which they sought to rule Mombasa and its environment.

How was Mombasa 'westernized' in this Portuguese phase? For one thing, architecture was partly influenced by the Portuguese as they built some of their own homes, which were emulated by the locals. The Portuguese language also had an impact on local languages. To the present day the Swahili words for slippers (*sapatu*), female undergarment (*shimizi*), a certain water kettle (*kindirinya*) are originally derived from the Portuguese language. The old Mombasa dialect even used the metaphor *mreno* (Portuguese person) to mean any kind of aristocrat.

Perhaps the most enduring cultural impact of the Portuguese was on the food culture of Mombasa, and subsequently of East Africa as a whole. Because of Portugal's links with the so-called New World of the Americas, the Portuguese in East Africa eventually brought maize and potatoes which assumed increasing importance in the diet of the local people. In time many of the indigenous people of the Coast (such as the Giriama) adopted *ugali* or maize-meal (powdered dry maize) as their staple food – a trend which subsequently spread to the hinterland of Kenya. The Waswahili of Mombasa continued to use rice as the staple, but they increased the use of potatoes as supportive diet and for minor meals of the day. Maize on the cob and *ugali* were also used for variation.

The Portuguese impact on the cuisine of Mombasa did not endure, except perhaps in the case of some desserts and puddings – an influence which was later reinforced by the British.[7]

Westernization under the Portuguese also meant the westernization of warfare for the first time in Mombasa. The use of gunpowder, cannons and guns entered a new phase in the city's history. Later on this became a case of 'nemesis' for the Portuguese – the use of western-style weapons to drive them out of Mombasa. This included the role of the Mazrui family in combating the Portuguese and finally driving them out of their fortress, Fort Jesus. Indeed the Mazrui family occupied the fort and ruled the Mombasa city-state from it, for about a hundred years from about the time of the French revolution in Europe.[8]

But clearly the most far-reaching period of the westernization of Mombasa was under British rule from the late nineteenth century until December 1963. British colonial policy for Mombasa was far more comprehensive than Portuguese. British policy included the building of primary and secondary schools for local children, the establishment of a legal system for the society as a whole, the demarcation of Kenya as a future nation-state and an elaborate system of accountability within a global British Empire.

Within every twenty-four hours the children of Mombasa crossed civilizations several times. They might speak Swahili (or Kiswahili) at home, take Arabic or Islamic lessons at the mosque, watch Indian films some weekends and be forced to speak English all the time at school.

Of these several civilizations under the British Raj, there was no doubt which was in the ascendancy in Mombasa. Western civilization exerted increasing influence at school, at the Kilindini harbour, in the new films at local cinemas, and as a direct result of the influence of British power.

The English language was implanted to a degree that the Portuguese language never was during Portugal's occupation of Mombasa. A school syllabus for British-style education was established linked to an empire-wide system based on examinations set by the University of Cambridge in England. School teachers in Mombasa included increasing numbers of men and women from the United Kingdom sent out to serve the British empire. Of course the white missionaries were also active, seeking to spread the Christian gospel through missionary schools, church services, and medical clinics bearing the cross.

The British helped to spread literacy not only in the English language but also in select indigenous languages in what became Kenya. In Mombasa the relevant indigenous language was Swahili (or Kiswahili). In the first half of the twentieth century newspapers began to appear in both languages in Mombasa. The *Mombasa Times*, published daily in English, was the most influential newspaper in the city. It was edited and run by Europeans. But other racial groups in Mombasa (African, Arab and Indian) developed weekly or monthly publications of their own in diverse languages. The languages were diverse, but the tradition of newspapers and weekly periodicals in *any* language reflected a process of westernization.

Under British rule Kenya became a white-settler colony. The colonial power encouraged large-scale white immigration to farm in the very fertile soils of what were overtly called 'the white highlands'. Although these highlands were several hundred miles away from Mombasa, there is no doubt that the transformation of Kenya into a white-settler colony had profound implications for Mombasa.

Although Mombasa was an ancient city, it was bypassed in order to build the capital of Kenya closer to the 'white highlands'. Nairobi was rapidly developed from a minor train-stop on the Uganda railway into a growing African metropolis. By the second half of the twentieth century Nairobi had outstripped Mombasa in size. What saved Mombasa from shrinking into insignificance was its continuing strategic value as the most important port in East Africa, regardless of where the Kenya capital was.

Mombasa and other parts of Kenya got westernized in more basic ways as well. Dress culture among the younger generation borrowed more and more from the West. Manners, etiquette and even forms of boasting became influenced by western norms. As John Plamenatz the late Oxford philosopher, once put it 'The vices of the strong acquire some of the prestige of strength'.[9]

Above all the colonial mentality looked towards the imperial metropole for a general standard of life and culture. Caliban sought the guidance of Prospero. The British way of life was for a while the ultimate standard of civilization to the colonized. Mombasa was in the shadow of this mental dependency.

And then the emulation of British ways included British standards of democratic life. Colonial rule was undemocratic – the imperial power was hoist with its own petard. Nationalists in Mombasa and other parts of Kenya started demanding 'One Man, One Vote' (*sic*). British standards of democracy by the second half of the twentieth century meant universal adult suffrage, leading on to full independence. By mid-December 1963, Mombasa was the proud port of independent Kenya. The old style colonialism was over.

It was during this postcolonial period that the epicentre of westernization in Mombasa shifted from a British focus to an American focus. The shift was neither sharp nor total. After all Britain and the United States were themselves close allies and were both English-speaking powers. Nevertheless, in the postcolonial world in Kenya capitalism mattered more than colonial ties. And the leader of the capitalist world was obviously the United States.

American influence in determining the prices of Kenya's agricultural products (especially coffee and tea); American influence with the World Bank and the International Monetary Fund; and American influence among the community of aid-donors generally contributed to this shift from Britannic westernization to Americo-centric westernization. This is quite apart from the expanding trade, aid and investment relations between the United States and Kenya more directly.

Further American influence came through the increasing impact of American music, television programmes, cinema shows and magazines which were making major cultural inroads into Mombasa and Nairobi. Young people also responded to American dress culture – with special reference to jeans and T-shirts. The American genius in fast food also affected parts of Mombasa street and restaurant culture. The hamburger had arrived on the African side of the Indian Ocean. So had Kentucky Fried Chicken or its equivalent. Competing with African, Arab and Indian snacks of old, there were now these new fast mini-meals from the food culture of the United States. Popular cuisine among the young in Mombasa was partly getting Americanized. The United States was clearly the new epicentre of this new burst of postcolonial westernization.

From this westernizing phase of Mombasa's historical experience (the Afro-Occidental phase) is an easy transition to the Afro-globalist phase. It is to this even more wide-ranging stage of Mombasa's historical evolution that we must now turn.

## THE AFRO-GLOBAL PHASE

Three forces contributed to the globalization of Mombasa – war, tourism and international politics. The wars ranged from World War II to the Mau Mau insurrection in Kenya. Tourism went back to the days of Theodore Roosevelt. International politics included the repercussions of the Cold War.

There were earlier stages in the globalization of Mombasa; and of course the first two phases in the history of Mombasa (oriental and occidental) were themselves stages towards a global scale. But there were other trends in the process. Mombasa as a major seaport acquired additional significance during World War II. It became important both in the defeat of Italy in the earlier phases of the war and in transporting African troops to Burma in the war against Japan. Mombasa was also important simply in relation to the flow of goods between Africa and Europe during that critical war-time period.

It is ironic that the ancient name of Mombasa was *Mvita*, meaning Isle of War, since it was fought over so often because of its strategic significance. In the 20th century Mombasa once again became *Mvita*, the Isle of War, but in a vastly different sense. It has been estimated that about five hundred thousand (half a million) African soldiers from British colonies alone served in World War II. They fought not only in the Horn of Africa and North Africa but also in Italy and Axis-occupied ports of the fertile crescent. Africa's heaviest casualties were in the war in Burma against the Japanese. A large proportion of those African soldiers sailed from Mombasa.

Almost none of those African soldiers who fought in World War II were ever allowed to rise above the rank of sergeant. They almost always had higher superior white officers. And while the contributions of Australians, New Zealanders and other Commonwealth combatants have repeatedly been celebrated (including during the 1994 D-Day extravaganza), very little tribute has ever been paid to the African heroes and martyrs of World War II. Mombasa was to many of those African soldiers what Portsmouth was to the soldiers who invaded Normandy on 6 June, 1944 – a point of departure on a momentous military mission.

When Italy's East African empire of Ethiopia and Eritrea was over-run by the British, Mombasa was used to accommodate many Italian prisoners of war, both men and women. Some of the earliest inter-racial dating experienced by the local African population in Mombasa was the dating between Mombasa men and the Italian women detained in Mombasa during World War II. That inter-racial dating must itself be counted as a stage in the globalization of Mombasa. Before World War II, sex between blacks and whites in Kenya was a crime. Curiously enough, inter-racial dating during the World War also included some Polish refugees temporarily encamped in Mombasa.

Later on Mombasa acquired a new value in relation to the Suez Canal. After World War II, Egyptian nationalists were putting increasing pressure on the British to vacate their military base near the Suez Canal. After the Egyptian revolution of 1952 these nationalist pressures against the British military presence in Egypt became irresistible. Mombasa in combination with Aden in Yemen acquired additional significance in British strategic calculations. The two ports constituted the fall-back position after the loss of the Egyptian military prize.

Mombasa was getting absorbed into wider and wider strategic politics of the world. Unfortunately for British planners, the year of the Egyptian revolution was also the year of the outbreak of the Mau Mau war in Kenya. Both events unleashed forces which evicted the British from both countries. The British were subjected to the same militant fate in Aden.

The Mau Mau war in Kenya was itself a globalizing experience. It gave the colonial politics of Kenya much more publicity than they had ever had before. And the name 'Jomo Kenyatta' became a household name in distant parts of the world. Although the war was fought mainly in central Kenya rather than at the Coast, it did of course affect Mombasa and must be seen as part of the wider forces of globalization at work. Of course, the British authorities also used Mombasa to bring in British troops, planes and ammunition for the war against the Mau Mau nationalists. In the end it was a victory of the vanquished. The Mau Mau were defeated militarily but their political cause of Black rule in Kenya prevailed. Kenya became independent in December 1963.

After Jimmy Carter was elected president of the United States in 1976, Mombasa acquired military significance to the United States for a while. The American concept of a 'rapid deployment force' in defence of the oil routes and the oil resources included a cluster of seaports which could be used by US ships either for refuelling or for 'morale-boosting' holidays for the servicemen and women who were guarding the approaches to the Red Sea and the Gulf. Before long the beginnings of an American military base began to be established in Mombasa. American naval ships stopped periodically during the 1980s and American serviceman disembarked. The shops, nightclubs, hawkers and whorehouses learnt the skills of catering for visiting American servicemen. Mombasa was absorbed into the more militarized side of the cold war.

Tourism as a globalizing experience in Kenya is, in a sense, older than war. In the first half of the century Mombasa was the main point of entry for all overseas tourists, but the Coast of Kenya was only a minor part of the attraction of the country at that stage. The big attraction for European and North American tourists in the first half of the century was the great *safari* – travelling into the bush tracking wild animals either to photograph them or to kill them. These were the days of animal trophies – the most ambitious being leopard skins, elephant tusks or the head of a lion. The white hunters came through Mombasa and left with their trophies from Mombasa. It was of course an age before the tourist airbus. One of the earliest tourists in Kenya this century was Theodore Roosevelt (1858–1919) of American presidential fame (26th president of the US, 1901–09). He came and left through Mombasa.

In the second half of the twentieth century Mombasa became more than simply a point of entry for tourists. The port and the Kenya Coast as a whole became a major part of the attraction of the country. Some of the major beach hotels were built in Mombasa – as were expensive beach chalets for longer-term rent. The safari and the wild beasts were still a major part of Kenya's tourist package, but the beaches and Mombasa's own very distinctive cultural mixture had become independent additional attractions for visitors. By the 1980s hunting in Kenya was outlawed – but the old style safari hunters had become only a tiny percentage of the tourists in any case.

With the coming of the jet age, Mombasa's importance as a point of entry for tourists had drastically declined – but Mombasa's significance itself as a major tourist attraction had risen dramatically. The globalization of Mombasa has continued unabated. The question arises whether the tourist globalization of Mombasa neutralized the previous Afro-orientalization of the city. It is true that the westernization had itself inevitably been partly at the expense of both African and Oriental ways. The new globalization is an ally of westernization, and both have continued to corrode both African and Oriental legacies in Mombasa.

As the city has learnt to cater for western tourists and for American service personnel, the pleasures of the evening have become increasingly westernized. More nightclubs, dance halls, bars, and western-style restaurants have opened. The old rhythms of African drums, the Arab *ud* and the Indian *tabla* and *sitar* have been giving way to the aggressive guitars and drums of the western world. Indeed, African music itself has become substantially westernized in the last twenty years.

One cruel irony is whether what would otherwise have been the relentless westernization of Mombasa even in the process of globalization is now being slowed down by the fears generated by the Acquired Immune Deficiency Syndrome (AIDS). Certainly sexual liberation as an aspect of westernization has become more circumspect in Mombasa in the 1990s. And the tourists who used to come from western Europe in search of 'white beaches, the blue ocean and black sex' have become much more careful about this third component. So have their former black partners, who regard white folks as the original carriers of AIDS into Africa.

It is one of the ironies of history that cultural westernization in Mombasa is being slowed down partly because of the fear of AIDS. The African and Oriental cultures of Mombasa may be the accidental beneficiaries of a terrible disease. The Bible used historical floods and famines to tell a moral story. One day historians may use AIDS to draw definitive cultural conclusions.

When did international politics begin the globalization of Mombasa? Again this is a process which inevitably includes some of the previous phases of Mombasa's historical experience. Certainly the anti-colonial struggle in Kenya became an experience in international politics. The name of Tom Mboya, the most prominent Kenyan politician after Jomo Kenyatta in the 1950s, became widely known in many circles in the United States as well as Great Britain. He lectured widely in both countries in defence of the Black nationalist cause in Kenya. Mboya was definitely an eloquent illustration of how internationalism contributed to globalization.

Even his assassination in 1969 in Nairobi was itself a form of internationalization, although his assassins were local. He was an important African friend of Martin Luther King Jr. who had himself been assassinated. In the early 1960s I had met Dr King in New York City. I already knew Tom Mboya personally at the time. Ironically, my only conversation with Martin Luther King had in fact been, in part, about Tom Mboya. Before the end of the decade both Mboya and King had fallen victim to an assassin's bullet.

In the 1950s Mombasa was important in Mboya's rise to national prominence in Kenya. He was a trade union leader who got involved in the vital dock strike in Mombasa of the 1950s. His combined skills of aggression and negotiation propelled him to national visibility. It was from within the ranks of trade unionism that he then entered wider anti-colonial politics.

After independence the cold war also became a major factor in the globalization of Mombasa. Although Jomo Kenyatta had been denounced by the British as 'leader into darkness and death', and had suffered as a 'Mau Mau' detainee, he emerged from prison ready to forgive and forget. He became one of Kenya's leading Anglophiles, and took the country firmly into the capitalist camp in the cold war.

However Mombasa as a port was serving more than just Kenya. Uganda under Milton Obote attempted a 'Move to the Left' ideologically and had tense relations with Kenya. Uganda needed Mombasa for its own exported goods and the goods it was importing from outside. Its relations with Kenya sometimes tempted Uganda to explore alternative points of access to the sea. Unfortunately for Uganda, Mombasa was still by far the best outlet to the sea.

Uganda under Idi Amin was, in domestic policy, capitalist; but its foreign policy became increasingly anti-western and pro-Soviet. There were also problems with the Kenyan government, which sometimes included Kenyan threats to withhold the port services of Mombasa from Uganda. Here a paradox emerged. Mombasa's role as a service for East Africa as a whole was sometimes compromised by the wider regional and global politics. The cold war cast its shadow on Mombasa directly and through inter-state rivalries in East Africa.

Globalization of Mombasa also occurred through the United Nations and its agencies. Certainly the United Nations High Commission for Refugees (UNHCR) needed Mombasa for some of the problems of refugees from Somalia – including refugee camps in Mombasa. The United Nations' Environmental Programme (UNEP) had its *global* headquarters in Nairobi. UNEP's concerns included oceanic ones in Mombasa and elsewhere at the Kenya Coast. The location of UNEP in Nairobi as the first UN agency to have its headquarters in Africa inevitably increased UNEP's consciousness of its own immediate environment, including the debate about pollution in the Indian Ocean from Kenya. How culpable is Mombasa in relation to the pollution of the sea?

Africa's internationalization has also meant inter-Africanization. During World War II Mombasa experienced what were perhaps its first visitors from West Africa – the soldiers from the Gold Coast (now Ghana). Mombasa also experienced white South Africans during World War II in uniform, on their way to battle areas elsewhere. The inter-Africanization of East Africa has reached new levels since the 1940s. Since Kenya has become one of the leading diplomatic and conference centres of Africa, Mombasa has inevitably been a pan-African beneficiary.

Paradoxically, Afro-globalization has also included a partial return to Afro-Orientalization. Islam in Mombasa in the 1990s became more politically radicalized, echoing tendencies towards Islamic militancy elsewhere in the world.

But no city exists independently of the state and nation to which it belongs. The state to which Mombasa now belongs is of course Kenya. While the City has gone through its three stages towards globalization, Kenya as a state has had a somewhat different transition. The national and state dilemmas have had implications for Mombasa. It is to this wider context of *Kenya* and its orientation that we must now turn.

## THE NATIONAL CONTEXT: BETWEEN THE ATLANTIC AND THE INDIAN OCEAN

Kenya is an *Indian Ocean power* (through Mombasa) which has been behaving as if it were an *Atlantic power* (through Nairobi). Perhaps of all

African countries Kenya evolved the most wide-ranging relationships with the leading countries of western Europe and North America. For a while Kenya was the darling of the West, not only because of its tourist attractions, but also because of its strategic importance. Ironically, Kenya's strategic value to the West was precisely because Kenya was an Indian Ocean power. It was located along one of the great sea routes of the world, and was also in close proximity to the oil reserves of the Middle East. It was a potential staging place for the rapid deployment of western forces in a critical area of the globe. It was vital that Kenya remained pro-western.

A paradox emerged. While the West flirted with Kenya because of its location on the Indian Ocean, western flirtations turned Kenya's eyes away from the Indian Ocean. The country became excessively western-oriented, and inadequately attentive to its Asian neighbours. The West embraced Kenya partly because the West valued the Indian Ocean; Kenya embraced the West and turned its back on the Indian Ocean. Mombasa was part and parcel of the paradox.

But now the honeymoon is over. Kenya's intimate embrace of the western world at the expense of all other relationships has at last to be reviewed. Kenya is a country which in the past was lukewarm about pan-Africanism, hostile to the People's Republic of China, profoundly distrustful of the Arabs, indifferent towards India, and cool towards the Soviet Union (or Russia). For the bulk of the first twenty-five years of the Kenya African National Union (KANU), Kenya's most intimate friends were the western powers (and Israel); and Kenya was often amply rewarded by these particular friends.

Now that the cold war is over, the West has itself reviewed its own relationship with Kenya. Many western countries have decided that they no longer have to humour the present KANU government simply because it is anti-communist. Western governments have at long last become friends of the cause of democracy in Kenya. Their pressures helped to force President Daniel arap Moi to accept the principle of multipartyism, though we must not underestimate the prior impact of domestic democratic pressures on President Moi's change of mind.

Whether KANU or some other party comes to power after the multiparty election, it is time that Kenya too embarked on a fundamental review of its wider global options. Just as Kenya is now of lesser strategic value to the West with the end of the cold war, so should the West become less fundamental to Kenya's global design in the wake of those wider developments.

On the ocean front in Mombasa, Kenya faces the Asian world rather than the European. Until the 1990s Kenya has been far more sensitive to the imperatives of history (the history of being an ex-colony of Britain) than to the imperatives of geography (proximity to Asia and the Middle East). It is time to redress this imbalance between postcolonial historical continuities and the older dictates of geographic proximity. First, Kenya has to recognize the fact that it is indeed an Indian Ocean power. In the past Kenya has tended to regard its own South Asian population at home as a historic liability (Indian immigrants in colonial Kenya go back beyond the building of the railway line to Uganda at the beginning of the century). Kenya should now learn to recognize its Asian population not as a politico-historical liability, but as an econo-geographical asset. In population India is the second largest country in the world after China – and therefore destined to become a superpower in the future. Pakistan is one of the leading Muslim and Third World powers on the world stage. Can Kenya work out a special relationship with both India and Pakistan? Kenya's Asian population can help forge economic, technological and educational ties.

The Kenya Coast is so culturally Indianized that the food culture of the Waswahili uses a lot of Indian spices, the music of the Coast Province shows evidence of South Asian impact, and Indian films are heavily patronized on the Kenyan Coast. This cultural influence of South Asia in Kenya could be converted into diplomatic currency in Kenya's economic relations with India, Pakistan and Bangladesh. Trade between Kenya and those countries could also be enhanced if careful thought was given to the nature of economic exchange for the future. We could learn a lot about intermediate technologies from our South Asian neighbours.

## KENYA AND THE ARABS

The KANU government's history of anti-Arabism has been even more costly to the country. Kenya's pro-Zionist orientation was often excessive and unnecessarily extreme. Arab travellers were often subjected to humiliating visa and customs policies. And yet arguably Kenya could have been the most attractive country for Arab investment in the whole of Black Africa. It is geographically close to the Arab world; it shares borders with two members of the Arab league (Sudan and Somalia); Kenya is itself the most stable country in Eastern Africa; it has a culturally Arabized population among its citizens (the Waswahili, the Somali and the other Muslims of Kenya); it has been economically prosperous since independence; it has exported both skilled and semi-skilled human power to the Arab world since its independence (including a former Kenyan Ambassador to Zaire who later became the Ambassador of the Sultanate of Oman to the People's Republic of China).

Kenya could easily have become a major magnet of Arab money had the KANU government not been so disproportionately pro-Zionist. Fences have been partly mended since the mid 1980s, but Kenya-Arab relations could do with a lot of improvement. Kenya's pro-Zionism was once so extreme that Kenya became the only Black African country which was a target for so-called 'Arab terrorism'. The Norfolk Hotel in Nairobi was bombed by an outraged Arab. Kenya was perceived as an ally of Israel militarily.

Future Kenyan governments will have to review their relations with the Arab world as a whole. In population the bulk of the Arab world is within Africa. The largest Arab country in population is Egypt, a fellow member of the Organization of African Unity (OAU). The largest country in Africa in square miles is Arabised Sudan, with which Kenya shares a border. Kenya's armed struggle for independence under Mau Mau overlapped in time with Algeria's armed struggle for independence under the National Liberation Front. And Algeria is an important member of both the OAU and the League of Arab States. Just as the concept of *Eurafrica* makes sense in Europe's special relationship with African states, so should the concept of *Afrabia* make sense in the context of the history and geography of African-Arab relations. Kenya has been a key country in the partnership of *Eurafrica*. Kenya could also be a key country in the solidarity of *Afrabia*. Kenyan goods, Arab oil and petro-dollars could do business with each other under more enlightened leadership from Nairobi.

## KENYA, CHINA AND JAPAN

China probably invented tea. Our Swahili word *chai* is, in all likelihood, Chinese in its ancestry. Will we be selling more Kenyan tea to China in the years ahead? It sounds like taking coal to Newcastle, or palm-dates to Muscat, Oman. But the issue simply dramatizes the immense potentialities of the Chinese market for Kenyan products. The Chinese have begun to diversify their tastes and consumption patterns – even to the extent of experimenting with new varieties of tea (Indian tea as well as Chinese). Some meat products and canned tropical fruit may also have a significant potential market in the People's Republic of China. On a visit to Beijing in the 1980s I was astonished by the number of businessmen and advertisers I met.

For at least two decades the KANU government treated the People's Republic of China with greater suspicion than was shown by the majority of western states towards China. The Kenyan government was often more anti-communist than western countries were. Kenyan courts still tend to regard works by Mao Tse-tung as 'subversive literature'. In a backstreet of Nairobi I once saw an exceptionally beautiful and elegantly bound edition of Mao's works in a dustbin. As a scholar I was strongly tempted to rescue that edition from the trashbin and take it to a library where it really belonged. But as a citizen I was reluctant to break the law, although I regarded the law as both unjust and absurd. In the end the citizen in me triumphed over the scholar on that particular occasion. With great reluctance I let Mao's works rot among the garbage in the backstreets of Nairobi – and walked away in painful ambivalence.

Even in China only a minority may still believe in Maoism, although many more continue to admire the man's contribution to the history of China and the world. A future Kenyan government has to recognize that one need not ban a book simply because one disagrees with it. A future Kenyan government may also have to be more diplomatic and considerate in its treatment of the People's Republic of China.

Kenyan businessmen are already eager to do business with Japan if at all possible. The next Kenyan government should go further than that. It should encourage some Kenyans to study Japan as a model of modernization and development. Here is one non-western country which has taken on the West at its own technological game – and given the West a run for its money. What is there in Japanese culture which permitted custom and tradition to be major engines of modernization? The next Kenyan government should encourage research into 'the culture of modernization and development'. If the Japanese could creatively and selectively learn from the western world, can Africa selectively and creatively learn from the Japanese? The Koreans have learnt from the Japanese. Is Kenya likely to become Africa's South Korea?

## BETWEEN GLOBALISM AND PAN-AFRICANISM

As for Kenya's relation with the rest of Africa, this has had a particularly strange dialectic. In many matters Kenya has been more globalist than pan-African. It has hosted such major global assemblies as that of women in 1985 and major international developmental conferences of the World Bank and the International Monetary Fund. But Nairobi has not been in the forefront as a host to the Organization of African Unity. Nairobi is the global capital of the United Nations Environmental Programme. It is also the African capital of the World Council of Churches through its affiliate, the All-Africa Conference of Churches. But Nairobi has hesitated about being the African capital of purely African organizations or activities. The headquarters of the Organization of African Unity are in Addis Ababa, Ethiopia; those of the African Development Bank are in Abidjan, Côte d'Ivoire; the headquarters of the Association of African Universities are in Accra, Ghana; the headquarters of the Africa Leadership Forum are in Ota, Nigeria. Nairobi is the most accessible capital in Black Africa, but it has not tried very hard to be the headquarters of major pan-African activities. In the first twenty-nine years of its postcolonial life, Kenya has at times tried to be globalist; but it has not tried hard enough to be Pan-African.

Kenya's virtue of globalism has been flawed by its excessive preoccupation with the western world. Kenya's neglect of pan-Africanism has been ameliorated by the respect in which Kenya's two presidents have been held as elder statesmen in a continent which is culturally sensitive to the elder tradition (*heshima ya uzee*). Both the late Mzee Jomo Kenyatta and President Daniel arap Moi have a record of earnest mediation in inter-African disputes – Zaire in the 1960s, Angola in the 1970s, Uganda in the 1980s, Mozambique and Somalia in the 1990s. The efforts by Mzee Kenyatta and President Moi to reconcile warring Africans have seldom been successful, but it is to the credit of the two presidents that they have been prepared to try. Kenya's Pan-African balance-sheet may be in the red, but our two presidents' roles as mediators are on the credit side of Kenya's Pan-African account.

As for the sad disintegration of the East African Community, there is enough blame to go around among the three old members – Tanzania, Uganda and Kenya. Charles Njonjo is widely regarded as the person who was responsible for the final act of destruction, the *coup de grâce*. It is true that Mr. Njonjo was no friend of the concept of an East African Community, but by the mid-1970s the Community had been greatly undermined and damaged by the policies of Tanzania, Uganda, as well as Kenya. The region as a whole remains guilty of having destroyed what stood a chance of becoming the most successful case of regional integration in the entire world. Can the East African community be revived before the end of the 20th century?

## CONCLUSION

But as Kenya tries to restore balance in its pan-African policies, and attempts to re-establish its credentials as an Indian Ocean power through Mombasa, what is to happen to its special relationship with the North Atlantic? Kenya still has many friends in the western world. The number of supporters it may have lost by becoming less strategically valuable to the West may be compensated by the new friends Kenya will make as it becomes truly democratic. In December 1991 I was privileged to meet the Prime Minister of Norway, Ms Gro Harlem Brundtland. Although diplomatic relations between Norway and Kenya were indeed broken, she emphasized to me that it was Nairobi which had decided on the diplomatic break. 'Norway believes in a democratic Kenya, not in isolating Kenya'. President Daniel arap Moi later capitulated to international and domestic pressures – and accepted the principle of multiparty politics. While Kenya may lose strategically-conscious westerners among its old partners, it may gain democratically-conscious westerners among its new friends.

Kenya may consolidate its role as an Indian Ocean power through Mombasa – without losing all the western gains it made when it behaved like an Atlantic power through Nairobi. The new equilibrium can indeed be accomplished. But it will need a new political will, a greater sense of history and a deeper sensibility to geography.

Much older than Kenya as a country is of course Mombasa as a city. Kenya is a 20th century political entity; Mombasa is a phenomenon of at least a millennium. Just as Mombasa is an ancient city while Kenya is a young nation, Mombasa is a global city while Kenya is still grappling with its basic dilemma between the geographical contiguities of the Indian Ocean and the historical continuities of the Atlantic legacy.

## NOTES

1.  See N. Chittick and R. I. Rotberg (eds), *East Africa and the Orient* (Africana Press, New York, 1975); also see B. A. Datoo, 'Influence of Monsoons on Movements of Dhows along the East African Coast', *East African Geographical Review*, vol. 12 (1974), pp. 23–33.
2.  See, for example, C. Sassoon, *Chinese Porcelain in Fort Jesus* (National Museum of Kenya, Mombasa, 1975).
3.  See R. Skene, 'Arab and Swahili Dances and Ceremonies', *Journal of the Royal Anthropological Institute* (London), vol. 47 (1917), pp. 413–34.
4.  See, T. O. Ranger, *Dance and Society in Eastern Africa, 1890–1970: The Beni Ngoma* (Heinemann, London, 1975).
5.  See, for example, J. de V. Allen, 'Ngoma: Music and Dance' in Mtoro bin Mwinyi Bakara and J. W. T. Allen (eds), *The Customs of the Swahili People: The Desturi za Waswahili* (University of California Press, Berkeley, CA, 1981), pp. 233–46.
6.  See, for example, R. L. Pouwels, *Horn and Crescent: Cultural Change and Traditional Islam on the East African Coast, 800–1900* (Cambridge University Press, 1987).
7.  See J. Strandes, *The Portuguese Period in East Africa* (East African Literature Bureau, Nairobi, 1961).
8.  See also G. A. Akinola, 'The Mazrui of Mombasa', *Tarikh*, vol. 2 no. 2 (1968), pp. 26–40, and C. R. Boxer and C de Azevedo, *Fort Jesus and the Portuguese in Mombasa 1593–1929* (Hollis and Carter, London, 1960).
9.  John Plamenatz, *On Alien Rule and Self-Government* (Longmans, London, 1960), p.111.

See also:

*   Allen Armstrong, 'Desperate Measures in an African City', *Town & Country Planning*, vol. 55 (October 1986), pp. 286–7.
*   Pauline Halpern Baker, *Urbanization and Political Change: The Politics of Lagos, 1917–1967* (University of California Press, Berkeley, 1974).
*   Frank Rosslyn Bradlow and Margaret Cairns, *The Early Cape Muslims: A Study of Their Mosques, Genealogy and Origins* (A. A. Balkema, Cape Town, 1978).
*   Frederick Cooper, *On the African Waterfront: Urban Disorder and the Transformation of Work in Colonial Mombasa* (Yale University Press, New Haven, 1987).

- J. de V. Allen, 'Town and Country in Swahili Culture', *Symposium Leo Frobenius* (Cologne, 1974), pp. 298–316.
- Harm J. de Blij, *Mombasa: An African City* (Northwestern University Press, Evanston, IL., 1968).
- Sir John Milner Gray, *The British in Mombasa, 1824–1826: Being the History of Captain Owen's Protectorate* (Macmillan, London & New York, 1957).
- B. S. Hoyle, *The Seaports of East Africa: A Geographical Study* (East African Pub. House, Nairobi, 1967).
- Hyder Kindy, *Life and Politics in Mombasa* (East African Pub. House, Nairobi, 1972).
- Anthony D. King, *Global Cities: Post-Imperialism and the Internationalization of London* (Routledge, London & New York, 1990).
- Richard V. Knight, and Gary Gappert (eds), *Cities in a Global Society* (Sage Publications, Newbury Park, CA, 1989).
- Josef W. Konvitz, 'Port Cities and Urban History', *Journal of Urban History*, vol. 19 (May 1993,) pp. 115–20.
- Peter Marris, *Family and Social Change in an African City: A Study of Rehousing in Lagos* (Northwestern University Press, Evanston, IL., 1962).
- kaje wa Mwenye Matano et al., *Wanawake watatu wa kiswahili: hadithi za maisha kutoka Mombasa, Kenya* (Indiana University Press, Bloomington, 1991).
- John Middleton, *The World of the Swahili: An African Mercantile Civilization* (Yale University Press, New Haven & London, 1992).
- Kevin Monroe, 'Tomorrow's cities are global cities', *American City and County*, vol. 107 (September 1992), pp. 42–4.
- C. Pama, *Bowler's Cape Town: Life at the Cape in Early Victorian Times, 1834–1868* 1st ed. (Tafelberg, Cape Town, 1977).
- Margaret Peil, *Lagos: The City is the People* (Belhaven, London, 1991).
- Aidan Southall, 'The African Port City: Docks and Suburbs' (review article), *Economic Development and Cultural Change*, vol. 38 (October 1989), pp. 167–89.
- Richard E. Stren, *Housing the Urban Poor in Africa: Policy, Politics, and Bureaucracy in Mombasa* (Institute of International Studies, University of California Press, Berkeley, 1978).
- Marc J. Swartz, *The Way the World is: Cultural Processes and Social Relations among the Mombasa Swahili* (University of California Press, Berkeley, 1991).
- Bernd Wiese, *Seaports and Port Cities of Southern Africa* (Steiner, Wiesbaden, 1981).
- Justin Willis, *Mombasa, the Swahili, and the Making of the Mijekenda* (Oxford University Press, New York, 1993).

# III

# URBAN CON-TEXTS: READING AND WRITING THE CITY

# 8

# This City Which is Not One

John Tagg

It may be difficult, even disrespectful, to try to respond to two such dense and informed contributions as those of Saskia Sassen and Sharon Zukin in the brief space given to me;[1] especially since I am not on a turf I know, coming from a different theoretical neighbourhood, where this built-up landscape is lived very differently. We have had so many questions put before us, questions thick with local implications, but also very large questions: In what sense does the New York City that has been constructed for us constitute a new formation and a paradigm for the rest of the urbanized world? Why can't we say that we are pressed to engage the same processes, conflicts and contradictions in analyzing the nineteenth-century metropolis? By what measure are 'global cities' defined and by what measure would we be disallowed from saying that, for example, Rome, or Mecca or Soweto could be 'global cities'? Are they not sites of a global stake, where the globe itself is staked?

But I shall leave such questions to those who come later, who are better equipped to ask them. Guided by the title of the conference, I want to get back to the mean streets I know, so my interest is caught by the way both papers speak of the urban field and constitute their object of knowledge because, to follow the lead of the title again, this must surely have consequences for the way we get from 'the city' to 'ethnicity', to 'capital' and, finally, to 'culture'.

Let me begin where I am led first: to 'Re-presenting' – the word broken, no doubt by the weight of meaning it has to bear, and dashed to pieces before our eyes. Or is it patched up, so it can go out into the streets again to do a job of work? It is striking how this damaged term continues to provide the theoretical armature on which the integrity of the arguments we have heard depends. For both authors of these papers there is a definite level at which the city is elaborated and at which it may be described and known; a level at which 'culture', 'style', 'design', and 'narrative'[2] are then 'attached',[3]

179

or across which they are deployed. The given level is that of political economy and the subsequent deployment is that of cultural systems as functional instruments. In the space between – a space of theoretical *liminality*, one might say[4] – the concept of 'representation' comes into play.[5] What holds the explanation together is therefore what cannot be spoken: the hyphen, which keeps the levels temporally and spatially apart, yet ensures that the secondary elaborations of meaning will still give access to the referent – the city – which is then wholly knowable to the subject of knowledge of political economy. For all the intended attention to 'culture', the accounts thus rest on a positivist conception of a real city, knowable to a certain subject, in a 'Master Narrative', one might say; a city which is then lived and experienced in different ways, and re-presented, expressed, masked or 'enhanced'[6] in a variety of urban cultures – the languages of modernism, postmodernism, the vernacular and so on, which are not effectively languages at all, but which merely embody the visual and spatial 'forms'[7] of an 'economic content'.[8]

Leaving these languages aside for the moment, we might note the languages in which the city is taken to be known – the languages of economics, sociology, statistics, surveys, case studies, demographics, cartography, photography, 'empirical documentation':[9] languages not only for describing the city, but languages *of* the city; languages that emerged with the city in the nineteenth century and through which the city emerged; languages embedded in the techniques and technologies of disciplinarity, about which Foucault, Deleuze and Guattari, Donzelot, Pasquino and others have said so much, and in which the city and its flows were constituted as knowable, graspable, harnessable and controllable. This was the fantasy of the city of the archive, the policed city, the city of surveillance, the city of health: a new 'landscape of power',[10] to use Sharon Zukin's term, one that enables an extraordinary take-off in productivity and governmentality, but one that is entirely irreducible to the drives of an 'economic dynamic' or an 'economic base'.[11]

The discourses of sociology and statistics emerged within the regime of disciplinarity that sought to saturate the city as an object of knowledge, transformation and control. Against this, the discourses of modernism and modernity emerged and wrote the city in the gendered field of spectacle. There is not time to make these statements mean much, but they suffice to make a point. To focus on the city as disciplinary field, or as spectacle, is to focus on the production of the city across specific discursive regimes, articulating the city as a space of new formations of power and pleasure, domination and desire. As discursive formations, the regimes of discipline and spectacle do not express interests, or re-present or mask a reality; they seek to produce the city and have no common, prior object. The discursivity of the city is indelibly multiple and heterogeneous, and the discursive regimes across which the city has been constituted do not coincide. This city, therefore, is not one: it is not identical with itself. 'A . . . city is a space of difference', as Saskia Sassen writes;[12] but its 'discontinuities' cannot be 'uncovered'.[13]

We must also add, however, that the regimes of spectacle and discourse do not work: they do not saturate the space of the urban; they are never coherent, exhaustive or closed in the ways they are fantasized as being. In effect they cannot finally constitute their object, 'separate, segregate and isolate' their Other, or stabilize their field. They cannot shed that ambivalence which always invades their fixities and unsettles their gaze. They are fissured and fractured; caught in a play of fear and desire they have to disavow. And this marks the spaces within their insistent fields in which resistance erupts or in which, like a *placa*, a difference is written that cannot be subsumed within their orders of otherness.[14]

I do not intend, however, to invoke at this point the nostalgic themes of 'production' over 'consumption' or of roots, place and fixity: 'the resistance of communities banded around their names and narratives'.[15] The regimes of the city are crossed over, graffitied, reworked, picked over like a trash heap, and used to different ends. They are plagued by unchannelled mobility and unwarranted consumption that feeds, unabashed, on excess in the sign value of commodities. And they can never encompass or exclude what is radically outside: the voices of what sociologists like to call 'sub-cultures'; the voices of evasion, separation, resistance and refusal; the inaudible or indecipherable voices that cannot speak in the city *as given*, but that are driven to go on speaking other cities, out of the pain of their silence, which the discourses of power – the discourses empowered to claim the Real – would impose on them forever.

## NOTES

1. This paper was written in response to the first two presentations of the 1992 symposium on which this volume is based and which were subsequently revised. Each respondent at the symposium was allocated ten minutes – *Editor*.
2. Saskia Sassen (this volume, chapter 1); and Sharon Zukin (this volume, chapter 2), passim.
3. Saskia Sassen (op. cit.), p. 24.
4. For 'liminality', see Sharon Zukin, *Landscapes of Power* (University of California Press, Berkeley and Los Angeles, 1991), pp. 28–9 et seq. *Editor*.
5. Saskia Sassen (op. cit.), p. 23; and Sharon Zukin (op. cit.), p. 43.
6. Sharon Zukin (op. cit.).
7. Saskia Sassen (op. cit.), p. 24.
8. Ibid., p. 25.
9. Ibid., p. 33.
10. Sharon Zukin (see note 4).
11. Saskia Sassen (op. cit.), pp. 26, 28.

12.   Ibid., p. 41.
13.   Ibid., pp. 25, 40, 41.
14.   Cf. John Tagg, 'The Pachuco's Flayed Hide: Mobility, Identity and *Buenas Garras*', (with Marcos Sanchez-Tranquilino) in John Tagg, *Grounds of Dispute: Art History, Cultural Politics and the Discursive Field* (University of Minnesota Press, Minneapolis, 1992), pp. 183–202.
15.   Jean-François Lyotard, *The Differend: Phrases in Dispute*, trans. George Van Den Abbeele (University of Minnesota Press, Minneapolis, 1988), section 262, p. 181. The argument about 'production' is, in effect, an argument about the primacy of *one form* of production over *another*.

# 9

# Analytic Borderlands: Race, Gender and Representation in the New City

Saskia Sassen

I speak here as a political economist in the hope of establishing an intellectual dialogue on the subject of race, gender and representation in the city. I begin with the facts and narratives about the economy of the city and move towards an attempt at theorizing the presences that are not represented in these accounts. In this attempt at theorizing I make use of elements from critical theory in feminism, art and architecture. I take liberties, because my intention is to use these elements to illuminate subjects and arenas which they have not addressed and are not meant to: the multiple presences and articulations of race and gender in the urban economy and their multiple absences in the dominant representations of that economy.

First a few clarifications and remarks to situate what I am trying to do. Feminist and other critical theories have contributed to a decentering of the subject and a valorizing of that decentering. I want to use this language to describe a basic transformation in the organization of the urban economy over the last twenty years, including a sharp distortion in the valorization dynamic of the economy, and to re-narrate what is now eviction as decentering. In so doing, I seek to valorize what has been evicted from the center.

In the last twenty years we have seen the expulsion and continuing exclusion from the center of significant components of the economy and a sharp increase in earnings inequality. Yet many of these components are actually servicing the center. Exclusion from the center makes economic survival precarious both for firms and workers. It also tends to make them either invisible or appear as backward, unnecessary, anachronistic. These devalorized components/subjects need to be recovered, and the center therewith transformed, brought down. This eviction and devaluing are embedded in a sharp demographic transformation as well: the growing presence of women, immigrants, and people of color generally in the urban economy. One important question is whether this demographic embeddedness has facilitated eviction and devalorization.

How do we valorize the evicted components of the economy in a system that values the center? There are here parallels with some issues in feminist theory, such as for example, the question of valorizing forms of knowledge associated with the female experience in a context where positivism and its variants are valued above all other forms of knowledge. Or, the debate on the positioned viewer and its assumption of one correct perspective. In economic analysis and in the narratives it produces there is one form of knowledge that is valued as the only correct one and one account that is considered to be a full rendering of the crucial elements in the economy. There is then, also, what one could think of as a positioned viewer behind the dominant narrative in economics.

What I have sought to do in much of my politico-economic work on cities is to valorize components of the economy that have been devalorized through their being evicted from the center or because they were never installed in the center. I have sought to show that they are articulated with sectors considered central, but are articulated in ways that present them as marginal, backward, unnecessary. Thus it is the form of this articulation which produces their representation as marginal. By revealing the facts of this articulation and the multiplicity of forms it assumes, I hope to begin the process of valorizing these various types of sectors, firms and workers that constitute the devalorized part of the urban economy.

It is also through a detailed examination of these devalued sectors that I hope to contribute to the specification of a multiplicity of femininities and racial identities, and to go beyond some of the dominant economic stereotypes, such as the white professional woman vs. the black welfare mother. There is a multiplicity of identities being formed and reproduced in these decentered spaces of the economy. Recognizing the representations being shaped by the constituents themselves is, clearly, a central task if we are to develop a political programmatics, in this particular case for revalorizing these spaces and presences of the economy.

How do we construct a narrative about the city, and particularly the economy of the city, that includes rather than evicts? For me as a political economist it has meant working in several systems of representation. Critical theory in feminism, art and architecture, each is a system of representation, with its own definitions, rules, boundaries, narratives. And so is economics. You may thus ask how one can use several of these systems, let alone have a dialogue across them. I recognize, further, that many would reject this possibility as not only unfeasible, but also undesirable.

Let me make three observations as to why I am interested in this kind of intellectual exploration. First, I think the time is ripe. To a much greater extent than in the past we have recognized the existence of multiple systems of representation, and there have been profound advances in their elaboration. The new politics of identity and the new cultural politics, especially evident in large cities, have brought this recognition into the everyday lives of people, onto the streets and out of theoretical texts.

A second observation is methodological. There are analytical moments when two systems of representation intersect. Such analytical moments are easily experienced as spaces of silence, of absence. One challenge, work that needs to be done, is to see what happens in those spaces; what operations (analytic, of power, of meaning) take place there. These operations may not be easy to recognize, either because they coexist in two different systems of representation, or because the intersection itself engenders a distinct third presence. It may require constructing a narrative about the operations that take place in these spaces of intersection. At a less theorized level, much of my own work on urban economies has consisted of exploring what I call analytic borderlands – the sharp discontinuities in the economy that lead me to posit that there is a multiplicity of economies. The narrative I have constructed about these analytic borderlands pivots on the question of circuits for the circulation and installation of economic operations. More on this later.

Third, the theoretical work on the body as a site of inscription opens up new possibilities for analyses of the sort I am exploring here. I would like to emphasize an aspect not usually developed in cultural analyses of the body and one that would serve the task of exploring the spaces of intersection I referred to above. This is the notion that the body is also inscribed by the workplace and specific work cultures. Beyond the variety of workplaces and cultures found in the 'western' tradition, there is the multiculturalism of large cities such as New York and Los Angeles today. It is not only a question of the corporate versus the factory workplace, but also of the different ways in which a particular workplace can be inscribed by specific cultural environments, for example, an all-Latino shopfloor in a garment factory. It seems to me that a focus on the body, culturally inscribed and inhabiting many different spaces in the city, may well be one of the elements facilitating the exploration of analytic borderlands.

These are the terrains and the instruments through which I want to re-read the city's economy in a way that recovers organizational, spatial and cultural dimensions that are now lost in representations of that economy. I do this in four sections. The first section briefly presents some of the key elements in the dominant narrative about the economy and argues that cities are useful arenas within which to explore the limitations of this narrative. The second section discusses how recovering place, particularly cities, in analyses of the economy allows us to see the multiplicity of economies and work cultures through which it is constituted. It also allows us to recover the concrete, localized processes through which globalization exists and argues that much of the multi-culturalism in large cities is no less a part of globalization than is international finance. The third section examines how space is inscribed in the urban economy, and particularly how the spaces of corporate culture, which are a representation of the space of power in today's cities, are actually contested spaces: they contain multiple presences even though their representation is exclusively corporate. The final section brings these various elements together in an effort to move from an economic narrative of eviction to one of inclusion. Conflicts of a profound nature become visible in this movement.

## THE DOMINANT ECONOMIC NARRATIVE

The dominant narrative about the economy has several key elements through which the system is constructed and explained. I will focus on three of them. Probably fundamental to it is the notion of continuous flow, also referred to as the trickle down: the idea that there are no structural barriers to the circulation of economic growth, or no discontinuities to be negotiated in this circulation and installation of economic growth. Thus growth emanates from the leading sectors and flows down to the rest of the economy via a series of mechanisms and intermediaries. Politically this establishes the superiority of the leading sectors; these are the ones that should receive support from the larger polity and the government when necessary. Sectors that lack technological development and have a preponderance of low-wage workers and small, low-profit firms, are considered as backward and not really belonging to an advanced economy. Hence the location of each component, whether at the top or at the bottom, reflects its value. In some sense one could say that the leading sector occupies the privileged location of the positioned viewer in theories of visuality. This account of the economy creates a 'white knight' theory of economic growth: one sector is privileged as the one that will rescue the economy. Again, you can see the resonances with accounts in other disciplines. In the US you can see this white knight version of economic growth in the hope and fanfare put onto high-tech industries in the 1970s and on finance in the 1980s as the sectors that would pull the economy ahead, make us strong, beautiful and happy.

There have been times when the center incorporated a majority of workers and firms under its regulatory umbrella and therewith empowered workers and their families – for example in the 1950s and 1960s, through well-paying unionized jobs and subsidized housing for the suburban middle class. When this protected center shrinks and begins to expel a growing number of workers and firms, then we are dealing with another situation.

And this distinction clearly is important within the conventional account and policy debate.[1] But it does not begin to touch on two issues central to this talk: that much of that expanded protected center in the economy – epitomized by the two decades after World War II – privileged men over women, and whites over blacks; and second, that exclusion and devalorization are embedded in a sharp demographic transformation in the urban workforce – women, immigrants and African-Americans now constitute a numerical majority in our large cities. But this is not the place to go into the policy issues.

A second aspect of importance here is economic internationalization. The account of the economy which takes off from the internationalization of transactions and firms is in many ways a more concrete account, one with lower scientific aspirations. It privileges certain elements and has only silences about others. The discussion about the internationalization of the economy privileges the reconstitution of capital as an internationalized presence; it emphasizes the vanguard character of this reconstitution.

At the same time it remains absolutely silent about another crucial element of this internationalization, one that some, like myself, see as the counterpart of the internationalization of capital: which is the internationalization of labor. We are still using the language of immigration to describe this process. Elsewhere I have argued at length that this language constructs immigration as a devalued process in so far as it describes the entry of people from generally poorer, disadvantaged countries, in search of the better lives that the receiving country can offer; it contains an implicit valorization of the receiving country and a devalorization of the sending country.[2] It is furthermore a language derived from an earlier historical period which proceeds as if the world economic system were the same today as it was one hundred years ago. What would happen to the representation of that process which we call immigration if we were to cast it in terms akin to those we use to describe the internationalization of capital, a process represented as imbued with economic rationality, technological advances and other attributes privileged in the mainstream narrative about the economy? What would happen if we did not privilege wealth over poverty, wealthy countries over poor countries? If we saw immigrants as using bridges built by the internationalization of capital or the internationalization of the military activities of dominant countries; if we saw immigrants as moving within an internationalized labor market?

A third aspect of the economic system and its representation has to do with the tendency towards concentration – concentration of power, of control, of appropriation of profits. This tendency, produced and reproduced through different historical periods under different specific forms and contents, clearly feeds the valorizing of the center of the economy. That is, it constitutes a center and then valorizes it. Elsewhere I have written in great detail about how this formation and reproduction of a center in the economy takes place through a variety of mechanisms and intermediaries (Sassen, 1988; 1993; see also my other chapter in this volume).[3,4] A general question we need to address is whether an economic system with strong tendencies towards concentration in ownership and control can have a space economy that lacks points of intense agglomeration.[5]

This dominant narrative of the economy can be usefully explored in large cities such as New York and Los Angeles, or any of the major West European cities. There are at least two reasons for this. First, cities are the site for concrete operations of the economy and we can distinguish two forms of this. One is about economic globalization and place. Cities are strategic places which concentrate command functions, global markets, and, I add, production sites for the new advanced information industries. The other form through which this concreteness can be captured is by an examination of the day to day work in the leading industrial complex, finance and specialized services. Such an examination makes it clear that a large share of the jobs involved in finance, for example, are lowly paid clerical and manual jobs, many held by women and immigrants. These types of workers and jobs do not fit the dominant representation of what the premier industry of this period is about.

Second, the city concentrates diversity.[6,7] Its spaces are inscribed with the dominant corporate culture but also with a multiplicity of other cultures and identities. The slippage is evident: the dominant culture can encompass only part of the city. And while corporate power inscribes these cultures and identities with 'otherness' thereby devaluing them, they are present everywhere. This presence is especially strong in our major cities which also have the largest concentrations of corporate power. We see here an interesting correspondence between great concentrations of corporate power and large concentrations of an amalgamated 'other'. It invites us to see that globalization is not only constituted in terms of capital (international finance, telecommunications, information flows) but also in terms of people and cultures.

## THE GLOBAL CITY

Changes in the geography, composition and institutional framework of economic globalization over the last two decades have led to sharp concentration of economic functions in major cities.[8,9,10] Some of this concentration reflects the reinvigoration of old functions; but much of it consists of new functions. Major cities have emerged as strategic places in the world economy (see also my other chapter in this volume). In the past cities were centers for imperial administration and international trade.[11]

Today they are transnational spaces for business and finance where firms and governments from many different countries can transact with each other, increasingly bypassing the firms of the 'host' country.

I note two other economic operations, not sufficiently recognized in the literature on economic globalization. One is that global cities are a new kind of production site. They contain the combination of industries, suppliers and markets, including labor markets, necessary for the production of highly specialized services: from financial innovations to international accounting models, international legal expertise, management and the coordination functions for just about any transborder flow. Emphasizing production brings to the fore a broad range of presences that are usually lost in discussions of globalization and the information economy. These presences range from the material conditions underlying global telecommunications to the various types of workers and firms we do not usually associate with globalization and the information economy: secretaries, manual workers, the truckers who deliver the state of the art software (and that old-fashioned xerox paper). It is particularly important, it seems to me, to effect these analytical operations in the case of the leading sectors of the information economy because the mainstream account of this economy is so radically distorting in its privileging of information flows over the material and concrete conditions through which it operates, in its privileging of the advanced professional workforce, in its exclusion of non-professional workers and firms.[12]

The third aspect that matters in the discussion is that global cities are also internationalized spaces in terms of people. The emphasis on production discussed above brings to the fore place-bound aspects of globalization.[13,14,15] And a recovery of place in a discussion of globalization brings forth the fact that it is not only firms from many different countries that can meet to do business. It is also the terrain where peoples from many different Third World countries are most likely to meet and a multiplicity of cultures come together. It's not only the material infrastructure, the jobs and firms: it is also the many different cultural environments in which these workers exist. One can no longer think of centers for international business and finance simply in terms of the corporate towers and corporate culture at its center.

From the perspective of the dominant narrative of the economy, there has been growing recognition of the formation of an international professional class of workers and of highly internationalized environments due to the presence of foreign firms and personnel, the formation of global markets in the arts, and the international circulation of high culture. What has not been recognized is the possibility that we are seeing an internationalized labor market for low-wage manual and service workers. This process continues to be couched in terms of immigration, a narrative rooted in an earlier historical period.

I think that there are representations of globality which have not been recognized as such or are 'contested representations of globality'.[16] Among these is the question of immigration, as well as the multiplicity of cultural environments to which it contributes in large cities, often subsumed under the notion of ethnicity. What we still narrate in the language of immigration and ethnicity I would argue is actually a series of processes having to do with the globalization of economic activity, of cultural activity, of identity formation.[17,18] Immigration and ethnicity are constituted as otherness. Understanding them as a set of processes whereby global elements are *localized*, international labor markets are constituted, and cultures from all over the world are de- and re-territorialized, puts them right there at the center along with the internationalization of capital as a fundamental aspect of globalization.[19] This way of narrating the migration events of the postwar era captures the ongoing weight of colonialism and postcolonial forms of empire on major processes of globalization today, and specifically those binding countries of emigration and immigration. The major immigration countries are not innocent bystanders; the specific genesis and contents of their responsibility will vary from case to case and period to period.

Today's global cities are in part the spaces of postcolonialism and indeed contain conditions for the formation of a postcolonialist discourse.[20,21] An interesting question concerns the nature of internationalization today in ex-colonial cities. King's analysis about the distinctive historical and unequal conditions in which the notion of the 'international' was constructed[22] is extremely important. It brings up, in part, the types of questions raised by Hall[23] in his observation that contemporary postcolonial and postimperialist critiques have emerged in the former centers of empires, and that they are silent about a range of conditions evident today in ex-colonial cities or countries. In many ways during the time of empire, the old colonies were far more internationalized than the metropolitan centers; yet the notion of internationalization as used today is rooted in the experience of the center. The idea that the international migrations now directed largely to the center from the former colonial territories, and neo-colonial versions in the case of the US and Japan,[24] might be the correlate of the internationalization of capital that began with colonialism is simply not part of the mainstream interpretation of that past and the present.

Methodologically speaking, this conception of the global city contains one way of addressing the question of the unit of analysis. The national society is a problematic category. But so is the 'world economy'.[25] Highly internationalized cities such as New York or London offer the possibility of examining globalization processes in great detail, within a bounded setting, and with all their multiple, often contradictory aspects. It would begin to address some of the questions raised by King about the need not only of a differentiated notion of culture, but also of the international and the global.[26]

We need to recognize the specific historical conditions for different conceptions of the international. There is a tendency to see the internationalization of the economy as a process operating at the center, embedded in the power of the multinational corporations today and colonial enterprises in the past.[27,28] One could note that the economies of many peripheral countries are thoroughly internationalized due to high levels of foreign investment in all economic sectors, and of heavy dependence on world markets for 'hard' currency. What center countries have is strategic concentrations of firms and markets that operate globally, the capability for global control and coordination, and power. This is a very different form of the international from that which we find in peripheral countries.

Globalization is a contradictory space; it is characterized by contestation, internal differentiation, continuous border crossings.[29] The global city is emblematic of this condition.


## CONTESTED SPACES IN THE CITY

Space in the city is inscribed with the dominant corporate culture. (See also my other chapter in this volume.) Sennett[30] observes that 'the space of authority in western culture has evolved as a space of precision'. And Giddens notes the centrality of 'expertise' in today's society, with the corresponding transfer of authority and trust to expert systems.[31]

Corporate culture is one representation of precision and expertise. Its space has become one of the main spaces of authority in today's cities. The dense concentrations of tall buildings in major downtowns or in the new edge cities are the site for corporate culture – though as I will argue later it is also the site for other forms of inhabitation, but they have been made invisible. The vertical grid of the corporate tower is imbued with the same neutrality and rationality attributed to the horizontal grid of American cities.

Much has been said about the protestant ethic as the culture through which the economic operations of capitalism are constituted in the daily life of people. Sennett opens up a whole new dimension both on the protestant ethic and on the American city by suggesting that what is experienced as a form of rational urban organization, the grid, is actually a far more charged event. It is 'the representation in urban design of a protestant language of self and space becoming a modern form of power'.[32] We can recognize that the neutralization of place brought about by the modern grid contains an aspiration to a modern space of precision. This same aspiration is evident in the self-inscription of corporate culture as neutral, as ordered by technology, economic efficiency, rationality. This is put in contrast to what is thought of as the culture of small businesses, or even more so, ethnic enterprises. Each of these is a partial representation, in one case of the city, in the other of the economy.

The dominant narrative presents the economy as ordered by technical and scientific efficiency principles, and in that sense as neutral. The emergence and consolidation of corporate power appears, then, as an inevitable form that economic growth takes under these ordering principles. The impressive engineering and architectural output evident in the tall corporate towers that dominate our downtowns are a physical embodiment of these principles. And the corporate culture that inhabits these towers and inscribes them is the organizational and behavioral correlate to these ordering principles.

Authority is thereby 'divorced from community. . . The visual forms of legibility in urban designs or space no longer suggest much about subjective life. . .'.[33] Subjective life is installed in a multiplicity of subjectivities, and this undermines the representation of the advanced modern economy as a space of neutrality, the neutrality that comes from technology and efficiency: the ordering principles of a modern economy.

We can easily recognize that both the neutralization of place through the grid in its aspiration to a modern space of precision, and the self-inscription of corporate culture as neutral, as ordered by technology and efficiency, are partial representations of the city and of the economy. This inscription needs to be produced and reproduced, and it can never be complete because of all the other presences in the city which are inscribed in urban space. The representation of the city contained in the dominant economic narrative can exclude large portions of the lived city and reconstitute them as some amalgamated 'other'.

The lived city contains a multiplicity of spatialities and identities many indeed articulated and very much a part of the economy, but represented as superfluous, anachronistic or marginal. Through immigration, a proliferation of originally highly localized cultures have now become presences in many large cities; cities whose elites think of themselves as cosmopolitan, that is transcending any locality.[34] An immense array of cultures from around the world, each rooted in a particular country or village, now are reterritorialized in a few single places, places such as New York, Los Angeles, Paris, London, and most recently Tokyo.[35]

The space of the amalgamated 'other' created by corporate culture is constituted as a devalued, downgraded space in the dominant economic narrative: social and physical decay, a burden. In today's New York or Los Angeles, this is the space of the immigrant community, of the black ghetto, and increasingly of the old manufacturing district. In its most extreme version it is the space of the 'underclass, full of welfare mothers and drug addicts'. Corporate culture collapses differences, some minute, some sharp, among the different socio-cultural contexts into one amorphous otherness;

an otherness that has no place in the economy; the other who holds the low-wage jobs that are supposedly, only marginally attached to the economy. It therewith reproduces the devaluing of those jobs and of those who hold the jobs. The dominant economic narrative, by leaving out these articulations, can present the economy as containing a higher-order unity by restricting it only to the centrally placed sectors of the economy.

The corporate economy evicts these other economies and workers from economic representation, and the corporate culture represents them as the other. It evicts other ways of being in the city and in the economy. What is not installed in a corporate center is devalued; will tend to be devalued. And what occupies the corporate building in non-corporate ways is made invisible. The fact that most of the people working in the corporate city during the day are low-paid secretaries, mostly women, many immigrant or African-American women, is not included in the representation of the corporate economy or corporate culture. And the fact that at night a whole other work force installs itself in these spaces, including the offices of the chief executives, and inscribes the space with a wholly different culture (manual labor, often music, lunch breaks at midnight) is an invisible event. (I have shown elsewhere the whole infrastructure of low-wage, non professional jobs and activities that constitute a crucial part of the so-called corporate economy).

In this sense, corporate architecture assumes a whole new meaning beyond the question of the economy of offices and real estate development. The built forms of the corporate economy are representative of its 'neutrality' – the fact that it is driven by technological development and efficiency, which are seen as neutral (there is a good literature, by the way, showing how this is not the case). Corporate architectural spatiality is one specific form assumed by the circulation of power in the economy, and specifically in the corporate economy. Wigley[36] notes that the house is not innocent of the violence inside it. And we now have an excellent literature showing how the design of different types of buildings – homes, factories, 'public' lobbies – is shaped by cultural values and social norms. This 'rational' organization of office space illustrates certain aspects of Foucault's microtechnologies of power (Rakatansky[37]).

But the changes in the details of habitation – institutional practices, the types and contents of buildings – indicate there is no univocal relation between these and built form. I agree with Rakatansky's observation that the play of ideologies in architectural form is complex. And I would add that this concept is essential if we are to allow for politics and agency in the built environment. Yes, in some sense buildings are frozen in time. But they can be re-inscribed. The only way we can think of these towers now is as corporate, *if* located downtown (and as failed public housing projects if they are in poor ghettos). Another dimension along which to explore some of these issues is the question of the body '. . . as the site of inscription for specific modes of subjectivity' (Grosz, 1991[38]). The body is citified, urbanized as a distinctively metropolitan body.

The particular geographical, architectural, municipal arrangements constituting a city are one particular ingredient in the social constitution of the body; Grosz adds that they are by no means the most important one. She argues that the structure and particularity of the family and neighborhoods is more influential, though the structure of the city is also contained therein.[39] I would add to this that the structure, spatiality and concrete localization of the economy are also influential. In these many ways the city is an active force that 'leaves its traces on the subject's corporeality'.

But it is citified in diverse ways: it is inscribed by the many socio-cultural environments present in the city, and it in turn inscribes these. There are two forms in which this weaves itself into the space of the economy. One is that these diverse ways in which the body is inscribed in the many socio-cultural contexts that exist in the city, works as a mechanism for segmenting and, in the end for devaluing, and it does so in very concrete ways. For example research by the anthropologist Philippe Bourgeois[40] shows us the case of an 18-year-old Puerto Rican from East Harlem who gets a job as a clerical attendant in an office in downtown Manhattan. He tells us that walking over to the xerox machine past all the secretaries is humiliating. The way he walks, the way he is dressed, the way he moves presents him to the office staff, secretaries and managers as someone from the ghetto; someone who 'doesn't know the proper ways'. This particular young man eventually fled the downtown world and entered the ghetto economy where at least his gait, speech and dress were the norm.

The other way in which this diversity weaves itself into the space of the economy is that it re-enters the space of the dominant economic sector as merchandise and as marketing. Of interest here is the fact that contemporary forms of globalization are different from earlier ones: the new global culture is absorptive, a continuously changing terrain that incorporates the new cultural elements whenever it can. In the earlier period, the culture of the empire epitomized by Englishness was exclusionary, seeking always to reproduce its difference (Hall, 1991[41]). At the same time, today's global culture cannot absorb everything, it is always a terrain for contestation, and its edges are certainly always in flux. The process of absorption can never be complete.

One question is whether the argument developed above regarding the neutralization of space brought about by the grid and the system of values it entails or seeks to produce in space, also occurs with cultural globalization. As with the grid, culture never fully succeeds in this neutralization; yet absorption does alter the absorbed. An interesting issue here that emerges out of my work on the urban economy is whether at some point all the 'others' (at its most extreme, the informal economy) carry enough weight to transform the center. In the case of culture one can see that the absorption of multiple cultural elements along with the cultural politics so evident in large cities, have transformed global culture. Yet it is still centered in the West, its technologies, its images, as Hall argues. Thus absorbed, the other cultures are neutralized. And yet they are also present.

We can perhaps see this most clearly in urban space, where a multiplicity of other work cultures, cultural environments, and culturally inscribed bodies increasingly inhabit a built terrain that has its origins visibly in another culture; the culture lying behind the grid.[42] Here again, I ask, at what point does the 'curve effect', as social scientists would put it, take hold and bring the center down.

## CONCLUSION: THE NEW FRONTIER

There are three important developments over the last twenty years which I believe set the stage for the re-reading of the city I am proposing here. One of them is the decentering of a growing share of economic activity with the ensuing shrinking of the center, as I discussed earlier. The second is what I describe as a dynamic of valorization which has sharply increased the distance between the devalorized and the valorized, indeed overvalorized, sectors of the economy. The third is the growing presence of women, immigrants and African-Americans in the urban economy of large cities, and their disproportionate concentration in the devalued sectors.

Large cities have emerged as strategic territories for these developments. On the one hand, they are crucial cogs in the new global economic system: they function as command points, global marketplaces for capital, and production sites for the information economy. On the other hand, they contain the multiplicity of economic activities and types of workers and cultural environments that are never represented as part of the global economy but are in fact as much a part of globalization as is international finance. These joint presences have made cities a contested terrain.

In the preceding sections I have tried to show that cities are of great importance to the dominant economic sectors; that these sectors represent themselves through narratives and spaces that are partial representations of what the economy and urban space are; that devalorized economic sectors are servicing the corporate center of the economy and hence are necessary to that center even though presented as marginal; that this devalorization of growing sectors of the economy has been embedded in a massive demographic transition towards a growing presence of women, African-Americans and third world immigrants in the urban workforce; and that the new politics of identity and the new cultural politics have brought many of these devalorized or marginal sectors into representation.

Secondly I have sought to argue that globalization needs to be thought of as a series of processes that are constituted by people as much as capital; for instance, it seems crucial to recognize that what we continue to think of as immigration is, today, an instance of globalization. There are consequences to this way of representing immigration. Our large cities, and increasingly the large cities in western Europe, are the terrain where a multiplicity of globalization processes assume concrete, localized forms. These localized forms are, in good part, what globalization is about. We can then think of cities also as the place where the contradictions of the internationalization of capital come to rest, or fight. If we consider, further, that large US cities especially also concentrate a growing share of African-Americans and Latinos, two populations that have suffered massive disadvantage in the economic system, then we can see that cities have become a strategic terrain for a whole series of conflicts and contradictions.

On the one hand they concentrate a disproportionate share of corporate power and are one of the key sites for the overvalorization of the corporate economy; on the other, they concentrate a disproportionate share of the disadvantaged and are one of the key sites for their devalorization. This joint presence happens in a context where the internationalization of the economy has grown sharply and cities have become increasingly strategic for global capital; and marginalized people have come into representation and are making claims on the city as well. This joint presence is further brought into focus by the sharpening of the distance between the two: white flight to the suburbs and the pronounced transformation in income distribution have reduced the mostly white middle class residing in the city, creating a series of intermediate spaces. Now the overvalorized center is smaller and its edges are sharper; and the devalorized others are far larger in number and inhabit a growing area of the city.

These conditions make it less and less likely that the hierarchical ordering that has up till now created the semblance of a unitary economic system, can be maintained. The center now concentrates immense power, a power that rests on the capability for global control and the nakedness of unencumbered greed. And marginality, notwithstanding weak economic and political power has become in Hall's words a 'powerful space'.

If cities were irrelevant to the globalization of economic activity, the center could simply abandon them and not be bothered by all of this. Indeed this is what some politicians are arguing – that cities have become hopeless reservoirs for all kinds of social despair. It is interesting to note again how the dominant economic narrative argues that place no longer matters, that firms can now move anywhere now thanks to telematics; that the dominant industries are information-based and hence not place-bound. This line of argument devalorizes cities at a time when they are a strategic terrain for the new cultural politics. And it makes it possible for the corporate economy to extract major concessions from city governments under the notion that firms can simply leave – which is not quite the case for a whole complex of firms.

In seeking to show that cities are strategic to economic globalization because they are command points, global marketplaces and production sites for the information economy; and also that many of the devalued sectors of the urban economy actually fulfill crucial functions for the center; I try to recover the importance of cities precisely in a globalized economic system and of those devalued sectors which rest largely on the labor of women, African-Americans and immigrants. It is all the intermediary sectors of the economy (routine office work; headquarters that are not geared to the world markets; the variety of services demanded by the largely suburbanized middle class) and of the urban population (the 'middle class') that can and have left cities. The two sectors that have remained, the center and the 'other', find in the city the strategic terrain for their operations. Because they find in the city such a terrain and because they matter to each other, we can think of cities as a new frontier charged with conflict between two opposites; charged with the possibility of fundamental transformation in the West. The global city is, perhaps, the premier arena for these battles – it is the new territory where the contemporary version of the colonial wars of independence are being fought. But today's battles lack clear boundaries and fields: there are many sites, many fronts, many forms, many politics. They are battles being fought in neighborhoods, schools, court rooms, public squares. They are fought around curriculums, rights, identity. Their sites of resistance are streets, parks, culture, the body.

## NOTES

1. The shrinking of the protected center has engendered considerable debate and caused much impoverishment. It is an important subject into itself, and there is a whole policy discussion that could become of interest eventually in the more theoretically oriented examination I am seeking to develop here.
2. S. Sassen, *The Mobility of Labor and Capital: A Study in International Investment and Labor Flow* (Cambridge University Press, New York, 1988).
3. Ibid.
4. S. Sassen, *The Global City: New York, London, Tokyo* (Princeton University Press, 1993).
5. Ibid., parts 1 and 2.
6. A. D. King, *Global Cities: Post-Imperialism and the Internationalization of London* (Routledge, London and New York, 1990).
7. An important point made by King (ibid.) is that during European colonization, it was in the colonial cities where different cultures and races

met. The cities of Europe and North America have only recently become places where such diversity is concentrated.

8.     The term globalization requires some clarification. Robertson (see note 9) posits that concepts of globalism are not economically fixed; I agree with this. Tagg agrees and adds that such concepts have 'no status outside the fields of discourse and practice that constitute them' (see note 10, p. 156). But he argues further that such concepts or representations of globality are not the expression of some 'real' process of globalization. In this discussion Tagg sees 'global' as having come to mean the world is 'systematic or one place' (ibid. p. 157). But this is merely one, albeit a very typical way of reading globalization. Such a world would indeed 'not be present to itself'. But authors as diverse as Hall on culture (see note 20) and me on the economy do not work with this version of the global. Detailed research on globalization makes it clear that it is a highly diversified and contested process, with a multiplicity of geographies and events, narratives and self-reflexive mechanisms (see Giddens, note 31, on the self-reflexivity of modernism). It seems to me that it is not simply a question of choosing between two extremes: either a singular, non-reflexive narrative of globalization, or a series of concepts that only exist in terms of the discourses that contain them and that can never be the expression of a real process of globalization. Once one begins to work with the clay of that multiplicity of geographies, events and contradictions that constitute globalization, one can indeed see the gravitation of discourses (see the discourse on the global information economy which I have sought to critique in much of my work), but also the concrete specifics of lived experience. I would certainly agree with Tagg's observation that '. . . the meaning and value of photographic practices cannot be adjudicated outside specific language games'. But what I call for is a differentiating of what the object being narrated is, rather than a universalizing. Photographic practices, yes, I can see that; manual work in a plantation or sweatshop, no: they leave their own inscription regardless of what discourse they are contained in. The question for me is how globalization is constituted, not just as a narrative but in terms of concrete specific, often place-bound, operations. Thus the narrative about globalization that is centered on the information economy and telematics is, in my analysis, a very partial and distorted representation because it leaves out a variety of elements that are part of globalization; and secondly, what it leaves out tends to be overwhelmingly that which lacks power.

9.     R. Robertson, 'Social Theory, Cultural Relativity and the Problem of Globality', in A. D. King (ed.), *Culture, Globalization and the World-System. Current Debates in Art History 3* (Department of Art & Art History, State University of New York at Binghamton, 1991), pp. 69–90.

10.   John Tagg, 'Globalization, Totalization and the Discursive Field', in A. D. King (ed.), *Culture, Globalization and the World-System. Current Debates in Art History 3* (Department of Art & Art History, State University of New York at Binghamton, 1991), pp. 155–60.

11.   King (see note 6) notes that a major instrument of European colonization was the colonial city. It played a different role from that of the imperial capital cities.

12.   In accounts of other sectors such as manufacturing or transportation, these 'other' types of workers, firms and places are less likely to be excluded, indeed they are often put at the center of the account and used to devalorise much of manufacturing. The exception is high-tech and here again we see a privileging

of the research and professional staff and a veiling of the production workforce which is mostly low wage, female and immigrant. Technology and the different classes of workers that embody, enact or use its components – whether technicians, professionals, clericals, manual workers – are not a pre-existing condition in the organization of the economy but are constituted by that economic organization.

13.    Cf. Robertson's notion of the world as a single place (see note 9), or the global human condition. I would say that globalization is also a process that produces differentiation, only the alignment of differences is of a very different kind from that associated with such differentiating notions as national character, national culture, national society. For example the corporate world today has a global geography, but it isn't everywhere in the world: in fact it has highly defined and structured spaces, and secondly it also is increasingly sharply differentiated from non-corporate segments in the economies of the particular locations (a city such as New York) or countries where it operates. There is homogenization along certain lines that cross national boundaries and sharp differentiation inside these boundaries. We can also see this in the geography of certain built forms; from the bungalow (King, see note 14) to the corporate complex (Sassen, note 4) or the landscapes of American theme parks (Zukin, note 15). We can see that these various built forms are both global yet highly localized in certain places. Globalized forms and processes tend to have a distinct geography.

14.    A. D. King, *The Bungalow: The Production of a Global Culture* (Routledge and Kegan Paul, London and New York, 1984).

15.    S. Zukin, *Landscapes of Power* (California University Press, Berkeley, 1991).

16.    U. Hannerz, 'Scenarios for Peripheral Cultures', in A. D. King (ed.), *Culture, Globalization and the World-System. Current Debates in Art History 3* (Department of Art & Art History, State University of New York at Binghamton, 1991), pp. 107–28.

17.    Elsewhere I have tried to argue that the current post-1945 period has distinct conditions for the formation and continuation of international flows of immigrants and refugees. I have sought to show that the specific forms of internationalization of capital we see over this period have contributed to mobilize people into migration streams and build bridges between countries of origin and the US. The first took place through the implantation of western development strategies, from the replacement of smallholder agriculture with export-oriented commercial agriculture to the westernization of educational systems. At the same time the administrative, commercial and development networks of the former European empires and the newer forms these networks assumed under the Pax Americana (international direct foreign investment, export processing zones, wars for democracy) have not only created bridges for the flow of capital, information and high level personnel from the center to the periphery but, I argue, also for the flow of migrants (Sassen, notes 2 and 18). On this last point, see also Hall's account of the postwar influx of people from the Commonwealth into Britain and his description of how England and Englishness were so present in his native Jamaica as to make people feel that London was the capital where they were all headed sooner or later (see note 20).

18.    S. Sassen (see note 4).

19.    That is why in a book mostly on immigration, I refused to use the concept immigration in the title and sought to link the internationalization of capital and labor.

20.    S. Hall, 'The Local and the Global: Globalization and Ethnicity', in Anthony
       D. King (ed.), *Culture, Globalization and the World-System: Contemporary
       Conditions for the Representation of Identity.Current Debates in Art History 3*
       (Department of Art and Art History, State University of New York at
       Binghamton, 1991).
21.    A. D. King (see note 6).
22.    A. D. King, *Urbanism, Colonialism, and the World Economy. Culture and
       Spatial Foundations of the World Urban System* (Routledge, London and New
       York, 1990), p. 78.
23.    S. Hall (see note 20).
24.    S. Sassen (see note 4).
25.    I would tend to agree with Robertson's comment (see note 9) that the
       proliferation of the ideas of nation, nationalism and national culture,
       especially in the twentieth century, is connected to globalization processes.
       Various forms of nationalism and sub-nationalism are speaking with
       increasingly loud voices today precisely because the nation-state and national
       society are eroding from within *and* without. This erosion assumes distinct
       modalities and degrees of intensity in different countries. It is by no means a
       uniform and universal process. The new nationalisms range from re-
       emergence of older nationalisms in extreme forms, as is evident in the former
       territories of Yugoslavia, to the renewed intensity of statements about the
       American people, the American character, and English as the official language
       in the last two decades in the US.
26.    A. D. King, 'The Global, the Urban, and the World', in A. D. King (ed.),
       *Culture, Globalization and the World-System. Current Debates in Art History 3*
       (Department of Art & Art History, State University of New York at
       Binghamton, 1991), pp. 4, 149–54.
27.    Similarly, in the social sciences the most common way to proceed is to study
       such categories as economic power, leading industries, or economic
       globalization, from the top down. I agree with Barabara Abou-El-Haj (see
       note 28) that we also need to proceed from the bottom up. The central
       assumption in much of my work has been that we learn something about
       power through its absence and by moving through or negotiating the borders
       and terrains that connect powerlessness to power. Power is not a silence at the
       bottom; its absence is present and has consequences. The terms and language
       of the debate force particular positions and pre-empt others.
28.    Barbara Abou-El-Haj, 'Languages and Models for Cultural Exchange', in
       A. D. King (ed.), *Culture, Globalization and the World-System. Current
       Debates in Art History 3* (Department of Art & Art History, State University
       of New York at Binghamton, 1991), pp. 139–40.
29.    There are many examples. Global mass culture homogenizes and is capable of
       absorbing an immense variety of local cultural elements. But this process is
       never complete. My analysis of data on electronic manufacturing shows that
       employment in leading sectors no longer inevitably constitutes membership in
       a labor aristocracy. Thus Third World women working in Export Processing
       Zones are not empowered: capitalism can work through difference. Yet
       another case is that of 'illegal' immigrants; here we see that national
       boundaries have the effect of creating and criminalizing difference. These
       kinds of differentiations are central to the formation of a world economic
       system. See, for example, I. Wallerstein, 'Culture as the Ideological Battle-
       ground of the Modern World-System', in Mike Featherstone (ed.), *Global*

*Culture: Nationalism, Globalization and Modernity* (Sage, London, Newbury Park, and Delhi, 1990).

30.   R. Sennett, *The Conscience of the Eye: The Design and Social Life of Cities*, paperback edition (Norton, New York, 1992).

31.   A. Giddens, *The Consequences of Modernity* (Polity Press, Oxford, UK, 1990), pp. 88–91.

32.   R. Sennett (see note 30).

33.   Ibid., p. 37.

34.   Hall (see note 20), makes an important observation when he uses the term ethnicity to describe that which is grounded and rooted, and notes two aspects: one, the inevitability of this if a group is to recover its own hidden history to enter into representation; and second that ethnicity, while necessary, is also about exclusion of all others. Politics should not be reduced to the politics of ethnicity as it risks becoming yet another form of fundamentalism. The discussion about culture as increasingly deterritorialized offers additional narratives to encompass certain aspects of the immigrant experience.

35.   Tokyo now has several, mostly working-class concentrations of legal and illegal immigrants coming from China, Bangladesh, Pakistan and the Philippines. This is quite remarkable in view of Japan's legal and cultural closure to immigrants. Is this simply a function of poverty in those countries? By itself it is not enough of an explanation, since they have long had poverty. I posit that the internationalization of the Japanese economy, including specific forms of investment in those countries and Japan's growing cultural influence there, have created bridges between those countries and Japan and reduced the subjective distance from Japan (see Sassen, note 4, Chapter 9).

36.   M. Wigley, 'Untitled: The Housing of Gender', in Beatriz Colomina (ed.), *Sexuality & Space*. Princeton Papers on Architecture (Princeton Architectural Press, 1992), pp. 327–90.

37.   M. Rakatansky, 'Spatial Narratives', in J. Whiteman, J. Kipnis and R. Burdett, *Strategies in Architectural Thinking* (The MIT Press, Cambridge, Chicago Institute for Architecture and Urbanism, 1992).

38.   E. Grosz, 'Bodies-Cities', in Beatriz Colomina (ed.), *Sexuality & Space*, Princeton Papers on Architecture (Princeton Architectural Press, 1992), pp. 241–53.

39.   Grosz (ibid.) suggests a model of the relation between bodies and cities that sees them not as distinct megalithic total entities but as assembles or collections of parts, capable of crossing the thresholds between substances to create new linkages. She does not stress the unity and integration of body and city, or posit their ecological balance. Rather, she posits a fundamentally disunified series of systems and interconnections, disparate flows, events, entities and spaces, brought together or drawn apart in more or less temporary alignments.

40.   P. Bourgeois, *In Search of Respect: Selling Crack in El Barrio*. Structural Analysis in the Social Sciences Series (Cambridge University Press, New York, forthcoming).

41.   S. Hall (see note 20).

42.   Similarly the informal economy when acknowledged, which is rare, is conceived of as a distortion, an import from the Third World. Elsewhere I have documented the diverse ways in which goods and services produced in the informal economy circulate in the mainstream economy and can be shown

to meet the needs of a broad variety of firms and households in that economy. Thus I posit that informalization is one way of organizing a range of activities that on the one hand produce goods and services in demand in the overall economy, and on the other hand have been devalorised and are hence under immense competitive pressure.

See also:.

- M. Castells, *The Informational City* (Blackwell, London, 1989).
- Beatriz Colomina (ed.), *Sexuality & Space.* Princeton Papers on Architecture (Princeton Architectural Press, 1992).
- B. Colomina, 'The Split Wall: Domestic Voyeurism', in Beatriz Colomina (ed.), *Sexuality & Space* Princeton Papers on Architecture (Princeton Architectural Press, 1992), pp. 73–128.
- M. Morris, 'Great Moments in Social Climbing: King Kong and the Human Fly', in Beatriz Colomina (ed.), *Sexuality & Space.* Princeton Papers on Architecture (Princeton Architectural Press, 1992).
- J. Whiteman, J. Kipnis and R. Burdett, *Strategies in Architectural Thinking* (The MIT Press, Cambridge, Chicago Institute for Architecture and Urbanism, 1992).
- S. Zukin, 'The Postmodern Debate over Urban Form', *Theory, Culture and Society*, 5 (2–3) 1988, pp. 431–46.

# 10

# Silent Itineraries: Making Places in Architectural History

Greig Crysler

The methods used to describe and analyze the spaces of the city have recently become subject to intense scrutiny and debate. *Re-presenting the City*, with its broad range of different and sometimes conflicting approaches, is an instance of this. Yet consideration of the way objects of knowledge are constituted is often reduced to acts of autonomous reason. In this chapter I will examine how a range of forces, both discursive and non-discursive, are intertwined in the production and dissemination of scholarly knowledge.[1]

In particular I want to examine how history is written about some of the specifically architectural spaces of the city, using *The Journal of the Society of Architectural Historians* (*JSAH*) as a case study. The *Journal* is published by the Society of Architectural Historians (SAH), an organization founded in 1940 to advance the cause of architectural history in the United States. Beginning as a small, regionally based organization, the Society has evolved into a fully bureaucratized knowledge corporation with a staff of seven, and a national headquarters housed in a historic building in Philadelphia.[2]

Although the Society operates as an independent organization, the majority of the writers for its *Journal* have been, and continue to be, employed as faculty members in university programs of architectural history. As mental labourers in the tertiary education system, the *JSAH*'s writers belong to a discursively constituted community whose existence is grounded in the production and dissemination of knowledge. The survival and strength of this community is linked to the continuing efficacy of a particular form of architectural knowledge. The *Journal*'s discourses on architectural history must therefore be examined as representations of interest, calculation and power.[3]

203

## A JOURNAL WITH CHAPTERS

The Society of Architectural Historians (SAH) was founded in 1940[4] when the relevance of history to architectural education was being questioned in the United States.[5] When responsibility for architectural training passed from the apprentice system to the universities in the late nineteenth century, the teaching of architectural history played a crucial role in differentiating architecture from other more technical disciplines, like engineering.[6] Architectural history, once only a subject amongst others within university art history programs, assumed a new role, and a seemingly secure institutional future, narrating the origins and history of the profession. Under the Beaux Arts regime that acted as the model for the first American schools,[7] architectural history was also closely tied to the studio, acting as a source for historical types in design projects. However by the 1940s, the privileged position of history in architectural education was well on the way to being overturned by a wave of modernist educators.[8]

Many of the founders of the SAH taught architectural history in schools of architecture.[9] The changing status of the discipline had a direct bearing on their careers. For example the appointment of Walter Gropius as head of the Harvard Design School in 1935 led to a reorganization of the curriculum which made the study of architectural history optional. Kenneth J. Conant, a well-known architectural historian at Harvard and the first president of the SAH, was transferred along with the entire subject of architectural history, out of the school of architecture and into the Fine Art Department. As early as 1932 the amount of time devoted to architectural history in some architectural programs had been reduced to as little as four per cent of total curriculum hours.[10]

The Society played a crucial role in helping to redefine and secure the professional identity of the architectural historian. A small network of regional chapters that slowly grew to a national scale after the war extended the legitimacy of architectural history beyond the university. Using American architecture as the common object of discussion, the Society built bridges between the 'interested lay person' and the professional architectural historian.[11] Members gave presentations on their architectural research, and illustrated talks about local monuments. Local chapters also organized weekend tours to those nearby buildings which were considered significant to American history.

The *Journal* also drew attention to American architectural history and the need to preserve it. A roundtable discussion on the importance of architectural preservation, held between prominent members of the architectural history establishment of the day, appears in the first volume;[12] in 1942 an entire issue was devoted to the subject. A special issue was also published in the first volume which examined how history could develop a new relevance within the emerging modernist curriculum.[13] This marked the beginning of a series of articles published throughout the 1940s which, in an effort to bolster the role of the historian in architectural education, re-examined the relationship between history and the design studio.

## PRESERVATION AND EXCISION

It is hard not to be struck by the emotional tone of articles on preservation published in the *Journal* in the 1940s and 1950s. Modernization, when it intruded on the newly emerging canon of American architecture, was considered tantamount to treasonable violence. The salvation of national heritage was linked to the knowledge of architectural historians in a manner that was at once both dramatic and juridical.[14] It was not long before several of the founding members of the *JSAH* were serving on federal advisory boards charged with drawing up lists of nationally 'important' buildings whose existence as monuments would be protected by law.[15]

Unlike the discourses of architectural history, those of preservation value not only monumental architecture but also the spaces of everyday life, including streets, urban landscapes and buildings not designed by architects. And just as preservation includes vernacular or everyday spaces amongst its objects of study, it also includes ordinary non-academic forms of speech as part of its mode of representation. It is a discourse frequently written without footnotes, performed by 'amateur' and professional historians alike, who speak passionately at public meetings, participate in local watchdog networks, and keep each other informed about possible threats to 'important' buildings. It is also an argument that the more scientific discourses of traditional architectural history cannot undertake without diluting and undermining their claims to reasoned objectivity.

In the *Journal*'s first two decades, descriptions of architecture, education, preservation and town planning fall together in an undifferentiated manner. A surprising number of articles, regardless of their subject matter, are not footnoted.[16] However in 1957, shorter and less 'scholarly' articles about American architecture were transferred to a new section called American Notes. This remained in place until 1967, when it was removed altogether. After the elimination of American Notes, articles that would previously have been published there appeared in the SAH Newsletter, or migrated to other publications devoted exclusively to preservation. Studies on 'high' architecture completed by American masters remained in the articles section as examples of the American contribution to a traditional canon of architectural history.

The disappearance of American Notes and the channeling of what has come to be known as 'vernacular' architecture into separate publications, sometimes with the less scholarly status of 'newsletter', illustrates the workings of a group of oppositional relations central to the construction and practice of architectural history: between what are seen on the one hand as architectural monuments, and on the other as buildings; between 'scholarly' and 'popular knowledge'; and finally between a discourse which seeks to transcend its national context to achieve a 'universal' character, and one which is plainly national in character and justifies its arguments through appeals to the imagined or constructed cultural criteria of national significance.

The separation of the different professional practices of preservation and history reflected not only irreconcilable differences between their modes of representation and objects of analysis, but also the varying institutional power and resources each was able to command from both the public and private sources. Architectural history no longer needed close proximity to preservation to underline the national relevance of the discipline as a whole. The great postwar expansion of university education was underway in the early 1950s. This, combined with a building boom that lasted nearly twenty years, resulted in the rapid growth of architectural education and with it programs in architectural history.[17]

The same forces that fueled the expansion of architectural education – the recycling and rebuilding of American cities to accommodate a new phase of capitalist investment and expansion – eventually brought preservation to new levels of prominence. As Osmund Overby has noted, the institutional tension that had developed in the *Journal* between 'traditional academic interests and some of the newer needs' of preservation was resolved by the latter's increasing 'maturity' as a discourse. As the preservation movement developed its own institutions and specializations, new publications emerged (often with SAH members in key roles) which catered to its interests. The preservationists gradually packed their intellectual bags and went elsewhere.[18]

## UNIVOCITY

As the *Journal*'s outlook narrowed, the balance between its taxonomic categories was refined. The knowledge categories of the *JSAH* are organized within the same boundaries of temporal periodization that have tradition-ally classified forms of teaching and research in the American university. The Eurocentric 'eras' of ancient-medieval-modern are further subdivided into a sequence that begins with ancient Greece, passes through the medieval, renaissance and baroque periods and culminates with nineteenth and twentieth century modernism.

Although based on morphological change and development,[19] and therefore putatively grounded in objective laws of measurement and observation,[20] the armature of neo-classical periodization[21] has been continually rebuilt in ways which expand some periods and diminish others, depending on who is mobilizing it, and for what purposes.

It is the way the regional is incorporated into the universal that typically defines differing versions of the system.[22] From its inception, the Society's members have been divided almost equally between those conducting research into European or into American topics. The *Journal* has gradually institutionalized this balance, and today maintains it as part of what it refers to as its 'international' outlook. Only a tiny percentage of the articles published in the *Journal* since its inception deal with research outside this axis. Though there is some discussion of seventeenth and eighteenth century buildings, architecture of the United States is represented mainly through a select set of buildings from the nineteenth and early twentieth century. Europe is represented through buildings dating primarily from the 16th to eighteenth century, though other European periods (particularly the medieval), have also risen and then faded in prominence over the years.[23]

An article entitled 'Where Architectural Historians Fear to Tread'[24] published in 1969 by John Maass, underscored the predominantly Euro-American emphasis of the *Journal*. Maass analysed the articles published in it between 1958 and 1967, and discovered that of the 450 articles and book reviews, only 11 dealt with non-western architecture, and that American architecture outnumbered all other subjects. A broader analysis of the *Journal*'s articles confirms a similar pattern. A study of 350 articles published from 1941 to 1993 inclusive revealed that 94 per cent were on topics located in either Western Europe or the United States. This degree of emphasis has remained constant over the life of the *Journal*.[25]

The *JSAH*'s bifurcation of periods along the geographical lines of the nation-state has the effect of making the United States the domain of 'modern' architectural history, and Europe the treasure trove of the past. Although separated geographically, these two periods are nevertheless linked by the underlying foundationalism of the entire system. American architecture, situated at the end of the morphological chain, is the 'uniquely American' conclusion to the development of Civilization.

The assertion of the United States as the apex of history occurred when postwar nationalism was at a peak, and the American economy was in a confident period of international expansion. At the same time, the professional identity of architects and architectural historians was under-going a change as profound as the 'great transformation'[26] which brought them into existence in the nineteenth century. In both cases professional sectors of the middle class were seeking to improve their position in changing stratifications of capitalist society. Legally enforced monopolies of practice depend on the parallel construction of a 'monopoly of credibility'[27] with the larger public. In the socially unstable period of the late nineteenth century, professional groups obtained public confidence through association with the norms and practices of an aristocratic European culture. The same groups conquered their markets in the post-World War II period by making themselves explorers, collectors, and guardians of the spaces of national identity.

A chain was formed linking the traditional canon of architectural history to American architecture, American architecture to preservation, and preservation to the law of the land. At one end of the chain were the local chapters of the Society, raising the alarm, and rallying fellow historians to fight the good fight;[28] at the other end were the academic architectural historians busy linking American architecture to historical developments extending back to ancient Greece. The chain served as a lifeline for the profession of architectural history, connecting it with a particular construction of American identity at one end, and an equally particular construction of Civilization at the other. In the process new roles for the historian were created in museums, local historical societies, civic trusts and the emerging heritage industry.

The gradual departure of discourses of preservation, along with other more informal voices, is matched by a growing 'statistical intoxication'[29] in the *Journal*. By the mid-1960s, an article's footnote text often came close to the length of the article itself.[30] Sibyl Moholy Nagy, in one of the several broadsides she launched against the *Journal* in the late 1960s and early 1970s, complains bitterly in a letter to the editor of the 'footnote test', by then well-established as a routine:

> . . . The footnote test demands that at least half of an article be printed out of context, and that at least half the footnotes prove that what the author has to say has already been said by someone else. The article by Carl F. Barnes Jr., on The Twelfth Century Transept of Soissons . . . goes the foregoing assumption one better. To 431 lines of text he has 341 lines of footnotes! . . .

With the settling of the balance between regional and universal, vernacular and scholarly, also came the delineation of a stable field of architectural objects.[31] There is a decline in the number of articles dealing with preservation, city planning, architectural education and architectural history, and an increase in those concerned with biographies of architectural careers, cathedrals, monasteries, villas, palaces, country houses, castles, museums and universities. Thus articles which examine the institutional and epistemological character of the field (architectural history, architectural education), or which tend to view architectural history from within other discourses (town planning, preservation) gradually assume less importance in the *Journal*. Attention turns almost exclusively to single buildings and their architects. In the periods extending from 1941 to 1963, and 1970 to 1993, the number about churches and palatial housing doubles between the first grouping and the second. Despite these changes, one factor has remained consistent throughout: in the 228 articles which establish architectural authorship, almost all are by white males.[32]

After two decades of lateral shifts and excisions, a univocal editorial voice emerged that, up to the present, remains largely unchanged.[33] It is a voice based on the hegemony of an absent third person narrator, firmly located in what Hayden White calls 'traditional history'.[34] Our way of looking at images and reading texts in the *Journal* is disciplined through the promotion of realism as a basic mode of reading. We read for 'a content that is modelled on reality at the expense of awareness of the signifying system of which the work is constructed. . .'[35] The narrative is treated as a neutral container of historical fact, 'naturally' suited to representing historical events directly, employing ordinary or natural, rather than technical languages to do so. The opinioned voice of the first person is confined to book reviews and letters to the editor, arenas where the historian evaluates other narratives according to what White calls the correspondence/coherence criteria.[36] The hegemony of the third person favors a 'scientific' voice that allows the 'I' to return only as an arbitrating expert, simultaneously judge and jury, whose knowledge permits (dis)qualifying judgments about other narratives based on abstract criteria of truth and logic, sanctioned by the standards of the profession.

## GENRES

Two narrative genres dominate in the *Journal*: the 'life-and-work' and 'the work'. The life-and-work is concerned with constituting professional subjectivities in relation to architectural space(s) through the trope of synecdoche ; that is, the building stands for the life of the architect (or vice-versa). 'Richardson's American Express Building', 'Palladio's Theory of Proportions', 'Louis Sullivan's Building for John D. Van Allen and Son', 'Vignola's Character and Achievement' – these apostrophized titles under-line the ownership to be established between architect and building. The architect's consciousness is situated as the point of mediation between what the historian chooses to constitute as influences (everything the architect experiences), and the presumed final product of that consciousness, the building. A typical example of this approach is the repeated attention given in the journal to determining the effects of Frank Lloyd Wright's kindergarten education on his later work.[37]

Because the synecdochical model requires that economic, social, political and building forces are somehow assembled in the consciousness of the architect, character-types frequently assume heroic proportions.[38] The architect may be an inventor: 'of new spatial concepts'; an infuser: 'history offers sources and prototypes, but it took the genius of Wright and le Corbusier to infuse mass architecture . . . with twentieth century meaning . . .'; a synthesizer: '. . . his ability [lay] not in the development of new ideas, but in a synthesis of a very high order. . .'; a personality: 'strong willed and determined'; a political ideologist: 'creator of fascist architecture'; or a visionary: 'a prophet of modernism'.

The genre of 'the work' is constructed out of a chain of elements which suppresses the centralizing function of the architect-as-author. Instead, the metonymic trope dominates, and a series of contiguities represents the whole. This genre is inherently less singular than that of the life-and-work because, in terms of explanation, it privileges a chain of dispersed elements. It therefore takes in a range of research methods, extending from the abstraction of typological studies of building forms, to the contextual studies of social history. However it is often the case in the *JSAH* that this genre is resorted to when the available data does not permit the use of the life-and-work model. Thus many of the objects that are narrated in the category of 'the work' are what might be described as 'mute' objects. They exist in the category of 'the work' as a stage in (re)searching for 'lives', or parts of lives, to pair them with.

Ambiguous authorship or date of origin assigns these objects to a historical purgatory. Here they must wait until sufficient evidence is compiled to establish 'attribution'. *Journal* articles pondering mute objects often present a range of documentary evidence in an effort to finalize the authorship or date of a building, as in this note appearing in italics at the beginning of an article about Amiens cathedral : 'the combination of a new measured plan, detailed investigation of building fabric and spaces, and a reinvestigation of textual sources . . .leads to a revised chronology and new interpretation. . .'[39]

Buildings that have the status of mute objects are often ones that were 'previously unknown', or at the very least unstudied and therefore unwritten. They are 'discovered' in the rubble of history, and in many cases do not actually exist in built form. They are historicized solely in two-dimensional representations and written texts; the discovery of a building is coincident with the discovery of representations of it. Thus the metonymic model of narration is informed by a metonymic model of investigation: a chain of events is pieced together that ultimately converges in a definitive statement. The starting point of the process is often research by other historians. A building may be treated as something which exists only as a proposition expressed through images; a second historian may decide to see if any such structures were actually built. Thus something as ephemeral as a shadow on an engraving provides 'evidence' of the existence of a building, a crucial first step in the metonymic process of reconstruction.[40]

The narrator must intervene to both inaugurate and close off the metonymic chain, which is no longer 'naturally' circumscribed by the life-and-death brackets of the architect-as-author. In effect, the contiguities of 'the work' are constituted as a collective author, which the narrator must bring to life and later silence. This genre therefore changes the way in which facts are dispersed, without challenging the epistemological status of the 'facts' themselves, or the author's role in arranging them.

## SPATIAL PRACTICES

The creation of a clearly demarcated past is essential to establishing it as a 'real' object of scientific research which appears to exist outside conscious-ness, observed and interpreted, rather than constructed by the historian. The text 'substitutes a representation of the past for an elucidation of the present institutional operations that manufacture the historian's text. It puts an appearance of the real (past) in place of the praxis (present) that produces it, thus developing an actual case of quid pro quo. . .'[41] The effacement or disappearance of the historian's presence as narrator is necessary for history to appear as though it is a mirror of the past. The facts are presented as though they speak for themselves; that is they are presented as a mimesis of the historical event. The disappearance of the narrator into the position of an absent third person thus describes a transition into the protocols of mimesis, where '. . .the quantity of information and the presence of the informant are in inverse ratio, mimesis being defined by a maximum of information and a minimum of the informant. . .'[42]

As Hayden White argues, the differing ways in which mimesis is constituted in historical narration defines differing forms of historical consciousness.[43] The text constructs a perceptual regime that allows us to 'see' history in a particular way, by directing us to take ensembles of representations as icons of events. In the *JSAH*, these ensembles are constituted through a combination of narrative and descriptive modes of discourse.[44] Narrative discourse is employed for the 'diachronic and discursive manifestation of events, things and beings'[45] and is successive in nature. Description, on the other hand, marks a resting point (and frequently the destination) of the narrative, where an object is viewed in a timeless present, as if it were 'always already visually present, fully ordered to full and potential speech'.[46] W. J. T. Mitchell states that although literary theory has traditionally categorized narrative discourse as temporal and descriptive discourse as spatial in character, both forms produce different spatialities: Narrative discourse constitutes linear forms of space, while description constitutes those which Mitchell describes as tectonic.[47]

There is an assimilation in the *JSAH* between language and space, between route and site, and their enunciated expression in linear and tectonic forms of discourse. The genres of the work and the life-and-work can also be described as itineraries and stories of pilgrimage. Narratives lead us on a journey to a place or places; descriptions wander over the surface of these places once we arrive. We travel along the path of a life, or part of a life, passing through spaces in which parts of the biography unfold temporally (the kindergarten playroom, the home, the university, the architectural office); we examine spaces which putatively influence the architect's design of a building. In the case of the work, multiple but contiguous routes lead to the final destination, a building.

Thus the pilgrimage narrative 'makes the complexity of the city readable, and immobilizes its opaque mobility in a transparent text'.[48] Fragments of the city are isolated and read as objective signs of the real/past. The historian/narrator becomes a guide who directs perception towards particular objects and events, at the same time demanding 'blindness' to other conditions – perhaps social, economic or political – in order to maintain discursive continuity. Each point on the itinerary is a step in the direction of a journey, 'by which is accomplished a desire triggered by a discursive process or narrative chain whose mapped text traces out its realization'.[49]

Many of the places of pilgrimage are in the past in the most tangible sense: they no longer exist. The architectural historian is therefore called upon to reconstruct them, assembling visual and textual data in a manner that will produce a convincing account of a 'real' place. A physical topography is formed through reference to other accounts and documents, affecting a 'domestication of textuality into a self-contained exercise of arranging and cataloguing . . .'[50] A building described in the *JSAH*'s architectural history is often, as with Edward Said's Orient, '. . . a topos: a set of references, a congerie of characteristics, that seems to have its origin in quotation . . .'[51]

In such cases, there is nowhere to travel to, only archives to write from. The result is a closed circle of representational practice, where one form of disciplinary truth statement (the orthogonal projection, for example) is used to supply evidence to support the truth claims of another (the historical narrative). Reception is predicated upon the disciplinary knowledge that allows the receiver to 'read' architectural drawings as direct transcriptions of physical objects. In this respect, the *Journal* does not simply transmit historical narratives; it inscribes and reinforces the methodological techniques of the discipline in both its readers and writers.


## EXPLICATORS OF HISTORY

From its founding until the late 1960s, the *JSAH* gradually demarcated a coherent field of knowledge drawing on the protocols of realist history. The extended period of stability connecting the late 1960s to the present, emerges as one of the most remarkable features of the *Journal*'s history. Eugene E. Matysek's analysis of citations for articles published in it between 1986 and

1990 confirms that recently published work shares many characteristics with the research of three decades ago.[52] Much of the current scholarship in the *JSAH* is built out of knowledge that dates from before 1970,[53] strengthening the *Journal*'s bond with the past, and separating its research from current developments in the field.

The list of most-cited monographs in Matysek's research is also revealing. The nine titles on the list include three from the *Pelican History of Art* surveys, two dealing with Great Britain and the third with modernism. The most cited authors include Nicholas Pevsner in the top position, followed by Frank Lloyd Wright, Frederick Law Olmsted and Richard Krautheimer. As Matysek has noted, the subject characteristics of these works correspond closely with the observations made by John Maass in his study of the *JSAH* between 1958 and 1967. Reflecting on the findings of his research, Matysek dryly states that 'the *JSAH* has apparently changed very little over the past 30 years'.[54]

This tendency towards atavism has occurred at a time when the institutional and discursive fields around the JSAH have altered dramatically. Architectural history is now characterized by a wide range of specializations, some of which fundamentally challenge the assumptions and practices of the *Journal*. This has not gone unnoticed. In a recent editorial entitled 'Celebrating Tradition and Change'[55] Nicholas Adams the current editor, lists some of the many sub-fields that have appeared in architectural history over the last two decades, including construction history, vernacular architecture, garden history, industrial archeology, urban history, military architecture and 'new methodologies' which 'blend architectural history with philosophy, literature, and literary criticism'. Adams argues that the *JSAH* should reposition itself as an integrative force in a rapidly fragmenting and diversifying discipline, working to 'engage the breadth of scholars' interests . . . to seek the margins as well as the center, the new-fashioned as well as the traditional . . .'[56]

Adams' remarks appeared in 1993, and it is too soon to say what effect his efforts will have on the direction of the *Journal*. Yet, if one can detect the outlines of a subtle change over the last 30 years, it may be found in a gradual movement away from the teleological patterns of classification and explanation conditioned by neoclassical periodization, and towards a positivist history which gives primacy to evidence. Research that does not follow the classical emphasis on monumental buildings and great architects has broadened to include such things as the North American shopping mall, military fortifications, and the history of construction techniques. Though the range of objects analyzed has expanded, the *Journal*'s commitment to the techniques and practices of realist history has remained constant.

It may thus be possible to suggest that the *JSAH* operates within an increasingly multifold context as an authoritative source of historical 'evidence', turning up, drawing attention to, and verifying archival material that subsequently becomes open to appropriation in a wide range of other discourses. Although 'untheorized' in the current sense of the term (concealing, rather than revealing its processes of signification), this research opens up sites for multiple paths of investigation.

The tendency towards specialization and diversification in academic research is not limited to the field of architectural history. Scholars have suggested that universities have passed from their roles as agents of cultural reproduction to that of producers of knowledge.[57] While the former model stressed the teaching of an ideologically unified canon, the latter places emphasis on research and its dissemination amongst peers. The university is no longer 'an integrated unit commanded by a concept of education so much as an administrative apparatus for managing a series of loosely-integrated activities'.[58] Scholars now work in 'knowledge communities' defined by highly specialized languages and research interests. In a highly competitive and overcrowded field, specialization and recognition have become intertwined. As Jonathan Culler notes, the definition of profession-alism in the academy:

> . . . ties one's identity to an expertise and to a field in which one might be judged an expert by one's peers. This induces a proliferation of sub-fields as the job market becomes tighter: as writers of letters of recommendation we find that we have a stake in defining some area – say psychoanalytic interpretations of Shakespeare – such that our candidate may be deemed one of its most accomplished experts . . .[59]

The type of knowledge the Society disseminates – factual evidence conveyed in the form of historical narratives which 'enrich the memory, whet the appetite, and satisfy the curiosity'[60] – is characteristic of what J. F. Lyotard has called the 'postmodern condition' of knowledge: that is knowledge which simultaneously establishes a social bond through 'traditional' narrative techniques, while at the same time using codified research methods to produce a wide range of 'solutions' to particular (historical) 'problems'. According to Lyotard, the development of an efficient information machinery which secures its own legitimation opens knowledge to mercantilization.[61] This interpretation suggests that the *JSAH* has carved out a unique place for its knowledge in a diversifying discipline.

Yet specialization has also been appropriated and deployed as a political tactic to resist hegemonic forms of knowledge. Beginning in the mid-1960s, the entry of women, blacks, and more recently immigrants from the Third World into the university system, combined with the increasing visibility of gays and lesbians, has resulted in a broad-based call for a fundamental transformation of racist, sexist and Eurocentric curriculums. As Chandra Talpade Mohanty states, the specialized programs set up to respond to the demands of these groups, although carrying with them the constant threat of incorporation, also created '. . .the possibility of counter-hegemonic discourse and oppositional analytic spaces within the institution. . .'[62]

In this case specialization is linked to forming spaces in which formerly subjugated knowledge can be uncovered and reclaimed. Such oppositional discourses are not interested in a cheerful plurality orchestrated by the 'traditional centers' of the university. Instead, they seek to provoke conflict. Competing discourses are understood as part of '. . . asymmetrical and incommensurable cultural spheres situated within relations of domination and resistance. . .'[63] This suggests nothing less than a reconceptualization of traditional categories of analysis, in order to specify the relations of power constructed by knowledge as part of larger political processes and systems. Claims to objectivity and exteriority need to be set aside in order to understand the connections between the 'historical configuration of social forms and the way they work subjectively'.[64] This alone may explain the dearth of such knowledge in the *JSAH*. It proposes a fundamental critique of the professional subjectivity at work in the *Journal*. When the editor states that his purpose in attempting to engage the 'margins as well as the center' is an objective 'exchange of information and methods',[65] it is clear that the margins are receiving an invitation from the center on terms specified by the center.

It is tempting to see the present character of the *Journal* as a defensive response towards all those 'other' discourses that question its legitimacy. Yet the *Journal* and the Society have always considered their audience to include a broader 'public' consisting of 'interested lay persons'. As a result both institutions have tended to see their purpose as simultaneously grounded within, and beyond, the academy. The pursuit of realist history may seem 'outdated' in certain academic contexts, where critiques of such methods have recently become well-established. However naturalistic history is flourishing in other settings – particularly the tourist and museum industries, where an interest in cultural specificity and historical continuity responds to the disintegrative forces of global economic restructuring and transnational migration.

The Society's current activities confirm its double focus on academia and what it perceives to be the general public. After many years of planning, it has recently published the first volumes of its encyclopedic guide to American buildings. Their appearance reflects the long-standing association the Society has forged over the years between travel and architectural history though its tradition of weekend excursions and annual architectural tours.

By 'reaching out' to a non-academic audience with its travel guides, the Society strengthens, rather than weakens, the legitimacy of its knowledge within the academy. At a time when state-sponsored research funds are declining, and universities are dependent upon outside funding for support, knowledge is increasingly subject to a test of 'social relevance'.[66] The Society appears to have passed this test by claiming the role of 'explicator' and public educator. As Nicholas Adams states in relation to the Guides:

> We welcome the public's interest in architecture and urbanism and we offer ourselves as their explicator through the Buildings of the United States. This is a powerful statement of confidence in our subject matter, and there is, so far as I know, nothing of a similar sort being undertaken in any American academic field at the present time . . . so far the Buildings of the United States takes public education seriously and sees buildings whole . . .[67]

The travel guides give a new coherence to the historical techniques implicit in much of the *JSAH*'s research. The narrative practices used to map buildings and guide the reader through space, have been collected together, objectified and standardized into an 'accessible' system that is repeated in each book. The result is a national grid of classification and display, imposed through the transparency of realist language onto the landscape. The grid itself becomes the site of pilgrimage, since without it there would be no 'Buildings of the United States'.

If we accept that disciplines like architectural history are no longer organized around a single hegemonic approach, but rather a range of competing approaches, it is difficult to suggest that the *Journal*'s discourse dominates any context outside the one which makes it identifiable as a specialized approach – in this case, the *Journal* itself. This argument also applies to the travel guides. Although the Society may provide a particular reading of history in the guides, it is quite likely that a keen architectural tourist would read them together with other materials, putting together a composite narrative by combining sources in a piecemeal fashion.

The Society anticipates just such combinations, and warns that its Guides do not provide all the knowledge necessary to understand the places they describe.[68] The Guides acknowledge other discourses and explanations. Such liberalism is intrinsic to attempts to incorporate, and thus benignly dominate, other historical voices. The Guides attempt to specify the terms of historical knowledge by claiming the position of exhaustive, authoritative overview; thus they appear as volumes in a 'monumental'[69] encyclopedia (the traditional form of total knowledge), and are laid out according to the geographic divisions of the United States with each volume corresponding to a separate state. Here as elsewhere, the struggle for the authority to define the norms of historical explanation is fought over the terms and conditions upon which 'other' voices will be heard.

Thus discourses of realist history (of which the *JSAH* and the travel guides are instances) operate together with a range of other historical discourses in specific settings. One discourse does not obtain a position of absolute hegemony over all others (though its practitioners may struggle to achieve such an end); nor does it have an identity independent from the knowledge which surrounds it. Instead, differing practices are woven together by institutions and agents to form an ensemble of knowledges that collectively impart a notion of what 'architectural history' constitutes in a particular context.

Architectural education is one of the locations where traditional discourses like those of the *JSAH* are woven together with other approaches. It is not possible to claim that the *Journal* is directly linked to the teaching of history in architectural schools in the way a survey textbook might be. Yet the range of signifying practices embodied in it are valued, considered useful, and disseminated through teaching and research in architectural schools. Through subscriptions, financial support and participation in the *Journal*'s research community, architectural schools – together with their faculty and graduate students – form part of the institutional support which allows the *Journal* to continue operating.[70]

Architectural education in the United States comprises a wide range of different approaches. Nevertheless, it is possible to speak in general terms about the architectural curriculum inasmuch as the National Architectural Accrediting Board (NAAB) encourages the generalization of a certain model of training, by imposing national standards to 'harmonize' credentials and ensure uniform qualifications amongst graduates. In order to retain their national accreditation, architectural schools must undergo periodic review by a visiting team from the NAAB. Student work must demonstrate competence in various forms of knowledge deemed necessary for the practice of architecture. Architectural history forms a part of this core of knowledge.[71]

The NAAB guidelines addresses architectural history under two headings: as part of the 'fundamental knowledge' students must gain of the 'social context for architecture',[72] and as part of the 'design' skills their work must demonstrate.[73] In this latter category, the NAAB requires that students must be able to 'be able to use architectural history and theory in the critical observation and discussion of architecture and bring an understanding of history to bear on the design of buildings and communities. . .'[74] Though the NAAB guidelines permit considerable flexibility in the design of a curriculum, all the schools have chosen to meet them through the use of three or four introductory level survey courses, divided according to an ancient-medieval-renaissance-modern grid emphasizing famous architects and their buildings, or what I have earlier characterized as the genre of the life-and-work.[75]

Dana Cuff has characterized the early years of architectural training as an 'intense indoctrination characteristic of an initiation right',[76] where students are isolated within the university, and required to spend long hours together either in the design studio, or completing a heavy load of required courses taught within the school. 'Here' Cuff remarks, 'in the earliest phase of becoming an architect, we see kernels of architects' later values, such as the principle of peer review and a developing segregation from the public. . .'[77] Architectural histories of the life-and-work help to define the terms of professional segregation and differentiation through idealized histories of its practice conveyed through the experiences of elders within the discipline. In this context, architectural history carries on the role it assumed when it was incorporated into architectural education in the nineteenth century, by providing a disciplinary myth of origins and historical development, and authenticating the jurisdiction of architectural expertise.

Because the life-and-work associates achievement in the field with the mystique of autonomous judgement, it also underpins one of the principal social relations in the school, between studio instructor and student. This is constructed as a relation between unique individuals, and becomes a model for later professional practice. The primacy of the individual:

> . . . is then carried into practice, promoting the explanation of everyday occurrences as matters of personality, talent, creativity, and convictions. Architects are thus not trained to be alert to significant relations of authority, economics, power, group decision-making processes, management . . . the structural conditions within which individuals must operate in practice are exempted from careful consideration by schools and from inclusion within the belief system . . .[78]

Thus the genre of the life-and-work plays a role in the first years of architectural education in the construction of professional subjectivity. Yet the emphasis on teaching architectural history in order to 'bring an understanding of history to bear on the design of buildings and communities' also suggests a continuing technical role for architectural history as a purveyor of types and precedents, in a manner reminiscent of Beaux Arts models of training; here narratives of 'the work' help to establish the limits to the possible range of solutions in the design process.

When such history – based almost exclusively on the experiences of Euro-American white males – is taught in a context which consistently portrays architecture as the result of individual will, it also tends to support racist and sexist stereotypes by implying that women and minorities have neither the will nor the ability to practice architecture. A segment of architectural educators has acknowledged this problem, and in recent years the terms of this debate have shifted to acknowledge not only the ignored contributions of women and minorities within the traditional canon, but to consider more broadly how educators and students might 'reconfigure the cultural political terrain to make the experiences of gender, race and class central to a reconceptualization of architectural education and pedagogy . . .'[79]

Yet the first three years of architectural education – the so-called 'boot camp for architects' – continues to be structured around a series of required courses that provide students with a common stock of skills and experiences considered essential to the production of expertise and cohesive professional identity.[80] This emphasis on transmitting pragmatic knowledge tends to limit openings for new analytical spaces in architectural history to the final years of training. Students are not permitted to 'break the rules' until they have mastered them. Precisely because architectural history is mandatory, and is taught in its traditional form as part of the 'fundamental knowledge' of architectural education, it assumes a foundational role in the curriculum, against which other forms of 'elective' knowledge are constructed.

Nevertheless, 'history for architects' is also an unstable formation. Gwendolyn Wright has described the way the discipline has shifted over the years to achieve a compatible relationship with ideologies of architectural practice.[81] Thus it may be possible to interpret the NAAB's recent interest in encouraging architectural schools to provide a survey course in 'world architecture'[82] as not only a recognition of the changing demographic composition of architectural schools, but also of the expanding international market for American architectural services.

While the inclusion of foundation courses on 'world' architecture would seem to suggest that a pluralistic expansion of the existing Eurocentric categories of analysis is underway, Stanley Tigerman has discerned a movement away from teaching history altogether. This development is presaged by the recent appearance of the architect as 'critical theorist'. He suggests that this identity has been articulated through displacement: the architect had to first 'invent typologically' a scholar 'compositely versed in criticism, philosophy, and linguistics (with just a touch of theology) – a 'critical theorist' – and attain a relation with this invention so as to ultimately displace it'.[83] The aim of this transaction was a redefinition of professional expertise:

> . . . Because the eighties were defined by an emerging sense of dislocative tendencies, who better than the critical theorist could architects displace to attain correspondence with the issues of the day? . . . even as the architectural studio critic has never had a problem in subsuming structures or history into a synthetic operation – the studio – so it was utterly simple for the architectural educator to subsume 'theory' into an operation innately ordered to continuously search elsewhere to perpetuate the dissimulative posture of self-determination . . .[84]

Thus the apparent separation of the *JSAH* from other discourses may define not so much a polarity as a dependent relation. In this respect, new positions (like poststructuralism in historical interpretation, or deconstruction in design), and the 'older' ones like those represented in the *Journal*, are mutually constitutive. The 'traditional' image of the architect-as-master allows new 'flexible' roles to proliferate through opposition to what is now regarded as a dying subjectivity. The production of difference gains both institutional and social legitimacy through reference to a stable past of homogeneity. The subjects of new professional strata narrate themselves moving forward from this past, adapting to the times, but only through endlessly constituting and then effacing an intractable bond between the living and the dead, the past and the present.

## NOTES

1. This chapter is based on material from my Ph.D dissertation, entitled 'Spaces of Representation/Representations of Space. Discourses of Architecture, Urbanism, and the Built Environment 1960-90'.
2. Osmund Overby, 'From 1947: The Society of Architectural Historians', *JSAH*, vol. XLIX (1990) no. 1, p. 12.
3. See John Frow, 'Knowledge and Class' *Cultural Studies*, vol. 7 (May 1993), no. 2, pp. 240–81; Barbara and John Ehrenreich, 'The Professional Managerial Class', in Pat Walker (ed.), *Between Labour and Capital* (South End Press, Boston, 1979); Pierre Bourdieu, *Homo Academicus* (Stanford University Pres, 1984); Alvin Gouldner, *The Future of Intellectuals and the Rise of the New Class: A Frame of Reference, Theses, Conjectures, Arguments, and an Historical Perspective on the Role of Intellectuals and Intelligentsia in the International Class Contest of the Modern Era* (Oxford University Press, New York, 1979); Daniel Bell, *The Coming of the Postindustrial Society: A Venture in Social Forecasting* (Basic Books, New York, 1973).
4. When The Society of Architectural Historians was founded, it was called the Society of American Architectural Historians. The word American was dropped when the Society was incorporated in 1947.
5. See J. A. Chewing, 'The Teaching of Architectural History during the Advent of Modernism, 1920s–1950s', in Elizabeth Blair MacDougall (ed.), *The Architectural Historian in America.* Studies in the History of Art 35 (Washington, D.C., 1990), p. 101. See also Gwendolyn Wright, 'History for Architects', in Gwendolyn Wright and Janet Parks (eds), *The History of History in American Schools of Architecture 1865–1975* (New York: Temple Hoyne Buell Center for the Study of American Architecture and Princeton Architectural Press, 1990); and Kenneth Frampton and Alessandra Latour, 'Notes on American Architectural Education', *Lotus* 27 (1980), no. 2, pp. 5–39.
6. Frampton, ibid., p. 7.
7. Wright, p. 13 (see note 5).
8. Ibid., p. 14.
9. Based on my analysis of the *Journal*. For the years 1941–44 inclusive, 74 per cent of the articles published in it were by writers who were teaching in schools of architecture; a small percentage of these writers were practicing architects. In the 1941 and 1942 volumes of the *Journal*, scholars teaching in schools of architecture outnumber all other writers by a margin of two to one.
   See also J. A. Chewing, p. 101 (note 5); O. Overby, p. 11 (note 2).
10. G. Wright (see note 5). Chewing disagrees with the claim that the amount of time devoted to history declined substantially in the 1940s; instead he rightly

emphasizes that the real change was in the changing content of courses and their role in the curriculum (p. 101, see note 5).

11. Turpin Bannister, the first editor of the *Journal*, described its audience in this way: 'Membership should be drawn from the staffs of professional schools of architecture and collegiate art departments, from practicing architects, from the governmental agencies dealing with the preservation of historic monuments, and from interested laymen. . .' as quoted in 'Summary of Round Table Discussion on the Preservation of Historic Architectural Monuments', *JSAH*, vol. 1 (April 1942), no. 2, p. 22.

12. Ibid., pp. 21–4. Among those present were noted historians Henry Russell Hitchcock, Richard Krautheimer, Paul Zucker, and officials from the National Parks Service then responsible for administering the Historic Sites Act, including Thomas Vint and Frederick D. Nichols.

13. *JSAH* vol. 2, no. 2. The issue published papers from a symposium held jointly with the Association of Collegiate Schools of Architecture entitled 'The Function of Architectural History in the Modern Professional Curriculum'. The editor, Turpin Bannister, stated in his contribution that he wished 'to survey the contributions that the study of the history of architecture can make to the students in our schools today, to help them master more completely the creative solution of contemporary problems . . .' (p. 5).

14. Hans Huth, writing in the July–October issue of the *Journal* in 1941, states that the American preservation movement began in 1864 when Congress declared Yosemite Valley a State Park, and 'war was declared against the vandals who threatened to destroy our cultural and national heritage . . .' (p. 5).

15. Fiske Kimball, a regular contributor to the *JSAH* in the 1940s, acted as architect for the restoration of, among other 'national' monuments, Monticello. He was also on the advisory boards of Colonial Williamsburg and the National Park Service, which was initially responsible for administering the Historic Sites Act.

16. In the period from 1941 to 1958 inclusive, 42 per cent of all articles do not have footnotes. For the first five years of this period, only 30 per cent have footnotes; from 1957 onwards, all articles are footnoted.

17. See Clausen Weatherhead, *The History of Collegiate Architecture in the United States* (The ACSA, New York, 1942); *The Architect at Mid-Century* (The AIA, Washington, 1952); Robert Gutman, *Architectural Practice: A Critical View* (Princeton Architectural Press, New York, 1988); and the SAH's *Graduate Degree Programs in Architectural History* (The Society of Architectural Historians, Philadelphia, 1992), for an indication of how architectural education has expanded since 1945. By 1955 the number of schools had increased by one third from the time of the last survey in 1935. Enrollment in first professional degree programs continued its upward climb until the 1970s, when it stabilized at approximately 15 000 students, an increase of two thirds over the 1940 level.

18. O. Overby, p. 15 (see note 2).

19. See William A. Green. 'Periodization and World History', *Journal of World History* (Spring 1992), pp. 13–53. Green stresses that the 'morphological exercise emphasizing disciplined concepts of change and continuity' is derived from the practices of eighteenth century botany. It is a mode of classification that relies on the comparative assessment of visible characteristics, and hence though it is putatively concerned with placing things in a chronological sequence, its method for establishing characteristics is based on observations of structure and form conducted 'outside time'. Universal, as opposed to particular manifestations in the object must be scrutinized (p. 14).

20.   See Stephen G. Nichols, 'Periodization and the Politics of Perception: A
      Romanesque Example', in *Poetics Today*, 10:1 (Spring 1989), pp. 131–54.
      Nichols describes how the eighteenth century naturalist Gerville developed his
      classification of Romanesque by referring to Jussieu's principles for studying
      and classifying plants. He determined the characteristics of Romanesque
      through the observation of relations in space, as though one were '. . .
      comparing plants in vegetal chains, or to a geographic map on which each
      being occupies a fixed point whose relationship to the whole may be
      determined . . . [or by] . . . a universal yardstick against which to measure and
      plot phenomena . . .' (p. 131).

21.   E. H. Gombrich has emphasized that although we accept the normative
      categories informing both art and architectural history, like 'Romanesque' as
      neutral and value-free, they are derived from discourses that favoured or
      opposed classicism. The terms of contemporary historical periodization
      evolved as terms of abuse related to one of these two positions. See E. H.
      Gombrich, *Norm and Form. Studies in the Art of the Renaissance* (Phaidon,
      London and New York, 1971), pp. 81–98. As Paul Rabinow has noted,
      although the opponents of anti-classicism were successful the categories
      remained, and were recuperated into a 'scientific' system of classification: '. . .
      much scholarly energy was . . . expended in seeking a scientific classification
      of form. Some historians sought universal morphological principles as the
      means to unify and ground the burgeoning historicist catalogue of difference.
      Others emphasized a plural unity within each of a multiplicity of cultural or
      historical periods; each era had its own internally coherent norm(s) and
      form(s) . . ., See Paul Rabinow, *French Modern. Norms and Forms of the
      Social Environment* (MIT Press, Cambridge, Mass., and London, 1989),
      pp. 7–8.

22.   Yasemin Aysan and Necdet Teymur. ' "Vernacularism" in Architectural
      Education', in Mete Turan (ed.), *Vernacular Architecture* (Avebury Press,
      Aldershot, 1990). Aysan and Teymur state that a 'parallel regionalism
      presenting itself within universalism exists within each Western discourse and
      education which consists of a selection of a very small proportion of the local
      production of artifacts and buildings assumed to qualify for the privileged title
      of Art or Architecture. It is this internalized universalism that provides the
      framework on which art and the architecture of different parts of the
      world are equally selectively judged in the name of "universal values". . .'
      (p. 308).

23.   The balance between American and European subjects has been present in the
      research activities of the Society's members at least since 1944. Progressive
      surveys of the members in 1944, 1949, 1956 and 1963 revealed that at least 50
      per cent of research was based on American topics, primarily in the nineteenth
      century. In 1967 a slightly higher proportion dealt with European subjects. In
      1990 the editor claimed that the typical balance between European and
      American subjects was still in place. See Tod Marder, 'Note From the Editor',
      *JSAH*, vol. XLIX (March 1990), no. 5, p. 5.

24.   John Maass, 'Where Architectural Historians Fear to Tread', *JSAH*, 28
      (March 1969), no. 1, pp. 3–8.

25.   I compiled the data for this sample from volumes for the following years:
      1941–43; 1950–52; 1960–63; 1970–73; 1980–83; 1990–93. In my survey I also
      found that since the 1980s the balance between Europe and North America
      has shifted, with articles on European topics outnumbering those based in
      America. In 1990–93, 67 per cent of the articles were on European subjects,
      while 29 per cent dealt with American topics.

26. Magali Sarfatti Larson, *The Rise of Professionalism. A Sociological Analysis* (University of California Press, Los Angeles, 1977), p. 4.

27. Ibid., p. 17.

28. In the 'Round Table on Architectural Preservation', H. R. Hitchcock suggests that a '. . . nationwide group of watchful historians could perform a valuable service in warning of danger weight (sic) with those responsible for an endangered building . . .' (p. 23).

29. Michel de Certeau, *Heterologies. Discourses on the Other* (University of Minnesota Press, Minneapolis, 1989).

30. Sibyl Moholy Nagy, 'Maass for Measure', *JSAH*, vol. XXIX (March 1970), no. 1, p. 61.

31. When the history of the *Journal* is considered as a whole, my research suggests that Christian religious monuments are the most common object of analysis in the *Journal* (18 per cent of all the articles in my survey were dedicated to this topic); this is followed by architectural biographies (14 per cent); and articles on villas, palaces, castles, country houses and modernist mansions (12 per cent). Articles on city planning took up 5 per cent of the total, while museums, government buildings and architectural style each comprised 5 per cent of the total; corporate office buildings, domestic architecture (row housing and mass housing) and architectural theory each registered 4 per cent.

32. While discussion of European architects is diffuse with very little repetition, the work of several American architects has attracted continuous attention in the *Journal*. Of the 228 articles which establish architectural authorship in my survey, the four most frequently analyzed are Frank Lloyd Wright (25), H. H. Richardson (12), Thomas Jefferson (8), and Louis Sullivan (7).

33. In his history of the *JSAH*, Osmund Overby suggests that its current form was established as early as 1951. He remarks that in response to a 1951 questionnaire respondents stated that 50 per cent of the *Journal*'s articles should be on American topics: 'In this, and most other ways as well, many of the salient and familiar features of the Society were in place by the 1950s'.

34. Hayden White, 'Historical Emplotment and the Problem of Truth', in Saul Friedlander (ed.), *Probing the Limits of Representation. Nazism and the Final Solution* (Harvard University Press, Cambridge, 1992), p. 37.

35. Mieke Bal, 'De-disciplining the Eye', *Critical Inquiry*, 16 (Spring, 1990), p. 506.

36. H. White, pp. 90–1 (see note 34).

37. See for example Stuart Wilson, 'The "Gifts" of Frederich Froebel', *JSAH*, vol. XXVI (Dec. 1967), no. 4, p. 238.

38. For an interesting study of the changing professional identities of the architect since the nineteenth century, see Andrew Saint's *The Image of the Architect* (Yale University Press, New Haven and London, 1983).

39. Steven Murray and James Addiss, 'Plan and Space at Amiens Cathedral: With a New Plan Drawn by James Addiss', *JSAH*, vol. XLIX (March 1990) pp. 44–66.

40. Clay Lancaster, 'The Philadelphia Centennial Towers', *JSAH*, vol. XXVI (October 1960), p. 11.

41. Michel de Certeau, *Heterologies. Discourse on the Other* (University of Minnesota Press, Minneapolis, 1989), p. 205.

42. Gerard Genette, *Narrative Discourse. An Essay in Method*, trans. by Jane E. Lewin (Cornell University Press, Ithaca, 1980), p. 166–7.

43. See Hayden White, *The Tropics of Discourse. Essays in Cultural Criticism* (The Johns Hopkins University Press, Baltimore, 1978). White claims that discourse is characterized by movement through archetypal modalities of figuration, which attempt to liken events to already known modes of

comprehension or consciousness. Discourse according to White 'is intended to constitute the ground whereon to decide what shall count as fact in the matters under consideration, and what mode of comprehension is best suited to the understanding of the facts thus constituted . . .', (p. 3) Because differing modes of comprehension are articulated through differing modalities of figuration, themselves forms of mimesis, mimetic text can be understood as representing a form of consciousness. 'Consciousness in its active, creative aspects, as against its passive, reflective aspects . . . is most directly apprehensible through discourse, and, moreover, in discourse guided by formulable goals, or aims of understanding . . .' (p. 20).

44.    I take this distinction from Louis Marin in *Utopics: The Semiological Play of Textual Spaces* (The Humanities Press, Atlantic Highlands, N.J., 1984), pp. 201–2.
45.    Ibid., p. 210.
46.    Ibid., p. 202.
47.    W. J. T. Mitchell, 'Spatial form in Literature: Towards a General Theory', in W. J. T. Mitchell (ed.), *The Language of Images* (University of Chicago Press, 1980), pp. 271–99.
48.    Michel de Certeau, *The Practice of Everyday Life* (University of California Press, Berkeley, 1984), p. 92.
49.    Marin, p. 206 (see note 44).
50.    Paul Rabinow, 'Representations Are Social Facts: Modernity and Post-Modernity in Anthropology', in J. Clifford and G. E. Marcus (eds), *Writing Culture* (The University of California Press, Berkeley and Los Angeles, 1986), p. 243.
51.    Edward Said, *Orientalism* (Phaidon, New York, 1977), p. 177.
52.    Eugene E. Matysek Jr., 'Three Recent Literatures in Architectural Research: A Citation Analysis, 1986–1990', unpublished student research paper, University of Maryland.
53.    According to Matysek, of the 98 articles published between 1986–90, 66 per cent of the monographs cited were published before 1970, and 13.2 per cent were published before 1900. Similarly, 56 per cent of the periodicals cited were published before 1950 (ibid., pp. 1–25).
54.    Matysek, ibid., p. 18.
55.    Nicholas Adams, 'Celebrating Tradition and Change', *JSAH*, vol. LII (June 1993), pp. 137–8.
56.    Ibid., p. 137.
57.    See for example, Sande Cohen, *Academia and the Lustre of Capital* (University of Minnesota Press, Minneapolis, 1993); Gayatri C. Spivak, *Outside in the Teaching Machine* (Routledge, New York and London, 1993); Régis Debray, *Teachers, Writers, Celebrities. The Intellectuals of Modern France* (New Left Books, London, 1979); Alaine Touraine, *The Academic System in American Society* (McGraw-Hill, New York, 1974).
58.    Jonathan Culler, 'Criticism and Institutions. The American University', in Derrick Attridge, Geoffrey Bennington, and Robert Young (eds), *Post-structuralism and the Question of History* (Cambridge University Press, 1987), p. 91.
59.    Ibid., p. 89.
60.    Nicholas Adams, 'Architectural Touring American Style', *JSAH*, 52 (September, 1993), p. 265.
61.    See Jean-François Lyotard, *The Postmodern Condition: A Report on Knowledge*, trans. Geoff Bennington and Brian Massumi (Manchester University Press, 1986).

62. Chandra Talpade Mohanty, 'On Race and Voice: Challenges for Liberal Education in the 1990s', *Cultural Critique* (Winter 1989–90), p. 188.
63. Ibid., p. 181.
64. Ibid., p. 185.
65. Nicholas Adams, 'Celebrating Tradition and Change', *JSAH*, vol. LII (June 1993), p. 137.
66. As Lyotard states, '. . . The relationship between suppliers and users of knowledge to the knowledge they supply and use is now tending, and will increasingly tend, to assume the form already taken by the relationship of commodity producers and consumers to the commodities they produce and consume – that is, the form of value. Knowledge is and will be produced in order to be sold, it is and will be consumed in order to be valorized in new production: in both cases, the goal is exchange. Knowledge ceases to be an end in itself, it loses its "use-value". . . See Jean-François Lyotard, *The Postmodern Condition: A Report on Knowledge*, trans. Geoff Bennington and Brian Massumi (Manchester University Press, 1986), p. 4.
67. Nicholas Adams, 'Architectural Touring American Style', *JSAH*, 52 (September 1993), p. 264.
68. See for example the Alaska Guide, where the author states that 'Readers who are travelling to Alaska will probably need additional guidebooks that explain the logistics of getting to places, available accommodations, and hours and fees of sites open to the public . . . For information on additional historic buildings, many towns distribute a walking tour guide. . .Sites open to the public also provide maps and other specific information . . .', Alison K. Hoagland, *Buildings of Alaska* (Oxford University Press, New York, Oxford, 1993), p. xiv.
69. Alfred K. Placzek, William H. Pierson, Jr. and Osmund Overby in their foreward to *Buildings of Alaska* state that the guide is '. . . among the first in a monumental series . . . dealing with a vast land of immense regional, geographic, climatic and ethnic diversity . . .' See Hoagland, p. v (note 68).
70. Over a third of the 'sustaining institutions', that contribute financially to the SAH are architectural schools; of the articles appearing in the *Journal* from 1990–93, for example, 19 were written by scholars working in schools of architecture, 15 came from art history departments, 15 from art or fine-art departments, and the remainder from history departments, graduate students, non-academics and contributors from outside North America.
71. See the NAAB *Conditions and Procedures* (The National Architectural Accrediting Board, New York, 1991).
72. Ibid., p. 16.
73. Ibid., p. 19.
74. Ibid., p. 19.
75. Conversation with J. Maudlin-Jeronimo, Executive Director of the NAAB, December 1, 1993.
76. Dana Cuff, *Architecture: The Story of Practice* (MIT Press, Cambridge, 1991), p. 118.
77. Ibid., p. 118.
78. Ibid., p. 45.
79. Thomas Dutton, 'Introduction: Architectural Education, Postmodernism and Critical Pedagogy', in Thomas Dutton (ed.), *Voices in Architectural Education: Cultural Politics and Pedagogy* (Bergin and Garvey, New York, 1991), p. xxiii. See also the themed issue of the *Journal of Architectural Education*, 'Gender and Multiculturalism in Architectural Education', *JAE* 47 (September 1993),

no. 1, and Greig Crysler, 'Critical Pedagogy and Architectural Education', *Journal of Architectural Education*, 48 (May 1995) in press.

80.   D. Cuff, p. 121 (see note 76).

81.   G. Wright, pp. 13–52 (see note 5).

82.   Conversation with J. Maudlin-Jeronimo, Executive Director of the NAAB, December 1, 1993. Though the NAAB would like to see the teaching of architectural history move towards the teaching of one general survey course on 'world architecture', followed by other more specialized topics, this has not yet happened although a small number of schools have begun courses in pre-Colombian , Oriental and Chinese architecture. This trend in fact is strikingly similar to the *JSAH*, which in recent years has also sought to expand its categories of analysis to include periods and places outside its Euro-American purview.

83.   Stanley Tigerman, 'Has Theory Displaced History as a Generator of Ideas in the Architectural Studio, or (More Importantly), Why Do Critics Continuously Displace Service Course Specialists?', *Journal of Architectural Education* (September 1992), p. 49.

84.   Ibid., p. 40.

# 11

# A Guide to Urban Representation and What to Do About It: Alternative Traditions of Urban Theory

Rob Shields

Debates over the ontological status of the city – is it 'real' or 'imagined'? – have kept academics busy for decades. Of course, most people usually don't bother with speculating about the real nature of the city. It is more useful to think of *whose* city it is. Where are the pleasant areas? Where is there danger? Such value-laden questions hint at the importance of representations for our understanding of environments which we characterize as 'urban'. To ourselves and to each other, we represent a complex environment which rarely has clear edges or boundaries as 'a city' or 'a town' or perhaps 'a neighbourhood'. While we may happily speak of the 'reality' of the city as a thing or form, they are the result of a cultural act of classification. We classify an environment as a city, and then 'reify' (see below) that city as a 'thing'. The notion of 'the city', *the city itself, is a representation*. It is a gloss on an environment which designates by fiat, resting only on an assertion of the self-evidence that a given environment *is* 'a city'. As an object of research, the city is always *aporetic*, a 'crisis-object' which destabilizes our certainty about 'the real'. Some have argued that the logical conclusions are that 'the urban' does not really exist or is an epiphenomenal distraction from 'real' issues, or that we should concentrate on studying individual buildings rather than urban environments, and people rather than neighbourhoods.[1,2] A more rigorous conclusion, however, would be that the role of representations in all matters urban needs to be re-examined.

In this chapter I shall survey different approaches to representation for clues to understanding representations of city life, townscapes both as 'cities' and as examples of 'the urban'. Here we are especially interested in the links between the visible that can be seen, and the articulable which is presented (or even made visible) by representations. Representations are argued to be complex formations of material, techniques and ideologies in which social practice is indissolubly linked to social thought and imagination. While 'ideological' they are therefore posited to be greater than 'ideology' and to outstrip the Cartesian divisions between the economic and cultural, and between thought and practice which are implicit in the terminology and theory of ideology.

## A WALK WITH DE CERTEAU AND BENJAMIN

Cities are not only the subject of representation but are 'objects' in representations. Representations of cities are like still life portraits. Consider planning documents, statistical profiles such as crime statistics, maps and 3-D models, respondents' sketch maps drawn for cognitive mapping research: these are like souvenirs of the lively urban environments in which most people live. Discussing planners' representations of the city, Michel De Certeau once remarked that from the height of a tall building like Toronto's CN Tower one can leave behind the everyday realities of living in a city and escape into an omniscient and objectifying planner's-eye view. From there:

> Icarus can ignore the tricks of Daedalus in his shifting and endless labyrinths. His altitude transforms him into a voyeur. It places him at a distance, it changes an enchanting world into a text. It allows him to read it, to become a solar Eye, a god's regard. The exaltation of a scopic . . . drive. Just to be this seeing point creates the fiction of knowledge. Must one then redescend into the sombre space through which crowds of people move about, crowds that, visible from above, cannot see there below? The fall of Icarus.[3]

Representations make the city available for analysis and replay. Their strange effect is that, like the snow falling in a souvenir snow-bubble, representations blanket the city, changing the way it appears to us. In Marxist terms, reality is obscured by ideology, which furthermore affects how we see ourselves and understand our actions. New York is metaphorically represented as 'the Big Apple', but other representations such as maps are understood to be realistic images for every city. In everyday life, we fashion and receive countless representations. Of course we all realize that a totally accurate representation – a perfect copy – is impossible. We are happy to settle for a good likeness. Like a still-life or *nature mort*, representations are arrangements of life – of nature *vivant*. Access to the environment in its crude 'real urban-ness' presumes that the city is a preformed and simply given object. A shroud of representations stands between us and even the concrete objects which are the elements of 'the city'.

Such problems are rarely issues in everyday life because most people are knowing, competent users of language and symbols. We focus on the resemblances between a given representation (such as a map of high-crime districts) and other representations (stories, urban myths, statistical reports), and balance them with our own experiences.[4] We make do with the representations we have at hand. In the bustle of everyday activities – including the pressurized atmosphere of city councils – we rarely have the time to turn our attention away from this practical focus to a more critical and even pessimistic study of the non-resemblance between different representations and the experience of everyday life.

If representations are souvenirs which serve to remind us of the city, on the other hand they replace or stand in for the city. Representations are treacherous metaphors, *summarizing* the complexity of the city in an elegant model. As de Certeau's example above hints, the city presented in planning documents is reified social process. In 'reification' we forget our own hand in producing representations, becoming alienated or estranged from our own production, and treat representations as natural objects. A plan is a frozen image of wandering footsteps and interactions which becomes preferred to physical interaction. The pedestrian and the idiosyncratic city of personal tastes vanishes or is at least thrown out of focus in representations such as plans. This might be contrasted with the stress some, such as Walter Benjamin (see Buck-Morss, 1989[5]), placed on the importance of flânerie ('prowling') for getting a 'fix' on the city and on the Other through a deep ethnography of attitudes and regimes of value.[6,7]

Representations are also metonymic in their tendency to *displace* the city completely so that one ends by not dealing with the physical level of direct social exchange and brute arrangements of objects but with a surrogate level of signs. This arrangement of signs is a simulacrum which presents itself as 'reality'. This is true whatever one's theoretical position on whether it makes any sense to talk of an objective, pre-representational 'reality'. Provided there are useful correspondences between this simulation and everyday practical experience, one accepts this substitution because it allows us to make useful conceptual shortcuts in our thinking and organizes experience and sensations in advance. Representations are linked to normative notions of what are appropriate social reactions to each of the myriad of possible events and encounters.[8] How? At the most simple, this occurs by re-coding (that is, translating and thus substituting) any given event or sensory experience as a social event or interaction of a specific kind. Representations tend to follow the formula of telling us 'what is really happening'. This process can become so complete that quite different representations of a given set of events and experiences are possible, especially when based on wider, culturally different, systems of representation.

In the notes he gathered over the 1930s for his uncompleted *Passagenwerk*[9] on the nineteenth century European city, Walter Benjamin pioneered this focus on 'individual footsteps'. He compiled dossiers on the archetypical 'figures' of the modern metropolis. In the shopping arcade, an early form of covered pedestrian mall, Benjamin defined people by their spatial activities: prostitutes, *flâneurs* or street prowlers,[10] onlookers who savour the view and sandwichmen wearing advertising placards who are so immersed in commercial exchange they become like commodities themselves. Benjamin's unconventional research procedure was to posit that people thought of their own, more mundane, activities in terms of ideal-typical figures (even if they were only urban myths). Rather than search for the statistical average 'arcade-user', he attempted to uncover the mythical structure of impulses, aspirations and anxieties which motivated the interactions of everyday street life. Benjamin used these 'nuggets' of everyday life to develop theories in which Marx's theory of capitalism was transformed to explain consumer society.

Benjamin argued that under modernity nostalgic representation produces corpses, and melancholic representation produces souvenirs. Benjamin characterizes the souvenir as an objectification of the moment of death. Celeste Olalquiaga[11] argues that we now experience this paradoxically: 'contemporary melancholia is capable of transforming nostalgic remains into souvenirs, as in the space-age comeback and the current delight in ruins and decay'.[12] We might revise and paraphrase her comments for the case of urban representations. Frozen in time, these representational 'corpses can only be understood spatially as volumes and textures [i.e. surfaces], promptly qualifying for an aesthetic scenification such as the one provided by dioramas', models, documentary film and other presentations of the urban.[13] 'A locus of conflict', sites of death and environments of suffering, can be 'aestheticized' in representations. For example, 'the camera – or the photographic gaze in general – . . . makes trophies of even the most gruesome images. In a reversal of straight hunting, photographic 'shooting' kills not the body but the life of things', leaving only representational carcasses.[14]

Perhaps this depressing observation is too nostalgic for a mythical golden age when reality was uncontaminated by representation. A time when things were things and thoughts were thoughts and the two never mixed. Yet this time when real and imaginary were perfectly separate probably never existed. Pure reality is an analytical construct which doesn't exist as far as social theory is concerned. Instead it appears that competing representations enliven the mute world of concrete and empirical interaction, giving meaning to places, cities and other urban areas. Without this element, urban conflicts would be factual and functional; instead they are symbolic and political.

In our 'walk' though the pages of Benjamin and de Certeau, we keep tripping over the concept of the city. Any archaeologist would argue that architecture and material culture can inform us about the society which constructed and used it. The city itself can be treated as a representation of the society which constructed it. For example the spatial divisions of the city are often indicators of the fault-lines of social relations which are spatialised, extruded into the arrangements of everyday living. This 'social spatialisation' includes not only habitual practices and representations of environments, but also the subtle spatial structuring of the social imaginary.[15] By this, people come to think of the world and cosmos in terms of their built environment and geographical experience. This is a 'second' nature because it overlays and partially effaces the original 'first' nature of the physical ecology[16] and provides the framework within which questions about both the universe and the structure of social relations are posed. Yet this cultural form, what I am calling a social spatialisation,[17] is a fractured, discontinuous and conflicting constellation.[18] It has order only for the analyst, and only for the fleeting time of analysis. We do not live in abstract categories, but in the lived space of *concrete* abstractions.[19,20] But the truth of 'the city' is that it is a 'concrete abstraction': an abstract form which nonetheless has concrete implications, such as the commodity. Hence the shortsightedness of *both* a simple empiricism which accepts the city as reality, not representation, and of cynical idealism which dismisses the 'equivalent to real' status of representations of the city. The city is a concept with a very concrete affect.

While the lives of individuals as well as the events of corporate powers can be included in a unified representation of space,[21] one town or any given building or architectural project, presents a much more restricted semiotic field. But even if the urban reveals much about its builders, it may be silent on the question of the 'unofficial text' which I have discussed above. Therefore we must pay attention to not only the visible and represented, but also the dark silences of urban constructions. It should also be warned that any such silences cannot simply be read-off from an eschatology of power or privilege. Silences are not necessarily intended. Nor are they necessarily consonant with class struggle, patriarchy or white domination.[22] Their meaning is ambiguous. First, this points to the *relative* autonomy of practices and processes of representation and the complexity of both processes of domination, of oppression and of the subjects involved.[23] It would be as foolish to reduce them in the last instance to other structural forces, as it would be to isolate them under the rubric of connoisseurship. Second, this points to the importance of interpretation. Within a system of interpretation, codes of reading and privileged positions of empathy with the object or work, channel perceptions and assumptions. Practices of meaning-production and of interpretation are inextricable parts of the sphere of ideas, discourses and representations.

## JACQUES DERRIDA DECONSTRUCTS REPRESENTATION

The very notion of 'representing the city' leads to philosophical questions of representation and of the definition of 'the city' and 'the urban'. Jacques Derrida's theory of deconstruction has been one of the most important influences on contemporary theory, going through several phases of reception in which it has been first trivialized and then later its radical potential retrieved. Deconstruction focusses on 'the political power of rhetorical operations – of tropes and metaphors in binary oppositions like white/black, good/bad, male/female, machine/nature, ruler/ruled, reality/appearance – showing how these. . .sustain hierarchical world views by devaluing the second terms. . .' (West, 1990[24]). Derrida's extreme doubt concerning the foundational dualisms of western thought results in the unravelling of the attempted closure of texts and the finality of meaning. These are not only philosophical texts but metaphoric texts like 'the urban' that de Certeau referred to above. Their meaning is questioned to reveal their implications, to dissolve their assumed authority and to transgress the conventional symbolic and political order of signs and meanings. Spivak puts it this way:

> . . . when a Jacques Derrida deconstructs the opposition between private and public, margin and centre, he touches the texture of language and tells how the old words would not resemble themselves anymore if a trick of rereading were learned. The trick is to recognize that . . . in the production of everyday explanation, there is the itinerary of a constantly thwarted desire to make the text [or a picture, or an object] explain.[25]

In simpler terms, in representing the city as a knowable, mappable thing the ironic and paradoxical aspects of the urban are elided, only to be rediscovered later as anomalies to, for example, theories of urban morphology. If the city is knowable, this will be on a rational basis (for academics at least)[26] and the city – even if hard to define – will be presumed to be a rational object: 'In incessantly explaining, we exclude the possibility of the existence of things so radically different they can't be explained within our system of rational thought'.[27]

In dualisms like urban-rural or public-private, each term is dependent on the other for its distinctness and definition. The city is conventionally defined as the opposite of the country.[28] Derrida labels this symbiotic relationship *différance*. In this system of meaning, the definition of terms and concepts ultimately is circular. Dictionaries of European and American languages define words in terms of other words. Their definitions eventually lead tautologically back to the first term. Derrida argues that it is necessary to go beyond defining terms to analyse the system of *différance* implicit in our definitions. For example debates on the meaning of the term 'community' became notorious in the late 1960s and early 1970s. Similarly the term 'urban', and even the more philosophically defined 'space' (as in social space), were endlessly debated through the 1980s. What is 'the urban'? Derrida's insight is to note that definitions rely on *différance*: the urban is what the non-urban (that is, the rural) is not and vice versa. In such a world half-way cases – suburbia, 'pre-urban' fringes or 'sprawl', and 'post-urban' ghost towns – are an abomination. Possibly such environments are widely condemned because they confuse us and the definitions by which we hold the world firmly and rationalize the evidence of our senses?[29] A more probing question is therefore to ask what operations must be brought to bear to distinguish the urban from the rural? What administrative procedures and authoritative powers define its boundaries marking 'the city' off from its surrounds? What technologies, sciences and other professions are brought into existence to accomplish this feat of definition? What are the implications of this legislative act? In particular, what in-between states (semi-urban or semi-rural) are neglected and therefore not studied, and their possibilities and potentials lost to us?

Yet a commitment to articulate *différance* merely creates the *possibility* of disturbing the conventional edifice of mutually supporting definitions. It does not accomplish social change. Like a biting joke that momentarily destabilizes accepted understandings or shows the irony in things, the challenge of deconstruction remains at the level of language and poetics. Alone, deconstruction does not replace or transform the prejudices of our system of cultural meaning. This project can become a never-ending series of repetitious deconstructions which reiterate the same lesson on new material again and again.

There is a second problem: like the metaphysical system of dualisms Derrida is critiquing, his work is ultimately logocentric in its focus on discourse. Deconstruction necessarily focuses on texts, words and ideas (e.g. definitions). These tend to become separated from their context. That is, a sociological or geographical vision of the practical context of language use and of language users has to be added to textual deconstruction. It is necessary to go beyond the symbolic operation of the universe of concepts to recognize that definitions and dualisms are signs 'implicated in specific historical and discursive conditions'.[30, 31] They have a time and, it must be added, *a place*. Dualistic concepts as *black/white* or *city/country* refer to lived material experiences and relationships as well as each other. Such terms take on different connotations when used in different practical, material circumstances. Used in the city, the city/country dualism often has the opposite sense from when used by a person who lives in the country. To the city cousin, it suggests that the city is better in every way than the country; to the country cousin, the countryside may be considered morally better than the cityscape. In the urban riots of the late 1960s, 'Black power' did not mean 'bad power' as it might if it was a phrase used in a sixteenth century Catholic mass where black would be counterposed to white as bad is to good. Spatial setting inflects the meanings of even the most basic metaphors of the most elementary moral division of good and bad (compare the critique of Werlen, 1992[32]). We could say that 'space' has communicative properties. Situation and context in time and space are communication factors which affect the meaning of even simple messages. Beyond territorial location and distance, representations are affected by built form, architectural style, volume, material and so on. This suggests that representations depend not only on linguistic and other cultural sign systems but also on material culture and the embodied materiality of culture which one finds in the practices of everyday life.[33, 34, 35]

Representations are thus often couched in such binary systems of *différance* but they are comprehensible only if one understands that they refer both to their opposite and to a non-discursive level of the city at the same time. The status of the city itself remains however always outside its representations. And without some sort of representation, a map, a generalisation, a guide, the purely non-discursive, positivistically empirical city is also unknowable. What a state science gets us into! Of course, this dualistic separation of the discursive and non-discursive has already been transgressed in an endnote, above. Michel de Certeau was cited at the beginning, muddying this distinction by contrasting the meaning of the city from the planner's bird's-eye viewpoint and the point of view of personal itineraries in space by which pedestrians actualize sites through their 'narrative footsteps' as spaces for this and spaces for that – a side*walk* for pedestrians and an *auto*route for cars which is to be only furtively crossed on foot.[36] The city is a 'metatext', or text of texts and of writers. The city crosses the line of discourse and action: it is '*trans-discursive*', to coin a term. In the city people are inscribed, but on it they leave their own everyday traces.[37] Heedful of this caveat let us turn to the issue of 'representing the city'.

## IN(THE)VISIBLE CITY OF REPRESENTATIONS

> . . . when the crisis of language and poetry is pushed beyond certain limits it ends up putting in question the very structure of society (*La Tour de Feu*, 82 (June 1964).[38]

'Re-presenting the City' is a curious phrase which conceptually sutures together representations of the city and the city as a concrete construction.

There are a series of paradoxes to this connection which weave together elements that are often placed in contrast by social theorists: ideological representations and urban realities. Representations versus Reality; Theory versus Practice; Art versus Life; Fiction versus Fact – a powerful string of dualisms unrolls. Shuttling back and forth between images and practical deeds, one might also imagine this in the way de Certeau does: a movement between the planar representational space of a picture frame, or a page of text, and the tactile space of everyday life. Urban environments are made selectively visible as 'cities' through representation. In such representations, cities are *presented* as primarily visual. Both the visibility and visuality of the city are always incomplete ciphers or parts of the tactile movement of urban life. The transactional city of direct interaction and exchange is the centrepiece of the sociologies of Simmel[39] and Goffman.[40] The 'condition of visibility', the logical and connotative system in which representations are formed, is so powerful as to effectively *create* the things that are the subjects of representation.[41] Only some parts are easily seen. What is un-represented and invisible? Often the relationship between the viewer and the representation itself is obscured. The city is kept in focus but not the representation's audience. Conditions of visibility refer to those factors such as power, and the social construction of reality through discourses on the real, which keep the city 'in focus' as a visible object, with us, researchers and audiences outside that focused frame.[42] Representation therefore raises the problem of the politics of what is visible and what is hidden.

The paradoxes of representing the city cannot be dismissed or avoided by simply revising this with a hyphen to 'Re-Presenting the City'. This would move it from a statement of what is done to an announcement. That is, the phrase changes from a speech-act of performance, to a presentation or proclamation with legislative overtones: the city *will* be seen (again) in a new light. In re-representing the city, the dilemmas of these dualisms merely 're-present' themselves. Our deconstruction reveals a series of crucial contradictions which cannot be solved by semantic, or scientific, 'fiddling'.

What is this object of representation and the subject of proclamation? As we have already found, 'The City' is a slippery notion. It slides back and forth between an abstract idea and concrete material; between the abstract universal of 'The (ideal) City' and concrete particular of 'This (my) City'. On the one hand it is an idea, on the other hand it is a thing. As an ideal-type the city is a general model of urban conglomeration and social centrality, for example, as discussed by Henri Lefebvre in *Le Droit à la ville*.[43] As a real 'thing', the city is a particular real-life arrangement of materials and constructions and/or social relationships as explored by Alan Pred in his examination of late 19th century working-class Stockholm.[44, 45] There is a pervasive intellectual tendency to forget the private spaces and life of the city in favour of its public, civic spaces. When we speak of 'the City', that is, when we attempt to represent this 'thing-idea', we inevitably engage in a subtle process of interweaving often unstated ideal-types with particular cases and situations we have experienced in specific cities. We blend the abstract and general with the concrete and particular in an easy and familiar notion of 'the city'. The city is part of a class of thing-ideas called *environments* which we conventionally and uncritically know can be understood from both the ground level of daily interaction and from the birds-eye view of, say, an urban planner.[46]

## DIFFERENCE AND VISIBILITY

One side-effect of the interest in Derridean *différence* has been to draw English-language researchers' attention to 'difference'. In the 'translation' the term has changed from being a political rather than theoretical term. Such a difference one accent makes. What is the role of difference in the city and representation? Feminist theorists[47, 48] have directed attention to the question of gender differences and male-domination of public life and urban public places. Without attention to gender there is a tendency to represent the city as a generally public space, that is to focus on its street life, leaving out the home life within the tenements, flats, dwellings and backyards in which family life takes place. This should not be taken to imply that women and children are or have been absent from public streets. Elizabeth Wilson, Christine Stansell (1986)[49, 50] and others have argued that the gendered distinction between male public and female private (domestic) life is too simply drawn. Both show the central role and celebrate the contribution of working-class women to public life both as 'figures on the street' and as service labourers in the economic public sphere, even though they might have been under-represented, even silenced, in the traditional political public sphere. Class, culture and local histories inflect this over-generalized male-public-female-private distinction. The admirable work of feminists in the field who attempt to restore the status of women *in the public spaces* of 'the city' is symptomatic of this cultural bias which underpins modernity and the ethical aesthetics of the middle class.[51, 52]

Nonetheless, the domestic sphere of women and men, and of children, adults and the elderly remains a 'third sector' unreached by almost all political economy.[53] The domestic remains *invisible* in representations of the city as a public 'space' which is thought of as merely the built analogue or architectural concretisation of the public 'sphere'.[54, 55, 56] The domestic is *made invisible* by such representations in the same way that women are made invisible in public. This pattern is confirmed at other levels of representation of the city, such as in academic journals concerned with urban studies which often repeat this bias of emphasis in the drawing of the limits of the topics they print.[57] Spaces of social activity such as the domestic are invisible due to their conventionally non-public character. Even much of sociology confines itself to a sociology of public space, relegating the sociology of private realms and spaces to the subdiscipline of 'family studies' and 'sociology of the family'. Although there is no space – pardon the pun – for it here, we begin to see the glimmerings of a theorisation of the domestic or private sphere which would be a corrective to the pattern of 'oppression of the domestic' by the stress on the public.[58]

'Postcolonial' critics have drawn attention to racial and ethnic difference, heavily accented by histories of political oppression, social domination and colonialism.[59, 60, 61] Ethnic oppression may have spatial manifestations – the ethnic or racial ghetto[62] being the classic case[63] where the identity of inhabitants may be inscribed in and ensured by municipal zoning and planning law.[64] The cases of 'Chinatowns'[65] or the Warsaw Jewish ghetto[66] are examples. The less systematically studied urban spatialisation is obviously the colonial city, especially the colonial capital[67, 68] of which Ottawa and Algiers[69] are cases.

The position and outlook of a person who hears, sees or reads a representation of a city or cities in general — their 'subject position' – is established on the basis of what is given to be heard, seen or read. Representations have the effect of 'positioning' people 'for or against' by building in assumptions about those receiving representations. To make sense or be believable, the 'spectator' or audience of a representation must place themselves in this 'subject position' – a positioning which is often criticised for being based on the viewpoint and desires of the white, urban, American or European professional male. This 'given to be seen is always exclusionary' and thus 'subject positions are always related to the negative, to that which cannot be or is not developed' within a representation. 'Therefore, subject positions are always partial'.[70] The importance of representations is that they are texts or images which, by revealing only specific aspects of the city and focussing our attention on these instead of on others, have the power to limit the courses of action which we will follow or to frame problems in such a way that only certain solutions are likely to occur to us.[71] For example many so-called dangerous areas of the city are only dangerous for certain people and at certain times, but by defining an area as 'dangerous' all people may avoid the area, causing business to suffer. In this spatialisation, fear is projected onto a space. A 'geography of fear'[72, 73] precipitates or furthers the decline of an area into a stereotypical landscape of 'inner city blight'.

This foregrounds the problem not just of the visible city, but of representation – what the city is represented as. Civic life 'in public' no longer conforms to the norms of the European bourgeoisie, analysed by Habermas,[74] Simmel[75] and Sennet.[76] But in general and normative terms, the accessible and easily visible city is the city of the old public sphere[77, 78] which dominates the private sphere or domestic.[79] It is the city of formal institutional and economic relations. This city is the political-economic city. Analyses abound of the importance of changing patterns of trade, communications and of the role of state apparatii in structuring the operation of markets, the conduct of social relations and the organisation of space through private property law, zoning, building codes and professional engineering and architectural practices. This is the city of streets, public institutions, sites of political encounter and debate, the consumption of commodities and symbols, of education, business and the conduct of neighbourly relations.

This social space is extended virtually in the form of the spaces of television broadcasts.[80, 81] However here the clarity of the schema of the 'public city' begins to break down as television messages penetrate into the private, supposedly less regulated domestic world of 'time-off', of the so-called 'reproduction of labour', of 'what life is all about': of family intimacy, care, dependency and emotion. Rather than a separate sphere, this is perhaps better understood through the musical metaphor of a shift in tonal register. The private sphere of the *domus* is the counterpoint, interwoven to the continuo of public life. This shift in register is indicated by the shift in terminology which occurs whenever we begin to speak profoundly of our intimate relations or of our alone-ness.[82, 83]

This private city is the invisible city of sociability[84] and everyday life. Often this set of urban relations, although intensified by the physical and social proximity of people, is masked by the visible architecture and spatial divisions of the urban built environment which provides an 'official text', as it were. The convergence of communications and transportation paths on the global city further expands this sense of proximity to include relatively great distances and far-away peoples.

The public and private are interlinked. This combination of the old notion of public 'civil society' and the internal life of households is the realm of 'everyday life' (see Lefebvre[85] and by contrast Maffesoli[86]). This is the realm of both the most insidious and most banal interpenetration of the political economic and the cultural. It is here on the terrain and in the spaces of everyday life that the analysis of the contemporary city must take root. As Maffesoli points out, there are now multiple public spaces where the provision of goods by the welfare state is contested. These range from institutional spaces such as hospital outpatient wards, public spaces such as street demonstrations and private spaces of provision for the needs of the disabled in the community. In the case of home care for the elderly, Yeatman argues that there is an:

> interpenetration of the state and everyday life in respect of areas of individual need usually reserved for what we would term personal privacy. It is an example which is outside the scope of the classical liberal and republican democratic polity of modernity. In this polity, needs of the

kind to which I am referring were left to the private and natural business of the internal life of households.[87]

Needs of this kind, and political struggles over their provision were not represented as part of public life in the city. Instead, they were relegated to private life or to the unofficial world of barter-exchange which Mikhail Bakhtin contrasts with the official representation of urban life.[88] Representations of the urban public sphere of the city focus on and make visible the political and economic sphere of civic interactions and official exchanges. Not all exchanges or interactions are political and economic, only those which are defined and recognized as productive, or production-oriented, and those which are guided by rationality. Thus consumption is the silent partner of production, women the silenced counterparts of men, and desire or non-rational thought the overlooked mirror of Reason. On the one hand, one might seek to synthesize such oppositions dialectically. But this assumes that a synthesis would be more stable and exempt from deconstructive critique. On the other hand it may be that one must defer to the liveliness of an irreducibly dialogical structure of polarities within concepts like the city and representation. This would involve attempting to maintain the co-presence of very different aspects whenever one represents the city.

## THE DIALOGICAL CITY: MIKHAIL BAKHTIN

The broad notion of *dialogism*, of contradictory elements locked in a permanently non-resolving arrangement, is used to characterize the work of the Russian philosopher and literary scholar Mikhail Bakhtin.[89, 90, 91, 92] The essence of dialogical opposition is the lack of promise of a synthesis. The 'dialogical' is quite different from the 'dialectical'. *Chronotope* is Bakhtin's term for the treatment of time and place characteristic of a literary genre such as the novel, or the epic.[93] Some have used 'chronotope' to develop the term 'chronotopography', the analysis of the time-space characteristics of a given mode of production or of colonialism.[94] There has been relatively little application of Bakhtin's work to urban studies or architecture. What exists is only the first sign of the analytical potential of dialogism. Notions such as chronotope have yet to be systematically compared to geographical concepts which foreground the social use and even construction of spaces by spatialising feelings, beliefs and activities.[95]

Geographers have made the most impressive applications to general discussions of the relationship between social life, peasant culture and landscape.[96] Bakhtin's work emphasizes the other-directedness of representations and of all communication. We are all implicated in a socio-cultural system for which language is the most obvious example and medium. In his

critique of Saussurian semiotics, Bakhtin shows that symbolic codes and
representations (for example, languages) are social: other people must
understand one's utterances and we are constantly judged by others on the
basis of our linguistic competence. As opposed to official culture and proper
language, Bakhtin demonstrates the fecundity and importance of what he
calls 'free-speech', the motley polyglot of spoken words in everyday life
which escape the control or censorship of officialdom. Central here is what
he calls 'Billingsgate', after the old London fish market, which is made up of
free forms of address (slang, insults, rough jibes) which do not acknowledge
distinctions of class or cultural politeness. This analysis of communication
and culture includes temporal and spatial categories. Billingsgate and other
forms of the carnivalesque are linked to specific sites such as the market-
square, theatre and fairground[97] and to an analysis of the time-space
characteristics of different genres of literature and story-telling. As a result
Bakhtin's work is rich in suggestive inferences for the student of urban life
and design. Yvonne Rainer comments that:

> the city . . . is a place full of sexual anxiety, obsession and verbal assault,
> litanies of sexual distress . . . [It is] a barrage – a veritable eruption – of
> ordinarily repressed material.[98]

A chronotopography goes beyond a time-space mapping such as
Hägerstrand's chronogeography (the best recent use is found in Pred,
1991[99]) or a study of cognitive maps[100, 101] because it is not grounded in a
functionalistic desire to describe or represent an empirical reality. It is
oriented to discovering the temporal and spatial character of cultures[102, 103, 104] which cross constantly between the 'real' and the represented. Because of the focus on oppositional discourse and practices (for
example, low culture versus high or official culture) and on moments of
inversion of norms (which Bakhtin terms the 'carnivalesque'), Bakhtin's
theoretical outlook is oriented towards the accommodation of difference
and opposing voices which, for example, represent the city in quite different
ways. Bakhtin's own representations of the city[105] are accounts of how
fragmented, partial and in conflict representations are in the hurly-burly
events of everyday 'unofficial' life. Such oppositions may produce synthetic
visions but more often than not, hybrid forms result which accommodate
the lived city to the ongoing tensions of the represented city. A classic
example of such a tension would be the balcony on the front facade of
bourgeois residences in many Mediterranean cultures, which allowed both
the expression of class difference and participation in city festivals and
processions.

In such sites and situations tensions remain not in a dialectical
arrangement (in which the resolution of contradictions in a synthesis is
emphasized) but a dialogical arrangement of unresolvable tensions and

paradox. As in a dialogue the difference between the positions is the motor of the conversation and the self-affirmation of the parties. The cultural goal may be just to 'keep the conversation going' rather than for one group or position to supersede or dominate the other. Dialogism describes the source of Benjamin's frisson of different cultures and figures experienced in the cosmopolitan arcades of late nineteenth century Paris. In Bakhtin's work, one finds a first taste of Derrida's exposure of the false dualism of 'real city life' and its representation.

## THE CITY IS A BODY WITHOUT ORGANS: DELEUZE

Gilles Deleuze and Félix Guattari have attacked the conventional Euro-American analytic focus on production and reason in their study of desire, the state and capitalism in their two volume *Capitalism and Schizophrenia* (*The Anti-Oedipus*, vol. 1 (1983) and *A Thousand Plateaus*, vol. 2 (1987).[106, 107] While the former is aimed at critiquing the practice of psychoanalysis, it begins with a spatialised 're-telling' of Marx's first volume of *Capital*. Like Derrida, they argue that the fascination of analysis – of seeing the truth – is linked to a scopophilia and voyeuristic desires for mastery. Here the visible is a product of desiring. Things must *mean*, and if they are paradoxical environments like 'the urban', they must be 'represented' for the purposes of analysis by surrogate visions, such as maps, models and images. Deleuze and Guattari provide a general theory of production and of the process of Reason in terms of these desires which are in turn linked to the social and the spatial.

> The truth of the matter is that *social production is purely and simply desiring production itself under determinate conditions.* We maintain that the social field is immediately invested by desire, that it is the historically determined product of desire, and that libido has no need of any mediation or sublimation, any psychic operation, any transformation, in order to invade and invest the productive forces and the relations of production. *There is only desire and the social, and nothing else.*[108]

Here desire is positive and constitutive, cast in the same manner as Foucault's notion of power which is implicit in everyday interaction, and constitutive of identities, not held apart from social action by the state. Deleuze and Guattari identify the Cartesian method of breaking problems and complex environments down into their small parts as central to the process which produces partial representations. A less pathological approach to understanding objects of analysis is summed up under the slogan of the 'body without organs'. Rather than dissecting an object of analysis, which merely renders new objects for further dissection (for example organs which explain the functioning of the first object of analysis, the body, but which themselves are later exposed as needing to be dissected and so on), objects must be understood at the ontological level at which they exist as such. They must be understood by their powers, surfaces and effects. We might recognize this as a rejection of depth hermeneutics,[109, 110] for example, realist explanations of urban 'appearances' by deep structures and forces which are posited to exist but are unprovable as such, only helpful tools for explanation (and for representing the city in a certain way as in, say, political economy). This new epistemology poses a challenge to what is, after all, a tradition of metaphoric representations sketched out in terms of the visible (using words like 'appearance' and 'surface', as if describing a canvas in a museum rather than the tactility of lived encounters).

The rational city of urban planning is one where the 'urban body' has been recoded or represented as a circulatory system of rationalized flows, traffic patterns and functional organ-like zones (spaces for this and spaces for that – see the critique by Otnes, 1990[111]). Applied to the city, this is an argument for an analysis of the urban *in se*. The questions now are: 'What is it that makes an urban conglomeration knowable as "a city"?' 'What are the powers of this 'urban body or thing'? These questions avoid dissolving the object of study into the operations which constitute it, such as the investment of capital, transportation links, political and economic activities, class antagonisms and so on. Rather than preferentially representing the urban as the public city only, this approach also focusses on the undivided and *undissected* city which is a complex surface of activities and interactions which are usually dismissed as anomalous in conventional representations of the urban.

This raises a new set of questions for students of the urban and presents the challenge of not dissolving the urban into its constituent processes, forces and objects. This would be a methodological break with the tradition of reductive Cartesian analysis. For example the relation between the visible built environment of the city and socio-economic relations is generally conceived as a relation between surface (appearance) and depth (structural forces). This allows the visible city to be re-presented as an artifact of socio-economic relations. Deleuze's critique can be used to argue that this relationship might be reconceived as a relationship between the visible and the articulable, between the visual (architecture, urban features) and the tactile (exchange and interaction) existing on the same epistemological plane with neither having analytical or explanatory priority over the other. If the city is a body without organs, what are its constitutive desires? How are these desires made manifest on this body? How is the play of desire as a productive, social force made visible on the face of the urban? If desire is the founding impulse of society, how are we to understand the affectual, emotional city (a kind of view from the slum) rather than focusing on the ideally-planned rational city (the view from city hall)? The emotional city is perhaps then closer to reality – to the essence of the urban – than the rational urban representation and ordering imposed by state functionaries.

Deleuze and Guattari sketch an initial answer in terms of state administrative technologies grounded in a state territory (ironically, a 'deterritorialized' spatialisation in which administrative codings of land as property or as a strategic site repress a prior spatialisation of the topography which is territorialized as a human landscape of meaningful places for dwelling) and nomadic organisational technologies which are also deterritorialized but in a different sense. They are grounded in flows of people and goods across space. The two are antithetical even if harnessed uneasily together in the form of the modern State. The former technology is cadastral in origin and finds its purest expression in municipal governance of the polis. The latter is numerical in origin (into legions and as in temporary encampments for example) and is expressed as 'pure war': the pirate ship or 'Barbarians' whose social organisation takes place not through peoples' belonging to a coded landscape but through their belonging to a mobile clan or military unit from which representative cadres report to a central leadership. The contradictory nature of the modern city derives from its dual organisation along both of these axes – the State and the Nomad. This is not a question of a state administration versus nomadic people but of the attempt by municipal administration to use both the organisational techniques of the State and of the Nomad together, and the appeal of both settled community life and anonymous crowd sociability to residents of the city. Thus on the one hand zoning, on the other hand the census. On the one hand identification through address and postal code, on the other hand the organisation of local militia units (as in countries with compulsory ongoing military service). On the one hand the identification of people by their neighbourhood of origin, on the other hand the mixing of people in clubs, cathedrals and political institutions, not to mention markets and shopping centres. On the one hand, settlement and belonging to the place, on the other hand the thrill of flows of people, goods and information which distinguish the urban milieu from the milieu and ethos of an isolated settlement. The city cannot be adequately represented as one or the other. This State-Nomad mixture is the motor of representations, the source of desires to fix, re-define and specify yet again 'the urban'. This mixture is the source of the paradoxical and 'Hybrid', syncretic quality of the urban which eludes the fixed categories and the 'presentation of the urban' in representations. Hybridity is one of the epistemological and ontological specificities of the urban which is often lost in representations. The city conceived of as a 'body without organs' is both grounded and sited within a place-based spatialisation, at the same time that it is presented and offers itself as a communications node in a wider, generalized space(s) of the flow of goods and information. Its hybrid quality affects its time-space character: it is always more than 'mine, here and now', it is 'theirs, then and there'.[112]

'The city' thus eludes definitions and our other attempts to possess it. Indeed a chronotopography of any city would be a representation which exceeded the conventional understanding of the specificity of 'the urban' because it would necessarily extend to include linkages and routes beyond the city itself.

## THE SITUATIONIST CITY

One final critique of the rational planning approach to understanding the city needs to be added, for it has the merit of having been applied historically. Bringing private desires into the public realm, giving the emotional and affectual a place in the urban environment was a project of the Situationist group[113, 114] with members in Strasbourg, Paris and Amsterdam between the mid 1950s and the end of the 1960s.[115] Turning the city from its productive orientation to being a centre for the consumption of environments, in which people lived by drifting from area to area and activity to activity depending on their moods rather than being regulated by instrumental rationality was certain to disrupt the modern city.[116] It culminated in the student led 'festival' of May 1968. For almost a month, such slogans as 'beneath the pavers, the beach' hinted at the ludic potential to change the even pragmatic road surfaces into dream sites. As during the rebellion of the Paris Commune in the Summer and Fall of 1871 (the historical precedent which served as a kind of template for the events of May 1968 and which the Situationists had carefully studied), sites symbolic of the existing social order were occupied and their functions changed.[117]

This project was dubbed '*psychogeography*' by the 'Situs'. The practice of psychogeography was *dérive*, literally 'drifting' and allowing themselves to be drawn by the chance attractions and encounters of the urban environment.[118, 119, 120] So the Situationists experimented by refusing to work and drifting themselves as the bohemians of 1960s Paris intellectuals. The key piece of Situationist writing on architecture, urbanism and the practice of space was Ivan Chtcheglov's 'Formulary for a New City', an essay written in 1953, when Chtcheglov was 19, and only published in 1958[121] under the pseudonym of Gilles Ivain in the first issue of *Internationale Situationniste*. Chtcheglov saw the city as the site of 'new visions of time and space'.[122] While this idea is strictly within the orbit of modernist urban and architectural projects such as those promoted by Le Corbusier in its attempt to use architecture as a means of changing the relations of everyday life, in Chtcheglov's new experimental city different districts would correspond to the 'diverse feelings that one encounters by chance in everyday life.' Inhabitants would spend their days in a 'continuous *dérive*', drifting through the multi-coloured quarters of the city as emotion and desire pulled them here and there. This is the origin of de Certeau's concern for a narrative of footsteps by which urban spaces are activated and used as places for this and places for that.

How is *dérive* relevant to a more general project of understanding urban representations, or any given city? *Dérive* highlights the emotive aspects of the city, where places are commonly characterised not just by physical data but by their powers of 'attraction': who hangs out where and when shapes the identity of sites and spaces. *Dérive* de-emphasises the dogma of urban theory and planning: that hidden economic forces shape experiences of the city. Instead we are confronted by the fractured logic of everyday life which superimposes a less rationalised experience of the city based on appearances, not essentialist socio-economic forces. *Dérive* arguably operates at the level of pragmatics, reversing the primacy of goal-oriented behaviour and intentions in favour of an emphasis on achieved effects and unanticipated results. *Dérive* and 'psychogeography' introduces an aesthetics of place and space purified of the traditional focus on architectural aesthetics (which becomes a kind of rhetoric focussed on the 'devices' of place- and space-making). As such this hints at the possibility of the reintroduction of concerns with aesthetics and thus of representations into urban planning, a field dominated by pragmatic transportation and economic concerns.


## CONCLUSION: WHAT TO DO ABOUT URBAN REPRESENTATIONS

Urban representations characterize not only academic theories but also the understandings of cities used in politics, planning and business investment. Representations are not simple fictions. If they are exposed as poetic, they are poetry written with peoples' interactions, social events and economic exchanges. The measure of success of a study of urban representations will lie in its fecundity to integrate theory with everyday practice and to generate new understandings and to transcend old dead-ends, such as the dualism erected between urban representations and the 'real city'. Rather than discard the urban because of its spatial hybridity; rather than disapprove of representations because of their treacherous selective vision of the city, we need to construct multi-dimensional analyses which, rather than imposing monological coherence and closure, allow parallel and conflicting representations to coexist in analysis. This leads us toward a dialogical approach to the spatialisation of the urban. This paper has reviewed several major but neglected sources for such a critical reconceptualisation of the urban. These form an alternative tradition of urban theory. All point towards the need to escape from representations of the urban in the form of one pole of a dualism, whether urban-rural, public-private (Derrida), Official-Unofficial (Benjamin, de Certeau, Bakhtin), or State-Nomad (Deleuze and Guattari). In each, the poles of such dualisms are shown to be locked together in representation. All of these approaches question the specificity of 'the urban' conceived in terms of 'the city'.

Any representation is always as much an attempt to incorporate and adjust the real, non-discursive material of everyday life, as an attempt to build an ideal discursive model outside of the plethora of disjunctures and variations, 'exceptions to the rule' in lived situations. Representation is thus plagued by instability internally. Long before one arrives at such conventional political questions as 'whose representation' and a consideration of representations 'made by whom for who?' one discovers the internal multiplicity of representation. Representations consist of dialogical contradictions in tension, which unite the discursive and non-discursive, the real and the representational. Representing the city is always a paradoxical project undertaken on shifting ground. In representations only some aspects are given to be seen, while others remain out of sight. Practices of representation are exercises of discursive definition, non-discursive presentation and of power. Because it can only be known through representation, the boundaries between authoritative text and authored (and partial) representation are confused in the case of the urban. Like any spatialisation, the 'trans-discursive' city thus transgresses easy Foucauldian division into discursive (codes) and non-discursive (practices); crosses the lines between the empirical and the fabricated; mixes the real with the imagined and the factual with the fictive. If the city, or rather the represented city, is thought of in the limited terms of a 'text' then it is a text which is read only by writing, and then only in part. If we accept the challenge of Deleuze and Guattari's 'body without organs', then we will require a broader, 'cultural-economic' analysis of the dialogism of urban environments. Let us guard a place for the paradox of street life, the irony of contrasting representations and the complexity of everyday life.

## NOTES

1.    A. Sayer, 'The Difference that Space Makes', in D. Gregory and J. Urry, *Social Relations and Spatial Structures* (Macmillan, London, 1985), pp. 49–66.
2.    P. Saunders, *Social Theory and the Urban Question* (Hutchinson, London, 1981).
3.    Michel de Certeau, 'Practices of Space', in Marshall Blonsky (1985) pp. 122–49 (see note 123).
4.    J. H Brunvand, *Curses! Broiled Again. The Hottest Urban Legends Going* (W. W. Norton, New York, 1989).

5. S. Buck-Morss, *The Dialectics of Seeing* (MIT Press, Cambridge, Mass., 1989).

6. R. Shields, 'Fancy Footwork: Walter Benjamin's Flâneur', in K. Tester (ed.) *The Flâneur* (Routledge, London, 1994).

7. C. Geertz, *Person, Time and Conduct in Bali: An Essay in Cultural Analysis* (Yale University Southeast Asia Studies, Cultural Report Series no. 14, Detroit, Mich., and The Cellar Book Shop, 1966).

8. P. Bourdieu, *Outline of a Theory of Practice*, R. Nice (trans.) *Esquisse d'un théorie de la pratique* 1977 (Cambridge University Press, 1980).

9. W. Benjamin, *Paris. Capital du XIX$^e$ Siècle: Le livre des passages*, R. Tiedemann (ed.), R. Lacoste, trans. (Ed. du CERF, Paris, 1989). Translation of W. Benjamin *Das Passagen-werk. Gesammelte Schriften vol. 5.* R. Tiedemann (ed.) (Suhrkamp Verlag, Frankfurt am Main, 1982).

10. R. Shields (see note 6).

11. Celeste Olalquiaga, *Megalopolis. Contemporary Cultural Sensibilities* (Minnesota University Press, Minneapolis, 1992).

12. Ibid., p. 58.

13. Consider the dioramas and models produced for recent Olympic bids. The *nature morte* style of documentary film making is commented on at length in the Peter Greenaway film *A Zed & Two Noughts.*

14. C. Olalquiaga, p. 58 (see note 11).

15. Rob Shields, *Places on the Margin* (Routledge, London, 1991).

16. Henri Lefebvre, *The Production of Space*, translation of *La Production de l'espace*, 1974 (Basil Blackwell, Oxford, 1991).

17. R. Shields (see note 15).

18. M. Foucault, 'Two Lectures', in *Power/Knowledge* (Pantheon, New York, 1980), pp. 78–108.

19. H. Lefebvre (see note 16).

20. Henri Lefebvre (ibid.) introduced the idea of lived space '*l'espace vecu*', in his 1974 discussion of the difference between the spatiotemporal understandings used in urban planning discourses, and in everyday life and embodied social interactions.

21. Ibid.

22. J. Donald and A. Rattansi (eds), '*Race', Culture and Difference* (Sage and The Open University, London, 1992).

23. Stuart Hall, 'New Ethnicities', chapter 11 in Donald and Rattansi, 1992, pp. 252–59 (see note 22).

24. Cornel West, 'The New Cultural Politics of Difference', in Ferguson et al., pp. 19–38 (see note 31).

25. Gayatri Chakravorty Spivak, 'Explanation and Culture: Marginalia', in Ferguson et al., 1990, pp. 377–92 (see note 31).

26. Compare the literary treatments of selected cities in which the city is known by the narrative footsteps of pedestrians, and any given person, character or narrator has only a partial knowledge of the urban. Only scratching the surface, recent fiction includes Raban (note 124) on 1970s London; Mendoza (note 125) on Post-World War I Barcelona and *City of Marvels* on pre-World War I Barcelona (note 126); Claudio Magris (note 127) on Interwar Trieste. Of course the Dickensian novel and the later edifice of European naturalist fiction (e.g. Zola, Balzac, Hoffmann) are directly concerned with and respond to the growth of metropolitan urban centres.

27. G. C. Spivak, p. 80 (see note 25).

28. R. Williams, *The Country and the City* (Chatto, London, 1973).

29.    The terms 'pre-urban', and 'post-urban', were suggested by Tony King. By contrast to the disapproving mainstream opinion on suburbia and urban fringes, see R. Venturi, D. Scott-Brown and S. Izenour, *Learning from Las Vegas* (Cambridge, Mass., 1972).

30.    See p. 73 of Homi Bhabha, 'The Other Question: Difference, Discrimination and the Discourse of Colonialism', in Ferguson et al., 1990, pp. 71–88 (see note 31 below).

31.    Russel Ferguson, Martha Gever, Trinh T. Minh-ha and Cornel West (eds), *Out There. Marginalization and Contemporary Cultures* (MIT Press and The New Museum of Contemporary Art, Cambridge Mass., 1990).

32.    Benno Werlen, *Society, Action and Space* (Routledge, London, 1992).

33.    I am grateful for the encouragement Tony King provided for this section of the paper on early drafts.

34.    R. Shields, 'The Logic of the Mall', in S. Riggins (ed.), *Material Culture* (Mouton de Gruyter, The Hague, 1994).

35.    Michel de Certeau, *The Practice of Everyday Life*. S. Rendall trans (Berkeley: University of California Press, 1984).

36.    M. de Certeau (see note 3).

37.    This point is implicit in de Certeau's earlier *Practices of Everyday Life* (see note 35) but is never presented clearly, nor are the implications of pedestrian 'resistance' developed for the urban and for the linguistic dualism of discursive and non-discursive.

38.    K. Knapp, 'The Blind Men and the Elephant (selected Opinions on the Situationists)', in K. Knapp (ed. and trans.), *Situationist International Anthology* (Bureau of Public Secrets, Berkeley, Cal., 1981), p. 381.

39.    Georg Simmel, *The Sociology of Georg Simmel*, K. H. Wolff trans. and ed. (Basic Books, New York, 1950).

40.    E. Goffman, *Behaviour in Public Places* (Free Press, Glencoe, Ill., 1963).

41.    Teresa de Lauretis, *Alice Doesn't: Feminism, Semiotics, Cinema* (Indiana University Press, Bloomington Ind., 1984), p. 68.

42.    Peggy Phelan, *Unmark(ed.) The Politics of Performance* (Routledge, London, 1993). See especially chapter 3, 'Spatial Envy: Yvonne Rainer's *The Man Who Envied Women*'.

43.    Henri Lefebvre, *Le Droit à la Ville* (Anthropos, Paris, 1975).

44.    Alan Pred, *Lost Words and Lost Worlds. Modernity and the Language of Everyday Life in Late Nineteenth-Century Stockholm* (Cambridge University Press, 1990).

45.    D. Gregory, 'Interventions in the Historical Geography of Modernity: Social Theory, Spatiality and the Politics of Representation', *Geografiska Annular*, 73b (1991), pp. 17–44.

46.    R. Shields (see note 34).

47.    J. Wolff, 'The Invisible *Flâneuse*: Women and the Literature of Modernity', in *Theory, Culture and Society*, 2:3 (1985), pp. 37–47.

48.    Elizabeth Wilson, *The Sphinx in the City: Urban Life, the Control of Disorder and Women* (University of California Press, Los Angeles, 1991).

49.    Ibid.

50.    C. Stansell, *City of Women: Sex and Class in New York 1789–1860* (Alfred Knopf, New York, 1986).

51.    M. Maffesoli, 'Homo Estheticus', in *Theory Culture and Society*, 8:1 (1991), p. 7.

52.    Rob Shields, 'Introduction to the Ethic of Aesthetics', in *Theory Culture and Society*, 8:1 (1991), pp. 1–6.

53.    R. Hart, *Children's Experience of Place* (Irvington, New York, 1979).

54.   Jürgen Habermas, *The Structural Transformation of the Public Sphere*, translation of *Strukturwandel der Oeffentlichkeit* (MIT Press, Cambridge, Mass., 1989).

55.   J. B Elshtain, *Public Man, Private Woman: Women in Social and Political Thought* (Martin Robertson, Oxford, 1981).

56.   If it is invisible in one discursive context the domestic is a mythical site of emotional 'belonging' in humanistic geographical literature (see Tuan, note 128 and Relph, note 129).

57.   The last 10 years have seen radical polemic and intellectual ferment. But consider the tables of contents over that period in *Environment and Planning D: Society and Space*; or *International Journal of Urban and Regional Research*. 'It is impossible to cover everything', plead the editors. And the recent birth of the journal *Gender and Space* is to be commended. Nonetheless a rigorous approach notes that in the absence of a self-consciously restricted definition, presumably 'urban studies' denotes all urban phenomena including the clear status of cities as places of family (in whatever form or definition) habitation. Comfortable behind my public-university barricade, it is indeed 'interesting' to observe that this will be one vector of a coming critique of the selective interdisciplinarity of fields such as urban studies.

58.   The 'oppression of the domestic sphere', is much complained about by women caught between moralizing discourses which on the one hand urge them to prioritize a career and on the other hand foreground social, religious and personal concerns for family. The theory remains mired in this debate, rather than broadening its concerns to include the forgotten and unexpected social consequences of the opening of the workplace to middle-class, often Anglo-Saxon, women. These include the expansion of a domestic labour force and infant 'day-care' service industry often staffed by non-Anglo Saxon women. In this female-female race-class oppression, old social hierarchies are repeated. Illegal immigrants or foreign 'guest workers', work for years without rights or representation hoping for citizenship. bell hooks has noted the difficulty that feminists have had incorporating analyses of race and class (see Childers and bell hooks, note 130).

59.   H. Bhabha (see note 30).

60.   Gayatri Chakravorty Spivak, *In Other Worlds: Essays in Cultural Politics* (Methuen, New York, 1987).

61.   M. H Krieger, 'Ethnicity and the frontier in Los Angeles', in *Society and Space*, 4 (1986), pp. 385–9.

62.   Here, 'racial', is intended in the sense of perceived differences in skin colour, for skin colour is a continuum, and races are not the homogenized groups that racist discourses (whether pro or contra-'racism') attribute to them (see Hall, note 23, pp. 253–55). Here 'ethnic difference' means cultural and social distinctions based on a cultural trait (including religious practices), usually heavily marked by both insiders and outsiders, which is used to establish group identity and inter-group difference (see Donald and Rattansi, note 22).

63.   Louis Wirth, *The Ghetto* (Chicago University Press, 1956).

64.   K. Anderson, ' "Chinatown Re-oriented": A Critical Analysis of Recent Redevelopment Schemes in a Melbourne and Sydney Enclave' in *Australian Geographical Studies*, 28:2 (1990), pp. 137–54.

65.   K. J. Anderson, 'Cultural Hegemony and the Race-Definition Process in Chinatown, Vancouver: 1880–1980', in *Society and Space*, 6:3 (1988), pp. 127–49.

66.   Stanslaw Adler, *In the Warsaw Ghetto, 1940–1943* (Yad Vaskem, Jerusalem, 1982).

67. Homi K. Bhabha, 'Remembering Fanon: Self, Psyche and the Colonial Condition', in B. Kruger and P. Mariani, (eds), *Remaking History. Discussions in Contemporary Culture* (Dia Art Foundation, Bay Press, Seattle, 1989).

68. Nihal Perera, 'DeColonizing Colombo: Explaining the Survival of the Colonial Landscape', mimeo paper presented to the CRCS Spring Symposium, Carleton University, Ottawa. 20–21 March, 1992.

69. Paul Rabinow, *French Modern; Norms and Forms of the Social Environment* (M.I.T. Press, Cambridge, Mass., 1989).

70. P. Phelan, p. 90 (see note 42).

71. R. Shields (see note 15).

72. Gill Valentine, 'The Geography of Women's Fear', in *Area*, 21:4 (1989), pp. 385–90.

73. Michael Dear and Jennifer Wolch, *Landscapes of Despair: From Deinstitutionalization to Homelessness* (Polity Press, Cambridge, 1987).

74. J. Habermas (see note 54).

75. G. Simmel (see note 39).

76. R. Sennett, *The Fall of Public Man* (Alfred Knopf, New York, 1977).

77. J. Landes, *Women and the Public Sphere* (Cornell Unversity Press, Ithaca, New York, 1988).

78. Audrey Kobayashi and Suzanne Mackenzie, *Remaking Human Geography* (Unwin, Boston, 1989).

79. Matrix, *Making Space* (Pluto Press, London). Chs 5, 9.

80. J. Meyrowitz, *No Sense of Place* (Oxford University Press, London, 1985).

81. J. Baudrillard, *In the Shadow of the Silent Majorities* (Semiotexte, New York, 1982).

82. Suzanne Mackenzie, *Visible Histories: Women and Environments in a Post-War British City* (McGill-Queen's University Press, Kingston, Ont., 1987).

83. Caroline Andrew and Beth Moore-Milroy, *Life Spaces; Gender, Household, Employment* (University of British Columbia, Vancouver (1988).

84. G. Simmel (see note 39).

85. Henri Lefebvre, *La Vie Quotidienne dans le Monde Moderne* (Gallimard, Paris, 1968).

86. M. Maffesoli, *Le Temps des Tribus* (Méridiens-Klinckseick, Paris, 1981).

87. Anna Yeatman, 'Postmodernity and Revisioning the Political', in A. Yeatman (ed.), *Postmodern Critical Theorising. Social Analysis No.30* (University of Adelaide Press, Adelaide, S. Aust., 1992), p. 118.

88. M. M Bakhtin, *The Dialogical Imagination*, Caryl Emerson and Michael Holquist trans. (University of Texas Press, Austin, 1981).

89. Ibid.

90. M. M Bakhtin, *Speech Genres and Other Late Essays*, Vern W. McGee, trans. Caryl Emerson and Michael Holquist (eds) (University of Texas Press, Austin, 1986)

91. Katerina Clark and Michael Holquist, *Mikhail Bakhtin* (University of Texas Press, Austin, 1984).

92. Gary Saul Morson (ed.), *Bakhtin, Essays and Dialogues on his Work.* (University of Chicago Press, Chicago, 1986).

93. M. Bakhtin, pp. 84–258 (see note 90).

94. Ian Roderick, *A Chronotopography of the Victorian Gazeteer*, Anthropology M.A. thesis, Dept. of Sociology and Anthropology, Carleton University, Ottawa Canada.

95. R. Shields, chapters 1 and 2 (see note 15).

96. Mireya Folch-Serra, 'Place voice space: Mikhail Bakhtin's dialogical landscape', in *Environment and Planning D: Society and Space*, 8 (1990) pp. 255–74.

97. P. Stallybrass and A. White, *The Politics and Poetics of Transgression* (Methuen, London, 1986).

98. Cited in P. Phelan, p. 81 (see note 42).

99. A. Pred (see note 44).

100. K. Lynch, *The Image of the City* (MIT Press, Cambridge, Mass., 1973).

101. D. Appleyard, 'Notes on urban perception and knowledge', in J. Archea and C. Eastman eds. *EDRA 2: Proceedings of the Second Annual Environmental Design Research Association Conference* (Dowden, Hutchinson and Ross, Strodsburg, Penn., 1970), pp. 97–101.

102. I. Roderick (see note 94).

103. S. Kern, *Cultures of Time and Space* (Weidenfeld and Nicolson, New York, 1983).

104. M. Folch-Serra (see note 96).

105. M. Bakhtin (see note 88).

106. Gilles Deleuze and Félix Guattari, *A Thousand Plateaus: Capitalism and Schizophrenia* (University of Minnesota Press, Minneapolis, 1987).

107. Gilles Deleuze and Félix Guattari, *The Anti-Oedipus: Capitalism and Schizophrenia* (University of Minnesota Press, Minneapolis, 1983).

108. Ibid., p. 26.

109. P. Ricoeur, 'The task of hermeneutics', in *Philosophy Today*, 17:2–4 (Summer 1973) pp. 112–28.

110. Hans-Georg Gadamer, *Truth and Method* (Sheed and Ward, London, 1975).

111. Per Otnes, 'The Conduit City. The Socio-Material Isolation of Urban Life', mimeo paper presented at ISA RC21 Conference, Gilleleje Denmark 5–9 May, 1990.

112. R. Shields, *Lifestyle Shopping. The Subject of Consumption* (Routledge, London, 1992).

113. K. Knapp (ed. and trans.) *Situationist International Anthology* (Bureau of Public Secrets, Berkeley, Cal., 1981).

114. The Situationists, led by Guy Debord, published an annual journal *Internationale Situationniste* from 1958–1969.

115. S. Plant, The Most Radical Gesture (Routledge, London & New York, 1992).

116. Ivan Chtcheglov, (Gilles Ivain), 'Formulary for a New Urbanism', in *Internationale Situationniste* 1 (June). 1. Translated in Knapp 1981a, p. 3 (see note 113).

117. A. Ross, *The Emergence of Social Space: Rimbaud and the Paris Commune* (University of Minnesota Press, Minneapolis, Minn., 1988).

118. Guy Debord, 'Theory of the Dérive', in *International Situationniste* 2 (December 1958). Translated in Knapp, 1981, p. 50 (see note 113).

119. K. Knapp, p. 50 (see note 113).

120. *Dérive* means drifting with the current, floating along, 'going with the flow', and more importantly, *diverted* to leeward or towards the lights, bustle and activity of one place or another. *Dérive* is a form of automatist urban flâneurie in which one allows oneself to be diverted by the 'solicitations of architecture and one's desires'. Substantively without any objective, the *formal* purpose of *dérive* is to find out where one ends up, to know what 'will have happened'.

121. I. Chtcheglov (see note 116).

122.    This obscure phrase, never worked out by the Situationists, hints at a
        fascinating intellectual history of mid-twentieth century thought on the city.
        While it resounds with Giedion's 1930s thesis of a modernist *Architecture of
        Time and Space*, Chtcheglov anticipated and perhaps inspired Lefebvre's
        work in the early 1970s on the city and on *The Production of Space* (see note
        16: originally published 1974), which in turn influenced David Harvey's
        development of a marxist geography (*Social Justice and the City*, London,
        Edward Arnold, 1973) and later provided the inspiration for Frederic
        Jameson's influential codification of postmodernity as a new mode of time
        and space ('Postmodernism, or the cultural logic of late capitalism', *New
        Left Review* 148, 1984, pp. 53–92).

123.    M. Blonsky, *On Signs* (Basil Blackwell, London, 1985).

124.    Jonathan Raban, *Soft City* (Fontana, London, 1974).

125.    Eduardo Mendoza, *The Truth About the Savolta Case*, Alfred Macadam
        trans. (Collins Harvill, London, 1993).

126.    E. Mendoza, *City of Marvels* (Harcourt Brace Jovanovich, San Diego,
        1988).

127.    Claudio Magris, *A Different Sea* (Harvill, London, 1993).

128.    Yi-Fu Tuan, *Space and Place: The Perspective of Experience* (Edward
        Arnold, London, 1977).

129.    E. Relph, *Place and Placelessness* (Pion, London, 1976).

130.    M. Childers and bell hooks (Gloria Watkins), 'A Conversation about Race
        and Class', in M. Hirsch and E. F. Keller (eds), *Conflicts in Feminism*
        (Routledge, London, 1990), pp. 60–81.

See also:

●   Augustin Berque, *Vivre l'espace au Japon* (Maison Franco-Japonaise,
    Presses Universitaires de France, Paris, 1982).

●   Bhabha, Homi 1990b. 'Dissemi-Nation: Time, Narrative and the
    Margins of the Modern Nation', in H. Bhabha (ed.) *Nation and
    Narration* (Routledge, London).

●   John Clammer, 1992. 'Aesthetics of the Self', in Shields 1992. 195–215.

●   Gilles Deleuze and Félix Guattari, *The Anti-Oedipus* (Minuit, Paris,
    1976).

●   M. Foucault, 'Space, Knowledge and Power', in *Skyline* (March 1982)
    reprinted in P. Rabinow (ed.) *The Foucault Reader* (Random House,
    New York, 1984), pp. 239–56.

●   Israel Gutman, *The Jews of Warsaw, 1939–1945* (Indiana University
    Press, Bloomington, 1982).

●   Masao Miyoshi and H. D Harootunian, *Postmodernism and Japan*
    (Duke University Press, Durham North Carolina, 1989).

●   Benita Parry, 'Problems in Current Theories of Colonial Discourse', in
    *Oxford Literary Review*, 9:1–2 (1987), pp. 27–58.

●   R. Shields, 'Culture Spoken Here: Cultural Studies and Transdiscipli-
    narity', keynote address 'Exploring Contemporary Discourse Analysis',
    conference, March 1993, Carleton University, Ottawa. (Mimeo copies
    available from Centre for Research on Culture and Society, Carleton
    University, Ottawa, Canada K1S 5B6.)

●   E. Soja, 'The Spatiality of Social Life: Towards a Transformative
    Retheorization', in D. Gregory and J. Urry (eds), *Social Relations and
    Spatial Structures* (Macmillan, London, 1985), pp. 90–127.

# 12

# Me(trope)olis: Or Hayden White Among the Urbanists

James S. Duncan

---

## INTRODUCTION

It is entirely possible that many of the urbanists who read this book will be unfamiliar with the work of Hayden White. This should come as no surprise since to my knowledge Professor White has never written about nor perhaps even given much thought to the problem of cities. As Presidential Professor of Historical Studies at the University of California at Santa Cruz, cities are not his problem, neither intellectually nor experientially. It is I, therefore, and not he, who has set him among the urbanists – like a cat amongst the pigeons. I have done so, not only to see feathers fly, but because I believe that the type of interpretive framework which he has so brilliantly applied to the writing of history can also be made to shed light on the writing of the city (although not without problematic consequences which I will address below). Actually it is not just White alone that I am setting among the urbanists; I use him, as one of the foremost contemporary exponents of what is broadly defined as discourse analysis, as a synecdoche for a whole interpretive tradition that problematizes the relationship between what we see and what we write. I use synechdoche to mean a tool of representation by which meaning is generated through the association of a part or microcosm to a macrocosmic whole for which the part stands.

Discourse analysis takes as its problematic, the unstable relationship between the data we collect and the interpretive structures which we erect to understand them. White[1] states the issue succinctly: 'Our discourse always tends to slip away from our data towards the structures of consciousness with which we are trying to grasp them . . .' This instability between the signified and signifier – between our data and our structures of consciousness – calls into question the issue of representation.

What do we mean when we say that we represent the city? Since a representation cannot, of course, literally reproduce the whole of what it seeks to represent, the interpretive process *necessarily* entails a selection and a movement – back and forth from presences to absences, from an area of experience which is felt to be understood, to one that is cognitively less secure. This discursive movement requires the use of various rhetorical strategies including tropes. Tropes such as metaphor, metonymy, synecdoche and irony, are figures of speech which construct meaning by transferring or deferring it from the realm of familiar experience into the realm of the unfamiliar. Pre-given reality is thus not so much a transparently viewed object of representation, as it is the material from which something new is fashioned. Recognition of the rhetorical basis of knowledge such as may be found in White's tropology, marks a shift from the positivist goal of mimesis to what Goodman[2] and some poststructuralists have called 'ways of worldmaking'. New 'worlds' are necessarily created through the use of language because there simply is no neutral discursive form with which to record reality. Some, including many marxists, however, would take an intermediate position, arguing that while their interpretations aim to be scientific, marxism and any other political project is nothing if it is not a way of world making. This position assumes that a recognition of power/ knowledge relations as socially constructed is not necessarily incompatible with realist representation.[3] Such a middleground position has much merit, for the problem with extreme relativism is, as Eco sees it,[4] solipsism; that is 'when everybody is right, everybody is wrong and I have the right to disregard everybody's point of view'. The danger and even immorality of the relativist position should be clear, especially when viewed in relation to events 'at the limits'.[5,6]

The choice, then, should not be between the false sense of a transparent world and an unnecessary sense of helplessness generated by a poststructural relativism that promises nothing but an irresolvable crisis of representation. Rather we should ask how we are to come to grips with the simultaneous demands made upon us by our data and by our interpretive framework. All of which brings us back to the title of my paper and to Hayden White. I have entitled my paper 'Me(trope)olis' in recognition of the tropology involved in every writing of the city.[7] I am applying White's methods of tropology to the way the city has been studied by several authors, each of whom forges their representation of the urban around a different primary trope.

The word trope comes from the Latin *tropus* meaning 'metaphor' or 'figure of speech'. Tropes constitute their objects of inquiry through figures of speech that generate meaning, not through literal description but by deviating from the expected conceptualization of reality which has become reified into common sense. Thus tropes are mind tricks which aim to produce fresh perceptions and insights. Tropes are also the allegedly bad characters our professors warned us to avoid if we aspired to move in respectable social scientific company. They are, to use White's terms, 'the shadow from which all realistic discourse tries to flee'.[8] He adds, however, that '[t]his flight. . .is futile; for tropics is the process by which all discourse *constitutes* the objects which it pretends only to describe realistically and analyze objectively'. Likewise he argues

> discourse is inescapable for it *constitute[s]* the ground whereon to decide *what shall count as a fact* in the matters under consideration and to determine *what mode of comprehension* is best suited to the understanding of the facts thus constituted. [emphasis in the original][9]

While White has applied tropology to historical discourse in the 1970s and 1980s,[10,11,12] it has in the 1980s and 1990s increasingly been applied in anthropology[13,14,15] and in geography.[16,17,18,19]

## DE-SCRIBING THE CITY

In this paper I will analyze three different authors' attempts to describe the city. The individuality of the authors are of little interest in this context, as is their corpus of writing, or for that matter the individuality of the cities they describe. My purpose here is not to judge the accuracy of the authors' conceptions of the city, but rather to discuss *how* they write the city through their use of different tropes. The first two authors not only describe the city but, I will argue, de-scribe it in the sense that they fail to call into question the elusive space between the city and their representation of it. Such a lack of self-consciousness about the rhetorical structure constitutes what Shapiro[20] has termed 'the delusional mode of writing'. The third author that I consider, is perhaps overly self-conscious about his writing of the city having come to the seemingly paralyzing conclusion that *all* writing is *inherently* delusional.

The first article I examine is E. W. Burgess's 'The growth of the city: an introduction to a research project'.[21] This article, a classic from the Chicago School of Human Ecology of the 1920s and 1930s, adopts what I term an objective/scientific mode of description. The 'master trope'[22,23] in this work is metaphor. The second article that I will examine is Mike Davis's 'Fortress Los Angeles: the militarization of urban space'.[24] He adopts what I call the tragic/Marxian mode of description. The 'master trope' in this work is synecdoche. Finally I turn to several of the essays in Roland Barthes's *Empire of Signs*.[25] Barthes writes in a playful/literary mode and the 'master trope' here is irony.

## E. W. Burgess and the Objective/Scientific Mode

'The Growth of the City' was written in 1925, in Burgess's words, in order to 'present the point of view and methods of investigation which the department of sociology is employing in its studies of the growth of the city. . .'[26] The paper would no doubt have sunk after a few years into the obscurity that awaits most academic papers, were it not for the fact that it introduced what Smith[27] has called the most famous diagram in social science, the concentric zone model of the city (see Figure 12.1). Burgess describes the diagram as follows:

> The typical processes of expansion of the city can best be illustrated, perhaps, by a series of concentric circles, which may be numbered to designate both the successive zones of urban extension and the types of areas differentiated in the process of expansion.
>
> This chart represents an ideal construction of the tendencies of any town or city to expand radially from its central business district. . .[28]

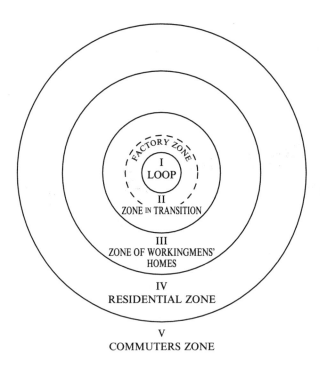

(E. W. Burgess in *The City* (University of Chicago Press, 1967))

FIGURE 12.1

This diagram, or chart as he prefers to call it, was generated inductively out of detailed field work in the neighborhoods of Chicago. Although Burgess admits that the diagram represents a schematic model of Chicago, he wishes to extend it to 'any town or city. . .' This urge to simplify in order to generalize is drawn from the practice of the natural sciences. The exponents of the relatively new discipline of sociology were keen to model their work upon the natural sciences and thereby make legitimate their discipline by sharing in the prestige of the latter. The language of science pervaded the work of the Chicago School as evidenced by the title of Park and Burgess' famous textbook of 1921, *An Introduction to the Science of Sociology*,[29] and members of the school commonly referred to the city as a 'laboratory'. Burgess assumed that natural science was the key to understanding the world and that the city could be explained through the application of scientific methods. He was ambitious both for himself and for Chicago sociology. He consequently did not want to simply map the form of the city, but rather to delineate the *processes* of expansion which produced that form. The problem he faced in discussing process, however, was how to translate it into the prestigious language of the natural sciences.

As Roberts points out,[30] because Burgess and other human ecologists found it difficult to specify the connections between the city and natural processes in scientific realist terms, they opted for an instrumentalist language which acknowledges the heuristic value of metaphor in science. Thus it was through the trope of metaphor that Burgess sought to link the city to natural science. The particular metaphor favored by Burgess and many other urbanists since, is that of a living organism. At times Burgess spoke of the city as functioning like the human body, and at other times he compared it to a plant community. As examples of the former, he suggests that urban growth should be thought of 'as a resultant of organization and disorganization analogous to the anabolic and katabolic processes of metabolism in the body'. For example, the great influx of 'southern Negroes' into northern cities after World War I was seen to cause 'disturbances of [urban] metabolism'; social disorganization was viewed as a product of 'the disordered social metabolism of the city', and:

> mobility may be thought of in more than a fanciful sense, as the 'pulse of the community'. Like the pulse of the human body, it is a process which reflects and is indicative of all the changes that are taking place in the community.[31]

In explaining his diagram, Burgess (1967, 50) employs the metaphor of the plant community:

> This chart brings out clearly the main fact of expansion, namely the tendency of each inner zone to extend its area by the invasion of the next

outer zone. This aspect of expansion may be called *succession*, a process which has been studied in detail in plant ecology [emphasis in the original].[32]


As one looks at this figure, it is not difficult to imagine those four concentric rings as the outline of a kind of organism whose structure is visible to the scientist peering through a microscope. In fact Burgess himself employs this very metaphor when he speaks of putting the city 'under the micro-scope'.[33,34,35] It is also not difficult, pursuing the analogy of plant ecology, to see this diagram as representing the concentric growth rings on a tree. Through his use of organic metaphors, Burgess attempts to convey his belief that the structure of the city is similar to structures found in nature. For example the tendency of each zone to invade its outer neighbor is seen as a natural process. In speaking of the central business district he writes, 'Quite *naturally*, almost inevitably, the economic, cultural, and political life centers here' [emphasis added]'.[36] The problematic usage of the language of nature has become obvious to contemporary readers who have witnessed the more recent abandonment of many of these functions in contemporary American downtowns. He goes on to refer to the 'natural . . . readjustment in the social organization', and 'natural economic and cultural groupings'.[37]

Certainly conceiving of the city as a natural entity did not begin or end with Burgess. Davison[38] points out that such conceptions were current in early nineteenth century Britain. The advances in nineteenth century biology, especially the enormous prestige of Darwinism, added weight to such perspectives. Although by the 1920s Social Darwinism was in decline in American thought, it remained as a powerful influence in the urban ecological perspective espoused by Park and Burgess.[39]

Roberts[40] argues that the Chicago School combined elements of Spencerian social evolutionism with ideas from plant ecology. While Burgess occasionally explains occupational selection by 'racial tempera-ment' as well as 'circumstance',[41] racial explanations do not characterize his work more generally. However one can see his reliance on evolutionism come into play in his description of social change. The pessimism of certain strands of social Darwinism is replaced in Burgess's writing by boundless naive optimism, for he held a teleological view that society and the city were evolving in inevitably progressive ways. Social organization and disorgani-zation, he believed, formed a 'moving equilibrium of social order toward an end vaguely or definitely regarded as progressive'.[42] Similarly what he termed the area of deterioration in the city, 'while essentially one of decay. . .is also one of regeneration' and even segregation 'limits develop-ment in certain directions, but releases it in others'.[43] The thrust of this line of argumentation was that the city evolves just as social organisms do. Somewhat paradoxically, however, such a belief did not discourage Burgess and other members of the Chicago School from assuming that intervention could limit the disorganizing forces within the evolutionary process.

Burgess employs the rhetoric of science not only through the metaphor of the organism, and in the claims to reduction and generalization, but also in the very organization of the paper which is neatly divided into sections on form and process. However reassured by the measured, distanced, value-neutral language of science, the reader may wonder about the metaphor of the organism which simultaneously constructs a bridge between Chicago and all other cities, while linking the practice of urban sociology to the discipline of biology. This bridge can be seen as highly deferential: all cities are made to defer to the form of Chicago. A measure of how influential this idea became is that several generations of geographers and sociologists devoted careers to searching for concentric zones all over the world.[44] Furthermore the organic metaphor not only defers meaning to the realm of the biological but also defers to the superior explanatory skill of the natural scientist. Through the deferential power of metaphor, 'social science' is rendered by implication as 'un-natural science', a lesser and distorted variant of a pure 'natural science'. Thus one could argue that Burgess uses metaphor as a language of deference assuming that academics in more prestigious fields can say what he wishes he could say of his subject matter but cannot. At least he cannot if he restricts himself to the literal language of urbanism. One is thus reminded of Harold Bloom's characterization of tropes as defenses against literal meaning; in fact Bloom goes so far as to see such defensive troping as similar to psychological repression or projection.[45]

### Mike Davis and the Tragic/Marxian Mode

'The city bristles with malice'. So begins Mike Davis' 'Fortress Los Angeles: the Militarization of Urban Space'.[46] But this is not a typical piece of anti-urbanism, damning the inherent evil of the city and lauding the virtues of the countryside. Rather the malice which Davis sees is not inherent in the city itself, but in the brutality of life under capitalism after the demise of liberalism. In this sense although Davis writes cogently about the city, his explanations of process, as with Burgess's, are deferred elsewhere. However while Burgess deferred to natural science through the 'master trope' of metaphor, Davis defers to Marxian analyses of capitalism through the 'master trope' of synechdoche. The city is thus seen as an essential part standing for the whole of capitalism, and consequently the problems of the city must be understood as identical with the broader problems of capitalism.

The city, as described by Davis, becomes the stage upon which that well known morality play 'class struggle' is enacted by the usual cast of characters, the bourgeoisie and the proletariat. Davis, following the favored Marxian emplotment, adopts the tragic mode of explication. The story that he tells of Los Angeles is an unrelenting tale of oppression, injustice and mean-spiritedness. The tragic effect is achieved by playing two classes off against one another in the battle for disputed territory. It is, as he says, '. . .open social warfare that pits the interests of the middle class against the welfare of the poor'.[47] The odds in this struggle are heavily weighted in favor of the bourgeoisie who control both the legal system which guarantees their privileges and the police who enforce that privilege. The poor fight back as best they can through urban guerilla warfare.

The language of warfare is meant to evoke the latter years of the Vietnam war, with the middle class playing the role of the Americans desperately trying to control increasingly fortified spaces, and the poor cast as the Viet Cong and North Vietnamese who are brutalized by superior firepower. A third of the way into his chapter, in case any of Davis' readers have not understood the point by then, he refers to Watts as the 'Mekong Delta'.

The bourgeoisie, according to Davis, are desperate and consequently adopt Draconian measures to protect their interests. 'Urban form', he writes, 'obediently follows repressive function'. The tragedy and ultimately the cause for profound pessimism is that the capitalist system requires repression. 'The pleasure domes of the elite Westside', he writes, 'rely upon the social imprisonment of a third world service proletariat in increasingly repressive ghettos and barrios'.[48] The system is represented as utterly ruthless, in that those whom capitalism does not need can be disposed of:

> By criminalizing every attempt by the poor – whether the Skid Row homeless or MacArthur Park vendors – to use public space for survival purposes, law-enforcement agencies have abolished the last informal safety net separating misery from catastrophe.[49]

The city which Davis describes is a place devoid of pleasure, for even the wealthy can not enjoy their ill-gotten gains. They 'cower behind walls with their gun-toting private police', and shop in malls which are 'prisons of consumerism'.[50]

Just as there is no pleasure in Davis's emplotment of Los Angeles, likewise there is no goodness. Amongst the bourgeoisie there are merely degrees of evil. For example, although 'post-liberal Los Angeles' is worse than liberal Los Angeles, liberals, far from being benevolent, are portrayed as apologists for an essentially repressive social order. He writes of 'the old liberal attempts at social control which at least tried to balance repression with reform' and calls politicians' attempts to have low income housing built in an area of the downtown which is to be redeveloped, a 'palliative'.[51] There seems to be no room left in his narrative for people who act in good faith to try to improve the lives of others. One suspects that Davis knows that such folk exist, but in the interest of the coherence of his narrative their existence is silenced.

The metaphor of invasion figures prominently both in Burgess's and Davis's articles. As we have seen, however, Burgess scripts the invasion of higher-income areas by the poor as a natural and progressive process which signifies the American dream come true; the inevitable movement of people outward in geographic space and upward in social space. Davis, on the other hand, scripts the invasion of public space by the poor and the subsequent armed resistance to it as an American tragedy. Unlike Burgess he is profoundly pessimistic, seeing invasion as productive of further repression and the denial of mobility. Violent resistance to police repression seems fruitless because '[e]ach incident, in turn, furnishes new pretexts for regulating crowds and preventing the invasion of outsiders'.[52]

The one illustration in Davis's article shows an African-American woman sitting with her back against a concrete block wall topped with fierce curved iron spears to keep people out. The caption reads, 'LA Skid Row Fortified Garbage'. This powerful image and poignant caption act as a synecdoche for a Los Angeles and more broadly a capitalist class which wishes to deny the poor even garbage. The fortified garbage also stands as a clever metaphor for the fortified residences and shops which Davis treats as moral garbage. But the photograph raises an awkward question that potentially disrupts the author's narrative. The woman in the photograph is scowling. Perhaps it is because she is being denied garbage, or because of the injustices committed by a white, racist society against her. Then again, it is possible that her scowl is a small act of resistance directed at the gaze of the middle-class male photographer whom she may understandably identify as someone who intends to exploit her plight, rather than as he intends, to expose and thereby alleviate it.

Burgess' rhetoric involved a taxonomic diagram of data, while Davis adopts a strong narrative structure. The sense of authorial neutrality one gets when reading Burgess is nowhere in evidence in Davis's writing. He clearly speaks for the underclass. We do not hear from them directly, however. In fact the only people other than Davis that we do hear from are those whom he parades before us to speak their highly edited 'confessions' and then marches out with a resounding 'guilty'. The implied readership who stand as jury to the author's prosecutor shake their heads sadly at these confessions. However it is clear that were these people not to be found guilty, they would not have been summoned to speak their lines. Such is the methodology of the show trial. While this strong narrative structure may lend illusory coherence to the plot, it may fail to produce the degree of 'reality effect' that an account more open to contradictory evidence might achieve. In this sense, an unintended consequence of too strict an adherence to the tragic mode of description is that it undermines the credibility of the account. This devaluation of the very real problems faced by the poor in Los Angeles is one of the tragic side effects of Davis's troping.

### Roland Barthes and the Playful/Literary Mode

Roland Barthes's *Empire of Signs*[53] is a quintessentially poststructural work in that its goal is to undermine the normally taken-for-granted relationship between signifiers (in this case Japanese cultural objects, including urban form), and their signifieds. Barthes accomplishes this by writing an entire book about Japanese landscapes, artifacts and cultural values, about a whole Japanese interrelated symbolic system that he claims is not actually *about* Japan. His claim, made on the first page of the book and reiterated in various places throughout the volume, purposely creates a tension in the reader, who finds it difficult to bear in mind that this book which appears to be all about Zen, haiku and the urban morphology of Tokyo, which is even illustrated with photographs and maps, is not really about Japan. This tension is meant to unsettle and impress the reader with the idea that there is no necessary relation between signifiers and referents thus pointing to the highly problematic notion of representation.

In this regard the work stands in stark opposition to Burgess's, for while Burgess wishes to 'naturalize' everything, Barthes treats 'nature' and the 'natural' as obfuscatory concepts which he dismissively assigns to the category of ideology. He differs in an important way from Davis as well; for while Davis' pessimism appears to offer little hope, he does at least believe that he can represent Los Angeles for us. In fact the only glimmer of hope that Davis offers lies in the idea that a compelling narrative might help to bring about social change for those who cannot help themselves. Barthes' pessimism is more profound in that not only does he despair of political solutions to a world gone wrong, but he no longer believes that one can even represent that world.

The 'master trope' which he employs to highlight with this double tragedy is irony. The task he sets himself, therefore, is to call attention to and comment upon his own impotence. He mocks the rhetoric of science by adopting the detached language of the third person. 'The author', he writes, 'has never, in any sense, photographed Japan. Rather, he has done the opposite: Japan has starred him with any number of "flashes". . .'[54] Again we can see an ironic distancing not only from the project of science and the camera which represents the ideal of representation, but also from the trope of synecdoche which presupposes a totality for which the part stands as an essence.

Barthes's writing draws neither on the dream of a taxonomy that can reproduce the structure of the natural world, nor that of the synecdoche standing for the totality, but rather in the fragment that alone survives when all certainty has disappeared. Barthes celebrates the fragmentary. The very structure of the volume is fragmentary, composed of essays often only a page or two in length, arranged in no rational order. I will focus upon the urban fragments. Barthes writes that the *Empire of Signs* is about 'an unheard of symbolic system, one altogether detached from our own'.[55] His chapter entitled 'City Center, empty center' produces a curious counterpoint to Burgess' and Davis' work. Barthes begins this chapter by referring to Los Angeles, and one assumes, but can one ever be sure, that he means the 'real' Los Angeles:

> Quadrangular, reticulated cities (Los Angeles, for instance) are said to produce a profound uneasiness: they offend our synthetic sentiment of the City, which requires that any urban space has a center to go to, to return from, a complete site to dream of and in relation to which to advance or retreat; in a word, to invent oneself.[56]

Here Los Angeles, rather than being a synecdoche, stands as an exception to the norm, and rather than serving as a stage upon which the tragic plays itself out, stands as an affront to people of taste. Adopting the language of the aesthetic, he writes the city off as a place that offends our sentiment. Unlike Los Angeles, most cities in the West have centers which are 'full'. The values of civilization are gathered in these centers and condensed, for here one finds the centers of spirituality, power, finance. 'To go downtown or to the center-city is to encounter the social "truth", to participate in the proud plenitude of "reality"'. To this dubious generalization Barthes adds the even more dubious statement that 'all . . . [the West's] cities are concentric'.[57] This sounds rather like Burgess's conception of the city. But Barthes does not attempt realist representation, instead he adopts irony in contrasting the empty center of Tokyo to the full western center:

> The entire city turns around a site both forbidden and indifferent, a residence concealed beneath the foliage, protected by moats, inhabited by an emperor who is never seen, which is to say literally, by no one knows who'.[58]

The center, he claims, can command only indifference, a 'sacred nothing'. Tokyo is a system of routes and spaces spread out in circular detours and returns which avoid the empty center. It is a system that does not radiate power, does not fire the imagination with its plenitude, but which supports urban morphology with its emptiness. It is this same emptiness which Barthes sees embodied in Japanese culture, in its art and in Zen Buddhism. Zen is seen as the force which 'writes' the landscape. It is not at all surprising to those who know Barthes's writing that he should be attracted to the Zen experience, in which emptiness plays such an important part. Much of Barthes's writings have been based on the duality empty/full and have involved a search for emptiness and the absence of meaning.[59] The concept of white writing which he outlines in *Writing Degree Zero* is an example.[60]

Fullness represents the core of western society and for him it is entirely negative:

> There is nothing more difficult to 'admit', for a Western mind, than this emptiness (which everything within us longs to fill up, through that obsession with the phallus, the father, the 'master-word' . . . fullness is remembrance (the past, the Father), while its neurotic form is repetition, and its social form is stereotype.[61]

Here we can begin to see where Barthes is going with this line of argument. Los Angeles is used as a foil to set up the western city, which in turn serves as a foil for Tokyo. But Barthes has already told us that although it may appear that he is describing Japan, this book is not really about Japan.

What is it about then? The answer is that it is about writing, or more precisely about Barthes's writing. The emptiness and the fragmentary nature of the Tokyo he describes is like his own theoretical project. The irony is that it is never clear where Tokyo ends and Barthes begins for they blur into one another. This in part is what he means when he tells us that this is and is not Tokyo. And yet the effect of this contradiction on the reader is very different from when Burgess produces his diagram of Chicago claiming that it is and is not Chicago. The difference is that many readers are less familiar with the poststructural problematizing of representation but are much more accustomed to the reductive and generalizing language of science adopted by Burgess when he writes that his diagram is of Chicago but also of 'the city', that is, of all those other cities that are not Chicago. Barthes's implicit claim is that if a taxonomy of cities were constructed, the urban spaces of Tokyo and the urbane writings of Barthes would occupy a single cell in the grid and western cities another. His description seems to be clearly of Japan, but it isn't, he says. And so he plays around with language: Tokyo is language, Japan is language, his writing is language, and language lies for it promises us a world that it can never deliver. The problem with this perspective is that while it is smart and it is fun, it is empty. For after Barthes tells us that he can tell us nothing for certain, he has nothing left to say. He has lead himself and his readers down a dead-end street.

## CONCLUSION

I have argued that the use of tropes is unavoidable in the representation of the city. I have further argued that representation is an intertextual process. The three authors whose writings I have examined use tropes in ways that link the meaning of their writings intertexually to intellectual traditions; natural science, Marxism, and poststructural literary theory. The tropes simultaneously produce meaning and defer it. Burgess defers meaning through metaphor beyond the city to biology, Davis defers it through synecdoche to Marxian political economy, and Barthes through irony permanently defers it into the endless empty circles of the poststructural crisis of representation. Each thereby acknowledges that the city cannot be described in terms of itself alone. It must be approached obliquely in terms of that which it can never be. In this sense the writing of the city always marks a lack. While each author employs intertextuality to carry his description of the city, that very act of displacement tends to undermine each of their accounts.

Burgess's dream of the happy unity of the natural and human sciences pushes him to transform Chicago into 'the city' in ways which stretch credulity. Furthermore through naturalization of spatial processes, he manages to depoliticize them. Davis' nightmare images of Los Angeles as the unmitigated evil which capitalists have wrought, by drawing such a uniformly dark picture, somehow obscures the more subtle and insidious evils that capitalism has produced. Finally Barthes's fantasy of Tokyo as nothing other than a crystallization on the earth of his own brand of poststructural writing, leaves us somewhat bemused as to his allegedly political intentions, for we know that there are millions of citizens of that city whose lives will remain forever untouched by the writings of one self-absorbed, hyper-intellectual Frenchman. It is only fair to add, however, that Barthes's notion of political action is broader than that held by the other two authors. His is neither an early twentieth century liberal politics as is Burgess's, nor a politics of opposition and reversal as with Davis, both of which Barthes would see as ultimately not effecting anything but superficial change. As he would argue, while power may change hands it never diminishes, it merely circulates. Rather Barthes's politics is one of transgression and parody which aims to short circuit power itself. His text, however, only reads as ironic and political to a particular implied readership.[62] This critical academic readership does not need to be convinced of the failures of the societies which it surveys, but could benefit from reflecting upon the social position which its members occupy when writing about those societies. The act of questioning academic representations through parody, like the woman returning the gaze in Davis's piece, is a small, but, Barthes would argue, nevertheless political act. However while his ironic denaturalization undermines conventional urban analysis for his readers, it may be difficult to export this unusual brand of radicalism very far beyond the academy.

Finally let me in closing briefly return to the issue of the goodness of interpretation raised by Eco. Although I have focused upon the rhetorical form of these various essays, I have also suggested that there may be related problems of content. In agreement with White, I believe that the employment of certain tropes brings with it unavoidable epistemological and political implications. These problems, I would suggest, stem in part from the strong authorial ambitions of the authors. Through tropes and intertextual reference each has persistently deferred meaning away from the data. What was often lacking was a certain deference to the data themselves. As White has pointed out, we cannot choose not to employ tropes, for they constitute the way we understand and explain data. We can, however, carefully reflect upon the implications of which primary tropes and narrative strategies we employ. For each choice situates our data in a different discursive field.

## NOTES

1.  H. White, *Tropics of Discourse: Essays in Cultural Criticism* (Johns Hopkins University Press, Baltimore, 1986), p. 1.
2.  N. Goodman, *Ways of Worldmaking* (Hackett, Indianapolis, 1978).
3.  A. Sayer, *Postmodernist Thought in Geography: A Realist View* (University of Sussex, Department of Geography, Research Paper 6, 1992).
4.  U. Eco, 'Reply', in S. Collini (ed.), *Umberto Eco: Interpretation and Overinterpretation* (Cambridge University Press, 1992), pp. 139–51.
5.  S. Friedlander, *Probing the Limits of Representation: Nazism and the 'Final Solution'* (Harvard University Press, Cambridge, Mass., 1992).
6.  Friedlander (ibid.) also questions the ethical basis of the historical relativism of White's tropological analyses.
7.  I am indebted to Joanne Sharp for suggesting the term 'Me(trope)olis' and to John Agnew, Nancy Duncan, Joanne Sharp and John Western for comments on an earlier draft of this paper.
8.  H. White, p. 2 (see note 1).
9.  Ibid., p. 3.
10. Ibid.
11. H. White, *Metahistory: The Historical Imagination in Nineteenth-Century Europe* (Johns Hopkins University Press, Baltimore, 1973).
12. H. White, *The Content of the Form: Narrative Discourse and Historical Representation* (Johns Hopkins University Press, Baltimore, 1987).
13. J. Clifford, *The Predicament of Culture: Twentieth Century Ethnography, Literature and Art* (Harvard University Press, Cambridge, Mass., 1988).
14. J. Clifford and G. E. Marcus (eds), *Writing Culture: the Politics and Poetics of Ethnography* (University of California Press, Berkeley, 1986).
15. J. W. Fernandez (ed.), *Beyond Metaphor: The Theory of Tropes in Anthropology* (Stanford University Press, Stanford, 1991).
16. J. S. Duncan, *The City as Text: The Politics of Landscape Interpretation in the Kandyan Kingdom* (Cambridge University Press, 1990).
17. T. J. Barnes and J. S. Duncan, *Writing Worlds: Discourse, Text and Metaphor in the Representation of Landscape* (Routledge, London, 1992).
18. J. S. Duncan and D. Ley, *Place/Culture/Representation* (Routledge, London, 1993).
19. J. Smith, 'Tropics of Geographical Discourse', *Annals, Association of American Geographers*, forthcoming.
20. M. J. Shapiro, *The Politics of Representation* (University of Wisconsin, Madison, 1988).

21. E. W. Burgess, (orig. 1925) 'The Growth of the City: an Introduction to a Research Project', in R. E. Park and E. W. Burgess (eds), *The City* (University of Chicago Press, 1967), pp. 47–62.

22. The term is Kenneth Burke's (see following note 23).

23. K. Burke, *A Grammar of Motives* (University of California Press, Berkeley, 1969).

24. M. Davis, 'Fortress Los Angeles: the Militarization of Urban Space', in M. Sorkin (ed.), *Variations on a Theme Park: The New American City and the End of Public Space* (Noonday Press, New York, 1992), pp. 154–80.

25. R. Barthes, *Empire of Signs*, trans. R. Howard (Hill and Wang, New York, 1982).

26. E. W. Burgess, p. 61 (see note 21)

27. D. Smith, *The Chicago School: A Liberal Critique of Capitalism* (Macmillan, London, 1988), p. 28.

28. E. W. Burgess, p. 50 (see note 21).

29. R. E. Park and E. W. Burgess, *An Introduction to the Science of Sociology* (University of Chicago Press, 1921).

30. S. Roberts, 'A Critical Evaluation of the City Life Cycle Idea', *Urban Geography*, 12 (1991), pp. 431–49.

31. E. W. Burgess, p. 53 (see note 21).

32. Ibid., p. 50.

33. Ibid., p. 62.

34. R. H. Schein, 'Representing Urban America: 19th-Century Views of Landscape, Space, and Power', *Environment and Planning D: Society and Space*, 11 (1993), pp. 7–21.

35. Schein (ibid.) describes another variant of such a 'god trick' when he explores the implications of the nineteenth-century bird's eye views of American cities. Such attempts to represent the city abstractly from a detached perspective may reflect a similar modernist scientific aesthetic.

36. E. W. Burgess, p. 52 (see note 21).

37. Ibid., pp. 53, 56.

38. G. Davison, 'The City as a Natural System: Theories of Urban Society in Early Nineteenth Century Britain', in D. Fraser and A. Sutcliffe (eds), *The Pursuit of Urban History* (Edward Arnold, London, 1983), pp. 349–70.

39. D. Smith, p. 119 (see note 27).

40. S. Roberts, p. 432 (see note 30).

41. E. W. Burgess, p. 57 (see note 21).

42. Ibid., p. 54.

43. Ibid., p. 56.

44. For an important study of the impact of the center-periphery metaphor in Italian urbanism see J. Agnew and K. Bolling, 'Two Romes or More? The Use and Abuse of the Center-Periphery Metaphor', *Urban Georgraphy*, 14 (1993), pp. 119–44.

45. H. Bloom, *A Map of Misreading* (Oxford University Press, New York, 1975).

46. M. Davis (see note 24).

47. Ibid., p. 155.

48. Ibid., p. 156.

49. Ibid., p. 166.

50. Ibid., p. 154.

51. Ibid., pp. 155, 165.

52. Ibid., p. 180.

53. R. Barthes (see note 25).

54.    Ibid., p. 4.
55.    Ibid., p. 3.
56.    Ibid., p. 30.
57.    Ibid.
58.    Ibid.
59.    R. Barthes, 'On S/Z and Empire of Signs', In *The Grain of the Voice: Interviews, 1962–80*, trans. L. Coverdale (Hill and Wang, New York, 1986), pp. 68–87.
60.    R. Barthes, *Writing Degree Zero*, trans. A. Lavers and C. Smith (Hill and Wang, New York, 1987).
61.    R. Barthes, 'Digressions', In *The Grain of the Voice: Interviews, 1962–80*, trans. L. Coverdale, (Hill and Wang, New York, 1986), pp. 113–27.
62.    J. Sharp, 'Ceci n'est pas Japon: Roland Barthes Detours the Orient', in J. Sharp (ed.), *Wondering Through the Tropics: Western Travel and the Geographing of Others* (Syracuse University Department of Geography Discussion Paper Series, 1993).

# Notes on Contributors

**Greig Crysler** is an architect and also editor of *A/R/C (Architecture/ Research/Criticism)*, Toronto. He is currently in the History and Theory of Art and Architecture doctoral program, Binghamton University, State University of New York.

**James S. Duncan** is Professor of Geography and Director of the Humanities Doctoral Program, Syracuse University. His most recent book is *Culture/ Place/Representation* (Routledge, 1993), edited with David Ley; he is also co-author (with Nancy Duncan) of the forthcoming *Deep Surburban Irony: Deconstructing History, Localism and Nature in a Westchester County Town*.

**Anthony D. King** is Professor of Art History and of Sociology, Binghamton University, State University of New York, and holds a fellowship from the American Council of Learned Societies (1994–95). His most recent (edited) book is *Culture, Globalization and the World-System* (Macmillan Education, London, and Art History, SUNY, Binghamton, 1991).

**Ali A. Mazrui** is Albert Schweitzer Professor in the Humanities and Director of the Institute of Global Cultural Studies, Binghamton University, State University of New York. He is also Albert Luthuli Professor-at-Large, University of Jos, Nigeria, and Senior Scholar and Andrew D. White Professor-at-Large Emeritus, Cornell University. His most recent books are *Cultural Forces in World Politics* (Heinemann, 1990) and *Africa Since 1935* (editor and co-author, UNESCO, 1993).

**Nkiru Nzegwu** is Assistant Professor in the Departments of Philosophy and Art History, Binghamton University, State University of New York. A visual artist, Dr. Nzegwu has had exhibitions in Lagos, Ottawa and New York, and contributed recent articles to *International Review of African American Art*, *American Anthropologist*, and the *Canadian Journal of Law and Jurisprudence*.

**Nihal Perera** is an architect planner from Colombo, Sri Lanka, where he was chief architect-planner for the Mahaweli Development Project. He recently completed his Ph.D. in the History and Theory of Art and

Architecture doctoral program, Binghamton University, State University of New York.

**Saskia Sassen** is Professor of Urban Planning, Columbia University. Her most recent books are *Cities in the World Economy* (Pine Forge/Sage, 1994) and *The Global City: New York, London, Tokyo* (Princeton University Press, 1991). In 1992, Saskia Sassen was Distinguished Visiting Scholar in Art History, State University of New York at Binghamton.

**Joseph Sciorra** is a Ph.D. candidate in the Department of Folklore and Folklife at the University of Pennsylvania. His most recent book is *R.I.P.: New York Spraycan Memorials*, with photographer Martha Cooper (Thames and Hudson, London; and Henry Holt and Company, New York, 1994).

**Rob Shields**, Associate Professor of Sociology and Co-director of the Center for Research on Culture and Society, Carleton University, is currently (1995) teaching in the Department of Sociology, University of Lancaster. His most recent books are *Places on the Margin: Alternate Geographies of Modernity* (Routledge, 1991) and *Lifestyle Shopping*, editor (Routledge, 1992).

**Neil Smith** is Professor of Geography and Chair, Rutgers University. He is the co-editor of *Gentrification of the City* (Allen & Unwin, 1986) and *Geography and Empire* (1994) and is completing a study of Isaiah Bowman, *The Geographical Pivot of History*.

**John Tagg** is Professor of Art History, Binghamton University, State University of New York. His most recent book is *Grounds of Dispute: Art History, Cultural Politics and the Discursive Field* (Macmillan, 1993).

**Sharon Zukin** is Professor of Sociology at Brooklyn College and the Graduate Center, City University of New York. Her most recent books are *Landscapes of Power* (University of California Press, 1991), winner of the C. Wright Mills Award and *The Culture of Cities* (Blackwell, 1995).

# Index

Aba, 134
Abeokuta, 116
Abeysinghe, A., 156
Abidjan, 173
Abou-El-Haj, B., 200
Abrams, R. D., 90, 91
Abu-Lughod, J., 135
Abuja, 11, 133, 134
Abyssinia, 160
Accra, 173
Adams, N., 213, 216, 224, 225
Addis Ababa, 173
Addiss, J., 224
Aden, 166
Adler, S., 250
*Afrabia*, 172
Africa, 158–78
Africa Leadership Forum, 173
Africa, -n, viii, 5, 12, 13, 66, 90, 112,
    119, 123, 127
African Development Bank, 73
African-American, -s, 101, 104, 187,
    193, 195, 197, 231
Agnew, J., 59, 266
Agudas, 123
AIDS, 103, 167, 168
Aig-Imoukhouede, F., 136
Aina, T. A., 123, 135, 136
Akinola, G. A., 175
Akinsemoyin, K., 135
Akitoye, 118
Alaska, 225
Alexander's, 48
Algeria, 172
Algiers, 237
Allah, 133
Allen, J.de V., 175, 176
Allen, J. W. T., 175
Alsayyad, N., 135
Altman's, 48

America, -n, -s, 11, 30, 50, 139, 142, 152,
    162, 164, 166, 167, 199, 204, 250,
    206, 207, 208, 209, 215, 216,
    218, 219, 222, 223, 225, 232, 237,
    260, 261
American Folklore Society, 86
Amerindian, 64, 66
Amiens, 210
Amis, P., 135
Amsterdam, 244
Anderson, K., 249, 250
André Hemmerich Gallery, 48
Andrew, C., 250
Anglo-Saxon, 138, 139, 249
Angola, 174
Anuradhapura, 150, 152
Apapa, 118
Aponte-Pares, L., 86
Apoupon, 128, 130
Appleyard, D., 251
Arab, -ic, 159, 160, 163, 165, 170, 171,
    172
Arabia, 160
Arap Moi, D., 170, 174
Archea, J., 251
Argentina, 6
Argentine, -an, 139
Armory, 39
Armstrong, A., 175
Armstrong, W., 157
ASEAN, 154
Asia, -n, viii, 5. 13, 138, 139, 142, 143,
    145, 156, 158, 159, 160, 170, 171
Association of African Universities, 173
Association of Collegiate Schools of
    Architecture (ACSA), 221
Atlanta, 102
Atlantic, 169
Attinasi, J., 88
Australia, -ns, 138, 141, 154, 156

Austria, 40
Awolowo, 128, 130
Awori, -s, 116, 134
Axis, 165
Aysan, Y., 222
Azeez, M., 153
Azevedo, C. de, 175

Babangida, President, 133
Bagh, C. V., 105
Bairoch, P., 156
Bakara, M. b. M., 175
Baker, P. H., 175
Bakhtin, M., 16, 64, 65, 87, 89, 90, 239,
    240, 245, 250, 251
Balogun, 130
Balzac, 247
Bamgbose, 127
Bandaranayake, S., 156
Baudrillard, J., 250
Bangladesh, 156, 171, 201
Bank of the North, 127
Bank of Ceylon, 144, 155
Bannister, T., 221
Bar On, B.A., ix
Baraka, A., 94
Barbados, -ians, 102
Barclay's Bank, 127
Barnes, C. F., 208
Barnes, T., 4, 18
Barnes, T. J., 266
Barthes, R., 17, 255, 262, 263, 264, 265,
    267, 268
Bartlett, S., 91
Basu, D. K., 156
Batavia, 138
Battery Park City, 53, 54
Beauregard, R., 94, 106
Beijing, 172
Belgium, 156
Bell, Daniel., 220
Bell, Don, ix
Benin, 119
Benitez, M., 90
Benitiz-Rojo, A., 91
Benjamin, W., 15, 16, 229, 230, 231,
    241, 245, 247
Bennet, J., 107
Berkshires, 58
Berlin, 13, 40
Bermann, M., 84, 89, 91
Berque, A., 252

Bhabha, H., 10, 12, 248, 249, 250, 252
Bhutan, 156
Biafra, -n, 133
Bible, 168
Billingsgate, 240
Black Africa, -n, 171
Blackmar, E., 59
*Blade Runner*, 48
Blaize, C. O., 136
Blonsky, M., 251
Bloom, H., 259, 267
Bloomingdale's, 48
Blumenthal, R., 106
Bocock, K., 17
Bolling, K., 267
Bonilla, F., 42
Borguwa, 119
Bourdieu, P., 200, 247
Bourgeois, P., 194, 201
Bourne, L. S., 93, 106
Boxer, C. R., 175
Boyer, C. M., 58
Bradlow, F. R., 175
Branco, 125
Brazil, 141
Brazilian Yoruba, 123, 125
Brecher, J., 41
Bristol Hotel, 119, 127
British, 2, 117, 120, 138, 139, 140, 144,
    145, 149, 152, 153, 155, 158, 163,
    164, 165, 168, 170
British Raj, 163
Broad Street, 119, 130
Broeze, F., 155
Bronner, S., 86
Bronx, 8, 73, 81, 84, 85, 86
Brooklyn, 55, 57, 75, 89, 99
Bruges, 7
Bruntland, G. M., 174
Brunvand, J. H., 246
Bryant, J., ix
Bryant Park, 55
Buck-Morss, S., 229, 247
Buddha, 150
Buddhist, 147, 149, 150, 151
Burdett, R., 201
Burgess, E. W., 17, 255, 256, 258, 259,
    262, 263, 264, 265, 267
Burghers, 147, 149
Burgos, V., 71
Burke, K., 267
Burma, 165
Byrne, M., 91

Cairns, M., 175
Cairo, 135
Calabar, 134
Caliban, 164
Campos Square, 118, 123
Canada, 6, 138, 139
Canary Wharf, 48, 49
Cape Town, 138
Caraballo, J., 81
Caribbean, 61, 63, 64, 65, 70, 73, 76
Carter Bridge, 119
Carter, J., 166
Cashdan, L., 91
Castagena, M., 76
Castells, M., 2, 13, 18, 19, 30, 41, 202
Cave, H. W., 157
Central Bank, 127, 130
Central Business District, 143
Central Park, 54, 55, 104
Ceylon, -ese, 138, 139, 140, 144, 150
Chad, 119
Chaney, E. M., 88
Chemical and Manufacturers' Hanover
    Bank, 48
Chewing, J. A., 220
Chicago, 17, 51, 257, 259, 264, 265
Chicago School of Human
    Ecology, 255, 258, 259
Chief Executive Officers (CEO), 132
Childe, J. B., 41
Childers, E., 248, 252
China, -ese, 102, 141, 170, 171, 172, 173,
    201
Chinatown, 103, 104, 237, 249
Chittick, N., 175
Choay, F., 19
Chrisman, L., 19
Christ, -ian, 147, 223
Christian Missionary Society, 136
Christianity, 158
Chtcheglov, I., 244, 251, 252
Church Avenue, 57
Cinnamon Gardens, 150
Cirese, A. M., 91
Civilian Review Board, 96
Clammer, J., 252
Clark, K., 250
Clemente, R., 73
Clifford, J., 19, 87, 244, 266
CN Tower (Toronto), 228
Cobbett, W., 9
Cohen, R. B., 154
Cohen, S., 224

Coker. F., 135
Colombia, -ns, 102
Colombo, 10, 11, 137–53, 156, 157
Colomina, B., 201
Columbia St., 75
Columbus, C., 139
Commonwealth, 165
Con Edison, 83
Conant, K. J., 204
Coney Island, 89
Constabulary, 119, 128
Cooper, F., 175
Cooper, M., ix, 62, 67, 72, 74, 80
Cooperative Bank, 127
Coras, 119
Cortes, F., 88
Côte d'Ivoire, 173
Coto, M., 81
Crown, 123
Crown Heights, 50
Crysler, G., vii, 14, 16, 203–26
Cuff, D., 217, 225
Culler, J., 214, 224
Cultural Triangle, 152
Cutter, J., 41

D-Day, 165
da Costa, J., 125
da Gama, V., 162
Daedalus, 228
Darwinism, 258
Datoo, B. A., 175
Davenport, M., 156
Davis, M., 17, 59, 95, 255, 259, 260,
    261, 263, 265
Davison, G., 258, 267
Dawodu, W. A., 136
de Blij, H. J., 134, 176
de Certeau, 15, 223, 224, 228, 229, 231,
    232, 234, 245, 246, 248
de Lauretis, T., 248
de Oviedo, G. F., 66
Dear, M., 154, 250
Debord, G., 251
Debray, R., 225
Deleuze, G., 16, 180, 241, 245, 246, 251
Democratic Socialists of America, 97
Denton Bridge, 119
Derrida, J., 16, 232, 233, 236, 241, 245
Deutsch, R., 58, 114, 135
Dhakka, 156
Dietz, J., 87, 88
Dinkins, D., 97, 100, 103, 104

Dinkinsville, 84, 99
Disney World, 57
Dissanayake, L., 155
Djakarta, 138
Dmochowskiz, R., 115, 135
DMZ, 98
Docklands, 46, 48, 53
Doherty, J.H., 136
Dolphin Estate, 130
Donald, J., 1, 3, 4, 17, 247
Donzelot, 180
Dresden, 61
Duncan, J., vii, 4, 5, 17, 18, 19,
    253–68
Duncan, N., 5, 19
Dutton, T., 225

East, 161
East Africa, 158, 159, 162, 164, 165,
    169, 171
East Asian Community, 174
East Harlem, 75, 194
East River, 99
East Side, 38
East Village, 97
Eastman, C., 251
Ebute Ero, 118, 130
Eco, U., 266, 265
Economic Intelligence Unit, 155
Edo, 116
Egan, T., 107
Egba, 119
Egypt, -ian, 54, 160, 166, 172
Ekiti, 119
*Eko*, 10, 116, 117, 119, 123, 128, 130,
    132, 134
El Balcon Boricuo, 81
El Barrio, 66, 75, 80, 82
El Fangito, 68
El Jaragual, 75
El Salvador, -ans, 102
Elder Dempster, 119, 127
Elegenza, 127
Elephant House, 123, 136
Elshtain, J.B., 249
*Empire of Signs*, 262
Engels, F., 7, 44, 106
England, -ish, 6, 138, 150, 163
*Environment and Planning D: Society
    and Space*, 249
Epstein, J., 59
Equitable Life, 51, 52, 54
Erhenreich, B.J., 220

Eritrea, 166
Espara, R., 84
Ethiopia, 158, 166, 173
*Eurafrica*, 172
Europe, -an, 2, 4, 13, 23, 119, 140, 149,
    152, 154, 155, 158, 159, 161, 163,
    170, 188, 196, 198, 207, 218, 222,
    232, 237
European Community, 13

Fainstein, N. and S., 155
Falcon, A., 88
Falomo Bridge, 132
Feagin, J.R., 154
Featherstone, M., 200
Federal Government, 130
Federal Mortgage Bank of
    Nigeria, 130
Fegley, L., ix
Ferguson, R., 135, 247
Ferguson, S., 98, 106
Fernandez, J.W., 90, 91
Ferrar, F., 84
Fewkes, J.W., 88
Figuero, J.B., 41
Figueroa, J.E., 89, 91
Filani, M., 134
Financial District, 102
Fine Art Department (Harvard), 204
First Bank, 127
Fischer, M.M.J., 87
Fisher, I., 107
Five Cowrie Creek, 119
Flatbush Avenue, 57
Flint, Mich., 44
Flores, J., 86, 87, 88, 92
Flushing, 57
Foch, C. ix
Foch-Serra, M., 251
Fort, 143
Fort Apache, 61
Fort Jesus, 162
Fortress Los Angeles, 255, 259
Foucault, M., -ian, 3, 14, 16, 180, 247,
    252
Frampton, K., 200
France, -ench, 40, 162
Franck, K.A., 19
Frankfurt, 23, 40,
Fraser, D., 267
French West Africa, 119
Friedan, B., 58, 59
Friedlander, M., 103

Friedlander, S., 223, 266
Friedmann, J., 18, 41, 142, 153, 154
Froebel, F., 223
Frow, J., 220
Fuentes, Z. O., 86
Fulani, 119

Gaber, J., 39, 42
Gambia, 119
Gangaramaya, 151
Gappert, G., 176
Geertz, C., 247
*Gender and Space*, 249
General Motors Building, 48
Genette, G., 224
Germany, 40, 156
Gerville, W., 222
Gever, M., 135, 248
Ghana, 119, 169, 173
Giddens, A., 201
Gilmore, R., 95, 105
Giulani, 104
Glover, J., 118, 135
Goffman, I., 235, 248
Goldman, F., ix
Gold Coast, 119, 169
Gombrich, E. H., 222
Gonzales, J. Judge, 84
Gonzales, J. L., 60, 63, 64, 76, 79, 87,
    88, 90, 91
Gooding-Williams, R., 106
Goodman, N., 254, 266
Gotbaum, B., 97
Gottdiener, M., 19
Gottschalk & Co., 119, 123
Gouldner, A., 220
Government Residential Area
    (GRA), 112, 128
Governor General, 123
Grammercy Park, 103, 104
Gramsci, A., 78, 90, 91
Grand Central Partnership, 56, 57
Grand Central Station, 51, 99
Graves, M., 51
Gray, J. M., 176
Great Britain, 213
Greater Antilles, 77
Greece, 206, 208
Green, W. A., 221
Greenfield, V., 89
Gregory, D., 248, 252
Gropius, W., 204
Grosz, E., 194, 201

Guattari, F., 16, 180, 241, 245, 246,
    251
Guggenheim Museum, 54
Gutman, I., 252
Gutman, R., 221
Guttierez, J., 76

Habermas, J., 237, 249, 250
Hall, P., 41
Hall, S., 190, 194, 195, 200, 201, 247
Handler, R., 90, 91, 92
Hannerz, U., 87, 199
Harlem, 57
Harold Washington Library, 51
Harris, N., 154
Hart, R., 249
Hartoonian, H. D., 252
Harvard Design School, 204
Harvey, D., 2, 18, 69, 88, 92, 251
Hausa, 119
Haussmann, 44
Hawthorne Avenue, 57
Held, A., 48
Hernandez, F., 83
Hertz, B-S., 86, 91
Hertzfeld, M., 90
Highway St., 58
*Hijra*, 160
Hindu, 147, 150, 157
Hirsch, M., 252
Hispaniola, 66
Hitchcock, H. R., 221, 223
Hoagland, A. K., 225
Hoffman, H., 247
Holdsworth, D., ix
Hollister, R. M., 18
Holquist, M., 250
Holt, J., 119
Home, R. K., 154, 156
Hong Kong, 156
hooks, b., 78, 86, 90, 248, 252
Hooverville, -s, 99
Horn of Africa, 165
Horvath, R., 139, 153
Houston, 154
Hoving, T., 54
Hoyle, B. S., 176
Hudson River, 53
Hufford, M., 90, 92
Hulugalle, H. A. J., 153, 156
Hunt, M., 92
Huth, H., 221
Hymes, D., 87, 91

Iberia, -n, 64
Ibibio, 119
Idejo, 118
Idumagbo, 120, 121, 132,
Idumota, 119, 130
Ife, 116
*Iga Idunganran*, 118, 123
Igbo, 119, 133, 134
Ijebu, 119
Ijesha, 119
Ikoyi, 118, 128, 130, 132, 133, 135
Ilesha, 116
India, -n, -s, 102, 153, 156, 159, 160, 163, 165, 170, 171
Indian Ocean, 138, 158, 164, 169, 170, 171, 174, 175
*International Journal of Urban and Regional Research*, 249
International Monetary Fund (IMF), 13, 31, 145, 173
*International Situationniste*, 244
Irigary, L., 13, 19
Isale Eko, 118, 119, 120, 125, 127, 128
Islam, 13, 158, 160, 161
Isle of War (Mvita), 165
Israel, 170
Istanbul, 160
Italy, -ies, 96, 165, 166
Itsekiri, 119
Ivan, G., 244
Iyaloda/Iyaloja, 126

Jackson Lears, T. J., 90
Jacobs, J., 3, 18, 19
Jaffna, 150
Jahn, H., 51
Jakande, L., 114
Jamaica, -s, 96, 102
Jameson, F., 18, 251
Janata Vimukti Peramuna (JVP), 149
Japan, -ese, 17, 40, 141, 142, 145, 154, 156, 165, 172, 173, 190, 201, 262, 264
Jayawardana, J. R., 150, 151
Jefferson, T., 223
Jerome, A., ix
Johannesburg, 142
Johnson, S., 135
Jopling, C. F., 88
*Journal of the Society of Architectural Historians* (JSAH), 203–25
Jussieu, 222

Kakawa, 125
Kalabari, 119
Kandy, 140, 149, 150, 151, 152
Kanuri, 119
Karasch, M., 141, 154
Kasamitz, P., 58
Katanayake, 143
Katz, C., 106
Kaufman, V., 41
Keeling, D., 154
Keith, M., 15, 19
Keller, E. F., 252
Kendal, M. S., 101, 106
Kentucky Fried Chicken, 164
Kenya, -n, 6, 12, 139, 158, 161–75
Kenya African National Union (KANU), 170, 172
Kenyatta, J., 166, 168, 174
Kern, S., 251
Kifner, J., 106
Kilindini, 163
Kimball, F., 221
Kimber, C. T., 90
Kindy, H., 176
King, A. D., viii, 1–19, 4, 14, 18, 19, 41, 59, 63, 86, 115, 135, 140, 153, 154, 156, 176, 190, 197, 198, 199, 200, 248
King, M. L., 168
King, R., 95
King, U., ix
Kingsway, 127
Kipins, J., 201
Kirshenblatt-Gimblett, B., 86, 89, 90, 92
Kiswahili, 13, 163
Knapp, K., 248, 251
Knight, R. V., 176
Knox, P., 13, 14, 154
Kobayashi, A., 250
Koch, 83, 84
Kokoli, O., ix
Kokomaiko, 119
Kolamba, 139
Konvitz, J. W., 176
Korea, -n, -s, 102
Kotte, 143, 149
Krautheimer, R., 213, 221
Krieger, M. H., 249
Kuala Lumpur, 142
Kugglemass, J., 86
Kuhn, Fr., 98, 103

*La Tour de Feu*, 234

Lacan, -ian, 3
Lafiaji, 118, 120, 127, 128, 132
Lagopoulos, A. P., 19
Lagos, 10, 11, 111, 112, 114, 115, 117, 118, 119, 123, 126, 127, 130, 131, 133, 134, 135, 138
Lancaster, C., 123, 224
Landes, J., 250
Langer, P., 3, 18
Lanka, *see* Sri Lanka
Laotna, A. B., 136
LaPerla, 68
Larson, M. S., 223
Lasekan, A., 112, 113, 119, 123, 124, 136
Latin America, 13
Latino, 104
Latour, A., 220
Lauria, A., 91
Le Bernardin Restaurant, 52
Le Corbusier, 209, 244
League of Arab States, 172
Lebanese, 119
Lefebvre, H., 16, 50, 59, 235, 238, 247, 248, 250
Legislative Assembly, 128
Lennox-Boyd, M., 155
Lewis, G. K., 87, 90, 92
Ley, D., 4, 18, 266
Liberation Tigers of Tamil Eelam (LTTE), 149, 151
Limon, J. E., 59, 91
Lindgren, H., 59
Lindsay, J., 55
Linnekin, J., 91
Lloyd, P., 135
Lombardi-Satriani, L., 91, 92
London, vii, 2, 8, 23, 26, 29, 32, 35, 40, 45, 139, 140, 141, 142, 152, 192
Long, L., 93
Los Angeles, vii, 10, 13, 17, 26, 40, 44, 57, 59, 95, 154, 188, 192, 260, 262, 263, 264, 265
Loven, S., 66, 88
Lowder, S., 126, 136
Lowell, Mass., 44
Lower East Side, 8, 61, 70, 71, 83, 84, 96, 98, 99, 100, 102, 103
Lynch, K., 89, 251
Lyotard, J-F., 182, 214

Maass, J., 207, 213, 222, 223
Mabogunje, A., 136

Macao, 13
MacArthur Park, 260
MacDougall, E. B., 220
Maciver & Co., 119
Mackenzie, S., 250
Macmillan, A., 135
Macy's, 48
Madame Tinubu, 126
Madison Ave., 47
Mafesoli, M., 16, 238, 248, 250
Mafia, 55
Maghreb, 160
Magris, C., 247, 252
Mahaweli, 155
Mahroof, M., 153
Maitama Suhe, Alhaji, 133
Malays, 147
Maldives, 156
Maloney, P., 98
Manchester, 7, 13, 44, 139
Mandelbaum, S., 154
Mandlin-Jeronimo, J., 226
Manhattan, 6, 8, 25, 26, 29, 37, 38, 39, 50, 75, 85, 89, 95, 97, 99, 194
Manzanet, J., 81, 84
Mao Tse-tung, 172
Marakkala, 138, 153
Marcus, G., 19, 87, 216, 224
Mardar, T., 222
Marin, L. M., 77, 224
Marina, 127, 130
Marris, P., 176
Marseille, 40
Martin, E., 130, 134, 119, 123
Marx, -ian, 230, 241, 255, 259, 264, 265
Matano, k.w. M., 176
Matrix, 250
Matysek, E. E., 212, 213, 224
Mau Mau, 165, 166, 168, 172
Mauritius, 141
Mazrui, A. A., ix, 6, 12, 13, 158–76
Mboya, T., 168
McDonald's, 51, 57
McGee, T., 154, 156, 157
McGregor, W., 118
Mecca, 14, 160, 179
Medina, 160
Mediterranean, 240
Mekong Delta, 260
Melbourne, 158
Melendez, E., 41, 42
Melucci, 238
Mendoza, E., 247, 252

Metropolitan Museum, 55
Mexico, -ans, 102
Meyrowitz, J., 250
Miami, 102
Middle Atlantic Folklife
    Association, 86
Middle East, -ern, 141, 160, 170
Middleton, J., 176
Miller Bros., N.S., 119, 136
Miller, R., 86
Million Houses Program, 155
Mills, C.W., 156
Minh-ha, T.T., 135, 248
Mintz, S., 75, 88, 90
Mission House, 125
Mitchell, W.J.T., 211, 224
Miyoshi, M., 252
Mobil Oil, 99
Modernist Movement, 127
Mohanty, C.T., 214, 225
Moholy-Nagy, S., 208, 223
Moloney, A., 116, 118, 121, 127, 132
Mombasa, 10, 12, 13, 139, 158, 159,
    161, 162, 163, 164, 165, 166, 167,
    168, 169, 170, 174
*Mombasa Times*, 163
Monroe, K., 176
Montano, M., 86
Monticello, 221
Montreal, 158
Moore-Milroy, B., 250
Morales, R., 42
Morgan Stanley, 49
Morgan, T., 107
Morocco, 160
Morris, M., 202
Morson, G.S., 87, 250
Moscoso, F., 88
Moscow, 7
Murphy, R., 150, 156
Murray, S., 224
Museum Mile, 54
Mushni, 147, 149
Muslim, 159, 160, 161, 171
Mvita, 159, 165
Myanmar, 141

Nairobi, 163, 164, 168, 169, 171, 173,
    174
Namda Azikewi, 127, 130
National Architectural Accrediting
    Board (NAAB), 217, 225, 226
National Electric Power Authority, 130

National Liberation Front, 172
National Parks Service, 221
National Public Radio, 97
Nehemiah Houses, 84
Nepa, 156
New Amsterdam, 138
New Calcutta, 86
New England, 87
New Jersey, 78
New Mexico, 138
New World, 162
New York City, vii, viii, 5, 7, 8, 10, 11,
    61, 63, 66, 68, 69, 70, 71, 74, 75, 76,
    77, 78, 79, 85, 93, 95, 102, 112, 114,
    115, 135, 137, 140, 141, 142, 143,
    146, 147, 148, 150, 151, 152, 179,
    188, 192, 228
*New York Times*, 53, 77, 97, 98, 100,
    103, 104
New Zealand, -ers, 138, 165
Newman, N., ix
Nichols, F.D., 221
Nichols, S.G., 222
Niger, 119
Nigeria, -n, 6, 10, 11, 115, 116, 119, 127,
    130, 132, 133, 139, 173
Nigerian Ports Authority (NPA), 130
Nigerian Telecommunications Office
    (NITEL), 130
Njonjo, C., 174
Norfolk Hotel, 171
Normandy, 166
North, 13
North Adams, Mass., 44
North Africa, 158, 160, 165
North America, viii, 13, 66, 73, 94, 138,
    170, 198, 213
North Atlantic, 174
North Vietnamese, 260
Norway, 174
Noyelle, T.J., 42
Nupe, 119
Nzegwu, N., vii, 6, 10, 11, 111–36, 156

Oba, 118, 125
Obalende, 119, 120, 132, 127
Obote, M., 168
O'Connor, Cardinal, 103
Odunlami, 127
Oke, Suna, 119, 127
Olaleye-Iponri, 135
Olalquiaga, C., 230, 247
Old Eko, 118

Oller, F., 77
Ollivant, G. B., 119, 123
Olmstead, F. L., 55, 213
Olowogbowa, 123
Olympia and York, 48, 49, 53
Oman, Sultanate of, 171
Ondo, 119
Onikan, 116, 128
Onikoyi, 135
Onitsha, 134
Onyemelukwe, J., 134
Operation Green Thumb, 73, 83
Operation Restore, 99
Organization of African (OAU), 172
Orient, -al, 160, 167
Oring, E., 92
Ortner, S., 90
Osaka, 40
Oshodi, 125
Ota, 173
Otnes, P., 242, 251
Ottawa, 237
Overby, O., 206, 220, 221, 223, 225
Oxford, 164
Oyo, 116, 119

Padilla, O., 79, 83
Pagan, A., 103, 104
Page, S., 156
PaineWebber, 52
Pakistan, 156, 160, 171.201
Palio Restaurant, 52
Palladio, 209
Paris, vii, 35, 40, 44, 140, 192, 241, 267
Park, R. E., 257, 267
Parker, S., ix
Parks, J., 220
Parliament, 143
Parma, C., 176
Parry, B., 252
Pasquino, 180
*Passagenwerk*, 230
Paterson and Zochonis (PZ), 123
Pearse, S. Hon., 125, 136
Pedraza, P., 88
Peil, M., 137–57, 176
Pelli, C., 53
Perera, N., ix, vii, 6, 10, 11, 12, 13, 19,
    137–57, 250
Perez, R., 92
Pevsner, N., 213
Phelan, P., 248, 250, 251

Philadelphia, 203, 224
Philippines, 142, 201
Phillip Morris, Building, 52, 54, 77
Phillips, E., 136
Phoenix Civic Center, 51
Pierson, W. H., 225
Pike, S., 15, 9
Pitkia Avenue, 57
Placzek, A. K., 225
Plamenatz, J., 164, 175
Plant, S., 251
Poland, -ish, 102
Polunnarurva, 152
Ponce, 74
Port Harcourt, 134
Portlandia Building, 51
Portsmouth, 165
Portugal, -uese, 139, 149, 153, 159, 161,
    162, 163
Pouwels, R. L., 175
Powell, A. C., 84
Pred, A., 235, 240, 248, 251
Premadasa, R., 151
Prophet Mohammed, 160
Prospect Park, 55
Prospero, 164
Public Library, 56
Public Works Department (PWD), 119,
    125
Puerto Rico, -ans, 6, 8, 10, 60, 63, 66,
    68, 70, 71, 73, 74, 75, 77, 78, 90,
    103, 114, 139, 140, 148, 194

Queen's, 57

Raban, J., 247, 252
Rabelais, 87
Rabinow, P., 19, 222, 224, 250
Rainer, Y., 240
Rakatansky, M., 193, 201
Ramirez, M. C., 90
Ranger, T. O., 175
Rattansi, A., 247
Red Sea, 166
Reed, L., 106
Relph, E., 249
Rent Assessment Board, 112
Richardson, H. R., 209, 223
Ricoeur, P., 251
Riggins, S., 248
Rincon Criollo, 81, 91
Ring Road, 130
Rio de Janeiro, 141, 154

Rios, P. N., 87, 92
Rist, C., 91
Rivera, A. Q. Q., 88
Rivera, C. R., 77
Rivera, F., 77
Rivera, I., 73, 78
Rivera, J., 81
Rivera, P. A., 86
Roberts, M., 155, 156
Roberts, S., 106
Roberts, S., 257, 258, 267
Robertson, R., 198, 199
Rockefeller Center, 51, 54, N., 53
Roderick, I., 251
Rodriguez, C., 41
Rodwin, L., 18
Rome, 13, 14, 179
Roosevelt, T., 165, 167
Rosenzweig, R., 59
Ross, A., 106, 251
Ross, R., 154
Rotberg, R. I., 175
Rushdie, S., 2, 18
Russia, -ns, 102, 170

Sada, P., 136
Safa, H., 90
Sagalyn, L. B., 58, 59
Said, E., 212, 224
Saint, A., 223
Saks, 48
Salinas, 85
Salvation Army, 39
San Francisco, 102
San Juan, 63, 66, 76, 96
Sanchez Korrol, V. E., 88
Sanchez, L. R., 89
Sanchez-Tranquilano, M., 182
Saussure, -ian, F., 240
Santa Cruz, 253
Santa Fe, 138
Sara Delano Roosevelt Park, 99
Saros, 123
Sassen, S., vii, viii, 6, 7, 8, 14, 15, 18, 19,
    23–42, 106, 134, 137, 139, 140, 141,
    153, 154, 179, 181, 183–202
Sassoon, C., 175
*Satanic Verses*, 2
Satler, G., 41, 42
Saunders, P., 246
Sayer, A., 246, 266
Schein, R. H., 267
Schneekloth, L., 19

Sciorra, J., ix, 8, 10, 60–92, 111, 114,
    115, 135, 140, 148
Scotland, 6
Scott, A., 154
Scott, J., ix
Seattle, 102
Sennett, R., 37, 41, 42, 59, 138, 153,
    191, 200, 201, 237, 250
Seoul, 142
Servin, J., 107
Seventh Avenue, 38
Shakespeare, W., 214
Shapiro, M. J., 266
Sharp, J., 266, 268
Shields, R., 4, 11, 15, 16, 17, 227–52
Sider, G. M., 91
Sierra Leone, 119, 123
Silmoric, S., 86
Simmel, G., 16, 235, 237, 248, 250
Simon, D., 112, 135, 150
Singapore, 142, 154, 155
Singhalese, 146, 147, 149, 151, 153,
Situationist, -s, 16, 244, 251
Skene, R., 175
Skid Row, 261
Sleeper, J., 89
Smith, D., 256, 267
Smith, J., 266
Smith, M. P., 41, 154
Smith, N., 9, 10, 15, 93–107, 111, 112,
    114, 115, 136, 140
Smuda, C., 18
Social Darwinism, 257
Société Commerciale et Industrielle de
    l'Afrique Occidentale, 119
Society of Architectural Historians
    (SAH), 16, 203, 204, 214, 215, 216,
    220, 221, 225
SoHo, 104
Soissons, 208
Soja, E., 154, 252
Solomon, A., 91
Somalia, 171
Sontag, S., 58
Sorkin, M., 58, 258
Soto, J. M., 77, 79
South Africa, 158
South Asia, 158, 160, 171
South Bronx, 61, 63, 71, 75, 76, 77, 84,
    89, 91
South Korea, 141, 145, 154, 156, 173
Southall, A., 176
Southern Negroes, 257

Soviet Union, 13, 170
Soweto, 14, 179
Spain, 13
Spencer, -ian, 258, 266
Spivak, G. C., 19, 224, 247, 249
Sri Jayawardanapura-Kotte, 143
Sri Lanka, 6, 11, 12, 137–57
St. Brigid's Church, 98, 101, 103
St. George, R. B., 87, 92
St. Patrick's Cathedral, 54
Stallybrass, P., 86, 251
Stanback, T. M., 42
Stanford St., 57
Stansell, C., 236, 248
Stein, P. R., 91
Steward, S., 87
Stock, H., 5
Strasbourg, 244
Stren, R. E., 176
Structural Adjustment Program
    (SAP), 132
Subic Bay, 142
Sudan, 171
Suez Canal, 166
Suleja, 133
Sullivan, D. G., 89
Sullivan, L., 209, 223
Surulere, 136
Sutcliffe, A., 267
Sutton, C. R., 88
Swahili, 160, 163, 172
Swartz, M. J., 176
Sydney, 158
Syrian, 119

Tafawa Balewa Square, 128, 129
Tagg, J., viii, 13, 14, 18, 19, 179–82, 198
Taino, 66
Taipei, 142, 154
Taiwan, -ese, 96, 141, 142, 145, 154, 156
Tamil, 146, 147, 149, 151, 157
Tanzania, 174
Taylor, P., 13, 14, 19, 154
Taylor, W., 59
Teilard de Chardin, 14
Telkamp, G., 154
Temple of Tooth Relic, 150
Temple of Dendur, 54
Teymur, N., 222
Thailand, -s, 102
Thich Nhat Hahn, 60
Third World, 9, 23, 32, 34, 35
Thomas, A. W. U., 125, 136

Thomas, C., 103
Thompson, E. P., 90, 91, 92
Thompson, K., 17
Thompson, R. F., 92
Thrift, N., 2, 18
Tigerman, S., 219, 226
Timbu Square, 127
Times Square, 46, 49, 54, 59
Tirado, A., 66, 71
Togo, 119
Tokumbo Street, 125
Tokyo, vii, 23, 29, 32, 35, 40, 141, 192,
    201, 262, 263, 264, 265
Tomich, D., ix
Tompkins Square Park, Neighborhood
    Association, 8, 84, 96, 97, 100, 101,
    103, 104
Tornin, M., 98
Toronto, 228
Touraine, A., 225
Township, 112
Transit Authority, 99
Tufino, 77
Tunji Oyegbeye, Chief, 128
Tuan, Y. F., 249
Turan, M., 222

Uganda, 153, 161, 163, 168, 169, 171,
    174
Unger, C., 106
Union Bank, 127
Union Square, 37, 39, 40
United Bank for Africa (UBA), 127
United Kingdom, 145, 163
United National Party, 145
United Nations, 154
United Nations Environmental
    Program (UNEP), 169
United Nations High Commissioner for
    Refugees (UNHCR), 169
United States, of America, 8, 10, 16, 17,
    23, 24, 42, 63, 65, 68, 94, 95, 102,
    138, 141, 144, 145, 146, 153, 155,
    156, 162, 164, 165, 166, 190, 196,
    203, 207, 216, 217
United Trading Company, 127
University of California, 253
University of Cambridge, 163
Upper Broad, 127
Urhobo, 119
Urry, J., 252
Urwick, W., 153
Uzelac, E., 105

Valásquez, J., 71, 75
Valentine, G., 250
Van Allen, J., 209
Vaughan-Richards, A., 135
Vaux, C., 55
Vázquez, O., ix, 86, 90
Venice, 7
Vernacular Architecture Forum, 86
Victoria Island, 118, 119, 130, 132, 133
Victoria Street, 119
Vienna, 40
Viet Cong, 260
Vietnam, 141, 260
Vignola, 209
Villa Allegre, 89
Villa El Gato, 75
Villa Hermosa, 89
Villa Puerto Rico, 72, 76, 81, 84, 85
*Village Voice*, 97, 103
Vint, T., 221
Vlach, J. M., 88
Volosnov, 64, 87

Walker, P., 220
Wallerstein, I., 156, 200
Walton, J., 3, 18
Warsaw Jewish Ghetto, 237
Washington, 10, 143, 150
Waswahili, 162, 171
Watts, 260
Weatherhead, C., 221
Weaver, M. A., 156
*Webster's Dictionary*, 97
Weissman, J., 83
Wellawetta, 146, 157
Werlen, B., 234
West, 161, 170, 173, 197
West, 2, 5, 15, 17
West Africa, 90
West Asia, 158
West, C., 135, 232, 247, 248
West Side, 260
West Side Highway, 99
West Village, 98, 104
Western Cameroon, 119
Western House, 127, 129
Western, J., 266
Westmacott, R., 92
White, A., 251
White, A., 86
White, H., 17, 209, 211, 223, 224, 253, 254, 255, 265, 266

White, L., 106
White, M., 106
Whiteman, J., 201
Whitney Museum, 51, 52
Wiese, B., 176
Wigley, M., 193, 201
Williams, L., 19
Williams, M. A., 87, 92
Williams, R., 78, 79, 90, 91, 248
Williamsburg (Colonial), 221
Williamsburg, 50, 89, 99
Willis, J., 176
Wilson, E., 59, 90, 236, 248
Wilson, H., 223
Wilson, W. A., 92
Winter Garden, 53
Wirth, L., 249
Wolch, J., 250
Wolff, G., 41
Wolff, J., 3, 18, 248
World Bank, 13, 145, 164, 173
World Council of Churches, 173
World Financial Center, 48, 53, 54
World Trade Center, 8, 95
World War I, 257
World War II, 165, 166, 169
Worldwide Plaza, 48
Wright, D., 91
Wright, F. L., 209, 213, 223
Wright, G., 219, 220, 226
*Writing Degree Zero*, 263

Yaba, 120
Yeatman, A., 250
Yemen, 166
Yen, 141
Yoruba, 10, 11
Yoruba, 111, 115, 116, 117, 118, 119, 123, 125, 133, 134
Yosemite Valley, 221
Young, M. J., 87
Yoyo Araromi, 125

Zaire, 171, 174
Zeitlin, S., 92
Zen Buddhism, 263
Zionism, 171
Zola, E., 247
Zukin, S., 1, 7, 8, 14, 18, 43–59, 105, 140, 179, 180, 199, 202
Zucker, P., 221